THE PEN
ENGLIS S

Faye Ca Waite

MARKET HOUSE BOOKS LIMITED

PENGUIN BOOKS

Penguin Books Ltd, Harmondsworth, Middlesex, England
Viking Penguin Inc., 40 West 23rd Street, New York, New York 10010, U.S.A.
Penguin Books Australia Ltd, Ringwood, Victoria, Australia
Penguin Books Canada Ltd, 2801 John Street, Markham, Ontario, Canada L3R 1B4
Penguin Books (N.Z.) Ltd, 182–190 Wairau Road, Auckland 10, New Zealand

First published 1985
Reprinted 1985

Printed and bound in Great Britain by
Cox & Wyman Ltd, Reading
Set in Times by
Market House Books Ltd

PREFACE

A thesaurus (from the Greek word for treasure) is what its name implies, a treasure-house of words. Unlike a dictionary, in which words are listed alphabetically and their meanings explained, a thesaurus consists of words grouped according to their meanings. The aim is to provide a source of words that express the same idea or closely related ideas.

An 'idea', of course, can be a material object, such as food or a machine; it can be a topic or area of activity, such as politics, the cinema, or language; or it can be abstract, such as willingness, innocence, or destruction.

A thesaurus paragraph dealing with a material object, topic, or activity lists the key words in that semantic area, providing a mini-vocabulary of a subject. A paragraph dealing with an abstract quality, on the other hand, lists related words, associations, figurative uses and idiomatic phrases showing different stylistic equivalents in formal or colloquial language. For example, a paragraph on an idea, such as *talkativeness*, will include formal words (*verbosity*), humorous and colloquial usages (*verbal diarrhoea* and *hot air*), and idiomatic phrases (*talk the hind leg off a donkey*).

Thus each paragraph on a particular topic contains a range of words covering different parts of speech and different levels of formality or informality. Vulgar and colloquial terms have all been appropriately labelled in this thesaurus. Words and phrases current on the other side of the Atlantic are labelled as Americanisms. Where necessary, cross-references to related paragraphs are also given. Since there is technically no such thing as a true synonym or exact equivalent, the thesaurus could be said to concentrate on areas of shared meaning, in which usages overlap and shade off into similar ideas. For example, the paragraph on *obstinacy* has cross-references to the paragraphs on *unwillingness* and *perseverance* – all different words related by a central core of common meaning.

This *Penguin English Thesaurus* is based on the original *Thesaurus* compiled by Peter Mark Roget in 1852. Roget's arrangement of ideas reflected the thinking and state of knowledge of his day; this framework was considered so obvious to his contemporaries that no index was provided. Over a century later, we order our language differently; priorities have changed, and new fields of knowledge have emerged. As a result it has been necessary to rearrange Roget's original sequence of ideas, and to provide a detailed index for the user. Entries in the index show both parts of speech and paragraph numbers.

As a thesaurus of this size cannot hope to be as exhaustive as Roget's, we have had to omit some rare and obscure terms. However, we have attempted to cover a comprehensive working vocabulary that takes in all levels of language. The end result, we hope, is sufficiently compact to provide a handy means of jogging a recalcitrant memory, while remaining sufficiently comprehensive to serve both as a vocabulary builder and as a source of many hours of useful browsing.

1 EXISTENCE

See also **3** (reality); **322** (life).

n. *existence*, being, life, essence, coexistence; *actuality*, reality, substance, fact, concreteness; *presence*, duration, entity; *universe*, creation, world, cosmos; *coming into being*, realization, materialization, actualization; *survival*, endurance, persistence, continuance; *metaphysics*, ontology, existentialism.

adj. *existing*, being, existent; *actual*, real, substantial, factual, material, physical, concrete; *present*, ongoing, current, prevalent; *surviving*, extant, enduring, lasting, abiding; *metaphysical*, ontological, existential.

vb. *exist*, be, have being, live, breathe; *coexist*, be found, be situated; *be present*, prevail, obtain; *survive*, subsist, remain, endure, continue, last, abide; *come into being*, come about, evolve, arise, take shape; *just exist*, vegetate, stagnate.

adv. *actually*, in (actual) fact, in point of fact, really, truly; *presently*, currently, at the moment; *in one's lifetime*, in all one's born days, man and boy.

2 NONEXISTENCE

See also **4** (unreality); **323** (death).

n. *nonexistence*, nonentity, absence, unreality; *nothingness*, emptiness, vacuum, void, limbo, blankness; *extinction*, death, oblivion, annihilation, nirvana; *nothing*, nil, love, zero; *nullification*, annulment, cancellation, obliteration; *disintegration*, dilapidation, decay, obsolescence; *nihilism*, negativism.

adj. *nonexistent*, absent, missing, minus; *vacant*, empty, blank, null, void; *unreal*, insubstantial, abstract, ideal; *extinct*, dead, defunct, dead and gone, past, obsolete; *nihilistic*, negative, destructive.

vb. *not exist*, be null and void, be over and done with; *cease to exist*, die, pass away, perish, die out; *disappear*, vanish, evaporate, fade, melt, dematerialize; *extinguish*, annihilate, demolish, wipe out, snuff out, quell; *nullify*, abolish, annul, cancel, obliterate, invalidate, neutralize, negate, veto; *disintegrate*, decay, decompose, go to rack and ruin.

3 REALITY

See also **1** (existence); **282** (material world).

n. *reality*, existence, the here and now; *objectivity*, corporeality, substance, tangibility, palpability, solidity, concreteness; *real world*, universe, creation, physical world, earth, matter; *actuality*, fact, historicity, validity, authenticity; *realism*, naturalism, verisimilitude, cinema vérité, documentary, kitchen sink drama, slice of life; *plausibility*, feasibility, practicality; *realities*, facts of life, home truths, basics, fundamentals, bottom line (*colloq.*), nitty-gritty (*colloq.*), brass tacks, crunch (*colloq.*); *materialism*, realism, empiricism, pragmatism.

adj. *real*, existing, substantial; *objective*, corporeal, tangible, palpable, solid, concrete, physical, material, natural; *actual*, factual, historical, true, valid, authentic; *realistic*, naturalistic, true-to-life, lifelike; *plausible*, feasible, practicable, likely; *practical*, down-to-earth, matter-of-fact, no-nonsense, realistic; *basic*, fundamental, crucial, primary, cardinal; *materialist*, realist, empirical, pragmatic.

vb. *be real*, weigh, bulk large, loom; *objectify*, embody, incarnate, body forth; *validate*, substantiate, corroborate, authenticate; *actualize*, materialize, realize.

adv. *really*, in reality, in fact; *in practice*, in all likelihood, when it comes to the crunch (*colloq.*), when the chips are down (*colloq.*).

4 UNREALITY

See also **2** (nonexistence); **457** (imagination).

n. *unreality*, nonexistence, insubstantiality, incorporeality, abstractness, intangibility, impalpability; *subjectivity*, fantasy, make-believe, fiction, dream world, maya, vision, hallucination, delusion, castle in Spain, pipe-dream; *illusion*, figment of the imagination, mirage, optical illusion, trompe l'oeil, fata morgana, ignis fatuus, will o' the wisp, jack o' lantern; *simulacrum*, shadow, phantom, chimera, ghost, spectre, ectoplasm; *bubble*, fool's paradise, fairy gold, tinsel, nine days' wonder, gossamer, cobweb; *a nothing*, a nobody, nonperson, unperson, hollow man, man of straw, broken reed, paper tiger, puppet; *vain hope*, empty promise, false dawn, pie in the sky (*colloq.*); *empty talk*, hot air (*colloq.*), cock and bull story, bullshit (*colloq.*).

adj. *unreal*, nonexistent, insubstantial, incorporeal, intangible, impapable; *abstract*, ideal, rarefied, bloodless; *subjective*, imaginary, fantastic, make-believe, fictional, dreamlike, hallucinatory, delusory, illusory, chimerical, ghostly, shadowy; *ephemeral*, fleeting, elusive, evanescent; *vague*, hazy, nebulous, tenuous; *spurious*, specious, phoney, flimsy, hollow, meretricious; *token*, nominal, honorary.

vb. *be unreal*, belie, deceive, delude; *idealize*, rarefy, etiolate; *imagine*, fantasize, hallucinate, daydream, hear/see things; *dissolve*, fade, melt, blur, cloud, mist; *falsify*, fudge, distort; *invent*, dissemble, fib, spin a yarn (*colloq.*), waffle (*colloq.*); *invalidate*, refute, puncture, expose, give the lie to.

adv. *ideally*, in theory; *in name*, superficially, to all appearances.

5 ESSENCE

See also **576** (importance).

n. *essence*, substance, gist, heart, stuff; *essential part*, prime constituent, main ingredient, property, attribute; *core*, kernel, backbone, nub, nucleus, marrow, pith, sap, lifeblood; *quintessence*, embodiment, incarnation, personification, epitome, soul; *character*, make-up, constitution, complexion, temperament, stamp, breed, stripe, humour, hue.

adj. *essential*, intrinsic, immanent, inherent; *innate*, inborn, inbred, deep-seated, deep-rooted, ingrained, bred-in-the-bone; *quintessential*, fundamental, constitutional, structural, organic; *integral*, inseparable, ineradicable, built-in.

vb. *be essential*, inhere, belong, be part and parcel of; *characterize*, stamp, inform, mark; *embody*, incarnate, personify, epitomize.

adv. *in essence*, essentially, intrinsically; *at heart*, at bottom, basically, fundamentally.

6 EXTRANEOUSNESS

See also **10** (unrelatedness); **54** (foreign body).

n. *extraneousness*, exteriority, externality; *exterior*, outside, surface, periphery, circumference; *objectification*, externalization, projection; *foreignness*, alienness, unrelatedness, irrelevance, contingency.

adj. *extraneous*, exterior, external, outer, superficial; *foreign*, alien, unrelated, unconnected; *irrelevant*, peripheral, tangential, contingent, incidental, circumstantial.

vb. *be extraneous*, externalize, realize, body forth, objectify; *be irrelevant*, miss the point, talk off the subject, digress.

adv. *outwardly*, on the outside, superficially, prima facie; *off the point*, beside the point, neither here nor there.

7 STATE

See also **5** (essence); **8** (circumstances).

n. *state*, condition, situation, circumstances, lot, plight, estate; *position*, status, standing, footing, rank; *sphere*, realm, world, orbit, walk of life, department (*colloq.*), line of country (*colloq.*); *mode*, manner, modality, modus operandi, modus vivendi; *state of mind*, frame of mind, mood, temper, disposition, attitude, morale, fettle, spirits; *physical condition*, form, shape (*colloq.*), repair, trim, nick (*colloq.*).

adj. *stative*, situational; *modal*, conditional.

vb. *be situated*, stand, lie, sit, be found; *situate*, contextualize, locate.

adv. *as things stand*, in the present situation, in the circumstances.

8 CIRCUMSTANCES

See also **7** (state).

n. *circumstances*, situation, state of affairs, status quo, set-up (*colloq.*); *position*, state of play, lie of the land, story so far; *conditions*, environment, surroundings, setting, milieu, context, background; *occasion*, occurrence, event, episode, incident, happening, coincidence; *stage*, point, juncture, stepping-stone, milestone, turning point, crisis, crossroads.

adj. *circumstantial*, relative, contingent, conditional, provisional, incidental; *surrounding*, environmental, contextual, situational.

adv. *in the circumstances*, as things stand; *in the event*, as it happened; *provisionally*, conditionally.

9 RELATEDNESS

See also **11** (reciprocity); **12** (family relations); **19** (accord); **24** (degree).

n. *relatedness*, relevance, pertinence, bearing, point, appositeness; *relationship*, affinity, kinship, affiliation, bond, tie, rapport; *connection*, relation, link, tie-up, association; *relativeness*, ratio, proportion, scale; *interrelatedness*, correlation, reciprocity, interdependence, cross-reference, complementarity; *correspondence*, agreement, similarity, parallel, comparison, analogy.

adj. *related*, relevant, pertinent, apposite, appropriate, germane, apropos; *corresponding*, connected, similar, parallel, comparable, analogous; *interrelated*, correlative, reciprocal, interdependent, complementary, mutual, respective; *relative*, proportional, commensurate.

vb. *be related*, belong, pertain; *touch*, concern, regard, involve, interest; *relate*, link, connect, tie up, tie in, bracket together; *correlate*, juxtapose, reconcile, compare, contrast, draw a parallel between, cross-refer; *correspond*, approximate, agree, match, accord, fit, tally; *be relevant*, address the question, stick to the point.

adv. *relatively*, proportionally, in proportion, to scale; *in contrast*; *by/in comparison*, comparatively; *respectively*, mutually.

prep. *relative to*, with respect to, with regard to, as regards, with reference to, concerning, in relation to, re, vis-a-vis.

10 UNRELATEDNESS

See also **6** (extraneousness); **20** (disparity).

n. *unrelatedness*, irrelevance, inappositeness, inappropriateness, extraneousness, red herring (*colloq.*), non sequitur; *unconnectedness*, separateness, dissociation, independence; *randomness*, arbitrariness, coincidence, long shot, shot in the dark, fluke; *disproportion*, disparity, imbalance, asymmetry, distortion.

adj. *unrelated*, irrelevant, inapposite, inappropriate, extraneous, foreign, alien; *unconnected*, incidental, tangential, peripheral, inessential, unimportant, immaterial; *random*, arbitrary, chance, coincidental; *disproportionate*, unbalanced, distorted, asymmetrical.

vb. *be unrelated*, have no bearing on, have nothing to do with; *digress*, miss the point, avoid the issue, get sidetracked.

adv. *beside the point*, off the point; *by the way*, incidentally, in parenthesis.

11 RECIPROCITY

See also **9** (relatedness); **129** (exchange).

n. *reciprocity*, correspondence, interrelation, interdependence, mutuality, interconnectedness, complementarity; *counterpart*, equivalent, opposite number, alter ego, mirror image; *interaction*, interchange, interplay, exchange; *alternation*, exchange, give and take, tit for tat, seesaw, vicissitudes, ups and downs, swings and roundabouts.

adj. *reciprocal*, interrelated, interdependent, mutual, interconnected, complementary; *equivalent*, interchangeable, corresponding; *alternating*, seesaw, ding-dong (*colloq.*), retaliatory.

vb. *reciprocate*, exchange, swap (*col-*

loq.), return in kind, give as good as one gets, retaliate; *interact*, interconnect, interrelate, interchange; *alternate*, seesaw, fluctuate, take turn about; *correspond*, match up, tally.
adv. *in turn*, turn and turn about, Box and Cox; *all things being equal*, on balance; *conversely*, on the other hand; *vice versa*, mutatis mutandis.

12 FAMILY RELATIONS

See also **9** (relatedness); **154** (parent).
n. *family relationships*, kinship. tribalism, nepotism, inbreeding, incest; *ancestry*, blood, lineage, descent, matriarchy, patriarchy, genealogy, distaff side, spear side; *family*, clan, folks (*colloq.*), kith and kin, one's own flesh and blood, next of kin, relatives, in-laws, nuclear family, extended family; *parenthood*, motherhood, fatherhood, parenting, fostering, adoption, artificial insemination; *parent*, mother, father, donor, surrogate mother, godparent, stepparent, grandparent; *offspring*, issue, son, daughter, bastardy, illegitimacy, natural child, love child, test-tube baby; *sibling*, brother, sister, half-brother, half-sister, stepbrother, stepsister, twin; *aunt*, uncle, niece, nephew, great-aunt, great-uncle, great-niece, great-nephew, cousin, second cousin; *heredity*, chromosome, gene, DNA, genetic engineering.
adj. *familial*, kindred, cognate, agnate, consanguineous, incestuous; *ancestral*, tribal, genealogical, matriarchal, patriarchal, matrilineal, patrilineal; *filial*; *sibling*, sisterly, brotherly, fraternal; *avuncular*; *hereditary*, inherited, congenital, genetic, inbred.
vb. *be related to*, be descended from, take after, favour; *father*, sire, beget, adopt, foster; *wed*, intermarry, interbreed; *be inherited*, run in the family, be in the blood.

13 SAMENESS

See also **15** (uniformity); **17** (similarity); **21** (imitation).
n. *sameness*, identity, equivalence, similarity, coincidence, congruence, agreement; *likeness*, double, Doppelganger, alter ego, second self, clone, lookalike, spitting image (*colloq.*), chip off the old block (*colloq.*), dead ringer (*colloq.*); *copy*, duplicate, replica, carbon copy, facsimile, analogue, fellow, mate, match, twin, Tweedledum and Tweedledee; *uniformity*, monotony, same old story, nothing new under the sun.
adj. *same*, identical, selfsame, indistinguishable, interchangeable; *similar*, equivalent, like, analogous, congruent; *uniform*, unvarying, monotonous, samey (*colloq.*).
vb. *be the same*, be identical, come to the same thing, be tantamount to; *merge*, coincide, coalesce; *mirror*, repeat, parrot, echo; *copy*, duplicate, replicate, match, twin, clone; *look alike*, be like two peas in a pod.
adv. *similarly*, by the same token, in the same way, likewise; *ditto*.

14 OPPOSITENESS

See also **18** (dissimilarity); **215** (contraposition); **632** (opposition).
n. *oppositeness*, contrariety, contraposition, polarity, contradiction, incompatibility; *opposite*, converse, opposite pole, other extreme, antipodes, antithesis, antonym, negative, counterpoint, foil, antidote; *opposition*, antagonism, hostility, antipathy, conflict, clash; *reverse*, mirror image, wrong side, other side, verso, countercurrent, contraflow; *diametric opposites*, day and night, chalk and cheese, oil and water, yin and yang.
adj. *opposite*, contrary, contradictory, incompatible, inverse, converse; *diametrically opposite*, antithetical, antipodean, contrapuntal, negative; *opposed*, antagonistic, hostile, antipathetic, adversarial; *reverse*, counter, anticlockwise.
vb. *be opposite*, contradict, contrast; *oppose*, antagonize, clash with, conflict with, challenge; *reverse*, negate, counteract, contravene, run counter to, turn the tables on.
adv. *on the contrary*, in contrast; *conversely*, on the other hand; *back to*

front, inside out, upside down, topsy turvy.

15 UNIFORMITY

See also **13** (sameness); **17** (similarity); **72** (conformity).

n. *uniformity*, evenness, consistency, homogeneity; *continuity*, regularity, constancy, stability; *identity*, accord, agreement, consensus, unison, unity; *conformity*, regimentation, standardization, normalization, mass-production; *mould*, pattern, stamp, stereotype, production line, conveyor belt; *sameness*, drabness, monotony, routine, daily round, groove, rut.

adj. *uniform*, even, consistent, homogeneous, alike, of a piece; *continuous*, constant, regular, unbroken, uninterrupted, rhythmic, stable, unchanging, unvarying; *identical*, mass-produced, unisex, off-the-peg, standard, stereotyped, typecast; *same*, monotonous, repetitive, dull, drab, monochrome, self-coloured; *undifferentiated*, unrelieved, monolithic.

vb. *make uniform*, level, even off, homogenize, grade, size; *regularize*, stabilize, normalize; *standardize*, stereotype, systematize, typecast, mass-produce; *align*, bring into line, rehabilitate, reeducate, drill, regiment.

adv. *uniformly*, across the board; *in line*, in keeping.

16 DIVERSITY

See also **18** (dissimilarity); **38** (mixture).

n. *diversity*, variety, heterogeneity, dissimilarity, contrast, relief, variegation; *nonuniformity*, inconsistency, irregularity, discontinuity, unevenness; *changeability*, instability, variability, versatility; *assortment*, medley, mixed bag, miscellany, motley crew, ragbag, patchwork, mosaic, kaleidoscope, rainbow, coat of many colours, chequered career, everything but the kitchen sink (*colloq.*).

adj. *diverse*, varied, heterogeneous, variegated, chequered; *nonuniform*, inconsistent, irregular, discontinuous, uneven; *changeable*, unstable, variable, kaleidoscopic; *assorted*, mixed, motley, divers, sundry, various, miscellaneous; *versatile*, all-round, multipurpose, multifaceted.

vb. *make diverse*, vary, contrast, variegate, chequer; *mix*, stir up, shake up, jumble, shuffle; *diversify*, have many strings to one's bow, have many irons in the fire, branch out, spread one's wings, broaden one's horizons.

adv. *all anyhow*, in a muddle, higgledy-piggledy (*colloq.*).

17 SIMILARITY

See also **13** (sameness); **15** (uniformity); **19** (accord); **21** (imitation).

n. *similarity*, sameness, synonymy, symmetry, similitude, resemblance, likeness, affinity; *correspondence*, equation, comparability, analogy, simile, parallel, alliteration, assonance, assimilation; *semblance*, simulation, imitation, dissimulation, disguise, camouflage; *counterpart*, twin, copy, clone, soulmate, kindred spirit, two of a king, birds of a feather; *sameness*, equivalence, approximation, much of a muchness (*colloq.*), six of one and half a dozen of the other.

adj. *similar*, same, synonymous, symmetrical, like; *corresponding*, comparable, analogous, parallel, equivalent, approximate, akin; *simulated*, imitation, artificial, cultured, ersatz, synthetic.

vb. *be similar*, resemble, take after, favour, suggest; *reflect*, mirror, echo, evoke, savour of, smack of, be redolent of; *make similar*, equalize, homogenize, assimilate, camouflage, disguise; *compare*, liken, draw a parallel between; *imitate*, emulate, copy, reproduce, duplicate, clone; *correspond*, accord, tally, match, coincide, agree.

adv. *all the same*, at the same time; *similarly*, by the same token, likewise; *in the style/manner of*, à la; *as it were*, so to speak; *in the same boat*, in a similar situation.

18 DISSIMILARITY

See also **14** (oppositeness); **16**

(diversity); **20** (disparity); **418** (discrimination).
n. *dissimilarity*, difference, disparity, diversity, discrepancy, divergence; *unlikeness*, incongruity, incompatibility, contrast, asymmetry, no comparison, nothing in common, another matter/story, different kettle of fish (*colloq.*); *differentiation*, discrimination, distinction, nuance, nicety, nit-picking (*colloq.*).
adj. *dissimilar*, different, disparate, divergent, diverse; *unlike*, incongruous, incompatible, contrasting, poles apart; *distinctive*, unusual, peculiar, out of the ordinary, singular; *discriminating*, discerning, selective, choosy (*colloq.*).
vb. *be dissimilar*, differ, diverge, deviate, depart from; *be unlike*, contrast, conflict, be at odds, be at variance; *differentiate*, distinguish, discriminate, split hairs, nit-pick (*colloq.*), separate the sheep from the goats, tell the men from the boys.
adv. *at different times*, variously; *in contrast*.

19 ACCORD

See also **15** (uniformity); **17** (similarity); **25** (equality); **436** (assent).
n. *accord*, agreement, concord, concert, chorus, harmony, understanding, reconciliation, arbitration; *consensus*, unanimity, unison, unity, cooperation, solidarity; *consistency*, uniformity, coherence, congruity, conformity; *aptness*, fitness, appropriateness, suitability, compatibility, timeliness, right moment, mot juste; *adaptation*, accommodation, adjustment, alignment, synchronization, fine tuning.
adj. *agreeing*, harmonious, reconciled; *unanimous*, united, concerted, joint, cooperative; *consistent*, uniform, coherent, congruent, of a piece; *apt*, appropriate, suitable, fitting, compatible, consonant, commensurate, timely, opportune; *adaptable*, accommodating, flexible, easygoing, conciliatory; *well-adjusted*, balanced, close-fitting, snug, made-to-measure.
vb. *accord*, agree, concur, consent, chorus, chime in, harmonize, reach an understanding; *cooperate*, get along, pull together, hit it off (*colloq.*), be on the same wavelength (*colloq.*), see eye to eye; *fit*, suit, fit the bill (*colloq.*), tally, square, match, dovetail, marry, coincide; *adapt*, adjust, accommodate, align, true up, synchronize, fine-tune.
adv. *in accord*, in chorus, in concert, in step, in phase, in tune, in unison; *in keeping*, in place, in context; *at home*, at ease, in one's element.

20 DISPARITY

See also **10** (unrelatedness); **18** (dissimilarity); **26** (unequality).
n. *disparity*, inequality, imbalance, difference, dissimilarity, divergence; *discrepancy*, inconsistency, gap, margin, overlap, shortfall, surplus, differential; *maladjustment*, mismatch, mésalliance, crossed line, cross-purposes, discord, dissonance, false note; *misfit*, odd man out, eccentric, freak, sport, square peg in a round hole, fish out of water; *unsuitability*, incompatibility, inappropriateness, untimeliness, irrelevancy.
adj. *disparate*, unequal, disproportionate, dissimilar, different, divergent, inconsistent; *discordant*, dissonant, jarring, grating, out-of-tune; *maladjusted*, unbalanced, deviant, eccentric, freakish, odd, ill-matched, ill-assorted; *unsuitable*, unfitting, unbecoming, inappropriate, untimely, inopportune, incompatible, irrelevant.
vb. *be disparate*, differ, diverge, contradict; *conflict*, clash, jar, grate, stick out like a sore thumb (*colloq.*); *misplace*, mistime, mishit, talk out of turn, drop a brick/clanger (*colloq.*).
adv. *out of step*, out of line, out of phase; *at odds*, at variance, at cross-purposes; *out of one's element*, out of place, out of keeping, out of season.

21 IMITATION

See also **13** (sameness); **17** (similarity); **151** (reproduction).
n. *imitation*, mimesis, onomatopoeia, emulation, plagiarism; *copy*, reproduction, duplicate, facsimile, photocopy, carbon copy, replica, clone; *fake*, forgery, counterfeit, sham, simulation,

disguise, camouflage; *mimicry*, mockery, travesty, satire, caricature, burlesque, parody, pastiche, impersonation, spoof (*colloq.*), send-up (*colloq.*), takeoff (*colloq.*); *imitator*, follower, emulator, disciple; *copyist*, plagiarist, impersonator, mime, echo, sheep, ape, parrot, copycat; *forger*, counterfeiter, fake, impostor, poseur, charlatan, mountebank; *mimic*, satirist, caricaturist, parodist.

adj. *imitative*, mimetic, onomatopoeic; *derivative*, second-hand, unoriginal, copycat, follow-my-leader; *fake*, counterfeit, false, sham, phoney, pseudo, artificial, synthetic, mock, ersatz, cultured.

vb. *imitate*, emulate, follow, model oneself on, pattern oneself after, follow in the footsteps of; *copy*, reproduce, duplicate, clone, photocopy, borrow, crib, plagiarize; *fake*, forge, counterfeit, sham, simulate, impersonate; *repeat*, echo, ape, parrot, chorus, follow the herd, jump/climb on the bandwagon (*colloq.*); *mimic*, mock, caricature, satirize, burlesque, parody, travesty, send up (*colloq.*), take off (*colloq.*).

adv. *word for word*, verbatim, parrot-fashion; *ditto*; *to the life*.

22 ORIGINALITY

See also **70** (speciality).

n. *originality*, creativity, imagination, inventiveness, innovation; *novelty*, individuality, uniqueness, freshness; *original*, source, model, pattern, mould, matrix, blueprint, prototype, archetype, paradigm, test case, precedent; *originator*, inventor, creator, innovator, deviser; *authenticity*, genuineness, real thing, genuine article, real McCoy (*colloq.*).

adj. *original*, creative, imaginative, inventive, innovative; *novel*, individual, unique, one-off, unparalleled, unprecedented, unheard-of, off-beat (*colloq.*), sui generis, inimitable, incomparable; *seminal*, prototypal, archetypal, stereotypical, standard, classic; *authentic*, genuine, real, echt, bona fide.

vb. *originate*, create, invent, devise, imagine, dream up, conceive, generate; *patent*, blueprint, copyright, trademark; *model*, mould, pattern, stereotype; *exemplify*, typify, represent.

adv. *from the beginning*, from scratch, ab ovo.

23 QUANTITY

See also **29** (greatness); **30** (smallness); **168** (size); **177** (measurement).

n. *quantity*, amount, amplitude, magnitude, bulk, mass; *dimensions*, longitude, length, latitude, breadth, width, girth, altitude, height, depth; *area*, extension, volume, capacity, weight, heaviness; *strength*, pressure, potential, tension, torque, stress, strain; *definite quantity*, quantum, measure, dose, ration, portion, helping, share, slice of the cake; *small quantity*, thimbleful, cupful, pinch, teaspoonful, ounce, milligram; *large quantity*, bucketful, sackful, armful, bundle, lorryload, hundredweight, kilo, stack, mountain.

adj. *quantitative*, high, long, wide, deep, broad; *large*, ample, bulky, massive, extensive, capacious, voluminous; *small*, compact, light, shallow, neat, diminutive.

vb. *quantify*, measure, estimate; *apportion*, ration, allot, distribute.

adv. *to the tune of*; *in the region of*, approximately, in the right ballpark (*U.S. colloq.*).

24 DEGREE

See also **9** (relatedness).

n. *degree*, extent, proportion, scale, ratio, rate, frequency; *stage*, level, step, rung, point, remove; *rank*, status, class, standing, footing; *gradation*, calibration, differential, interval, nuance; *hierarchy*, taxonomy, series; *gauge*, grid, graph, sliding scale, ladder.

adj. *gradational*, serial, hierarchical; *proportional*, relative, comparative; *gradual*, staggered.

vb. *graduate*, calibrate, measure off, grade, scale, size; *class*, sort, rank, rate.

adv. *by degrees*, gradually, bit by bit,

step by step, little by little; *in some degree*, to some extent, somewhat.

25 EQUALITY

See also **19** (accord); **28** (compensation).

n. *equality*, equivalence, equal footing, identity, sameness, symmetry; *parity*, par, quits, level pegging, six of one and half a dozen of the other; *equilibrium*, balance, poise, even keel, equation, balance of power, balance of terror, mutually assured destruction; *stability*, status quo, stasis, stalemate, deadlock, hung jury; *draw*, tie, dead heat, photo finish (*colloq.*), cliffhanger (*colloq.*); *equalizer*, makeweight, counterweight, ballast, stopgap; *equal*, peer, match, mate, twin, fellow, counterpart, opposite number, oppo (*colloq.*); *egalitarianism*, democracy, equal rights, equal opportunity, positive discrimination, justice.

adj. *equal*, same, equilateral, equidistant, coextensive, identical; *even*, stable, static, self-righting, self-regulating, homoeostatic; *symmetrical*, half-and-half, fifty-fifty, parallel, one-to-one, ding-dong (*colloq.*); *egalitarian*, democratic, equitable, just, fair, impartial.

vb. *be equal*, tie, draw, even out, tally, balance; *equalize*, synchronize, level up/down, round up/down; *compensate*, make good, offset, rob Peter to pay Paul; *stabilize*, strike a balance, redress the balance.

adv. *equally*, by the same token; *on equal terms*, pari passu; *neck and neck*, abreast.

26 INEQUALITY

See also **20** (disparity).

n. *inequality*, disparity, difference, discrepancy, disproportion; *imbalance*, overload, overkill, top-heaviness, shortage, shortfall, deficiency; *handicap*, disadvantage, loaded dice, advantage, privilege, head start; *unevenness*, asymmetry, tilt, camber, list, lopsidedness, odd number, casting vote; *inequity*, injustice, discrimination, prejudice, bias.

adj. *unequal*, disparate, different, disproportionate; *unbalanced*, overweight, underweight, top-heavy, overshot, undershot; *uneven*, asymmetrical, askew, awry, lopsided, skewwhiff (*colloq.*); *inequitable*, undemocratic, unfair, unjust, discriminatory, biased, prejudiced.

vb. *be unequal*, be above/below par, overcompensate, overshoot, fall short; *outweigh*, outrank, outclass, outstrip, outvote; *unbalance*, upset, capsize, destabilize; *bias*, prejudice, skew, disadvantage, handicap, tip the scales.

adv. *of balance*, on the light/heavy side; *at a disadvantage*, up against it, with the odds stacked against one; *at an advantage*, out in front.

27 AVERAGE

See also **63** (middle); **69** (generality).

n. *average*, mean, median, norm, par; *moderation*, middle course, golden mean, happy medium, best of both worlds; *midpoint*, midway, halfway, halfway house, middle age, middle class, middle distance, mid-life crisis; *averageness*, mediocrity, ordinariness, lowest common denominator, middle of the road, common run, common man, man in the street, Joe Bloggs (*colloq.*); *neutrality*, impartiality, mugwumpery, silent majority, floating vote, don't knows.

adj. *average*, mean, median, normal, standard, par for the course; *moderate*, middling, middle-aged, middlebrow, middle-class, middle-of-the-road; *mediocre*, ordinary, commonplace, run-of-the-mill, passable, adequate, so-so (*colloq.*); *neutral*, impartial, tepid, lukewarm, Laodicean.

vb. *average out*, balance out, even out; *take an average*, go halves, split the difference; *be moderate*, strike a balance between, see both sides of the question, sit on the fence (*colloq.*).

adv. *on average*, in general, as a rule, on the whole; *all in all*, on balance, all things considered, at the end of the day; *up to the mark*, up to scratch (*colloq.*), up to snuff (*colloq.*).

come up to scratch (*colloq.*), not be a patch on (*colloq,*), not be in the running; *sink*, slump, bottom out, go through the floor (*colloq.*), hit rock bottom.

adv. *below par*, below average; *under someone's heel*, under someone's thumb.

33 INCREASE

See also **35** (addition).

n. *increase*, addition, increment, augmentation, supplement, accretion, accumulation, appreciation, intensification; *growth*, development, advance, progression, acceleration, crescendo, rise, buildup, inflation; *spread*, expansion, enlargement, proliferation multiplication; *sudden increase*, escalation, explosion, bulge, boom, boost, spiral, climb, rising tide, quantum leap; *extra*, bonus, profit, rake-off (*colloq.*).

adj. *increasing*, growing, escalating; *progressive*, cumulative, incremental; *additional*, supplementary, extra; *spiralling*, inflationary.

vb. *increase*, add, accrue, accumulate, appreciate, augment; *grow*, develop, burgeon, sprout, thrive, prosper, advance, progress, accelerate, rise, inflate, wax; *spread*, expand, enlarge, mushroom, proliferate, multiply; *escalate*, climb, spiral, rocket, take off; *intensify*, redouble, treble, step up, hot up (*colloq.*); *boost*, swell, stoke, reinforce, bolster, pad out, flesh out, beef up (*colloq.*).

adv. *increasingly*, more and more; *on the increase*, on the up and up; *into the bargain*, with interest, with knobs on (*colloq.*).

34 DECREASE

See also **36** (subtraction).

n. *decrease*, diminution, abatement, reduction, deduction, subtraction, loss, depreciation, decline; *contraction*, shrinkage, cutback, rundown, retrenchment, deceleration; *recession*, slump, depression, squeeze, freeze, restraint, deflation; *gradual decrease*, diminuendo, decrescendo, ebb, leakage, evaporation, erosion, attrition; *sudden decrease*, fall, dip, drop, plunge, slide, tumble, crash.

adj. *decreasing*, diminishing, dwindling; *reductive*, subtractive; *depressive*, deflationary.

vb. *decrease*, diminish, reduce, deduct, subtract, lose, depreciate, decline; *contract*, shrink, cut back, retrench, tighten one's belt, deflate, depress, squeeze, freeze; *lessen*, dwindle, ebb, recede, abate, subside, wane, slacken, decelerate; *fall*, dip, drop, plunge, slide, slump, tumble, crash; *cut*, axe, slash, curtail, decimate.

adv. *decreasingly*, less and less; *in decline*, on the wane.

35 ADDITION

See also **33** (increase).

n. *addition*, increase, increment, appendage; *adjunct*, attachment, annexe, extension, arm, wing; *appendix*, supplement, postscript, coda, codicil, addendum, footnote, rider, pendant; *insertion*, interjection, interpolation, parenthesis, filling, padding; *reinforcement*, auxiliary, supernumerary, reserve, backup; *accretion*, agglomeration, agglutination, concatenation; *additive*, admixture, ingredient, seasoning; *accompaniment*, extras, trappings, accessories, trimmings, frills (*colloq.*); *bonus*, perk (*colloq.*), overtime, profit, gain, interest, percentage, golden handshake, windfall; *sequel*, follow-up, encore, epilogue, afterthought.

adj. *additional*, accessory, supplementary; *extra*, spare, reserve, auxiliary, ancillary, supernumerary.

vb. *add*, affix, annex, attach, append; *supplement*, augment, swell, reinforce, pad out, flesh out, top up, beef up (*colloq.*); *insert*, interject, introduce, interpose, interpolate, throw in, chip in (*colloq.*); *add on*, tack on, join on, slap on (*colloq.*), superimpose, overlay, graft.

adv. *in addition*, moreover, furthermore; *plus*, with interest, over the odds; *into the bargain*, to boot; *to the good*, in profit, in the black.

36 SUBTRACTION

See also **34** (decrease).

n. *subtraction*, deduction, removal, withdrawal, elimination, deletion, expurgation, bowdlerization; *curtailment*, cutback, contraction, retrenchment; *reduction*, discount, rebate, loss, decrement, tare; *abridgment*, abbreviation, condensation, summary, precis; *amputation*, excision, decapitation, castration; *erosion*, abrasion, attrition.

vb. *subtract*, deduct, remove, withdraw, eliminate, delete, censor, blue-pencil, expurgate, bowdlerize; *curtail*, decrease, cut, cut back, prune, pare, whittle, trim, slim down, dock, chop, axe, slash; *reduce*, abridge, abbreviate, condense, summarize; *amputate*, excise, decapitate, behead, castrate, geld, spay; *erode*, abrade, wear away, grind down.

adv. *less*, minus, without; *at a discount*, at a loss; *out of pocket*, down, in the red.

37 REMAINDER

See also **60** (sequence).

n. *remainder*, residue, remains, remnant, relic; *surplus*, balance, profit, net; *trace*, track, trail, footprint, spoor, vestige; *ruins*, shell, shadow, wreck, husk, skeleton, fossil, ashes; *debris*, detritus, slough, scurf, refuse, litter, rubbish, sewage, excrement; *sediment*, dregs, lees, grounds, scum, dross; *leavings*, leftovers, scraps, scrapings, off-scourings, gleanings, stubble, chaff; *rump*, stump, offcut, tail end, fag end (*colloq.*), odds and ends, odds and sods (*colloq.*); *wake*, aftermath, aftereffect, fallout, hangover, by-product, spin-off; *survivor*, orphan, widow, widower, relict, heir, successor.

adj. *remaining*, leftover, residual, vestigial; *surplus*, spare, odd, net, outstanding, superfluous; *sedimentary*, alluvial; *surviving*, alive, extant.

vb. *remain*, survive, outlast, persist, endure.

adv. *to spare*, in hand, to play with (*colloq.*); *on the shelf* (*colloq.*).

38 MIXTURE

See also **16** (diversity); **45** (combination).

n. *mixture*, combination, compound, concoction, infusion, confection; *amalgam*, alloy, blend, fusion, merger; *assortment*, mixed bag, motley crew, miscellany, melange, medley, kaleidoscope, mosaic, patchwork, pot pourri, cocktail, punch; *mishmash*, hotchpotch, ragbag, farrago, job lot, jumble, gallimaufry, ragout, witches' brew, everything but the kitchen sink (*colloq.*); *mixer*, blender, liquidizer, melting pot, crucible; *hybrid*, cross, mongrel, chimera, half-breed, mulatto, creole, androgyne, hermaphrodite, bisexual, transsexual; *admixture*, tinge, trace, dash, sprinkling, hint, soupçon.

adj. *mixed*, combined, composite; *assorted*, miscellaneous, heterogeneous, catholic, eclectic, syncretic; *variegated*, dappled, mottled, brindled, piebald, skewbald, motley, rainbow, kaleidoscopic, psychedelic, technicolour; *hybrid*, mongrel, half-caste, crossbred, bionic, androgynous, bisexual, transsexual, hermaphroditic.

vb. *mix*, combine, amalgamate, fuse, merge; *blend*, shake, stir, dilute, brew, knead, mash, liquidize, homogenize; *mingle*, intersperse, interlard, interlace, interweave, intertwine; *suffuse*, pervade, imbue, impregnate, infuse, permeate; *tinge*, season, spice, sprinkle, lace, spike, adulterate; *intermarry*, interbreed.

adv. *among*, amidst; *pell-mell*, higgledy-piggledy (*colloq.*).

39 PURITY

See also **586** (cleanness).

n. *purity*, homogeneity, integrity, immaculateness; *wholeness*, wholefood, health food, macrobiotics; *essence*, distillate, concentrate, extract; *cleanliness*, antisepsis, hygiene, sanitation, pasteurization, sterilization; *purification*, clarification, filtration, distillation; *purgative*, laxative, cathartic.

adj. *pure*, simple, single, unalloyed, irreducible, homogeneous; *integral*, intact, immaculate, pristine, virgin;

natural, whole, raw, unadulterated, unprocessed, untreated, macrobiotic; *clean*, antiseptic, hygienic, sterile, unpolluted, sanitized; *undiluted*, neat, straight; *purebred*, thoroughbred, pedigree.
vb. *purify*, simplify, refine, distil, clarify, concentrate; *filter*, sieve, sift, winnow, weed; *clean*, wash, sterilize, disinfect, pasteurize, purge, flush out, cleanse the Augean stables.
adv. *purely*, simply, merely; *neat*, straight, on the rocks.

40 UNION

See also **42** (connection); **43** (adhesion); **66** (assembly).
n. *union*, combination, conjunction, confluence, convergence, merger, fusion, synthesis; *alliance*, coalition, association, league, brotherhood, guild, trade union, syndicate, cooperative; *meeting*, reunion, gathering, congress, conference; *joint*, link, bond, connection, tie-in, hookup, linkup, ligature, suture, seal, bracket, seam, splice, weld, coupling, yoke; *junction*, intersection, node, nexus, crossroads, interface, hinge, pivot; *consolidation*, compaction, coagulation, coalescence, conglomeration, concretion; *coordination*, cooperation, communication, teamwork, solidarity, symbiosis; *marriage*, wedlock, matrimony; *sexual union*, coitus, coition, coupling, pairing, mating, copulation, sexual intercourse, carnal knowledge, intimacy, nooky (*colloq.*), fucking (*vulg.*), screwing (*vulg.*).
adj. *united*, combined, composite, conjoined, coordinated, interlinked, online; *allied*, associated, joint, symbiotic, corporate, communal, cooperative; *connective*, conjunctive, adhesive, cohesive, copulative; *compact*, close-set, dense, solid, firm, immovable, inextricable; *married*, wed, matrimonial, marital; *coital*, sexual, venereal, intimate.
vb. *unite*, combine, conjoin, compound, coalesce, blend, fuse, merge, incorporate, amalgamate, converge; *ally*, associate, join forces, team up, organize; *join*, bond, link, connect, bridge, span, straddle; *couple*, harness, hitch, yoke, pair, bracket, lump together; *cement*, solder, seal, splice, tie, knit, sew, bind, lash, stitch, lock, bolt, clamp, staple; *attach*, secure, fasten, nail, hook, pin, screw, stick, gum, plaster; *hinge*, dovetail, mitre, rabbet; *moor*, tether, hobble, fetter, shackle, manacle, handcuff; *marry*, wed, get hitched (*colloq.*), get spliced (*colloq.*); *copulate*, mate, pair, couple, mount, cover, serve, have sex with, know, enjoy, possess, make love to, sleep with, bed, lay (*vulg.*), screw (*vulg.*), fuck (*vulg.*), have it off with (*colloq.*), make it with (*colloq.*), get one's oats, get one's leg over (*colloq.*).
adv. *arm in arm*, hand in hand; *side by side*, shoulder to shoulder, as one man; *hand in glove*, in league, as thick as thieves.

41 SEPARATION

see also **44** (nonadhesion); **46** (disintegration); **67** (dispersion); **790** (unsociability).
n. *separation*, disintegration, fragmentation, decomposition, dissection, analysis; *division*, partition, demarcation, cleavage, dichotomy, divergence, polarization, parting of the ways; *breach*, break, rupture, fracture, split, fission, severance, divorce; *dissociation*, dissolution, disbandment, demobilization, breakup, dispersion, diaspora; *cleft*, crack, fissure, rent, crevasse, chasm; *separatism*, segregation, apartheid, purdah, secession, ghettoism, isolationism, insularity, nonalignment; *seclusion*, quarantine, ghetto, enclave, oasis, reserve; *schism*, sect, faction, splinter group, breakaway group, offshoot, branch; *exclusion*, embargo, boycott, blacklist, blackballing, ostracism.
adj. *separate*, distinct, discrete, unattached, disengaged, free, free-standing; *solitary*, alone, aloof, detached, insular, self-contained, self-sufficient, independent; *apart*, asunder, cleft, cloven, broken, torn, rent; *separatist*, segregationist, isolatinist, secessionist, sectarian,

dissident, breakaway; *divisive*, controversial, contentious, polemical.
vb. *separate*, disintegrate, fragment, decompose, dissolve; *break*, breach, rupture, fracture, splinter, split, crack; *dissociate*, disband, disperse, scatter, diverge, divorce, polarize, go one's separate ways; *divide*, halve, split, sever, partition, hive off; *seclude*, sequester, quarantine, segregate, isolate, insulate, cut off; *exclude*, expel, bar, blacklist, blackball, ostracize, send to Coventry, cold-shoulder (*colloq.*); *part*, rend, cleave, sunder, tear, slash, gash, score, slit, scratch, lacerate, chip, shred; *cut down*, hack, chop, dock, clip, shear, prune, fell, scythe, mow.
adv. *apart*, asunder, in two, in twain; *in pieces*, in bits, to shreds, to tatters, to smithereens (*colloq.*), limb from limb.

42 CONNECTION

See also **40** (union).
n. *connection*, association, relation, link, tie, nexus; *bond*, affinity, sympathy, fellow-feeling, rapport; *bridge*, aqueduct, span, arch, stepping-stone, neck, isthmus, causeway, ladder, companionway; *channel*, route, passage, corridor, tunnel, duct, pipeline; *linkup*, hookup, tie-up, hot line (*colloq.*), switchboard, bleeper, intercom, walkie-talkie; *intermediary*, link-man, go-between, middleman, broker, matchmaker, negotiator, pig-in-the-middle (*colloq.*); *fastener*, buckle, hasp, clasp, brooch, bracket, bolt, padlock, latch, nail, peg, dowel, adhesive, glue; *cable*, rope, ligament, tendon, muscle, leash, halter, harness, rein, chain, fetter, manacle, shackle, yoke; *junction*, knot, ligature, suture, seam, hinge, pivot.
adj., vb., adv. *See* **40** (union).

43 ADHESION

See also **40** (union); **539** (resolution); **540** (perseverance); **633** (cooperation).
n. *adhesion*, accretion, agglomeration, consolidation; *cohesiveness*, stickiness, tackiness, viscosity, density, solidity; *association*, adherence, affiliation, membership, enrolment, matriculation; *solidarity*, esprit de corps, team spirit, serried ranks, united front, phalanx; *mass*, cluster, clump, clot, clod, cake; *adhesive*, gum, glue, paste, fixative, cement, mortar, solder, seal, sticky tape, flypaper; *grasp*, clutch, grip, hug, foothold, toehold, stranglehold; *limpet*, barnacle, leech, bur, clinging vine; *tenacity*, perseverance, resolution, stamina, staying power; *commitment*, dedication, zeal, militancy.
adj. *adhesive*, sticky, gummy, tacky, gluey, viscous, gooey (*colloq.*); *cohesive*, dense, close, solid, compact; *adhering*, clinging, tight-fitting, skintight; *united*, associated, inseparable, indivisible, inextricable; *tenacious*, firm, unshakable, unwavering, persistent, resolute; *committed*, dedicated, engagé, card-carrying, zealous, militant.
vb. *adhere*, stick, cling, cleave; *cohere*, bunch, mass, congeal, cluster, cake, coagulate, set, solidify; *associate*, affiliate, join, enrol, matriculate, subscribe to, adopt, wed, espouse; *glue*, gum, paste, plaster, cement, solder, weld; *grasp*, grip, clutch, clasp, hug, intertwine, interlace, interlock; *persevere*, hold out, stand firm, stay the course; *commit oneself*, take sides, take the plunge (*colloq.*), nail one's colours to the mast, come down on the side of.
adv. *side by side*, shoulder to shoulder, cheek by jowl.

44 NONADHESION

See also **41** (separation); **541** (vacillation).
n. *nonadhesion*, smoothness, slipperiness, runniness, wateriness, looseness, slackness, separateness, detachedness; *independence*, individualism, aloofness, self-sufficiency, nonalignment, separatism, maverick, free spirit, renegade; *irresolution*, vacillation, fickleness, inconstancy, defection; *apathy*, indifference, floating vote, don't knows.
adj. *nonadhesive*, smooth, slippery, runny, watery; *separate*, loose, free, free-floating, flyaway, floppy, slack, baggy; *independent*, aloof, self-sufficient, individualist, nonaligned, separa-

tist; *irresolute*, vacillating, fickle, volatile, inconstant; *uncommitted*, apathetic, indifferent, lukewarm, wishy-washy (*colloq.*).
vb. *not adhere*, slide, slip, flow, thaw, melt, hang, dangle, flap; *unstick*, free, loosen, slacken, release; *be independent*, go it alone, do one's own thing (*colloq.*), stand on one's own two feet, paddle one's own canoe (*colloq.*); *be irresolute*, waver, vacillate, fluctuate, be in two minds, have second thoughts; *be uncommitted*, sit on the fence (*colloq.*), face both ways, hedge one's bets.
adv. *apart*, asunder.

45 COMBINATION

See also **38** (mixture); **633** (cooperation).
n. *combination*, fusion, blend, alloy, amalgam, mixture, merger, synthesis; *union*, marriage, alliance, association, league, confederation, corporation, combine, cartel, cabal, clique, unholy alliance, conspiracy; *cooperation*, partnership, teamwork, joint effort, job-sharing, collective, cooperative; *compilation*, anthology, compendium, miscellany, *composition*, collage, jigsaw, mosaic, patchwork; *unification*, integration, incorporation, absorption, assimilation.
adj. *combined*, corporate, joint, allied, united; *cooperative*, communal, collaborative, symbiotic.
vb. *combine*, mix, fuse, alloy, blend, amalgamate, merge; *unify*, lump together, incorporate, synthesize, assemble, marry up, integrate, homogenize; *unite*, ally, associate, band together, join forces, pool one's resources, team up, get together, pair off.
adv. *in addition*, plus, moreover, on top of that; *in league*, in tandem, in cahoots (*colloq.*), in partnership, in the same boat (*colloq.*).

46 DISINTEGRATION

See also **41** (separation); **593** (deterioration).
n. *disintegration*, fragmentation, fission, breakup, collapse; *decomposition*, decay, dilapidation, erosion, corrosion; *dissection*, analysis, breakdown, anatomization; *dispersal*, disbandment, dissolution, atomization, pulverization.
adj. *disintegrated*, fragmented, shattered, broken, brittle, fissile; *soluble*, biodegradable, disposable, recyclable; *decomposed*, decaying, dilapidated, crumbling.
vb. *disintegrate*, fragment, break up, collapse, fall apart, go to pieces (*colloq.*), crack up (*colloq.*); *split*, fracture, crack, splinter, shatter, shiver, smash, explode; *decompose*, decay, erode, corrode, crumble, degenerate; *dissect*, analyse, break down, dismantle, dismember, anatomize, put under the microscope; *disperse*, disband, dissolve, scatter, atomize, pulverize.
adv. *apart*, asunder, into pieces, into smithereens (*colloq.*).

47 WHOLE

See also **29** (greatness); **49** (completeness); **51** (inclusion).
n. *whole*, entity, unit, ensemble, complex, total, sum, aggregate, corpus; *wholeness*, unity, integrity, entirety, completeness, totality, universality, fullness, comprehensiveness; *universe*, world, cosmos, globe, microcosm; *panorama*, survey, overview, bird's eye view, synopsis; *everything*, the lot (*colloq.*), the works (*colloq.*), the whole shooting match (*colloq.*), the whole kit and caboodle (*colloq.*); *everyone*, Tom, Dick, and Harry, all the world and his wife.
adj. *whole*, entire, complete, full, total, aggregate, gross; *integral*, organic, intact, virgin, pristine, flawless, seamless, unadulterated, undiluted, unabridged, unedited; *universal*, all-embracing, cosmic, global, holistic, panoramic, omnibus; *comprehensive*, catch-all, sweeping, blanket, exhaustive, wholesale, outright.
vb. *See* **49** (completeness).
adv. *wholly*, entirely, totally, fully, unreservedly, body and soul, one hundred per cent; *outright*, lock, stock, and barrel, hook, line, and sinker, in

one fell swoop, at a stroke; *altogether*, all told, in all, as a whole, en masse.

48 PART

See also **50** (incompleteness); **53** (component); **78** (fraction).

n. *part*, portion, segment, section, sector; *share*, cut, whack (*colloq.*), slice of the cake, lion's share; *subdivision*, category, class, branch, offshoot, tributary, feeder, department, compartment; *component*, element, ingredient, constituent, factor, item, detail; *proportion*, percentage, fraction, minority, majority; *instalment*, issue, number, volume, partwork, part-payment, deposit, down payment; *body part*, member, limb, organ, appendage, trunk, torso; *piece*, wedge, chunk, slab, hunk, wodge (*colloq.*); *passage*, extract, snippet, gobbet, excerpt, clip; *small piece*, scrap, morsel, shred, crumb, drop, bite; *fragment*, sliver, shard, splinter, flake, chip, granule.

adj. *partial*, incomplete, unfinished, fragmentary, piecemeal; *scrappy*, bitty, patchy, uneven; *divided*, segmented, fractional, sectional, departmental, compartmentalized.

vb. *part*, split, divide, bisect, section, segment, partition; *subdivide*, branch, ramify, fork, radiate; *disintegrate*, fragment, disband, dissolve, break up; *dissect*, take apart, dismember, dismantle, anatomize, cannibalize.

adv. *partly*, in part; *partially*, incompletely, in some degree; *bit by bit*, piecemeal, in dribs and drabs (*colloq.*), in fits and starts, in snatches.

49 COMPLETENESS

See also **29** (greatness); **47** (whole); **653** (completion).

n. *completeness*, wholeness, entirety, totality; *fullness*, plenitude, repleteness, satiety, bellyful (*colloq.*), skinful (*colloq.*); *refill*, top-up, finishing/last touch, second helping; *maximum*, upper limit, ceiling, summit, acme, crowning glory, ne plus ultra, culmination, apotheosis, saturation point, last straw, clincher (*colloq.*); *comprehensiveness*, exhaustiveness, thoroughness, inclusiveness, A to Z, alpha and omega, gamut, everything but the kitchen sink (*colloq.*); *all-rounder*, polymath, Renaissance man, jack of all trades, superman, superwoman.

adj. *whole*, entire, total, full-length, full-time, full-scale, full-blown; *replete*, full, sated, brim-full, bursting at the seams, jam-packed, crammed, stuffed, bulging, chock-a-block (*colloq.*); *comprehensive*, exhaustive, inclusive, all-embracing, in-depth, encyclopedic, all-round, wide-ranging; *absolute*, utter, thoroughgoing, radical, wholesale, unmitigated, unqualified, unstinting, wholehearted, unreserved, downright, out-and-out; *sheer*, pure, arrant, rank, gross, regular, arch, dyed-in-the-wool.

vb. *complete*, finish off, follow up/through, round off, put the finishing touches to, perfect, clinch (*colloq.*), set the seal on, despatch, polish off, mop up; *sate*, satisfy, gorge, stuff, cram, pack, fill; *replenish*, refill, top up; *saturate*, swamp, drown, overrun, overwhelm; *do one's utmost*, go all out, go the whole hog (*colloq.*), go for broke (*colloq.*), pull out all the stops, leave no stone unturned.

adv. *completely*, fully, thoroughly, to the hilt, to the top of one's bent, body and soul, down to the ground; *entirely*, root and branch, hook, line, and sinker, lock, stock, and barrel; *absolutely*, unreservedly, wholeheartedly, head and shoulders; *utterly*, wholly, downright, thoroughly, plain, clean, stark, to the core, through and through; *all over*, high and low, far and wide, from top to toe.

50 INCOMPLETENESS

See also **48** (part); **65** (discontinuity); **585** (imperfection); **655** (non-completion).

n. *incompleteness*, inadequacy, deficiency, defectiveness, scantiness, meagreness; *insufficiency*, deficit, shortage, shortfall, short measure, lack, want, need; *superficiality*, perfunctoriness, cursoriness, half measures; *immaturity*, rawness, callowness, greenness, crudity; *unevenness*, scrappiness, patchiness, bittiness, sketchiness, loose ends, curate's egg; *outline*, rough copy, rough draft, sketch, jottings, notes; *gap*, break, breach, hiatus, hole, flaw, omission, lacuna, missing link.

adj. *incomplete*, insufficient, scanty, meagre, underweight, under strength; *inadequate*, deficient, defective, wanting, lacking, missing; *superficial*, perfunctory, cursory, cosmetic; *immature*, raw, green, callow, ill-digested, half-baked (*colloq.*); *uneven*, patchy, scrappy, bitty, sketchy, fragmentary; *provisional*, temporary, makeshift, crude, rough and ready; *unfinished*, half-finished, unpolished, ragged, rough-hewn, uncut, unrefined, coarse.

vb. *be incomplete*, lack, need, want, miss, fall short, leave something to be desired, not come up to scratch, not make the grade; *not complete*, skimp, scamp, bodge, patch up, paper over the cracks; *interrupt*, leave off, break off, leave hanging; *omit*, skip, jump, miss out, skate over.

adv. *incompletely*, partially, nearly, almost, all but, virtually; *in preparation*, under way, nearing completion, on the stocks.

51 INCLUSION

See also **47** (whole); **69** (generality).

n. *inclusion*, incorporation, integration, assimilation, absorption; *inclusiveness*, comprehensiveness, encyclopedicity, blanket coverage, catch-all, package deal; *universality*, catholicity, eclecticness, ecumenicism, broad church, something for everyone; *admission*, membership, admissibility, eligibility.

adj. *including*, comprising, containing, consisting of; *inclusive*, all-in, all-embracing, comprehensive, overall; *universal*, catholic, eclectic, broad-based.

vb. *include*, comprise, subsume, contain, comprehend; *incorporate*, encapsulate, cover, assimilate, encompass, embrace; *admit*, accommodate, receive, number among, count in.

adv. *inclusive*, across the board, from A to Z.

52 EXCLUSION

See also **790** (unsociability).

n. *exclusion*, expulsion, eviction, rejection, banishment, exile, extradition, deportation, excommunication; *prohibition*, ban, embargo, boycott, blockade; *segregation*, colour bar, apartheid, quarantine, ostracism; *barrier*, barricade, closed door, lockout, partition, Iron Curtain, Bamboo Curtain, Berlin Wall, no-man's-land, demilitarized zone, exclusion zone, no-go area; *exclusiveness*, cliquishness, clannishness, freemasonry; *clique*, coterie, in-group, clan, inner circle, elect; *monopoly*, cartel, closed shop, restrictive practices.

adj. *excluding*, debarring, prohibitive, restrictive, monopolistic, protectionist; *exclusive*, clannish, cliquey, snobbish, up-market; *excluded*, inadmissible, struck off, disallowed, debarred.

vb. *exclude*, evict, expel, deport, reject, banish, exile, extradite, outlaw, excommunicate; *prohibit*, ban, boycott, blockade, black, blacklist, blackball; *segregate*, quarantine, demarcate, cordon off, lock out, ostracize, send to Coventry, cold-shoulder (*colloq.*); *except*, omit, pass over, count out, leave out, rule out of court; *prevent*, preclude, forestall, obviate; *monopolize*, corner, hog (*colloq.*), bag (*colloq.*).

adv. *excluding*, barring, excepting, save; *out of the running*, out of the reckoning.

53 COMPONENT

See also **48** (part).

n. *component*, part, piece, element, ingredient, constituent; *unit*, module, building block, Lego (*tdmk.*), Meccano (*tdmk.*); *attachment*, fixture, accessory, spare part; *member*, associate, colleague, cog in the wheel, organization man, party hack, apparatchik; *machinery*, works, innards, insides, guts.

adj. *component*, constituent, essential, intrinsic, inherent; *integral*, fitted, built-in, modular.

vb. *compose*, comprise, make up, constitute; *belong to*, inhere, reside in, consist in, be part and parcel of; *con-*

struct, assemble, compile, fashion, knock together (*colloq.*).

54 FOREIGN BODY

See also **6** (extraneousness); **331** (nationality).

n. *foreign body*, extraneous element, reject, discard, spanner in the works; *foreignness*, ethnicity, alienness, extraneousness, undesirability, superfluousness, irrelevance; *foreigner*, alien, stranger, barbarian, immigrant, incomer, new face, refugee, expatriate, colonial; *intruder*, interloper, trespasser, squatter, gatecrasher, cuckoo in the nest; *misfit*, outsider, black sheep, fish out of water, pariah, leper; *extraterrestrial*, alien, Martian, little green men; *abroad*, overseas, foreign parts, exotica.

adj. *foreign*, alien, extraneous, superfluous, irrelevant, unwanted, undesirable; *strange*, exotic, outlandish, imported, borrowed, ethnic; *extraterrestrial*, alien, space-age, futuristic.

vb. *be foreign*, be out of one's element, stick out like a sore thumb (*colloq.*); *introduce*, borrow, import, naturalize, assimilate; *intrude*, trespass, squat, gatecrash.

adv. *abroad*, overseas.

55 ORDER

See also **57** (arrangement); **64** (consecutiveness); **68** (class).

n. *order*, arrangement, array, disposition, layout; *orderliness*, tidiness, neatness, apple-pie order, alignment; *system*, method, organization, routine, pattern, coordination, regularity, uniformity, coherence; *harmony*, quiet, peace, calm, law and order, rule of law, discipline, stability; *rank*, series, hierarchy, gradation, ascending/descending order, pecking order.

adj. *orderly*, tidy, neat, all shipshape and Bristol fashion, spruce, trim, groomed, dapper, smart, not a hair out of place; *disciplined*, law-abiding, peaceable, docile, well-behaved, obedient; *harmonious*, quiet, peaceful, calm, stable; *serial*, hierarchical, gradational, ordinal; *systematic*, methodical, organized.

vb. *order*, arrange, dispose, deploy, align; *organize*, sort, sift, classify, systematize, rationalize; *tidy*, neaten, smarten up, spruce up, groom, put to rights, lick/knock into shape (*colloq.*); *restore order*, pacify, discipline, control, police, tighten up on, take in hand; *be in order*, function, work, go like clockwork.

adv. *in order*, O.K., all present and correct, under control; *methodically*, systematically, step by step.

56 DISORDER

See also **58** (disturbance).

n. *disorder*, disarray, untidiness, unkemptness, scruffiness, neglect; *confusion*, muddle, welter, jumble, mix-up, mess, cock-up (*colloq.*), balls-up (*vulg.*); *litter*, clutter, shambles, pigsty, midden, dump (*colloq.*), tip (*colloq.*); *tangle*, snarl, web, warren, jungle, maze, labyrinth; *commotion*, uproar, to-do, trouble, hubbub, hullabaloo, bedlam, babel, pandemonium; *tumult*, turmoil, turbulence, chaos, upheaval, ferment, free-for-all, fracas, melee, rumpus, roughhouse, brawl, punchup (*colloq.*), dustup (*colloq.*), aggro (*colloq.*), breach of the peace, affray, disturbance, riot, anarchy, mob rule.

adj. *disordered*, untidy, unkempt, scruffy, dishevelled, bedraggled, tousled, windswept; *confused*, muddle-headed, incoherent, featherbrained, scatterbrained, disorganized; *careless*, slipshod, neglectful, messy, sloppy, shambolic (*colloq.*); *intricate*, complex, involved, tangled, convoluted, labyrinthine; *random*, desultory, haphazard, rambling, wandering; *turbulent*, tumultuous, chaotic, hell-raising, riotous, disorderly, wild, unruly, undisciplined, harum-scarum, lawless, anarchic.

vb. *make disordered*, untidy, rumple, ruffle, dishevel, bedraggle, tousle; *disorganize*, upset, disperse, throw into disarray, randomize, shuffle, scatter; *confuse*, muddle, botch, mess up, foul up, cock up (*colloq.*), balls up (*vulg.*); *complicate*, entangle, embroil, ensnare;

be disorderly, riot, rampage, storm, mob, run wild/amuck, get out of hand. **adv.** *in disorder*, in disarray, pell-mell, haywire, higgledy-piggledy (*colloq.*), all anyhow, upside down, topsy turvy, arsy versy (*colloq.*); *confusedly*, at sixes and sevens, at cross-purposes; *out of order*, off the rails, kaput, on the blink (*colloq.*).

57 ARRANGEMENT

See also **55** (order); **76** (list); **559** (preparation).

n. *arrangement*, order, disposition, layout, line-up (*colloq.*), distribution, composition, organization, structure; *classification*, categorization, listing, hierarchy, taxonomy, paradigm, pattern, system; *catalogue*, directory, list, table, index, inventory, checklist, register, file, slot, niche, pigeonhole; *chart*, diagram, schema, programme, agenda, timetable, schedule, graph, flow chart, critical path.

adj. *arranged*, ordered, classified, graded, sorted; *schematic*, diagrammatic, tabular, paradigmatic; *systematic*, methodical, organizational.

vb. *arrange*, order, dispose, array, marshal, group, deploy, distribute, sort, label, rank, range, grade, size, alphabetize; *catalogue*, tabulate, programme, index, timetable, schedule, cross-refer, file, pigeonhole, compartmentalize.

adv. *in place*, in line, in order.

58 DISTURBANCE

See also **56** (disorder); **161** (displacement); **447** (insanity).

n. *disturbance*, displacement, dislocation, dislodgment, derailment, disorientation, dispersion; *upset*, upheaval, convulsion, perturbation, agitation; *interference*, interruption, perversion, subversion, agitprop, sabotage; *derangement*, madness, insanity, a screw loose (*colloq.*).

adj. *disturbed*, displaced, dislocated, disorientated, dispersed; *upset*, perturbed, agitated, confused, disconcerted; *deranged*, mad, unhinged, unbalanced, insane.

vb. *disturb*, displace, dislocate, dislodge, derail, unseat, disorientate, throw off course; *upset*, agitate, discompose, disconcert, perturb, ruffle, fluster, put off one's stride/stroke; *disperse*, scatter, shuffle, jumble, randomize; *interfere*, interrupt, pervert, subvert, sabotage, throw out of joint, throw a spanner in the works; *derange*, unhinge, unbalance, drive insane, drive round the bend (*colloq.*).

adv. *on the wrong track*, off the rails, off course; *out of gear*, out of joint, out of place.

59 PRECEDENCE

See also **61** (beginning); **99** (priority).

n. *precedence*, antecedence, ancestry, pedigree, primogeniture; *priority*, pride of place, head start, initiative, first come first served, front of the queue, forefront, avant-garde, vanguard; *forerunner*, eldest, firstborn, ancestor, precursor, senior, predecessor; *guide*, scout, outrider, pilot, beacon, harbinger, messenger, pioneer, trail-blazer, pathfinder, trendsetter; *precedent*, antecedent, example, sample, preview, foretaste, forecast, prognosis, trailer, prequel; *introduction*, initiation, inauguration, baptism of fire, christening; *preliminary*, preface, prologue, foreword, frontispiece, prelude, preamble, overture, curtain-raiser, aperitif, starter, appetizer.

adj. *preceding*, antecedent, anterior, prior, former, previous, foregoing, aforementioned; *leading*, foremost, avant-garde, pioneering, innovative, exploratory; *introductory*, initial, preliminary, prefatory, initiatory, inaugural, baptismal; *elder*, senior, superior.

vb. *precede*, antedate, predate, anticipate, preempt, preclude, forestall; *lead*, go before, front, head, spearhead, pioneer, explore, blaze a trail; *announce*, herald, forecast, presage, foretell, usher in, advertise, trail (*colloq.*); *introduce*, preface, initiate, baptize, christen, inaugurate, blood.

adv. *first*, above all, first and foremost; *ahead*, in front, upfront (*colloq.*); *in advance*, previously, beforehand.

60 SEQUENCE

See also **37** (remainder); **64** (consecutiveness); **100** (succession).

n. *sequence*, series, succession, chain, string, progression; *posterity*, line, lineage, issue, progeny, offspring; *consequence*, effect, end result, outcome, upshot, legacy, by-product, spin-off, aftereffect, aftermath, sequel, hangover (*colloq.*), fallout; *appendage*, follow-up, tailpiece, epilogue, afterword, postscript, coda, afterthought, supplement, post mortem, dessert, afters (*colloq.*); *rear*, posterior, train, trail, wake, tail; *rearguard*, runner-up, straggler, sweeper, tail-end Charlie (*colloq.*), last man in, booby prize, wooden spoon.

adj. *sequential*, successive, consecutive, serial; *succeeding*, following, subsequent, next, later, resulting, ensuing; *rear*, posterior, hindmost.

vb. *succeed*, come after, follow, come in the wake of, tread on the heels of, follow in the footsteps of, step into someone's shoes, supplant, supersede; *pursue*, tail, trail, shadow, dog someone's footsteps; *result*, ensue, turn out, come to pass; *come last*, bring up the rear, lag, dawdle.

adv. *in succession*, in turn, one after the other, back to back (*colloq.*); *in sequence*, in order; *next*, then, afterwards, subsequently; *in consequence*, as a result, therefore; *behind*, in someone's wake/train.

61 BEGINNING

See also **59** (precedence); **132** (cause).

n. *beginning*, start, commencement, onset; *foundation*, inception, inauguration, instigation, institution; *initiation*, christening, baptism, honeymoon, debut, first night, premiere, maiden speech, maiden voyage, launch, housewarming, send-off; *starting-point*, outset, first base, first lap, first round, qualifier, square one, zero, alpha, kick-off (*colloq.*); *introduction*, opening gambit, preliminaries, lead-in, foreword, preface; *preparation*, rudiments, first principles, groundwork, spadework (*colloq.*), trial run, teething troubles, growing pains, birth pangs; *origin*, birth, infancy, dawn, morning, cradle, genesis; *germ*, seed, bud, embryo, nucleus, primordial soup; *beginner*, apprentice, learner, novice, tyro, probationer, new boy, new bug (*colloq.*).

adj. *beginning*, primary, initial, first; *primal*, primordial, primeval, aboriginal; *introductory*, preliminary, prefatory, initiatory, preparatory, inaugural, baptismal; *fundamental*, rudimentary, elementary, basic; *infant*, embryonic, budding, incipient, nascent.

vb. *begin*, start, commence, make a start, set about, get under way, set in motion, tackle, broach; *set out*, kick off (*colloq.*), set the ball rolling, blast off, fire away, take the plunge, break the ice, pull one's finger out (*colloq.*), get weaving/cracking (*colloq.*), clock in; *initiate*, inaugurate, instigate, found, institute, launch, christen, baptize, be in on the ground floor; *originate*, generate, provoke, prompt, sow the seeds of, trigger off, spark off; *pioneer*, explore, embark on, break new ground, blaze a trail; *arise*, appear, emerge, see the light of day, spring up, crop up; *recommence*, resume, make a fresh start, go back to square one, go back to the drawing board.

adv. *from the beginning*, ab ovo, from scratch (*colloq.*), from the word go (*colloq.*); *in the beginning*, at first, at the outset, initially, early on, to begin with; *in the first place*, firstly, for a start, for a kick-off (*colloq.*).

62 END

See also **60** (sequence); **133** (effect); **323** (death).

n. *end*, cessation, termination, completion, conclusion, end result, payoff, expiry; *ending*, final, finale, death, demise, last words, last gasp, swansong; *end point*, terminus, goal, omega, last lap, last round, home stretch, end of the road; *extremity*, boundary, limit, peak, summit; *finality*, final offer, ultimatum, deadline, last orders, time up, closing time, close of play, closedown, adjournment, dissolution; *climax*, resolution, denouement, death blow, coup de grâce, clincher (*colloq.*); *last judgment*, last trump, doomsday, apocalypse, twilight of the gods, holocaust.

adj. *final*, last, terminal, ultimate, concluding; *rear*, back, hindmost, posterior; *finished*, ended, over and done with, played out, kaput (*colloq.*), clapped out (*colloq.*), washed up (*colloq.*); *apocalyptic*, eschatological.

vb. *end*, finish, cease, stop, terminate, conclude, close down, ring down the curtain, shut up shop, sign off, clock off, call it a day; *come to an end*, die, expire, run one's course, run out of time, fade out, peter out, fizzle out (*colloq.*), tail off; *bring to an end*, conclude, terminate, discontinue, dispose of, drop, write off, wash one's hands of, wind up (*colloq.*), wrap up (*colloq.*); *complete*, finish off, round off.

adv. *in the end*, finally, at last, at the end of the day, in the final analysis, in the long run, when the chips are down (*colloq.*); *once and for all*, for good, forever, conclusively, definitively.

63 MIDDLE

See also **27** (average).

n. *middle*, midst, centre, thick, heart, core, kernel, marrow, focus, hub, nucleus, pivot, fulcrum; *midpoint*, midway, midweek, midsummer, midwinter, midstream, middle distance, equator, midriff, middle age, mid-life crisis, halfway house; *average*, mean, median, happy medium; *mediation*, intervention, arbitration, compromise, no-man's-land, middle ground, grey area, borderline case; *intermediary*, middleman, agent, broker, mediator, go-between, buffer, arbitrator, third force, pig-in-the-middle (*colloq.*).

adj. *middle*, central, mid, medial, median, interim, equidistant; *mean*, average, middle-of-the-road; *intermediate*, neutral, halfway, grey, indeterminate.

vb. *straddle*, lie betwixt and between, hold the centre, occupy the middle ground; *compromise*, meet someone halfway, steer a middle course, fall between two stools, be neither fish nor fowl; *intervene*, mediate, come between; *split down the middle*, halve, divide fifty-fifty, bisect.

adv. *midway*, halfway; *amidst*, among; *in between*, between Scylla and Charybdis, between the devil and the deep blue sea.

64 CONSECUTIVENESS

See also **55** (order); **60** (sequence).

n. *consecutiveness*, sequence, succession, causality, cause and effect, domino theory, knock-on effect, repercussion; *continuity*, stability, routine, flow, trend, run; *series*, string, chain, ladder, suite, scale, arpeggio, spectrum, hierarchy, colonnade, dynasty, line, family tree; *one of a series*, instalment, row, tier, storey, echelon, rank, course; *continuum*, assembly line, conveyor belt, treadmill, endless band, Mobius strip, vicious circle; *procession*, column, cortege, train, caravan, queue, crocodile, tailback.

adj. *consecutive*, successive, following, serial; *continuous*, perpetual, endless, nonstop, unbroken, seamless, running, ongoing; *progressive*, linear, gradual.

vb. *be consecutive*, succeed, run on, follow on, overlap; *continue*, extend, run, flow, persist, endure; *arrange in succession*, range, rank, line up, stagger.

adv. *consecutively*, successively, one after another, back to back (*colloq.*), in succession, in turn; *continuously*, nonstop, day in day out, round the clock, on the trot (*colloq.*); *end to end*, nose to tail, bumper to bumper.

65 DISCONTINUITY

See also **50** (incompleteness).

n. *discontinuity*, disconnectedness, disjointedness, alternation, unevenness, sporadicness, jerkiness; *disruption*, break, gap, breach, interval, caesura, hiatus, pause, stopover, time lag, time-warp, missing link, non sequitur, anacoluthon; *interruption*, digression, parenthesis, interjection, interpolation; *irregularity*, collage, patchwork, crazy paving.

adj. *discontinuous*, discrete, broken,

uneven, distinct; *disconnected*, disjointed, fitful, jerky, spasmodic, sporadic, episodic; *intermittent*, desultory, irregular, alternate, periodic, stop-go, on-off; *digressive*, parenthetical, interjectional.

vb. *discontinue*, suspend, terminate, interrupt; *break off*, leave off, stop off/over, digress, pause, take time out (*colloq.*); *interject*, interpose, intervene, cut in, butt in, chip in, put one's oar in; *omit*, miss out, jump, skip, leapfrog (*colloq.*); *alternate*, oscillate, fluctuate, blow hot and cold (*colloq.*).

adv. *discontinuously*, periodically, now and then, occasionally, off and on, at intervals; *by degrees*, by fits and starts, in dribs and drabs (*colloq.*).

66 ASSEMBLY

See also **40** (union).

n. *assembly*, meeting, rally, convention, conference, company, congregation, caucus, party, rendezvous, tryst, get-together (*colloq.*); *collection*, compilation, compendium, anthology, roundup (*colloq.*); *group*, band, troupe, collective, syndicate, union, guild, team, stable, string, squad, crew, posse, force, regiment; *social group*, circle, family, clan, tribe, peer group, age group, generation, clique, coterie, mafia; *crowd*, throng, mob, press, huddle, scrum, crush, swarm, bevy, gang; *multitude*, host, galaxy, constellation, storm, shower, hail, volley, deluge, spate, flood, slew (*colloq.*), raft (*colloq.*); *bunch*, bouquet, spray, knot, clump, cluster, bundle, parcel, bale, roll, bolt, skein, hank, truss, sheaf, conglomeration, heap, pile, mass; *flock*, herd, shoal, pack, drove, brood, school, clutch, litter, covey (partridges), flight/gaggle/skein (geese), pride (lions), leap (leopards), kindle (kittens), skulk (foxes), charm (goldfinches), exaltation (larks).

adj. *assembled*, gathered, congregated; *crowded*, congested, packed, teeming, milling, seething, crawling (*colloq.*), chock-a-block (*colloq.*); *converging*, centripetal.

vb. *assemble*, collect, forgather, meet, unite, congregate, get together, rendezvous, fall in, join forces, team up, band together, gang up; *crowd*, flock, mass, mill, seethe, swarm, teem, pack, huddle, throng; *bring together*, summon, convoke, convene, rally, mobilize, herd, muster, shepherd, round up; *bunch*, bundle, parcel, package, clump, knot, cluster, bind, truss; *accumulate*, amass, agglomerate, stack, heap, pile; *compress*, cram, crush, squash, stuff, squeeze.

adv. *collectively*, all together, as one, in a body, en masse.

67 DISPERSION

See also **41** (separation).

n. *dispersion*, diffusion, dissemination, propagation, distribution, spread; *disbandment*, dissolution, breakup, demobilization, decentralization; *divergence*, branching, radiation, ramification; *emigration*, exodus, diaspora, population drift, overspill, new town, suburbia, urban sprawl, ribbon development.

adj. *dispersed*, scattered, far-flung, widespread; *sparse*, strung out, dotted about, sporadic, few and far between, thin on the ground; *loose*, stray, straggling, wandering, sprawling; *divergent*, branching, radiating, centrifugal.

vb. *disperse*, diffuse, spread, disseminate, propagate, broadcast, distribute; *disband*, disintegrate, dissolve, break up, fall out, demobilize, decentralize; *scatter*, strew, sprinkle, litter, spatter; *emigrate*, wander, drift, stray, straggle, sprawl; *diverge*, branch, radiate, ramify, fan out, hive off.

adv. *here and there*, round and about; *in all directions*, to the four winds, to the four corners of the earth.

68 CLASS

See also **55** (order).

n. *class*, category, variety, kind, sort, strain, brand, make, marque; *division*, group, species, genus, order, phylum; *type*, manner, stamp, mould, stripe, breed, race, tribe, ilk, kidney, cast, colour, complexion, hue; *classification*,

rank, order, system, hierarchy, taxonomy.
adj. *classificatory*, hierarchical, taxonomic; *typical*, representative, generic, stereotypical.
vb. *class*, group, divide, sort, grade, range, rank; *classify*, typify, categorize, identify, label, brand, stamp.

69 GENERALITY

See also **27** (average); **51** (inclusion).
n. *generality*, universality, comprehensiveness, inclusiveness, catholicity, ecumenicalism, broad church, eclecticism, cosmopolitanism; *nonspecificness*, broad canvas, broad spectrum, blanket coverage, catch-all, dragnet, grapeshot, panacea, cure-all, open house, open meeting, open letter, circular, something for everyone; *average*, ordinariness, common run, lowest common denominator; *everyman*, man in the street, man on the Clapham omnibus, Joe Bloggs, Tom, Dick, and Harry, every man Jack; *common people*, general public, masses, admass, grassroots, vox populi.
adj. *general*, nonspecific, generic, representative, typical, standard; *universal*, comprehensive, all-inclusive, blanket, across-the-board; *common*, ordinary, popular, middlebrow, vernacular, vulgar, down-market; *prevalent*, widespread, ubiquitous, worldwide, global, endemic; *multipurpose*, versatile, adaptable.
vb. *generalize*, spread, broaden, widen, popularize, vulgarize, broadcast, disseminate; *prevail*, obtain, predominate.
adv. *generally*, in general, as a rule, by and large, in the main, broadly speaking, typically.

70 SPECIALITY

See also **22** (originality); **79** (one).
n. *speciality*, individuality, originality, uniqueness, particularity, singularity, distinctiveness, specificity; *feature*, attribute, trait, peculiarity, characteristic, quirk, idiosyncrasy, hallmark, trademark; *particulars*, specifications, details, minutiae, ins and outs (*colloq.*); *exception*, special case, one-off, nonce word, rara avis; *subjectivity*, individualism, egoism, self, number one, ego-trip (*colloq.*), solipsism, me generation.
adj. *special*, particular, peculiar, specific, unique, singular, distinctive, original, individual; *characteristic*, idiomatic, peculiar, typical, personal, idiosyncratic, quirky, eccentric; *exceptional*, one-off, unique, sui generis, inimitable, esoteric, way-out (*colloq.*); *exclusive*, bespoke, made-to-order, made-to-measure, custom-made, personalized, own-brand; *subjective*, individualistic, self-centred, egotistical, solipsistic.
vb. *specify*, enumerate, list, detail, itemize, spell out; *particularize*, cite, mention, quote, name names; *isolate*, distinguish, individuate, pick out, single out, highlight, pinpoint, put one's finger on (*colloq.*); *stand out*, shine, excel, be in a class of one's own, be out of the ordinary, be off the beaten track.
adv. *especially*, in particular, above all; *specifically*, namely, respectively; *personally*, ad hominem.

71 RULE

See also **549** (habit); **657** (authority); **852** (legality).
n. *rule*, regulation, ruling, standing order, injunction, law, degree, edict, statute, bylaw; *code*, canon, rulebook, charter, statute book, constitution; *precept*, guideline, criterion, standard, benchmark, litmus test, principle, tenet, prescription, precedent; *procedure*, system, method, practice, drill, routine, form.
adj. *regulatory*, normative, prescriptive; *legal*, compulsory, obligatory, de rigueur, statutory, mandatory; *standard*, normal, conventional, orthodox, canonical; *procedural*, routine, formulaic, copybook.
vb. *rule*, prescribe, ordain, decree, lay down the law; *regulate*, standardize, normalize, bring into line, regularize; *obey orders*, stick to the rules, keep to the straight and narrow, keep one's

nose clean (*colloq.*), toe the line (*colloq.*), work to rule, mind one's Ps and Qs.
adv. *according to the rules*, by the book.

72 CONFORMITY

See also **15** (uniformity); **549** (habit).
n. *conformity*, agreement, harmony, consistency, compatibility; *usage*, convention, orthodoxy, conservatism, traditionalism, Babbitry, conventional wisdom, done thing, order of the day, received idea, party line; *assimilation*, absorption, levelling, acclimatization, adaptation, indoctrination, reeducation, rehabilitation; *pattern*, mould, stereotype, matrix; *conformist*, traditionalist, silent majority, herd, sheep, copycat, running dog, yes-man, company man, timeserver, party hack, apparatchik.
adj. *conformist*, conventional, orthodox, conservative, law-abiding, traditionalist, bourgeois; *consistent*, compatible, harmonious, consonant; *typical*, stock, standard, identikit, average, common or garden, unexceptional; *adaptable*, flexible, malleable, compliant, pliable.
vb. *conform*, accord, agree, correspond, match, tally, run true to form; *make conform*, standardize, stereotype, process, assimilate, bring into line, adapt, adjust, mould; *indoctrinate*, brainwash, reeducate, rehabilitate; *follow suit*, fall into line, follow the crowd, keep up appearances, keep up with the Joneses, jump on the bandwagon, swim with the tide.
adv. *in place*, in keeping, in line.

73 NONCONFORMITY

See also **20** (disparity).
n. *nonconformity*, disparity, disagreement, inconsistency, incompatibility, incongruity, contrast; *nonconformism*, unorthodoxy, heresy, schism, iconoclasm, revolt, dissent, protest, deviationism; *unconventionality*, eccentricity, oddity, rarity, singularity; *nonconformist*, maverick, renegade, lone wolf, outsider, outlaw, outcast, pariah, blackleg, scab, marginal, lunatic fringe; *rebel*, Bohemian, hippie, drop-out, angry young man, dissident, young Turk, radical, freethinker, iconoclast, heretic; *exception*, anomaly, aberration, abnormality, special case, odd man out; *eccentric*, character, card (*colloq.*), crank, weirdo (*colloq.*), oddball, freak, misfit, deviant; *homosexual*, gay, lesbian, dyke (*colloq.*), queer (*colloq.*), poofter (*colloq*), woofter (*colloq.*), pansy (*colloq.*), fairy (*colloq.*), bisexual, transvestite, crossdresser, transsexual, hermaphrodite.
adj. *nonconformist*, inconsistent, incompatible, incongruous, contrasting; *unorthodox*, independent, freethinking, radical, iconoclastic, heretical; *rebellious*, Bohemian, dissident, deviationist; *eccentric*, unconventional, odd, rare, unusual, exotic, out-of-the-ordinary, fringe, outlandish, offbeat (*colloq.*), way-out (*colloq.*), weird; *exceptional*, anomalous, aberrant, abnormal, deviant; *homosexual*, gay, lesbian, queer (*colloq.*), bent (*colloq.*), bisexual, AC/DC (*colloq.*).
vb. *not conform*, diverge, dissent, protest, rebel, kick over the traces, rock the boat (*colloq.*); *be independent*, deviate, break ranks, step out of line, go one's own way, do one's own thing (*colloq.*), break the mould, drop out (*colloq.*).
adv. *out of step*, out of keeping, out of line, out on a limb; *out of the way*, out of the common run, off the beaten track.

74 NUMBER

See also **75** (calculation).
n. *number*, numeral, digit, figure, integer, character, cipher, decimal; *sum*, total, aggregate, remainder; *factor*, multiple, quotient, product, function, variable, expression, coefficient, formula; *fraction*, numerator, denominator, vulgar fraction, common fraction; *power*, exponent, root, square, logarithm, mantissa.
adj. *numerical*, digital, prime, whole, real, even, odd, cardinal, ordinal, binary, decimal.

vb. *number*, enumerate, count, tell, reckon, tick off (*colloq.*); *amount to*, total, come to, make, notch up (*colloq.*).

75 CALCULATION

See also **74** (number).

n. *calculation*, estimation, computation, numeration, addition, subtraction, multiplication, division; *count*, score, tally, census, poll, head-count, stocktaking, roll call; *mathematics*, arithmetic, calculus, algebra, geometry, trigonometry, statistics; *data processing*, computing, numbercrunching (*colloq.*), information retrieval, cybernetics; *computer*, mainframe, microcomputer, minicomputer, personal/desk computer, microprocessor, chip, circuit, hardware, visual display unit, printout, core, memory, floppy disk, software, program, machine code; *abacus*, ready reckoner, slide rule, calculator; *numerator*, mathematician, accountant, actuary, teller, statistician, programmer, systems analyst, liveware.

adj. *computational*, actuarial, mathematical, arithmetical, statistical, geometric, algebraic.

vb. *calculate*, estimate, compute, add, subtract, multiply, divide, square, cube; *automate*, computerize, process, input, throughput, program.

76 LIST

See also **57** (arrangement).

n. *list*, record, register, table, file, listing; *index*, catalogue, directory, inventory, checklist, bibliography, filmography, discography; *agenda*, programme, timetable, schedule, bill of fare, table of contents, prospectus; *vocabulary*, glossary, lexicon, dictionary, thesaurus, gazetteer, almanac, yearbook; *roll*, roster, rota, short list, waiting list, blacklist, dramatis personae, credits.

vb. *list*, enter, log, register, record, table, file; *catalogue*, index, inventorize, schedule, timetable, minute; *enrol*, inscribe, enlist, matriculate, sign on.

77 ZERO

n. *zero*, nothing, none, naught, nix, nada, zilch (*colloq.*), sweet f.a. (*colloq.*); *nought*, nil, null, love, duck; *nullity*, nothingness, blank, cipher, void.

adj. *zero*, no, nil.

78 FRACTION

See also **30** (smallness); **48** (part).

n. *fraction*, part, piece, portion, section, segment, percentage, proportion; *fragment*, particle, atom, iota, scrap, shred, whit, jot; *less than one*, quarter, half, three quarters.

adj. *fractional*, small, tiny, slight, infinitesimal; *partial*, fragmentary, incomplete.

adv. *fractionally*, slightly, marginally, partially.

79 ONE

See also **40** (union); **70** (speciality).

n. *one*, ace, unit, entity, individual, atom, monad; *item*, detail, bit, isolated instance; *oneness*, unity, wholeness, integrity, indivisibility, indissolubility; *individualism*, separatism, isolationism, unilateralism; *solitariness*, isolation, aloneness, solitude, loneliness; *soloist*, one-man band, one-man show, solo effort, monologue, soliloquy; *single person*, spinster, bachelor, bachelor girl, single parent, widow, widower, celibacy, monogamy; *monopoly*, cartel, multinational.

adj. *one*, solo, single, mono, unified, whole, indivisible, indissoluble; *individual*, separatist, isolationist, unilateralist, insular; *solo*, single-handed, alone, isolated, solitary; *single*, unmarried, celibate, monogamous.

vb. *be one*, stand alone, plough a lonely furrow, stand on one's own two feet, do one's own thing (*colloq.*), paddle one's own canoe (*colloq.*); *become one*, unite, cohere, combine, merge, fuse; *isolate*, single out, specify, prick out.

adv. *one by one*, singly, one at a time; *on one's own*, by oneself, on one's tod (*colloq.*); *solely*, only, merely, simply; *in unison*, as one.

80 PLURALITY

See also **86** (multitude).

n. *plurality*, majority, multiple; *variety*, multiplicity, multifariousness, multilateralism, polygamy, polysemy, pluralism; *all-rounder*, polymath, Renaissance man, pluralist.

adj. *plural*, many, numerous, multiple; *various*, divers, sundry, several; *versatile*, multifarious, multipurpose, pluralist, multilateralist, polygamous, polysemous, polytheist.

81 TWO

n. *two*, deuce, pair, couple, duo, brace, span, twosome, twins; *double*, couplet, doublet, duet, two-hander, diptych, double-decker, tandem, two-seater, two-wheeler, bicycle, biplane; *duality*, dichotomy, polarity, dualism, bilingualism, bisexuality, ambidexterity, ambiguity, ambivalence, duplicity, double-dealing; *duplication*, doubling, repetition, reproduction; *bisection*, bifurcation, fork, branch, swallowtail; *half*, moiety, hemisphere, semicircle, semitone, semibreve.

adj. *dual*, double, binary, duple, duplex, twofold, double-barrelled, biennial, biannual; *both*, amphibious, ambidextrous, bilingual, bisexual, ambiguous, ambivalent, double-edged, duplicitous, double-dealing, two-faced; *two-way*, dual-purpose, reciprocal, bilateral, bipartite, binaural, split, cloven; *duplicate*, second, repeat, twin.

vb. *double*, duplicate, repeat, copy, mirror, echo, second; *pair*, twin, match, mate; *bisect*, halve, bifurcate, split, cleave; *go halves*, go fifty-fifty; *have it both ways*, have the best of both worlds, have one's cake and eat it (*colloq.*).

adv. *twice*, twofold, as much again, doubly.

82 THREE

n. *three*, triad, trio, trinity, triune, threesome, troika, triumvirate; *treble*, triplet, tercet, trilogy, three-decker, three-hander, triangle, triptych, three-wheeler, tricycle, trident, tripod, trimester, hat trick; *third*, tierce, third party, Third World.

adj. *triple*, ternary, triplex, threefold, triplicate, three-ply, three-dimensional; *three-way*, triangular, trilateral, tripartite; *third*, tertiary.

vb. *triple*, treble, cube, triplicate.

adv. *thrice*, trebly, threefold, in triplicate.

83 FOUR

n. *four*, quartet, tetrad, foursome, quaternity, quadriga, four-in-hand, four-poster; *quadruplicate*, quadrangle, square, tetrahedron, quadruped, quadruplet, quad, tetralogy, quatrain, tetrameter, four-letter word; *quarter*, fourth, quarterly, quarto, tetrarch.

adj. *quadruple*, quaternary, fourfold; *square*, foursquare, quadrate, quadrilateral, tetrahedral; *quarterly*, quadraphonic, quadrennial.

vb. *quadruple*, quadruplicate, square, quadrate; *quarter*.

adv. *fourfold*; *squarely*, foursquare.

84 FIVE AND OVER

n. *five*, quintet, quintuplet, quin, fiver (*colloq.*), pentad, pentagon, pentangle, quincunx, pentameter, Pentateuch, pentathlon; *six*, half a dozen, sextet, sextuplet, sixer, hexad, hexagon, hexameter, sestina, Hexateuch; *seven*, heptad, septet, heptagon, Sabbath, sabbatical, Heptateuch; *eight*, octet, octad, octagon, octave, octoroon, octopus, octavo; *nine*, nonet, nonagon, novena; *ten*, tenner (*colloq.*), decade, decalogue, decagon, decathlon, tenth, decimal, tithe; *eleven*, double figures; *twelve*, dozen, dodecahedron, alexandrine; *thirteen*, baker's dozen, long dozen, teens; *twenty and over*, score, fifty, quinquagenarian, sixty, sexagenarian, seventy, septuagenarian, eighty, octogenarian, ninety, nonagenarian; *hundred*, centenarian, century, three figures, gross, bicentenary, tercentenary, quadricentennial, quincentenary; *thousand*, K, millennium, grand (*colloq.*); *million*, billion, trillion.

adj. *fifth*, fivefold etc., quintuple, sixth, sextuple, seventh, septuple, eighth,

octuple, ninth, nonary, tenth, decimal, twelfth, duodecimal, centennial, millionth, billionth.
vb. *quintuple etc.*, multiply; *decimate*, decimalize.
adv. *fivefold* etc., hundredfold.

85 ACCOMPANIMENT

See also **35** (addition); **789** (sociability); **793** (friendship).
n. *accompaniment*, coexistence, symbiosis, conjunction, cohabitation, company, society, fellowship, companionship, friendship, togetherness, mateyness (*colloq.*); *companion*, friend, comrade, mate, buddy (*colloq.*), colleague, partner, cohabitee, consort; *escort*, guide, convoy, outrider, attendant, chaperon, bodyguard, minder (*colloq.*); *follower*, dependant, satellite, hanger-on, camp follower, shadow, tail; *concomitant*, attribute, feature, symptom, accessory, appurtenance, appendage, corollary, sine qua non, prerequisite.
adj. *accompanying*, attendant, associated, concomitant, accessory, incidental; *parallel*, simultaneous, contemporaneous, coexistent; *inseparable*, thick as thieves, symbiotic.
vb. *accompany*, escort, guide, convoy, attend, partner, chaperon, squire, mind (*colloq.*); *attach oneself to*, dance attendance on, tag along, string along, dog the footsteps of, shadow, tail, track; *belong with*, complement, go together, go hand in hand; *associate*, consort, frequent, hobnob (*colloq.*), socialize, club together, team up, gang up.
adv. *together*, in a body; *in convoy*, in tow, in someone's wake, on someone's coat-tails.

86 MULTITUDE

See also **29** (greatness); **80** (plurality).
n. *multitude*, multiplicity, infinity, myriad, zillions (*colloq.*); *host*, army, legion, horde, fleet, swarm, brood, sea, forest, galaxy; *throng*, crowd, masses, mob, press, crush.
adj. *multitudinous*, countless, numberless, innumerable, myriad; *endless*, infinite, boundless, vast, untold, inexhaustible; *numerous*, many, manifold, ample, abundant, profuse, plenty, bumper, umpteen (*colloq.*), galore (*colloq.*); *crowded*, packed, overcrowded, overmanned, overpopulated, high-density, thick on the ground.
vb. *crowd*, throng, flock, troop, pour, flood, stream; *swarm*, crawl, infest, mill, seethe, teem, pullulate, multiply; *overrun*, outnumber, swamp, snow under.
adv. *in droves*, en masse, thick and fast.

87 FEW

See also **30** (smallness).
n. *few*, handful, trickle, sprinkling, minority, low turnout; *scarcity*, paucity, shortage, scantiness; *sparseness*, rarity, infrequency.
adj. *few*, scant, scarce, straggly, wispy, few and far between; *sparse*, infrequent, intermittent, dotted about, strung out, scattered; *underpopulated*, low-density, thin on the ground, understaffed, undermanned.
vb. *scatter*, sprinkle, dot; *thin*, reduce, rarefy, weed out, eliminate, decimate.
adv. *thinly*, in ones and twos, in dribs and drabs (*colloq.*); *seldom*, rarely, infrequently, occasionally.

88 REPETITION

See also **119** (regularity).
n. *repetition*, recapitulation, reiteration, tautology, reproduction, duplication; *renewal*, resumption, reprise, rehearsal, repeat, rerun, replay, reprint, remake, reissue, rehash; *recurrence*, reappearance, renaissance, rebirth, return, cycle, revival, relapse, reversion; *regularity*, rhythm, beat, pulse, rhyme, alliteration, assonance; *refrain*, chorus, encore, repeat performance, second helping; *repetitiveness*, routine, monotony, familiarity, cliché, chestnut (*colloq.*), same old story, mixture as before.
adj. *repetitive*, reiterative, tautological, repetitious; *recurrent*, regular, rhythmical, periodic, cyclical; *monotonous*,

routine, familiar, stale, hackneyed, trite.
vb. *repeat*, recapitulate, reiterate, restate, reemphasize, hammer into, din into, harp, nag; *reproduce*, copy, mirror, duplicate, echo, chorus, parrot; *renew*, resume, revive, reprise, rehearse, rerun, replay, remake, reissue, reprint, rehash, recycle; *recur*, reappear, return, crop up; *relapse*, regress, revert, retrace one's steps, go back over old ground.
adv. *repeatedly*, again and again, time after time, over and over, ad nauseam; *once more*, da capo.

89 INFINITY

See also **95** (eternity).
n. *infinity*, infinitude, immensity, boundlessness, limitlessness, vastness, abyss; *eternity*, perpetuity, immortality, everlastingness.
adj. *infinite*, boundless, limitless, bottomless, immeasurable, vast, unfathomable, ineffable; *countless*, innumerable, incalculable, numberless, untold; *endless*, indefinite, open-ended, neverending, interminable, inexhaustible; *eternal*, immortal, perpetual, everlasting.
vb. *be infinite*, know no bounds, go on and on, last forever.
adv. *infinitely*, immeasurably, incalculably, vastly, ineffably; *ad infinitum*, to the nth degree, forever, eternally, perpetually; *indefinitely*, sine die.

90 TIME

See also **92** (period); **97** (timekeeping).
n. *time*, spacetime, duration, continuity; *age*, epoch, aeon, century, lifetime, time immemorial, time out of mind; *period*, span, course, season, spell, phase; *interim*, meanwhile, meantime, interval, interlude, time lag, timewarp; *hour*, zero hour, moment, point in time, local time, time zone, standard time, summer time, man hour, flexitime, overtime.
adj. *temporal*, periodical, seasonal; *continual*, ongoing, present, current, pending.
vb. *pass*, elapse, continue, run, roll, glide; *pause*, take time out, mark time, bide one's time, stand still, tick over, vegetate; *spend*, while away, kill (*colloq.*), waste, idle, fritter, squander.
adv. *meanwhile*, in the meantime, in the interim, for the time being; *at present*, now, currently; *soon*, in time, one fine day; *sometimes*, from time to time, at times; *once*, once upon a time, at one time.

91 TIMELESSNESS

See also **95** (eternity).
n. *timelessness*, eternity, perpetuity, unchangingness, immutability; *immortality*, agelessness, datelessness, everlastingness.
adj. *timeless*, eternal, perpetual, unchanging, immutable; *immortal*, ageless, dateless, classic, evergreen.
adv. *never*, at no time, not in a month of Sundays, over one's dead body; *indefinitely*, sine die, till the cows come home (*colloq.*).

92 PERIOD

See also **90** (time); **120** (irregularity).
n. *period*, season, cycle, span, spell, phase, stint, watch, stretch, bout, round, innings; *term*, quarter, trimester, semester; *hour*, rush hour, lunch hour, witching hour, small hours; *day*, weekday, rest day, red-letter day; *week*, fortnight, month, calendar month, lunar month; *year*, twelvemonth, leap year, light-year, solar year; *decade*, century, millennium; *anniversary*, birthday, saint's day, jubilee, centenary, bicentenary, tercentenary; *age*, epoch, generation, aeon.
adj. *periodic*, seasonal, cyclical; *daily*, quotidian, weekly, hebdomadal, fortnightly, monthly, menstrual, quarterly, biannual, yearly, annual, biennial, centennial, perennial.
vb. *be periodic*, recur, come round, go in phases; *alternate*, take one's turn.
adv. *periodically*, from time to time, sometimes, now and then, at times.

93 DURATION

See also **95** (eternity); **124** (continuity).

n. duration, continuance, permanence; *long time*, lifetime, ages, month of Sundays (*colloq.*), donkey's years (*colloq.*), yonks (*colloq.*), long haul, marathon; *protraction*, prolongation, filibustering, stonewalling; *durability*, toughness, endurance, stamina, staying power, persistence, survival instinct.

adj. *lasting*, abiding, enduring, continuing, ongoing, permanent, surviving; *long-term*, long-haul, long-standing, lifelong; *protracted*, long-drawn-out, time-consuming, longwinded, interminable; *durable*, tough, long-lasting, imperishable, evergreen, perennial.

vb. *last*, abide, endure, continue, remain, persist; *survive*, outlast, outstay, outlive, have nine lives; *protract*, prolong, spin out, linger, dawdle, take forever, play for time, temporize, filibuster, stonewall.

adv. *for a long time*, at length, for ages; *in the long run*, in the end, at the end of the day.

94 TRANSIENCE

See also **130** (changeableness).

n. *transience*, impermanence, evanescence, brevity, instantaneity; *changeability*, volatility, instability, precariousness, fragility, brittleness, perishability; *shooting star*, bubble, spindrift, flare, flicker, shifting sand, nomad, bird of passage, ship that passes in the night, nine days' wonder, flash in the pan (*colloq.*).

adj. *transient*, ephemeral, shortlived, evanescent, passing, fleeting, brief, cursory, momentary, transitory; *temporary*, makeshift, provisional, ad hoc, short-term, impermanent, disposable, throwaway; *changeable*, volatile, mutable, perishable, fragile, brittle; *precarious*, unstable, unsettled, drifting, rootless, nomadic.

vb. *pass*, fade, die, expire, disappear, vanish, melt, evaporate; *flare*, flicker, flash, spurt, explode.

adv. *briefly*, momentarily; *temporarily*, provisionally, for the time being.

95 ETERNITY

See also **89** (infinity); **91** (timelessness); **93** (duration).

n. *eternity*, perpetuity, infinity, forever; *timelessness*, agelessness, immortality, imperishability, indestructibiity, permanence, endurance.

adj. *eternal*, perpetual, sempiternal, everlasting; *immortal*, deathless, undying, imperishable, indestructible, self-perpetuating; *timeless*, ageless, classic, evergreen; *endless*, ceaseless, neverending, unremitting, relentless.

vb. *perpetuate*, immortalize; *preserve*, conserve, freeze, embalm, mummify.

adv. *eternally*, for ever, for ever and a day, for good, for keeps (*colloq.*), till doomsday, for good and all; *endlessly*, incessantly, nonstop, relentlessly, around the clock.

96 IMMEDIACY

See also **94** (transience); **245** (speed).

n. *immediacy*, instantaneousness, simultaneity, suddenness, abruptness; *promptness*, speediness, alacrity, spontaneity, impulsiveness.

adj. *immediate*, instant, instantaneous, simultaneous; *sudden*, abrupt, spontaneous, impulsive, unpremeditated; *prompt*, punctual, speedy, rapid-fire, staccato.

vb. *act on impulse*, improvise, extemporize, ad-lib; *start*, dart, flit, bolt, pelt, flash, dash.

adv. *immediately*, forthwith, pronto (*colloq.*), overnight; *suddenly*, in a flash, on the spur of the moment, at the drop of a hat, off the cuff; *at once*, at a stroke, in one fell swoop; *punctually*, on time, to the second, on the dot (*colloq.*), on the nail.

97 TIMEKEEPING

See also **90** (time).

n. *timekeeping*, horology, chronometry, timing, clockwatching; *dateline*, time zone, meridian, daylight saving, local time, standard time; *chronology*, calendar, almanac, agenda, timetable, schedule, timesheet, journal, diary, logbook, chronicle, annals; *timepiece*, chronometer, sundial, waterclock, hourglass, siren, hooter, time signal, gong, chimes, speaking clock, metronome; *clock*, grandfather clock, alarm, repeater, fobwatch, hunter, turnip, wristwatch, digital watch, stopwatch, dial, face, hand, pendulum, escapement, mainspring.

adj. *timekeeping*, chronometrical, horological; *chronological*, temporal, historical.

vb. *record*, chronicle, log, clock up, time, timetable, schedule.

adv. *clockwise*; *around the clock*, twenty-four-hours a day; *anticlockwise*, against the clock, out of time.

98 WRONG TIME

n. *wrong time*, mistiming, bad timing, untimeliness, wrong moment; *anachronism*, precocity, prematurity, outdatedness, unfashionableness.

adj. *mistimed*, untimely, unseasonable, inopportune; *unpunctual*, late, tardy, dilatory, behindhand, early, previous; *anachronistic*, precocious, premature, overdue, outdated, posthumous, old-fashioned.

vb. *mistime*, bring forward, antedate, jump the gun (*colloq.*); *delay*, retard, postdate, hold up, tarry, be slow off the mark, be behind the times, put the clock back, regress.

adv. *in advance*, prematurely, ahead of time; *belatedly*, tardily, late in the day.

99 PRIORITY

See also **59** (precedence).

n. *priority*, anteriority, preexistence, prehistory; *precedence*, primogeniture, antecedence, right of way, early bird, first come first served; *firstborn*, eldest, antecedent, forbear, precursor; *premonition*, presentiment, forewarning, briefing, prior notice, foresight.

adj. *prior*, previous, preexisting, anterior, antecedent, earlier, first; *former*, onetime, erstwhile, sometime; *preemptive*, preventive, anticipatory.

vb. *precede*, predate, preexist, predecease; *foreshadow*, presage, anticipate, forestall, obviate, prevent; *preempt*, preclude, steal a march on, jump the queue, present with a fait accompli.

adv. *before*, beforehand, in advance, previously.

100 SUCCESSION

See also **60** (sequence).

n. *succession*, posterity, issue, inheritance, legacy; *aftereffect*, aftermath, fallout, upshot, outcome; *youngest*, junior, benjamin, latecomer; *successor*, heir, descendant, inheritor; *afterthought*, hindsight, second thoughts, post mortem, debriefing.

adj. *successive*, subsequent, following, last, posterior, next, rear; *future*, budding, would-be, elect, designate; *posthumous*.

vb. *succeed*, follow, take over from, inherit the mantle of, step into the shoes of; *defer*, put off, postpone, postdate.

adv. *after*, afterwards, subsequently, thereafter, thereupon.

101 PRESENT TIME

See also **96** (immediacy); **103** (same time); **106** (newness).

n. *present time*, present, simultaneity, contemporaneousness, present day, here and now, modern times; *contemporary*, one's generation, age group, peer group; *topicality*, currency, current affairs, news; *present event*, happening, occurrence, incident, episode, development, affair, matter, concern, transaction; *crisis*, turn of events, emergency, chapter of accidents, vicissitudes, ups and downs (*colloq.*).

adj. *present*, existing, extant, ongoing, actual, current, contemporaneous, simultaneous, live; *present-day*, contemporary, modern, up-to-date, topical, latest, up-to-the-minute, now (*colloq.*); *temporary*, provisional, ad hoc, makeshift, stopgap.

vb. *be present*, be in the air, be in the wind; *exist*, live from hand to mouth, live for the present; *attend*, show up, put in an appearance, turn up; *take place*, happen, occur, come about, coincide, arise, spring up, crop up

(*colloq.*), transpire, supervene; *experience*, encounter, undergo, go through.
adv. *at present*, at the moment, today, nowadays, these days, in this day and age; *now*, now or never, immediately, instantly, on the spot; *until now*, hitherto, to date; *for the present*, for the time being, temporarily, provisionally.

102 DIFFERENT TIME

See also **98** (wrong time).
n. *different time*, another time, alternative date; *past*, days gone by, better days; *future*, days to come, distant future.
adj. *out-of-date*, anachronistic, behind the times, overdue, advanced, futuristic.
adv. *not now*, later, some time, one of these days, one fine day, sooner or later; *then*, earlier, previously, at one time; *out of step*, out of phase, out of sync.

103 SAME TIME

See also **101** (present time).
n. *same time*, synchronism, coexistence, coincidence, simultaneity, clash, concurrence, contemporaneusness, unison, chorus; *same age*, vintage, generation, peer group, age group, contemporary, coeval; *synchronization*, sync, meridian, time zone, dead heat, photo finish.
adj. *synchronous*, synchronic, simultaneous, contemporaneous, concurrent, coexistent, coincidental; *contemporary*, coeval, isochronous.
vb. *synchronize*, tune, phase, align; *coincide*, come together, clash, double-book; *chorus*, chime, chant; *keep up*, keep abreast, keep in step.
adv. *at the same time*, simultaneously, concurrently, in the same breath; *in step*, in phase, in sync, in concert, in unison.

104 FUTURE TIME

See also **100** (succession); **450** (expectation).
n. *future time*, futurity, tomorrow, morrow, time to come; *future*, prospect, outlook, expectation, lookout (*colloq.*); *potential*, promise, raw material; *imminence*, proximity, approach, advent; *fate*, destiny, karma, predestination, inevitability; *horoscope*, stars, forecast, prediction, divination, futurology, crystal-gazing; *afterlife*, hereafter, next world, millennium, doomsday.
adj. *future*, coming, approaching, impending, imminent, due, ahead; *potential*, promising, budding, aspiring, would-be, prospective; *predestined*, fated, doomed, inevitable, inescapable.
vb. *lie ahead*, threaten, loom, draw nigh, be just around the corner; *anticipate*, foresee, foreshadow, predict, divine.
adv. *in future*, henceforth, from now on; *eventually*, in due course, in the fullness of time, in the long run; *at hand*, in view, in the offing, on the horizon, on the cards, on the agenda.

105 PAST TIME

See also **107** (oldness).
n. *past time*, bygone days, yesteryear, days of yore, good old days, auld lang syne; *souvenir*, memento, retrospective, golden oldie (*colloq.*), blast from the past (*colloq.*); *recollection*, memory, remembrance, nostalgia, hindsight; *regression*, atavism, reversion, relapse, throw-back; *obsoleteness*, antiquity, time immemorial, prehistory, Dark Ages, Stone Age; *relic*, archaism, antique, fossil, dinosaur, ruin, ancient monument, museum, archive; *archaeology*, palaeology, palaeography, antiquarianism; *thing of the past*, dead letter, ancient history, old news, has-been (*colloq.*), yesterday's man; *revival*, resurrection, resuscitation, exhumation.
adj. *past*, bygone, archaic, antiquated, obsolete, extinct; *retrospective*, nostalgic, retroactive, regressive, atavistic; *ancient*, prehistoric, Stone-Age, antediluvian; *lapsed*, date-expired, finished with, over and done with, irrevocable, irreversible; *former*, late, erstwhile, onetime, sometime, previous.
vb. *be past*, have run its course, have had its day, have seen better days; *pass*, elapse, expire, run out, die out,

fade away, blow over (*colloq.*); *recollect*, remember, recall, look back, hark back, put the clock back, go over old ground, regress, revert; *revive*, exhume, resurrect, resuscitate.

adv. *in the past*, formerly, previously, before, at one time, time was; *long ago*, once upon a time, in the dim and distant past.

106 NEWNESS

See also **101** (present time); **111** (youth).

n. *newness*, recentness, freshness, bloom; *novelty*, innovation, neologism, scoop, exclusive; *modernity*, up-to-dateness, topicality, currency, trendiness, latest thing, last word, dernier cri, flavour of the month (*colloq.*); *avant-garde*, modernism, new wave, futurism; *modernization*, revolution, renovation, restoration, facelift, overhaul, update, new edition, new look, revision; *immaturity*, greenness, rawness, callowness, inexperience; *novice*, raw recruit, tyro, fledgling, apprentice, greenhorn (*colloq.*), new boy, new bug (*colloq.*), newcomer, new broom, new blood; *rising generation*, bright young thing (*colloq.*), trendy (*colloq.*), upstart, parvenu, nouveaux riches.

adj. *new*, brand-new, born-again, fresh, virgin, pristine, evergreen; *novel*, innovative, new-minted, hot off the press; *modern*, up-to-date, current, topical, up-to-the-minute, fashionable, trendy (*colloq.*), with-it (*colloq.*); *immature*, green, callow, raw, inexperienced, untried, new to the game, budding.

vb. *make new*, modernize, renew, renovate, refurbish, rejuvenate, freshen up, give a new lease of life, update, revise, overhaul; *innovate*, introduce, invent, patent, coin, mint.

adv. *newly*, recently, lately, of late; *as new*, in mint condition; *anew*, afresh.

107 OLDNESS

See also **105** (past time); **112** (age).

n. *oldness*, age, antiquity, archaism, obsolescence, obsoleteness; *antique*, heirloom, collector's piece, museum piece, relic, fossil; *tradition*, custom, oral history, folklore, mythology; *maturity*, ripeness, experience, seniority, wisdom; *veteran*, old hand, old-timer (*colloq.*), doyen, father figure; *old age*, longevity, senility, senescence; *decay*, decline, dilapidation, erosion, ruin.

adj. *old*, age-old, ancient, olden, bygone, antique, vintage, old-world, archaic, obsolescent, obsolete, antediluvian; *traditional*, time-honoured, long-standing, historical, old as the hills, mythological, primordial; *outdated*, outmoded, antiquated, superannuated, passé, disused, discontinued, old hat (*colloq.*), out of the ark (*colloq.*); *dilapidated*, mouldering, crumbling, motheaten, threadbare, clapped out (*colloq.*), rusty, musty, distressed; *aged*, venerable, hoary, geriatric, past it (*colloq.*), senile, gaga (*colloq.*).

vb. *grow old*, age, wither, fade, crumble, moulder, decay, rust.

adv. *for ages* (*colloq.*), since the year dot, since Adam was a boy.

108 SEASON

n. *season*, high/low season, close season; *spring*, springtime, seedtime, youth, vernal equinox; *summer*, summertime, midsummer, high summer, dog days, summer solstice; *autumn*, fall (*U.S.*), back end, Indian summer, autumn equinox; *winter*, wintertime, Christmas, yuletide, festive season, midwinter, hibernation, decline, decay, winter solstice.

adj. *seasonal*, springlike, vernal, burgeoning, summery, aestival, autumnal, equinoctial, wintry, hibernal, bleak.

109 MORNING

n. *morning*, morn, daybreak, dawn, sunrise, Aurora, cockcrow, sunup; *forenoon*, elevenses, noon, midday, high noon; *dawn chorus*, early bird, early riser, reveille, matins.

adj. *morning*, matutinal, daytime, diurnal.

adv. *a.m.*, ante meridiem; *at first light*, at the crack of dawn, with the lark.

110 EVENING

n. *evening*, eventide, eve, sunset, sundown, twilight, half-light, dusk, gloaming, cockshut; *night*, nightfall, nighttime, darkness, moonrise, dead of night, midnight, witching hour, small hours; *afternoon*, matinée, soiree, cocktail, sundowner, evensong, vespers, lights out, curfew, lighting-up time, last post, bedtime, night hawk, night owl, moonlight flit.
adj. *nightly*, nocturnal, dark, twilight, crepuscular, overnight.
adv. *p.m.*, post meridiem; *by night*, overnight, under cover of darkness.

111 YOUTH

See also **106** (newness).
n. *youth*, springtime, heyday, salad days; *youthfulness*, freshness, immaturity, callowness; *babyhood*, infancy, childhood, tender years, formative years; *adolescence*, teens, puberty, awkward age, pubescence, growing pains; *cradle*, nursery, kindergarten, playschool; *pupillage*, nonage, tutelage, wardship; *youngster*, infant, babe in arms, suckling, toddler, tot, mite; *child*, kid (*colloq.*), brat (*colloq.*), urchin, nipper (*colloq.*), minx, madam, moppet; *adolescent*, juvenile, teenager, delinquent, whippersnapper (*colloq.*), stripling, tearaway, skinhead, yob (*colloq.*), lass, teenybopper, tomboy, nymphet, Lolita; *pupil*, ward, minor.
adj. *young*, youthful, fresh, young-at-heart, ageless; *immature*, green, callow, wet behind the ears (*colloq.*); *newborn*, babyish, infantile, preschool, childish, puerile, adolescent, pubescent, virginal, coltish, junior, teenage.

112 AGE

See also **107** (oldness).
n. *age*, older generation, adulthood, manhood, legal age, majority, seniority; *middle age*, prime, maturity, menopause, climacteric, change of life, mid-life crisis, mutton dressed as lamb, no spring chicken (*colloq.*); *old age*, longevity, ripe old age, declining years, evening of one's life, second childhood, senility, dotage; *old person*, adult, grown-up, matriarch, matron, patriarch, oldster (*colloq.*), old-age pensioner, senior citizen, grandfather, grandad (*colloq.*), old boy (*colloq.*), old fogy, old buffer (*colloq.*), greybeard, grandmother, granny (*colloq.*), old dear (*colloq.*), crone, hag, Darby and Joan; *old hand*, veteran, expert, old-timer, elder, elder statesman, grand old man, doyen, grande dame, doyenne; *gerontocracy*, gerontology, geriatrics, old folks' home, granny flat.
adj. *old*, adult, grown-up, mature; *middle-aged*, menopausal, matronly, of a certain age, ageing, getting on (*colloq.*), long in the tooth (*colloq.*); *aged*, elderly, sprightly, geriatric, doddering, failing, senile, gaga (*colloq.*), white-haired, with one foot in the grave (*colloq.*).

113 EARLINESS

See also **99** (priority).
n. *earliness*, promptness, dispatch, timeliness, immediacy, punctuality; *prematurity*, precocity, forwardness; *immaturity*, unreadiness, unpreparedness, unripeness; *foresight*, anticipation, preparedness, forward planning, prior warning, head start.
adj. *early*, prompt, immediate, punctual, timely; *premature*, precocious, previous, forward, advanced; *immature*, unripe, unready, unprepared; *preliminary*, preparatory, anticipatory.
vb. *be early*, reserve, book, get in first, jump the queue, jump the gun (*colloq.*); *preempt*, take the initiative, forestall, nip in the bud; *dispatch*, expedite, lose no time, take time by the forelock.
adv. *early on*, first thing; *beforehand*, in advance, before one's time, out of turn.

114 LATENESS

See also **100** (succession).
n. *lateness*, late hour, small hours, eleventh hour, last minute, high time, brinksmanship; *tardiness*, slowness, delayed reaction, time lag, afterthought; *dilatoriness*, unpunctuality, delay, holdup, latecomer; *backward-*

ness, retardation, slow starter, late developer; *postponement*, adjournment, deferment, procrastination, suspension, reprieve, moratorium.

adj. *late*, late in the day, last-minute, deathbed, posthumous; *belated*, overdue, behindhand, tardy, dilatory, unpunctual; *backward*, retarded, slow; *postponed*, deferred, suspended.

vb. *be late*, oversleep, keep late hours, burn the midnight oil; *be slow*, linger, dawdle, tarry, loiter, dilly-dally (*colloq.*); *postpone*, put off, defer, adjourn, shelve, mothball, put on ice/in cold storage, procrastinate; *delay*, stall, stonewall, filibuster, play for time, suspend, hang fire, sleep on it, take one's time, cool one's heels, wait and see.

adv. *late*, till all hours; *at last*, ultimately, in the end; *tardily*, belatedly, at the last minute, in the nick of time.

115 TIMELINESS

See also **580** (convenience).

n. *timeliness*, opportuneness, convenience, expediency, right moment; *opportunity*, golden opportunity, chance, break (*colloq.*), piece of luck, opening; *key moment*, psychological moment, moment of truth, pinch (*colloq.*), push (*colloq.*), crunch (*colloq.*); *critical point*, crux, turning point, crisis, emergency, narrow escape, close shave.

adj. *timely*, welcome, seasonable, fortuitous, well-timed, auspicious, opportune, providential, propitious, heaven-sent; *convenient*, handy, expedient, advantageous.

vb. *seize one's opportunity*, profit by, take advantage of, exploit, turn to good account, capitalize on, strike while the iron is hot, make hay while the sun shines.

adv. *at the right moment*, conveniently, not before time, in the nick of time.

116 UNTIMELINESS

See also **581** (inconvenience).

n. *untimeliness*, inconvenience, inopportuneness, wrong moment, evil hour, off-day, one of those days; *mistiming*, intrusion, interruption, misjudgment, blunder, clanger (*colloq.*).

adj. *untimely*, inopportune, inauspicious, untoward, disadvantageous, unlucky, ill-starred; *mistimed*, intrusive, misjudged, malapropos, awkward, inconvenient.

vb. *mistime*, misjudge, miss one's opportunity, miss the boat (*colloq.*), blow it (*colloq.*); *intrude*, break in on, talk out of turn, put one's foot in it (*colloq.*), drop a brick (*colloq.*).

adv. *at a bad time*, at the wrong moment, inopportunely, inconveniently.

117 FREQUENCY

See also **88** (repetition); **119** (regularity).

n. *frequency*, recurrence, regularity, repetition, rhythm; *predictability*, familiarity, commonness, monotony, banality.

adj. *frequent*, numerous, recurrent, periodic, regular, repeated, rhythmic; *continual*, sustained, constant, monotonous, relentless, remorseless; *predictable*, familiar, common, prevalent, banal, two a penny.

vb. *be frequent*, recur, keep on, continue.

adv. *frequently*, often, many a time; *repeatedly*, constantly, again and again, time and time again, regularly, continually; *commonly*, generally, more often than not.

118 INFREQUENCY

See also **87** (few); **120** (irregularity).

n. *infrequency*, rarity, scarcity, scantness, sparseness; *intermittence*, irregularity, unpredictability.

adj. *infrequent*, rare, few and far between, spaced out, occasional, scarce, sparse; *intermittent*, irregular, unpredictable, uncommon, unusual.

adv. *infrequently*, rarely, seldom; *occasionally*, once in a while, every now and then, once in a blue moon (*colloq.*); *intermittently*, off and on, now and then.

119 REGULARITY

See also **88** (repetition); **92** (period); **117** (frequency).

n. *regularity*, rhythm, recurrence, repetition, periodicity; *reliability*, steadiness, constancy, predictability, uniformity; *beat*, throb, tick, pulse, measure, refrain, chorus; *alternation*, ebb and flow, to and fro, shuttle service, swing, pendulum, piston; *rotation*, rota, roster, revolution, circuit, cycle, menstruation, biorhythms; *routine*, daily round, nine to five, treadmill; *anniversary*, birthday, leap year, immovable feast.

adj. *regular*, rhythmic, repeated, recurring, periodic; *reliable*, predictable, steady, constant, uniform, even, measured; *alternating*, seasonal, cyclical, rotational.

vb. *recur*, come round again, revolve, rotate, alternate, reciprocate, take turn about; *be rhythmic*, beat, throb, tick, chime, swing; *go to and fro*, ply, commute.

adv. *regularly*, at regular intervals, seasonally, cyclically; *periodically*, at intervals, now and again; *alternately*, in rotation, in turn; *to and fro*, back and forwards.

120 IRREGULARITY

See also **118** (infrequency).

n. *irregularity*, variability, unpredictability, randomness, inconstancy, capriciousness; *unevenness*, unsteadiness, fitfulness, jerkiness, sporadicness, spasmodicness, fluctuation; *caprice*, whim, variable, unknown quantity, movable feast.

adj. *irregular*, variable, unpredictable, random, changeable, capricious, erratic; *uneven*, unsteady, fitful, jerky, sporadic, spasmodic, intermittent, arhythmic, stop-go.

vb. *be irregular*, vary, change, waver, flicker, fluctuate, come and go.

adv. *irregularly*, off and on, spasmodically, in fits and starts.

121 CHANGE

See also **125** (conversion); **127** (revolution); **130** (changeableness).

n. *change*, alteration, modification, version, adjustment, modulation, inflection, mutation; *transformation*, transfiguration, transmogrification, metamorphosis, conversion; *adaptation*, variation, permutation, shift; *transition*, changeover, switch, substitution, transposition, transference; *flux*, flow, mobility, impermanence, instability, vicissitudes, ups and downs (*colloq.*); *improvement*, reformation, revision, upturn, change for the better/worse, deterioration, degeneration, downturn; *fluctuation*, seesaw, change of mind, vacillation, change of direction, deviation, diversion, U-turn, volte-face, about-turn; *revolution*, overthrow, upheaval, sea change, wind of change, innovation, reform, reconstruction, reorganization; *adapter*, alterant, transformer, catalyst, metabolism, alchemy, enzyme, leaven, yeast; *reformer*, radical, revolutionary, agitator, new broom.

adj. *changing*, fluid, plastic, mobile, unstable, protean, impermanent, volatile; *transitional*, provisional, temporary, interim, ad hoc; *revolutionary*, radical, progressive, innovative, reformist.

vb. *change*, alter, modify, adjust, temper, modulate, inflect, mutate; *transform*, transfigure, transmogrify, transmute, metamorphose, convert, metabolize; *vary*, diversify, adapt, ring the changes; *improve*, reform, turnover a new leaf, change for the better/worse, deteriorate, degenerate, fall away; *fluctuate*, vacillate, change one's tune, shift, veer, chop and change, blow hot and cold (*colloq.*); *interchange*, swap (*colloq.*), switch, change round, substitute, transpose, transfer; *revolutionize*, revamp, remodel, reconstruct, refurbish, reorganize, revise; *process*, treat, adulterate, denature, doctor, massage.

adv. *mutatis mutandis*, vice versa.

122 PERMANENCE

See also **131** (stability).

n. *permanence*, unchangingness, immutability, fixity, immobility, stasis;

endurance, continuity, persistence, subsistence, survival; *stability*, steadiness, constancy, firmness, bedrock, solidity; *tradition*, custom, habit, routine, status quo, conservatism, laissez-faire; *conservative*, reactionary, hawk, diehard, stick-in-the-mud (*colloq.*); *invariability*, inflexibility, rigidity, immovableness, stubborness, obstinacy.

adj. *permanent*, unchanging, immutable, fixed, stationary, immobile, static; *enduring*, persistent, continuing, lasting, surviving; *stable*, steady, constant, firm, solid, unbudgeable, unwavering, steadfast; *invariable*, inflexible, rigid, immovable, stubborn, obstinate.

vb. *be permanent*, endure, last, abide, subsist, persist, survive; *remain*, stay, tarry, stay put, stand still, dig in one's toes, tread water, mark time; *settle*, establish, fix, entrench, put down roots; *maintain*, sustain, uphold, persevere, conserve.

adv. *permanently*, for good, for ever.

123 CESSATION

See also **235** (motionlessness).

n. *cessation*, discontinuation, termination, closure, shutdown, closedown, collapse, failure, crash; *stop*, halt, standstill, deadlock, stasis, stalemate, checkmate; *hitch*, check, holdup, snag, hiccup, blockage, bottleneck, jam; *stoppage*, walkout, strike, work-to-rule, go-slow, lockout, sit-in; *pause*, lull, break, interruption, letup, rest, breather (*colloq.*), respite, cooling-off period; *suspension*, freeze, abeyance, moratorium, truce, ceasefire, armistice, amnesty; *end*, conclusion, expiry, end-date, terminus, end of the road.

vb. *cease*, stop, desist, refrain, hold off; *halt*, stop short, stop in one's tracks, pull up, baulk, stall, seize up; *discontinue*, pause, break off, leave off, ring off, knock off (*colloq.*); *strike*, walk out, down tools, come out, work to rule, go slow, occupy; *check*, arrest, stem, block, veto, thwart, foil, parry, checkmate; *suspend*, drop, hold over, put on ice, freeze, shelve, mothball; *end*, terminate, finish, conclude, expire, run out, peter out, fizzle out (*colloq.*); *collapse*, fail, fold, go into liquidation, wind up, shut up shop, ring down the curtain; *retire*, resign, stand down, pull out, withdraw, scratch.

124 CONTINUITY

See also **93** (duration).

n. *continuity*, continuation, perpetuation, maintenance, prolongation; *flow*, run, course, progress, current; *regularity*, constancy, uniformity, steadiness, smoothness, monotony; *link*, bridge, stopgap, potboiler (*colloq.*), filler, padding.

adj. *continuous*, uninterrupted, unbroken, nonstop, ongoing, flowing, seamless; *perpetual*, unceasing, incessant, neverending, inexhaustible, undying; *continual*, steady, constant, uniform, regular, recurrent, monotonous, unremitting, relentless.

vb. *continue*, proceed, progress, advance, carry on, keep on; *maintain*, uphold, sustain, preserve, conserve, perpetuate; *endure*, persist, persevere, hang on, plod on, peg away (*colloq.*), stick; *prolong*, protract, extend, spin out, drag out.

adv. *continuously*, on and on, to the bitter end; *continually*, repeatedly.

125 CONVERSION

See also **121** (change).

n. *conversion*, mutation, switch, changeover, transformation, metamorphosis; *processing*, treatment, chemistry, alchemy, evaporation, liquefaction, crystallization, solidification; *convertibility*, adaptability, versatility, flexibility; *laboratory*, melting pot, crucible, test tube; *convert*, proselyte, neophyte, apostate, turncoat, deserter.

adj. *convertible*, mutable, adaptable, versatile, flexible, recyclable, biodegradable; *converted*, reborn, born-again, reformed; *proselytizing*, evangelical, crusading, missionary, revivalist.

vb. *convert*, adapt, change, assimilate, mutate, metamorphose, transform; *process*, treat, liquefy, evaporate, solidify, crystallize, recycle, break down; *proselytize*, evangelize, win over, persuade; *be converted*, change one's mind, defect, go over to the other side, desert.

126 REVERSION

See also **254** (backward motion).

n. *reversion*, return, regression, atavism, throwback; *relapse*, recidivism, backsliding, recurrence, recrudescence; *reaction*, response, feedback, backlash, whiplash, recoil, retaliation, repercussion, reverberation; *reversal*, overthrow, overturn, upset, about-turn, U-turn, volte-face, swing of the pendulum; *restoration*, recovery, retrieval, restitution, reinstatement; *retreat*, withdrawal, retraction, retrogression, retrenchment, recession.

adj. *reverted*, reflexive, retrogressive, retroactive; *retrograde*, reactionary, unreconstructed, backward-looking, retrospective, regressive; *reacting*, responsive, reflex, repercussive, reverberative; *reversible*, convertible, inverted, two-way.

vb. *revert*, return, relapse, regress, retrace one's steps, retreat, recede, withdraw; *undo*, unmake, overthrow, overturn, upset; *react*, respond, retort, counter, recoil, rebound; *restore*, reinstate, redress, recover, retrieve.

adv. *inside out*, back to front, upside down; *as you were*, back to square one, back to the drawing board.

127 REVOLUTION

See also **121** (change); **662** (disobedience).

n. *revolution*, unpheaval, upset, convulsion, shakeup, coup d'état, overthrow; *rotation*, full circle, circuit, lap, turn; *revolt*, uprising, insurrection, rebellion, insurgency, mutiny; *extremism*, militancy, radicalism, agitprop, entryism, subversion, sedition; *complete change*, clean sweep, clean slate, tabula rasa, new dawn; *revolutionary*, militant, radical, extremist, fanatic, rebel, insurgent, guerrilla, freedom fighter, fifth column.

adj. *revolutionary*, radical, extreme, far-reaching, sweeping, thoroughgoing, draconian, root and branch; *rebellious*, mutinous, bolshie (*colloq.*), militant, extremist, insurgent, underground, seditious, subversive, entryist, anarchistic.

vb. *revolutionize*, shake up, change the face of, remodel, reconstruct; *overturn*, overthrow, subvert, undermine, infiltrate; *revolt*, rebel, rise up, mutiny, kick over the traces.

128 SUBSTITUTION

See also **129** (exchange).

n. *substitution*, exchange, switch, swap (*colloq.*), changeround, shuffle, musical chairs; *substitute*, agent, deputy, proxy, replacement, stand-in, surrogate, understudy, relief, reserve, locum, whipping boy, scapegoat; *equivalent*, approximation, imitation, second best, makeshift, expedient, stopgap.

adj. *substitutable*, surrogate, alternative, equivalent, interchangeable, vicarious; *substitute*, imitation, fake, ersatz, mock.

vb. *substitute*, exchange, switch, swap (*colloq.*), change round, shuffle; *replace*, supplant, oust, supersede, take over from; *deputize*, stand in for, understudy, cover up for, impersonate.

adv. *instead*, in lieu; *in one's place/stead*, in one's shoes, by proxy.

129 EXCHANGE

See also **11** (reciprocity); **128** (substitution).

n. *exchange*, barter, trade, handover, transfer, swap (*colloq.*); *reciprocity*, give and take, mutuality, quid pro quo, retort, rejoinder, riposte, repartee, dialogue; *interaction*, interplay, interchange, cooperation; *substitution*, transposition, transliteration, transcription; *retaliation*, requittal, reprisals, tit for tat (*colloq.*).

adj. *exchanged*, mutual, reciprocal, cooperative, two-way; *interchangeable*, substitutable, equivalent, convertible.

vb. *exchange*, barter, trade, swap (*colloq.*), hand over, transfer; *reciprocate*, retaliate, retort, bandy words; *interchange*, switch, transpose, transcribe, shuffle, substitute.

adv. *in exchange*, instead, in kind, in return.

130 CHANGEABLENESS

See also **94** (transience); **121** (change).

n. *changeableness*, changeability, mutability, variability; *fluidity*, plasticity, malleability, flexibility, versatility, adaptability; *inconstancy*, impermanence, instability, volatility, unreliability, unpredictability, waywardness, fickleness, capriciousness; *fluctuation*, vacillation, hesitation, indecision, irresolution; *mobility*, restlessness, unease, fidgetiness, *changeable thing*, kaleidoscope, prism, chameleon, mercury, quicksilver, shot silk.

adj. *changeable*, mutable, variable, unstable, impermanent; *fluid*, plastic, malleable, flexible, versatile, adaptable, quick-change, protean, mercurial; *inconstant*, volatile, fickle, flighty, unreliable, wayward, capricious, erratic, unpredictable; *vacillating*, hesitant, indecisive, irresolute, uncertain; *mobile*, restless, shifty, fidgety, uneasy; *desultory*, fitful, spasmodic, sporadic.

vb. *vary*, change, shift, fluctuate, waver, vacillate, hesitate, blow hot and cold (*colloq.*); *move*, dart, dance, flit, flicker, twinkle, gutter, shimmer.

adv. *spasmodically*, off and on.

131 STABILITY

See also **122** (permanence).

n. *stability*, steadiness, firmness, fixity, permanence, solidity, immobility; *balance*, equilibrium, homoeostasis, self-regulation, self-control, composure, even-temperedness, even keel; *reliability*, predictability, invariability, constancy, regularity, sureness; *stabilizer*, ballast, counterweight, prop, buttress, foundation, pillar, bedrock, anchor, mooring; *confirmation*, ratification, validation, corroboration.

adj. *stable*, steady, firm, fixed, permanent, immobile; *balanced*, homoeostatic, self-regulating, self-controlled, calm, composed, even-tempered; *immovable*, entrenched, solid, unwavering, inalterable, unshakable, unassailable; *reliable*, predictable, invariable, constant, regular, perennial; *indelible*, fast, ingrained, deep-rooted, deep-seated, ineradicable.

vb. *be stable*, stand firm/fast, stay put, dig in, settle down, put down roots; *stabilize*, support, buttress, shore up, prop up, anchor, embed, entrench, fix; *confirm*, establish, validate, ratify, corroborate.

132 CAUSE

See also **61** (beginning); **134** (motive).

n. *cause*, motive, reason, casus belli, ground, explanation, rationale, factor, influence, determinant; *causality*, instrumentality, aetiology, necessity, determinism; *motivation*, mainspring, provocation, stimulus, impetus, encouragement, inducement; *creator*, prime mover, author, inventor, originator, founder, architect; *source*, fount, fountainhead, cradle, womb, nursery, seed bed, breeding ground, hotbed; *genesis*, origin, ancestry, roots, derivation, etymology; *instrument*, means, motor, pivot, lever, hinge, dynamo; *germ*, seed, fetus, embryo, raw material.

adj. *causal*, instrumental, determinant, pivotal, influential, formative; *basic*, original, primary, fundamental, elemental, embryonic; *creative*, dynamic, innovative, inventive, productive, generative, fertile, seminal.

vb. *cause*, give rise to, create, generate, produce, originate; *found*, establish, institute, launch, initiate; *bring about*, occasion, unleash, precipitate, trigger; *organize*, set up, engineer, stage-manage; *provoke*, elicit, evoke, release; *stimulate*, kindle, inspire, encourage, foster, promote; *determine*, decide, entail, require, necessitate.

prep. *because of*, owing to, due to, as a result of.

133 EFFECT

See also **62** (end).

n. *effect*, consequence, result, end result, development, outcome, upshot; *aftereffect*, sequel, aftermath, fallout, reaction, backlash, ripple effect, knock-on effect, chain reaction; *prod-*

uct, produce, crop, harvest, fruit, output; *derivative*, by-product, side effect, spin-off, legacy.
adj. *resultant*, consequent, subsequent, secondary, ensuing; *dependent*, contingent, concomitant; *derivative*, inherited, hereditary, genetic.
vb. *result*, develop, arise, unfold, evolve, spring up, issue, emerge; *derive from*, emanate from, go back to, originate in, have one's roots in; *depend on*, hinge, pivot, turn, hang.
adv. *consequently*, hence, as a result, in consequence.

134 MOTIVE

See also **132** (cause); **551** (persuasion).
n. *motive*, reason, hypothesis, theory, inference, assumption, grounds, basis; *explanation*, occasion, pretext, excuse, justification, rationale; *motivation*, impetus, driving force, impulsion, mainspring, trigger, inspiration, inducement, carrot; incentive; *attribution*, imputation, responsibility, accountability, credit, blame.
adj. *motivated*, caused, inspired, occasioned; *attributable*, assignable, ascribable, accountable, responsible, culpable; *inferred*, assumed, hypothetical, putative.
vb. *motivate*, cause, occasion, instigate, inspire; *attribute*, ascribe, assign, put down to, lay at the door of, blame, implicate; *explain*, account for, justify, interpret; *assume*, infer, derive, hypothesize.
adv. *hence*, for this reason; *therefore*, consequently.
prep. *owing to*, on account of, because of.

135 LACK OF MOTIVE

See also **554** (chance).
n. *lack of motive*, fortuitousness, gratuitousness, arbitrariness, randomness; *chance*, luck, fortune, pot luck, hazard, accident, fluke; *unaccountability*, unpredictability, coincidence, haphazardness, indeterminacy.
adj. *motiveless*, groundless, causeless, gratuitous, uncalled-for, arbitrary, random; *unmotivated*, unintentional, accidental, coincidental, fortuitous, lucky; *unpredictable*, unaccountable, inexplicable, unexpected, chance, haphazard.
vb. *chance*, light upon, stumble upon, hit upon.
adv. *by chance*, accidentally, coincidentally; *unpredictably*, unexpectedly, out of the blue.

136 OPERATION

See also **138** (instrumentality); **567** (means).
n. *operation*, action, agency, influence, power, stress, pressure; *execution*, implementation, performance, application, effect, force; *process*, function, working, running, handling, administration.
adj. *operative*, effective, conducive, influential; *operational*, functional, working, active, live, on-stream; *practical*, feasible, applicable, manageable; *executive*, administrative, managerial.
vb. *operate*, work, function, run, tick over, idle; *execute*, perform, carry out, put into effect/practice; *affect*, influence, work on, act on, take effect; *activate*, power, drive, run, switch on, plug in, wind up.
adv. *into action*, into operation, into force, into play.

137 COUNTERACTION

See also **28** (compensation); **632** (opposition).
n. *counteraction*, opposition, retaliation, reprisals, counterattack, counterblast, counterrevolution; *reaction*, response, retort, riposte, repercussion, backlash; *recoil*, resistance, friction, drag; *compensation*, counterbalance, counterweight, foil, corrective, checks and balances, antidote, remedy, cure.
adj. *counteractive*, counter, contrary, counterproductive, opposing, retaliatory; *reactionary*, counterrevolutionary, resistant, recalcitrant; *compensatory*, countervailing, makeweight; *restorative*, corrective, remedial, curative.
vb. *counteract*, counter, oppose, combat, militate against; *react*, retaliate, respond, answer, riposte, retort; *com-*

pensate, offset, make up for, counterbalance, neutralize, defuse, cancel out; *check*, prevent, foil, thwart, cross, obviate; *remedy*, cure, restore, correct.

138 INSTRUMENTALITY

See also **136** (operation); **568** (tool); **631** (help).

n. *instrumentality*, agency, means, services, action, aid, assistance; *intervention*, intercession, mediation, intermediary; *mechanism*, device, contrivance, deus ex machina, means to an end; *utility*, usefulness, helpfulness, serviceability, convenience, handiness.

adj. *instrumental*, effective, influential, conducive; *useful*, serviceable, practicable, convenient, handy; *helpful*, contributory, favourable, supportive.

vb. *be instrumental*, work, act, influence, affect; *serve*, help, encourage, support, promote, foster, advance; *intervene*, intercede, interpose, mediate, have a hand in.

prep. *by means of*, through, via, per; *thanks to*, courtesy of; *on behalf of*, for the sake of.

139 INFLUENCE

See also **551** (persuasion).

n. *influence*, dominance, sway, ascendancy, power, hegemony; *leverage*, pull, weight, clout (*colloq.*), whip hand, upper hand, casting vote; *persuasion*, suggestion, manipulation, string-pulling, lobbying, propaganda, soft sell, brainwashing; *charm*, magnetism, charisma, hypnotism, mesmerism, sorcery, magic, seduction, fascination; *patronage*, nepotism, freemasonry, old-boy network, friend at court, powers that be, Establishment; *moving force*, lobby, pressure group, ginger group, power behind the throne, grey eminence, agent provocateur, mole; *infiltration*, subversion, entryism.

adj. *influential*, important, dominant, prevailing, powerful, pervasive; *persuasive*, suggestive, convincing, manipulative, subversive; *charming*, charismatic, magnetic, hypnotic, mesmeric, bewitching, fascinating.

vb. *influence*, dominate, override, outweigh, master, subdue, have under one's thumb. *have influence*, count, tell, weigh, matter, carry weight, wear the trousers, call the tune; *persuade*, convince, manipulate, sway, have the ear of, work on, lean on, prevail on, pressurize, lobby; *charm*, mesmerize, hypnotize, bewitch, fascinate, captivate; *permeate*, infiltrate, penetrate, subvert, undermine.

140 TENDENCY

See also **430** (misjudgment).

n. *tendency*, trend, tenor, course, direction, mainstream, current; *inclination*, leaning, penchant, proclivity, propensity, predilection, soft spot; *predisposition*, cast, bent, bias, prejudice; *proneness*, liability, susceptibility, likelihood, vulnerability; *aptitude*, instinct, flair, gift.

adj. *tending*, conducive, leading, tendentious, biased, partisan, partial; *predisposed*, inclined, prone, apt, liable, susceptible, likely.

vb. *tend*, incline, lean, gravitate, verge; *predispose*, bias, prejudice, influence.

141 POWER

See also **143** (strength); **145** (vigour).

n. *power*, might, omnipotence, rule, authority, dominance, ascendancy, hegemony, influence, sway; *strength*, forcefulness, cogency, impact, effectiveness, teeth, muscle; *vigour*, life, energy, dynamism, drive, overdrive; *ability*, capability, potential, competence, reach, grasp, aptitude; *powerful person*, chief, mandarin, mogul, magnate, tycoon, big battalions, power behind the throne, linchpin, moving spirit, driving force; *energy*, impetus, momentum, propulsion, drive, thrust, pressure, horsepower, locomotion; *energy source*, fuel, gas, electricity, atomic power, wave power, solar energy, fossil fuel, hydroelectricity; *motor*, engine, generator, turbine, dynamo, battery, reactor, power station.

adj. *powerful*, mighty, all-powerful, omnipotent, dominant, influential, authoritative; *strong*, forceful, cogent,

telling, hard-hitting, effective; *able*, capable, competent, efficacious, adequate; *powered*, locomotive, automated, self-propelled, souped-up; *active*, live, operative, on-stream, working.
vb. *power*, drive, charge, propel, electrify, automate, mechanize; *activate*, plug in, switch on, wire up; *strengthen*, invigorate, energize, galvanize, boost; *dominate*, rule, govern, hold sway, prevail, pull rank, rule the roost, wear the trousers (*colloq.*).
adv. *in power*, in force, in operation.

142 POWERLESSNESS

See also **144** (weakness); **593** (deterioration).
n. *powerlessness*, impotence, helplessness, defencelessness, vulnerability; *weakness*, frailness, feebleness, debility, disablement, handicap, senility; *inability*, incapacity, incompetence, unfitness, ineffectiveness, inadequacy; *prostration*, exhaustion, paralysis, lifelessness, torpor, inertia, atrophy; *broken reed*, sitting duck, lame duck, paper tiger, man of straw.
adj. *powerless*, impotent, helpless, defenceless, vulnerable; *weak*, frail, feeble, disabled, handicapped, hamstrung, senile, debilitated, incapacitated; *prostrate*, inert, paralysed, lifeless, torpid, comatose, exhausted, all in, laid up, invalid, bedridden; *unable*, incompetent, ineffectual, unfit, inadequate, spineless, toothless.
vb. *make powerless*, disarm, disable, put out of action, neutralize, invalidate; *weaken*, undermine, sap, cripple, handicap, cramp someone's style, put a spoke in someone's wheel; *prostrate*, exhaust, paralyse, atrophy, drain.
adv. *out of commission*, hors de combat, in dock (*colloq.*).

143 STRENGTH

See also **141** (power); **664** (compulsion).
n. *strength*, might, brute force, muscle, brawn, toughness, hardness, steel, iron; *potency*, virility, manliness, ruggedness, fitness, health, soundness; *endurance*, resistance, durability, stamina, staying power, grit, backbone, guts, bottle (*colloq.*), pluck; *vigour*, force, energy, assertiveness, strength of character, resolution; *invulnerability*, impregnability, impermeability, indomitability, resilience; *athleticism*, gymnastics, weightlifting, body building, pumping iron (*colloq.*); *weightlifter*, strong man, amazon, Samson, Tarzan, Hercules, muscleman, he-man (*colloq.*), beefcake (*colloq.*); *support*, reinforcement, rampant, buttress, mainstay, pillar, tower of strenth.
adj. *strong*, powerful, mighty, well-armed, tough, hard, steely; *potent*, virile, manly, rugged, robust, fit, healthy, sound; *vigorous*, energetic, dynamic, forceful, assertive, resolute; *invulnerable*, impregnable, impermeable, indestructible, durable; *resilient*, plucky, indomitable, unflagging, staunch, stalwart, doughty; *athletic*, able-bodied, muscular, brawny, burly, hefty, strapping, amazonian.
vb. *strengthen*, reinforce, fortify, buttress, brace, steel, nerve, gird one's loins; *assert*, affirm, stress, underline, emphasize; *invigorate*, energize, hearten, enliven, animate.
adv. *strongly*, with might and main, forcefully.

144 WEAKNESS

See also **142** (powerlessness).
n. *weakness*, feebleness, puniness, slightness, frailty; *flimsiness*, fragility, brittleness, delicacy, fineness; *ineffectiveness*, impotence, powerlessness, helplessness, vulnerability, uselessness; *softness*, tenderness, womanliness, effeminacy, effeteness; *limpness*, flaccidity, flabbiness, slackness, sponginess; *debility*, infirmity, weakliness, decrepitude, sickliness, invalidism, valetudinarianism; *prostration*, fatigue, languor, listlessness, lethargy, lassitude; *insipidness*, tastelessness, wateriness, thinness, pallor, bloodlessness, anaemia; *instability*, insecurity, shakiness, unsteadiness, precariousness, house of cards, matchwood; *weak point*, soft spot, foible, Achilles' heel,

inadequacy, defect, flaw, weak link, chink in someone's armour; *weakling*, milksop, sissy, lame duck, invalid, jellyfish, doormat, wet (*colloq.*), wimp (*colloq.*), drip (*colloq.*), weed (*colloq.*).

adj. *weak*, feeble, puny, slight, frail, fragile, brittle, delicate, flimsy; *ineffectual*, impotent, powerless, helpless, unarmed, unaided, vulnerable; *soft*, tender, womanly, effeminate, babyish, effete; *weak-willed*, irresolute, gutless, weak-kneed, spineless, wet (*colloq.*), drippy (*colloq.*), wimpish (*colloq.*); *limp*, flaccid, flabby, slack, spongy; *infirm*, sickly, weakly, decrepit, invalid, disabled, lame, halt; *prostrate*, weary, languid, spent, listless, lethargic, burnt-out; *insipid*, tasteless, watery, thin, pale, anaemic, dilute, wishy-washy (*colloq.*), washed out; *unstable*, insecure, shaky, wobbly, rocky, rickety, precarious, ramshackle, gimcrack.

vb. *weaken*, sap, undermine, disarm; *disable*, maim, lame, cripple, enfeeble, debilitate, enervate; *decline*, dwindle, fade, wither, wilt, languish, flag, sag, slacken; *mitigate*, extenuate, lessen, soften, cushion, muffle, blunt; *dilute*, thin, water down, adulterate, tone down, moderate; *shake*, waver, quaver, tremble, totter, teeter, dodder.

145 VIGOUR

See also **141** (power); **507** (emphasis).

n. *vigour*, energy, life, vitality, dynamism, dash, elan, liveliness, impetus, vim, pep (*colloq.*), zap (*colloq.*), oomph (*colloq.*); *enthusiasm*, fervour, zest, joie de vivre, gusto, relish; *enterprise*, initiative, drive, dynamism, aggressiveness, thrust, punch, attack, verve, get-up-and-go (*colloq.*); *spirit*, mettle, fire, guts (*colloq.*), pluck, spunk (*colloq.*), bottle (*colloq.*); *stimulus*, boost, shot in the arm, fillip, tonic, stimulant, pick-me-up (*colloq.*), upper (*colloq.*), pep talk (*colloq.*); *whiz kid*, livewire (*colloq.*), bright spark (*colloq.*), self-starter, go-getter (*colloq.*).

adj. *vigorous*, energetic, lively, animated, racy, spirited, zappy (*colloq.*); *enthusiastic*, keen, go-ahead, enterprising, high-powered; *forceful*, aggressive, thrusting, punchy (*colloq.*); *stimulating*, invigorating, bracing, tonic, brisk, no-nonsense (*colloq.*).

vb. *invigorate*, enliven, animate, energize, vitalize, galvanize, electrify, ginger up, put a bomb under (*colloq.*); *stimulate*, rouse, encourage, boost, kindle, inflame, intoxicate; *drive*, thrust, push, attack, go at, pull out all the stops; *be vigorous*, thrive, blossom, bloom, flourish, be in fine fettle.

adv. *vigorously*, hard, full steam ahead.

146 INERTNESS

See also **144** (weakness); **608** (inaction); **610** (inactivity).

n. *inertness*, inactivity, languor, sluggishness, lethargy, inertia, torpor, lifelessness; *immobility*, stillness, stagnation, hibernation, dormancy; *dullness*, apathy, passivity, sloth, indolence, laziness, stolidity, impassivity, nonchalance.

adj. *inert*, inactive, languid, lethargic, sluggish, torpid; *immobile*, still, stagnant, dormant, fallow; *lifeless*, heavy, sleepy, numb, paralysed; *dull*, apathetic, lazy, idle, slothful, indolent, passive, indifferent, nonchalant, stolid.

vb. *be inert*, stagnate, vegetate, tick over, idle; *sleep*, doze, slumber, hibernate.

147 VIOLENCE

See also **639** (attack).

n. *violence*, vehemence, intensity, force, power; *outbreak*, outburst, spasm, paroxysm, convulsion, eruption, earthquake, upheaval, explosion, cataclysm; *onrush*, torrent, tidal wave, hurricane, storm, tempest; *turbulence*, turmoil, uproar, furore; *ferocity*, savagery, brutality, frenzy, rage, passion; *assault*, hammering (*colloq.*), thrashing, grievous bodily harm, rape, battering, mugging; *fight*, punchup (*colloq.*), dustup (*colloq.*), brawl, melee, aggro (*colloq.*), bovver (*colloq.*), hooliganism, thuggery, riot, mayhem, mob rule; *killing*, murder, homicide, massacre, slaughter, carnage; *brute*, beast, savage, barbarian, thug, hooligan, ruffian, bully, yob (*colloq.*); *killer*, assassin, murderer, butcher, axeman, hatchetman; *fury*, spitfire, termagant, virago, hothead, firebrand.

adj. *violent*, vehement, intense, forceful, powerful; *turbulent*, tumultuous, cataclysmic, explosive, convulsive, volcanic; *wild*, frenzied, frantic, hysterical, unrestrained, unbridled, sweeping, overwhelming; *rampant*, raging, rabid, fuming, tempestuous, stormy; *fierce*, ferocious, vicious, brutal, savage, murderous, bloodthirsty; *aggressive*, belligerent, tough, rowdy, boisterous, riotous.

vb. *be violent*, convulse, erupt, explode, burst, let fly, lash out; *rage*, storm, fume, rant, see red, go berserk; *charge*, stampede, rampage, riot, run amuck; *surge*, gush, flood, inundate, overwhelm; *dash*, hurtle, rush, fling, pelt, hurl; *smash*, crash, break, shatter, demolish, pulverize, crush; *assault*, rape, violate, strike, punch, mug, lay into, beat up, thrash, hammer (*colloq.*), batter, work over, dust up (*colloq.*); *make violent*, rouse, goad, lash, whip up, exasperate, infuriate, enrage, madden.

adv. *violently*, tooth and nail, hammer and tongs; *precipitately*, headlong, headfirst, at full tilt.

148 MODERATION

See also **63** (middle); **733** (impassivity).

n. *moderation*, reasonableness, rationality, sanity, sobriety, common sense; *calmness*, composure, restraint, self-control, cool-headedness, impassivity; *middle way*, golden mean, happy medium, middle of the road; *mildness*, harmlessness, innocuousness, gentleness, blandness; *alleviation*, mitigation, abatement, relief, easing, relaxation; *pacification*, mollification, appeasement; *palliative*, balm, emollient, lubricant, salve, sedative, tranquillizer, opiate, downer (*colloq.*), analgesic; *mediator*, peacemaker, arbitrator, conciliator; *brake*, check, curb, rein, damper, cushion, wet blanket (*colloq.*); *moderate*, centrist, reformist, pinko (*colloq.*), woolly liberal (*colloq.*).

adj. *moderate*, reasonable, rational, sensible, sane, sober; *calm*, composed, impassive, restrained, low-key, subdued, tame; *mild*, gentle, soothing, bland, anodyne, insipid; *average*, middlebrow, middle-of-the-road.

vb. *moderate*, temper, mitigate, lessen, tone down, dampen, muffle, blunt, take the edge off; *curb*, check, quell, subdue, tame, bring to heel; *alleviate*, allay, assuage, relieve, deaden, numb, dull; *pacify*, calm, appease, lull, soothe, pour oil on troubled waters.

adv. *in moderation*, within reason, within bounds; *gradually*, softly softly (*colloq.*).

149 PRODUCTION

See also **152** (fertility); **611** (work).

n. *production*, creation, origination, generation, invention; *manufacture*, fabrication, concoction, preparation, formation, construction; *industrialization*, mass production, factory farming, assembly line, automation, new technology; *industry*, trade, craft, skill, cottage industry, homeworking; *product*, end-product, output, throughput, yield, productivity, produce, crop, harvest, by-product, waste, extract; *artefact*, handiwork, ware, goods, merchandise, finished article; *composition*, piece, opus, oeuvre, work of art, chef d'oeuvre, masterpiece, brainchild; *handicrafts*, ceramics, pottery, metalworking, silversmithing, weaving, tapestry, embroidery, patchwork, crochet, knitting, macramé; *producer*, creator, maker, originator, inventor, founder, author, architect, engineer, composer, designer; *manufacturer*, industrialist, workman, labourer, craftsman, artisan; *farmer*, grower, breeder, market gardener.

adj. *productive*, creative, generative, inventive, constructive; *fruitful*, rich, prolific, fertile, profitable; *synthetic*, artificial, man-made, ready-made.

vb. *produce*, create, originate, generate, invent, devise, conceive, design; *make*, fabricate, concoct, frame, fashion, forge, cast, coin, mint, cobble together; *craft*, sew, knit, spin, weave, embroider; *manufacture*, machine, synthesize, process, treat, mass-produce, assemble, turn out; *accomplish*, achieve, contrive, engineer, develop, exploit; *farm*, grow, breed, cultivate, propagate.

150 DESTRUCTION

See also **324** (killing); **593** (deterioration).

n. *destruction*, obliteration, nullification, abolition, deterioration, erosion, eradication, extirpation; *extinction*, annihilation, extermination, liquidation, decimation, assassination, murder, slaughter, massacre, genocide; *demolition*, bombardment, blitz, scorched-earth policy, defoliation; *disaster*, catastrophe, cataclysm, holocaust, earthquake, flood, disaster area; *devastation*, chaos, ruin, wreckage, damage, harm, ravages, shambles; *collapse*, smash-up, crash, collision, wreck; *destructiveness*, vandalism, sabotage, arson, character assassination, smear campaign; *destroyer*, vandal, wrecker, arsonist, saboteur, killer, assassin, butcher, hitman (*colloq.*); *blight*, bane, cancer, canker, poison, toxin, corrosive; *battering ram*, bulldozer, steamroller, juggernaut.

adj. *destructive*, disastrous, catastrophic, cataclysmic, ruinous, fatal, terminal; *harmful*, injurious, pernicious, corrosive; *murderous*, homicidal, suicidal, deadly, lethal, self-destructive; *destroyed*, ruined, undone, washed up, burnt-out, kaput (*colloq.*), done for (*colloq.*).

vb. *destroy*, harm, damage, injure, erode; *obliterate*, nullify, delete, expunge, erase, cancel out, undo, unmake; *abolish*, extinguish, eradicate, extirpate, stamp out, wipe out, annihilate; *exterminate*, liquidate, assassinate, decimate, murder, massacre, slaughter, butcher, do in (*colloq.*); *engulf*, consume, devour, swallow up, swamp, drown; *devastate*, ravage, despoil, ransack, pillage, lay waste; *flatten*, blitz, raze, level, bulldoze, demolish; *ruin*, wreck, vandalize, sabotage, torpedo, sink, scuttle, scupper (*colloq.*), put the mockers/kibosh on (*colloq.*); *dismantle*, scrap, shred, pulp, break up, make mincemeat of (*colloq.*); *crash*, collide, write off, smash up, shatter; *suppress*, quell, quash, smother, stifle, strangle, suffocate, nip in the bud; *be destroyed*, go under/down, go to rack and ruin, go to the wall, succumb, go to the dogs (*colloq.*).

adv. *on the scrapheap*, on the rocks (*colloq.*).

151 REPRODUCTION

See also **21** (imitation); **88** (repetition).

n. *reproduction*, procreation, regeneration, reincarnation; *reduplication*, repetition, multiplication, mass production; *remake*, reprint, reissue, repeat, copy; *renewal*, revitalization, resurgence, renaissance, rebirth, resuscitation, revival.

adj. *reproductive*, regenerative, procreative, prolific; *resurgent*, born-again, rejuvenated.

vb. *reproduce*, procreate, breed, multiply; *repeat*, duplicate, copy, mass-produce, churn out; *remake*, rebuild, reprint, reissue; *renew*, revive, resurrect, resuscitate.

152 FERTILITY

See also **149** (production).

n. *fertility*, fecundity, virility, potency; *procreation*, propagation, proliferation, multiplication, reproduction, facts of life, birds and the bees (*colloq.*); *productiveness*, abundance, richness, glut, cornucopia, horn of plenty, baby boom, population explosion; *motherhood*, maternity, childbearing, midwifery, obstetrics; *fertilization*, insemination, pollination, irrigation, artificial insemination, conception, gestation, pregnancy, test-tube baby; *childbirth*, birthing, parturition, confinement, delivery, happy event, stillbirth, miscarriage; *womb*, uterus, ovary, cervix, loins; *ovum*, seed, sperm, semen, pollen; *genitals*, private parts, vagina, cunt (*vulg.*), twat (*vulg.*), fanny (*colloq.*), pudenda, penis, phallus, pizzle,

cock (vulg.), prick (*vulg.*), dick (*colloq.*), testicles, balls (*vulg.*), bollocks (*vulg.*), goolies (*vulg.*).
adj. *fertile*, fecund, procreative, potent, virile, productive, seminal; *pregnant*, gravid, expecting, broody, with child, antenatal, obstetric; *abundant*, copious, rich, plentiful, fruitful.
vb. *fertilize*, impregnate, inseminate, pollinate, irrigate, manure; *procreate*, propagate, breed, spawn, cultivate, rear, multiply, increase; *conceive*, fall, beget, engender, sire; *give birth*, bring forth, drop, lamb, farrow, whelp, pup, litter, hatch; *proliferate*, sprout, mushroom, blossom, burgeon, bloom, flourish.
adv. *with child*, in the family way, up the spout (*colloq.*), in the club (*colloq.*).

153 INFERTILITY

See also **579** (uselessness).
n. *infertility*, sterility, impotence, barrenness, unproductiveness, aridity; *fruitlessness*, futility, unprofitability, zero growth, stagnation; *desolation*, desert, tundra, wasteland, dustbowl, famine, dearth; *contraception*, family planning, birth control, abortion, sterilization, vasectomy, menopause, castration; *eunuch*, castrato, gelding, neuter, freemartin, hermaphrodite.
adj. *infertile*, sterile, impotent, barren, childless, subfertile; *unproductive*, fruitless, arid, unprofitable, fallow, stillborn.
vb. *be unproductive*, lie fallow, stagnate, wither on the vine, abort, miscarry, die aborning; *sterilize*, castrate, emasculate, geld, neuter, spay.

154 PARENT

See also **12** (family relations).
n. *parent*, parenthood, parenting, single parent, one-parent family, donor, godparent, foster parent, guardian; *family*, blood, stock, strain, line, pedigree, extraction, ancestry; *motherhood*, maternity, mother-to-be, earth mother, surrogate mother, mum (*colloq.*), mater, mamma, matron, matriarch; *fatherhood*, paternity, sire, progenitor, dad (*colloq.*), pater, papa, paterfamilias, patriarch.
adj. *parental*, familial, ancestral; *maternal*, motherly, matronly, matriarchal; *paternal*, fatherly, patriarchal.
vb. *father*, sire, beget.
adv. in loco parentis.

155 OFFSPRING

See also **111** (youth).
n. *offspring*, progeny, issue, young, spawn, litter, brood; *heir*, heiress, successor, descendant, posterity, offshoot, branch, scion, love child, bastard; *descent*, lineage, succession, dynasty, illegitimacy.
adj. *familial*, lineal, filial, hereditary, genetic.

156 SPACE

See also **157** (region).
n. *space*, space-time, extension, outer space; *dimensions*, proportions, size, extent, area, volume, capacity, circumference; *range*, span, compass, coverage, radius, sweep, scope, spread; *region*, expanse, tract, reach, stretch; *room*, latitude, margin, clearance, leeway, legroom, headroom, accommodation.
adj. *spatial*, three-dimensional, spatiotemporal; *extensive*, widespread, far-reaching, global, worldwide; *spacious*, roomy, capacious, voluminous, commodious, expansive.
vb. *extend*, range, spread, stretch, sweep; *span*, straddle, cover, enclose, encompass, contain, accommodate.
adv. *extensively*, far and wide, all over, high and low.

157 REGION

See also **156** (space).
n. *region*, locality, area, zone, belt, heartland, parallel, latitudes, climes, parts, neck of the woods (*colloq.*); *sphere*, field, domain, arena, theatre; *territory*, enclave, ghetto, exclusion zone, precinct; *state*, realm, kingdom, dominion, protectorate, colony, dependency, republic; *district*, county, province, shire, parish, ward, borough, hamlet, village; *city*, town, built-up

area, new town, conurbation, inner city, city centre, quarter; *suburb*, dormitory town, green belt, stockbroker belt; *environs*, neighbourhood, vicinity, outskirts, hinterland.
adj. *regional*, zonal, provincial; *local*, municipal, parochial, urban, suburban.

158 LOCATION
See also **165** (habitat).
n. *location*, situation, site, whereabouts, seat; *haunt*, habitat, patch, pitch, beat, territory, stamping ground; *abode*, residence, quarters, address, premises; *place*, spot, corner, nook, niche, hole, slot, groove; *enclosure*, stockade, compound, pen, paddock, field, quadrangle, courtyard; *compartment*, recess, alcove, cubicle, locker, pigeonhole.
vb. *locate*, site, situate, place; *quarter*, billet, station, post; *reside in*, inhabit, frequent, haunt; *pinpoint*, track, home in, zero in.
adv. *locally*, on the spot.

159 SITUATION
See also **160** (placement).
n. *situation*, position, setting, locale, scene, venue; *orientation*, direction, bearings, standpoint, viewpoint; *geography*, topography, orienteering, mapreading.
adj. *situated*, orientated, positioned, located; *geographical*, topographical, directional.
vb. *situate*, site, position, station, post, locate; *orientate*, direct, head.
adv. *in place*, in situ, on site; *on course*, on the right track.

160 PLACEMENT
See also **159** (situation).
n. *placement*, emplacement, installation, settlement, establishment; *post*, position, station, base, depot, camp, encampment, depot; *niche*, resting-place, berth, anchorage, garage, storehouse, repository.
adj. *placed*, lodged, installed, ensconced, entrenched, dug in.
vb. *place*, position, install, station, post; *lodge*, establish, embed, fix, house; *anchor*, moor, tether, berth, dock, park; *settle*, colonize, encamp, camp, dig in, pitch, squat.
adv. *in position*, in place; *at rest*, at anchor.

161 DISPLACEMENT
See also **58** (disturbance); **266** (expulsion).
n. *displacement*, dislocation, dislodgment, disturbance; *transfer*, transposition, removal, relocation, evacuation; *deposition*, overthrow, coup, takeover, palace revolution; *relegation*, demotion, expulsion, banishment, exile, eviction, homelessness; *dismissal*, sacking, redundancy, lay-off; *displaced person*, refugee, evacuee, waif, stray, guest worker, immigrant.
adj. *displaced*, dislocated, disturbed; *disorientated*, uprooted, rootless, homeless; *misplaced*, mislaid, lost, gone astray.
vb. *displace*, dislocate, dislodge, disturb; *transfer*, transpose, shunt, remove, relocate, evacuate; *depose*, unseat, dethrone, usurp, oust, supersede; *relegate*, demote, dismiss, lay off, sack, fire, kick upstairs (*colloq.*), banish, exile, expel; *misplace*, mislay, lose.
adv. *out of place*, out of joint; *out of the running*, out of the picture, out in the cold (*colloq.*), in limbo.

162 PRESENCE
See also **85** (accompaniment).
n. *presence*, existence, pervasiveness, omnipresence, ubiquitousness; *situation*, location, position, whereabouts; *availability*, readiness, handiness, convenience; *attendance*, appearance, participation, accompaniment; *residence*, occupancy, habitation; *conspicuousness*, obviousness, visibility; *spectator*, onlooker, audience, bystander, eye-witness, participant.
adj. *present*, existent, pervasive, omnipresent, ubiquitous; *available*, ready, handy, convenient; *attendant*, participant, concomitant, accompanying; *resident*, live-in, in-house, residential; *conspicuous*, obvious, visible, eye-catching.
vb. *be present*, pervade, permeate, imbue; *reside*, occupy, inhabit, live in;

participate, take part, watch, witness, assist at, spectate; *attend*, turn up, present oneself, show up, put in an appearance, look in; *be conspicuous*, stand out, stick out like a sore thumb (*colloq.*), make one's presence felt.
adv. *at hand*, on the spot, on the ground; *to hand*, within reach, on call, on tap; *close to*, under one's nose, to one's face, before one's very eyes; *in person*, live; *at home*, in town, on the premises.

163 ABSENCE

See also **2** (nonexistence).
n. *absence*, nonexistence, disappearance, loss; *nonappearance*, nonattendance, absenteeism, truancy, desertion, defection, French leave; *emptiness*, vacuum, blankness, void, vacancy, gap, omission; *lack*, shortage, want, scarcity, deficiency; *absentee*, nonperson, missing person, defector, deserter; *leave of absence*, furlough, holiday, vacation.
adj. *absent*, nonexistent, gone, lost, flown, fled; *away*, out, unavailable, off (*colloq.*); *empty*, vacant, void, blank, vacuous, hollow; *lacking*, missing, minus, devoid, deficient, short; *unoccupied*, deserted, abandoned, depopulated, godforsaken.
vb. *be absent*, stay away, be conspicuous by one's absence, vote with one's feet; *depart*, withdraw, retreat, absent oneself, make oneself scarce (*colloq.*); *abandon*, desert, defect, forsake, walk out on; *miss*, skip, go AWOL, play hooky (*colloq.*).
adv. *in one's absence*, in absentia, behind one's back; *off the premises*, out of house; *on leave*, on vacation, on holiday, out of town.

164 INHABITANT

See also **165** (habitat).
n. *inhabitant*, dweller, citizen, denizen; *occupant*, resident, householder, owner-occupier; *tenant*, lodger, boarder, paying guest, au pair; *inmate*, incumbent, in-patient; *native*, aborigine, local, villager, parishioner, townee, suburbanite, commuter, city slicker (*colloq.*); *cottager*, crofter, smallholder, peasant, rustic, yokel, country bumpkin; *incomer*, immigrant, settler, colonist, squatter; *household*, ménage, commune, colony, community, population.
adj. *inhabited*, occupied, rented, leased; *native*, indigenous, aboriginal, ethnic, vernacular; *domestic*, local, household, home.

165 HABITAT

See also **158** (location); **164** (inhabitant); **762** (recreation).
n. *habitat*, abode, dwelling, domicile, residence, haunt, hang-out (*colloq.*); *base*, headquarters, seat, camp, bivouac, pad (*colloq.*); *accommodation*, quarters, billet, lodgings, digs (*colloq.*), squat, hostel, dormitory, dosshouse (*colloq.*); *home*, hearth, fireside, homestead, cradle, home town, birthplace, stamping ground, motherland, fatherland; *lair*, den, burrow, warren, earth, sett, holt, nest, drey, aviary, apiary; *house*, villa, bungalow, chalet, prefab, townhouse, houseboat, caravan, mobile home; *cottage*, cabin, shack, hovel, lean-to, outhouse; *flat*, maisonette, studio, apartment, mews, penthouse, pied-à-terre, bedsitter, granny flat; *mansion*, seat, hall, grange, manor, chateau, stately home; *housing*, conurbation, housing estate/scheme, tower block, slum, shanty town; *stable*, byre, cowshed, sty, kennel, fold, stall, coop, hutch; *hotel*, bed & breakfast, motel, roadhouse, inn, tavern, public house, pub, hostelry, local (*colloq.*), boozer (*colloq.*); *restaurant*, wine bar, bistro, brasserie, trattoria; *cafe*, cafeteria, snack bar, tearoom, canteen, buffet, takeaway, diner; *retreat*, haven, refuge, sanctuary, halfway house, hospice; *park*, gardens, allotment, arbour, pergola, gazebo, folly, conservatory, glasshouse.
adj. *residential*, built-up, metropolitan, urban, surburban; *detached*, semidetached, terraced, purpose-built, multistorey, high/low rise; *rural*, rustic, countrified; *local*, parochial, municipal.
vb. *inhabit*, occupy, people, settle, colonize, populate; *reside*, dwell, sojourn,

lodge, put up at, doss down (*colloq.*), crash (*colloq.*), camp; *frequent*, haunt, visit, hang out at (*colloq.*).

166 CONTENTS

See also **53** (component).

n. *contents*, ingredients, components, stuffing, filling, centre; *insides*, guts, entrails, bowels, pith, marrow; *containment*, load, cargo, shipment, freight.

vb. *contain*, hold, enclose, conceal; *insert*, stuff, pack, cram; *take in*, absorb, assimilate, ingest; *containerize*, load, freight, ship, transport.

167 CONTAINER

n. *container*, receptacle, holder, frame; *cover*, case, envelope, wrapper, packaging, sheath, cocoon; *depository*, reservoir, store, warehouse, treasury; *boxroom*, cloakroom, strongroom, cellar, bunker, attic; *compartment*, locker, cupboard, cabinet, closet; *box*, chest, casket, coffer, crate, hamper, basket, punnet; *suitcase*, overnight bag, holdall, grip, trunk, baggage; *capsule*, pillbox, canister, carton, caddy, tin, can, tub; *bag*, knapsack, rucksack, haversack, backpack, kitbag, duffel bag; *satchel*, pannier, creel, saddlebag; *purse*, wallet, money-belt, briefcase, attaché case, file, portfolio; *vessel*, barrel, cask, vat, tun, tank, keg, cistern; *vase*, jug, pitcher, carafe, decanter, vial, phial, flagon, carboy; *bucket*, pail, bin, hopper, silo; *basin*, ewer, pan, pot, urn, kettle, cauldron; *cup*, chalice, goblet, wineglass, schooner, beaker, tumbler, tankard, mug; *bottle*, demijohn, magnum, jeroboam, rehoboam, methuselah; *bowl*, porringer, ramekin, tureen; *plate*, platter, charger, salver.

168 SIZE

See also **23** (quantity); **29** (greatness).

n. *size*, proportions, dimensions, amplitude, girth, bulk, magnitude; *extent*, area, volume, mass, weight; *largeness*, bigness, hugeness, vastness, immensity, enormity; *colossus*, mountain, skyscraper, pyramid, mausoleum; *giant*, monster, leviathan, whale, whopper (*colloq.*); *fatness*, obesity, corpulence, portliness, fleshiness, corporation, beer belly, midriff bulge, spare tyre (*colloq.*), flab (*colloq.*); *fat person*, fattie (*colloq.*), hulk, Falstaff, Billy Bunter, slimmer, weight watcher.

adj. *large*, big, sizable, considerable, hefty (*colloq.*); *large-scale*, life-size, full-grown, king-size, mammoth, jumbo, outsize, giant; *massive*, bulky, huge, enormous, hulking, whopping (*colloq.*); *gigantic*, colossal, monumental, immense, vast, astronomical, gargantuan, Brobdingnagian; *fat*, stout, corpulent, obese, overweight, portly, rotund, plump, chubby, podgy, roly-poly, tubby, buxom, pot-bellied, Falstaffian.

169 LITTLENESS

See also **30** (smallness); **179** (shortness).

n. *littleness*, diminutiveness, minuteness, smallness; *scantiness*, meagreness, paucity, skimpiness; *miniature*, mini, baby, microcosm, pinhead, atom, particle, molecule; *dwarf*, midget, manikin, pygmy, Tom Thumb, homunculus; *gnat*, flea, sprat, tiddler, minnow, shrimp, runt, small fry; *microorganism*, microbe, germ, virus, bacterium; *microelectronics*, microcomputer, microprocessor, integrated circuit; *spot*, fleck, dot, speck, mote, crumb, grain, granule, drop, shred.

adj. *little*, small, diminutive, minute, tiny, petite, dainty, dinky (*colloq.*); *small-scale*, toy, baby, mini, miniaturized, pint-sized, wee, titchy (*colloq.*), Lilliputian; *dwarfish*, puny, runty, stunted, undersized; *scanty*, meagre, insufficient, skimpy.

170 EXPANSION

See also **33** (increase); **180** (breadth).

n. *expansion*, increase, enlargement, augmentation, amplification, aggrandizement; *development*, spread, deployment, sweep, sprawl; *inflation*, distension, swollenness, inflammation, tumescence, puffiness, turgidity, dilation; *extensibility*, elasticity, stretchiness, give; *padding*, stuffing, wadding, waffle (*colloq.*), bombast.

adj. *expanded*, inflated, bloated, distended, dilated, taut; *expandable*, stretchy, elastic, extensible; *swollen*, turgid, overblown, tumescent, tumid, bulbous, distended, pot-bellied; *wide*, gaping, flared, bell-bottomed, splayed, spreadeagled, outstretched.

vb. *expand*, broaden, widen, flare, splay; *increase*, augment, enlarge, magnify, wax, amplify; *spread*, develop fan out, deploy, sprawl, mushroom; *inflate*, balloon, belly, dilate, distend, puff up, swell, inflame; *pad*, stuff, bulk up, beef up (*colloq.*).

171 CONTRACTION

See also **34** (decrease); **179** (shortness).

n. *contraction*, shrinkage, reduction, abatement, diminution, decrease, attenuation; *curtailment*, abbreviation, abridgment, constriction, compaction, compression; *decline*, falling-off, slump, recession, squeeze; *compressor*, constrictor, tourniquet, straitjacket, corset.

adj. *contracted*, shrunk, compacted, condensed, abridged, compressed; *constricted*, pinched, drawn, wizened, shrivelled, stunted; *astringent*, tight, constricting, binding.

vb. *contract*, diminish, lessen, decrease, reduce, curtail; *compress*, condense, abridge, abbreviate, boil down; *constrict*, nip, pinch, tighten, clench; *compact*, pack, squeeze, bind, cramp, squash, flatten; *narrow*, taper, attenuate, thin, slim, extrude; *shrivel*, wrinkle, wizen, pucker, crease; *dwarf*, stunt, shorten.

172 DISTANCE

See also **178** (length).

n. *distance*, farness, remoteness, inaccessibility; *extent*, range, reach, span, sweep, coverage; *long distance*, long haul, trek, marathon; *outskirts*, purlieus, periphery, frontier, outback, back of beyond; *horizon*, skyline, background, middle distance; *aloofness*, detachedness, reserve, stand-offishness.

adj. *distant*, far, far-away, far-off, far-flung, farthest; *remote*, outlying, offshore, peripheral, inaccessible, out-of-the-way, godforsaken; *foreign*, antipodean, overseas, exotic; *long-distance*, long-range, long-haul; *aloof*, stand-offish, unapproachable, reserved.

vb. *distance*, outdistance, outstrip, outrun, outdo; *carry*, extend, stretch, reach; *keep one's distance*, keep clear of, give a wide berth to, not touch with a bargepole (*colloq.*).

adv. *afar*, far afield, far off, far and wide, to the ends of the earth; *off the beaten track*, in the middle of nowhere, out in the sticks (*colloq.*); *at a distance*, at arm's length; *out of range*, out of sight, out of earshot.

173 NEARNESS

See also **176** (juxtaposition).

n. *nearness*, proximity, propinquity, juxtaposition, closeness; *locality*, vicinity, neighbourhood, environs; *close range*, close quarters, pointblank range, foreground, ringside seat; *edge*, brink, verge, border; *short distance*, shortcut, beeline, walking distance, hop, step, and jump, stone's throw, spitting distance, hair's breadth; *closeness*, intimacy, understanding, rapport, affection.

adj. *near*, close, approximate, rough; *nearby*, adjoining, local, neighbouring, accessible, handy; *short-distance*, short-range, short-haul; *close*, affectionate, intimate, inseparable; *crowded*, packed, serried.

vb. *be near*, hug, skirt, brush, graze, skim; *approximate*, approach, be in the right ballpark (*colloq.*); *adjoin*, abut, border, verge, touch; *close up*, close ranks, huddle, press, crowd, jostle, elbow, rub shoulders; *follow*, shadow, tail, dog someone's footsteps, tread on someone's heels.

adv. *nearly*, almost, approximately, circa, thereabouts; *nearby*, close to, face to face, eyeball to eyeball; *within range*, within earshot, in view; *nigh*, at hand; *practically*, virtually, to all intents and purposes.

174 INTERVAL
See also **65** (discontinuity).
n. *interval*, space, gap, interstice, hole, lacuna; *breach*, break, fissure, rupture, crevice, crack, rift, chasm, gulf; *network*, lattice, mesh, trellis, reticulation; *margin*, clearance, leeway, headroom.
adj. *spaced out*, intermittent, sporadic, periodic; *latticed*, criss-cross, gap-toothed, crenellated, filigree, lacy.
vb. *space out*, stagger, intersperse; *gape*, yawn, split, tear, rend, crack; *lattice*, mesh, criss-cross, reticulate, interweave.
adv. *at intervals*, now and then, off and on, here and there.

175 LAYER
See also **202** (covering).
n. *layer*, stratum, bed, course, string, vein, seam, band; *level*, floor, storey, tier; *thickness*, ply, coat, overlay, top-coat, veneer; *lamina*, sheet, strip, foil, leaf; *flake*, scale, wafer, slice, lamella, shavings, peelings, parings; *sandwich*, double-decker, onion, Chinese boxes, nest of tables.
adj. *layered*, laminated, lamellate; *flaky*, peeling, scaly, squamose; *overlaid*, overlapping, shingled, clinker-built.
vb. *layer*, laminate, stratify, deck; *overlay*, plate, veneer, coat; *flake*, peel, pare, shave; *overlap*, tile, flag, shingle.

176 JUXTAPOSITION
see also **173** (nearness); **207** (interface).
n. *juxtaposition*, contiguity, contact, tangency, proximity; *border*, dividing line, demarcation, watershed, interface, meeting, junction.
adj. *juxtaposed*, adjacent, coterminous, contiguous, adjoining, interconnecting.
vb. *juxtapose*, bring together, butt, dovetail, overlap; *adjoin*, border, abut, skirt, fringe, hem.
adv. *side by side*, cheek by jowl, arm in arm, abreast; *end to end*, bumper to bumper.

177 MEASUREMENT
See also **23** (quantity).
n. *measurement*, mensuration, triangulation, calculation, computation, quantification; *valuation*, estimation, assessment, appreciation, appraisal; *geometry*, trigonometry, surveying, sounding; *measure*, gauge, scales, balance, ruler, yardstick, footrule, tape measure; *compass*, callipers, protractor, sextant, quadrant, theodolite; *meter*, thermometer, barometer, speedometer, tacheograph, metronome, Geiger counter; *reference point*, grid, water line, tidemark, Plimsoll line, bench mark.
adj. *metric*, imperial, avoirdupois, troy, SI.
vb. *measure*, mensurate, compute, calculate, quantify; *estimate*, sound, reckon, weigh up, pace out, valuate, assess, gauge; *rule*, graduate, calibrate, mark off.

178 LENGTH
See also **172** (distance).
n. *length*, extent, expanse, reach, stretch, span; *lengthening*, elongation, extension, extrusion; *protraction*, prolongation, slowness, longueur, tedium; *line*, queue, file, string, crocodile; *longitude*, parallel, wavelength, waveband, frequency.
adj. *long*, longitudinal, extended, elongated, extruded; *lengthy*, protracted, prolonged, long-drawn-out, long-winded, tedious; *full-length*, uncut, unabridged.
vb. *lengthen*, elongate, extend, extrude, stretch, expand; *protract*, prolong, draw out, spin out, drag out.
adv. *lengthways*, from stem to stern, from top to toe; *at length*, lengthily, long.

179 SHORTNESS
See also **169** (littleness); **171** (contraction).
n. *shortness*, scarcity, scantiness, skimpiness; *abridgment*, condensation, summary, precis, résumé; *conciseness*, compression, succintness, terseness, ellipsis, thumbnail sketch; *brevity*,

transience, fleetingness; *squatness*, dumpiness, stockiness, stubbiness.
adj. *short*, scanty, scarce, insufficient, skimpy; *abridged*, condensed, potted, cut; *concise*, terse, succinct, elliptical, laconic, curt; *brief*, transient, fleeting, short-lived; *curtailed*, foreshortened, truncated, headless, retroussé, blunt; *squat*, dumpy, stocky, petite, stubby, stunted.
vb. *shorten*, cut, curtail, reduce, contract; *abridge*, abbreviate, condense, summarize, precis, telescope, compress; *cut short*, interrupt, truncate, guillotine, behead, foreshorten, dock, prune, lop.
adv. *in short*, briefly, in sum, to cut a long story short, in a nutshell.

180 BREADTH

See also **170** (expansion).
n. *breadth*, width, girth, latitude, span, diameter; *amplitude*, scope, range, extent; *expanse*, panorama, vista, sweep; *broad-mindedness*, tolerance, permissiveness, liberalness.
adj. *broad*, wide, wide-angle, wide-bodied, broad in the beam, broad-shouldered, flared, bell-bottomed; *wide-ranging*, extensive, sweeping, far-reaching; *expansive*, roomy, spacious, ample; *broad-minded*, liberal, tolerant, permissive.
vb. *broaden*, widen, extend, stretch, spread one's wings; *splay*, sprawl, spreadeagle, flare, bell.
adv. *widthways*, across; *broadly*, loosely, roughly.

181 NARROWNESS

See also **171** (contraction); **183** (thinness).
n. *narrowness*, tightness, constriction, compression, contraction; *confinement*, restrictedness, crampedness, overcrowding, tight fit, tight squeeze, no room to swing a cat; *narrow space*, corner, cranny, nook, crack, cleft, chink, crevice; *strait*, gully, gorge, ravine, pass, defile; *neck*, isthmus, chimney, funnel, bottleneck, hourglass; *line*, path, strip, vein, streak, stripe, ribbon, knife-edge, pinhead; *narrow-mindedness*, intolerance, prejudice, bigotry.
adj. *narrow*, tight, constricted, compressed, pinched; *skin-tight*, figure-hugging, clinging, slinky; *confined*, overcrowded, cramped, restricted, straitened; *narrow-minded*, intolerant, prejudiced, bigoted.
vb. *narrow*, converge, streamline, taper, funnel; *tighten*, contract, pinch, squeeze, constrict; *confine*, cramp, restrict, tether, hobble, fetter; *cling*, hug, cleave, adhere, stick like glue.

182 THICKNESS

See also **168** (size): **317** (semiliquid).
n. *thickness*, solidity, massiveness, bulk, body, density, consistency; *breadth*, ampleness, generosity, fullness, abundance; *viscosity*, tackiness, lumpiness, stodginess, clottedness, pulpiness, soupiness; *sediment*, mud, silt, jelly, curd, soup, pulp; *thickener*, padding, wadding, stuffing, bulk, starch, emulsifier; *thick-headedness*, dullness, stolidness, crassness, stupidity.
adj. *thick*, solid, massive, bulky, dense; *ample*, generous, lavish, full, plentiful, abundant, thick on the ground; *clotted*, lumpy, stodgy, starchy, soupy, pulpy, viscous, tacky; *thick-headed*, dull, stolid, obtuse, crass, stupid, block-headed.
vb. *thicken*, fatten, pad, wad, stuff, bulk up; *solidify*, coagulate, clot, curdle, congeal, gel.

183 THINNESS

See also **171** (contraction); **181** (narrowness).
n. *thinness*, slimness, slenderness, leanness, skinniness, emaciation, anorexia; *thin person*, beanpole, rake, scarecrow, anorexic; *filament*, stalk, tendril, antenna, wire, thread, fibre, capillary; *streak*, strand, splinter, sliver, wafer, shavings; *fineness*, delicacy, transparency, translucency, sheerness; *gauze*, tulle, chiffon, gossamer, cobweb, eggshell; *sparseness*, rarity, infrequency.
adj. *thin*, slim, slender, svelte, willowy,

lissom, lithe, leggy, lean, wiry, sinewy, spare; *underweight*, skinny, skeletal, emaciated, anorexic, spindly, lanky, scraggy, scrawny, gaunt, haggard, raw-boned; *threadlike*, filamentous, fine-spun, stringy, fibrous, streaky; *flimsy*, fragile, delicate, transparent, translucent, sheer, diaphanous; *fluid*, runny, watery, dilute, weak; *sparse*, infrequent, thin on the ground.
vb. *thin*, reduce, slim down, streamline, prune, weed out; *rarefy*, attenuate, dilute, water down, liquefy, melt; *contract*, narrow, taper, shrink.

184 HEIGHT

See also **188** (summit); **190** (verticality); **274** (ascent); **276** (raising).
n. *height*, altitude, elevation, stature, tallness, loftiness, verticality, steepness; *high point*, summit, climax, zenith, ceiling, heavens, sky; *vantage point*, bird's eye view, overview, watchtower, lookout, crow's nest, platform, dais, rostrum; *heights*, highland, upland, mountain, alp, peak, crest, Everest; *cliff*, precipice, bluff, escarpment, slope, gradient, incline; *tower*, spire, steeple, mast, skyscraper, tower block, penthouse, attic, rooftop, Empire State Building; *ascent*, climb, rise, takeoff.
adj. *high*, sky-high, aerial, elevated, lofty; *steep*, vertical, vertiginous, precipitous; *mountainous*, alpine, multistorey, high-rise, towering, soaring; *tall*, lanky, rangy, gangly.
vb. *heighten*, raise, elevate, uplift; *tower*, soar, hover, overlook, overhang; *ascend*, rise, climb, scale, mount.
adv. *above*, overhead, upstairs, on high, aloft.

185 LOWNESS

See also **189** (base); **275** (descent); **277** (lowering).
n. *lowness*, smallness, squatness, dwarfishness; *flatness*, floor, sea level, plain, foothills, depression, flats, lowland, valley; *low point*, nadir, base, rock bottom, plinth, foot, ground; *underneath*, underside, underbelly, worm's eye view; *descent*, dip, fall, drop, decline.
adj. *low*, supine, prostrate, laid low, flat out; *bent*, hunched, bowed, stooping, crouched; *small*, squat, petite, stunted, dwarfish; *low-lying*, flat, level, sunken, depressed, subterranean, underground.
vb. *lower*, depress, flatten, level, raze, lay low; *bend*, stoop, hunch, crouch, cower, duck, crawl, kneel, knuckle under, bow; *descend*, fall, tumble, dip, plunge.
adv. *below*, underfoot, underneath, underground, downstairs.

186 DEPTH

See also **277** (lowering).
n. *depth*, deep end, depression, hollow, crater, pit, shaft, well, mine, excavation; *depths*, the deep, abyss, chasm, bowels, underworld; *plunge*, dive, immersion, submersion; *cellar*, basement, vault, crypt, dungeon; *profundity*, deep thought, searching, thoroughness.
adj. *deep*, profound, thorough, probing, in-depth; *cavernous*, yawning, gaping, bottomless, fathomless, unplumbed; *entrenched*, embedded, deep-seated, deep-rooted; *buried*, underground, subterranean, deep-sea, underwater.
vb. *deepen*, darken, worsen, intensify; *excavate*, dig, hollow, gouge out; *sound*, probe, fathom, plumb the depths; *bury*, entrench, embed, entomb; *sink*, submerge, plummet, dive, plunge.
adv. *deeply*, profoundly, intensely; *at bottom*, deep down; *out of one's depth*, over one's head, in deep water.

187 SHALLOWNESS

See also **577** (unimportance).
n. *shallowness*, slightness, cursoriness, superficiality, triviality; *shallows*, shoals, ford, puddle; *surface*, facade, overlay, topcoat, veneer, gloss; *surface wound*, scratch, pinprick, graze, scrape.
adj. *shallow*, slight, perfunctory, cursory, trivial, lightweight; *surface*, skin-

deep, cosmetic; *thin*, light, sparse, meagre.
vb. *be shallow*, skim, graze, scrape, brush, tickle; *dabble*, paddle, tinker, scratch the surface, make no impression on; *face*, coat, gloss, veneer, touch up.

188 SUMMIT

See also **184** (height).
n. *summit*, brow, top, peak, crest, pinnacle, tip, crown, apex, vertex; *high point*, zenith, acme, apogee, apotheosis, culmination, climax; *maximum*, high-water mark, ceiling, upper limit; *roof*, coping, capstone, steeple, spire; *head*, pate, poll, noddle (*colloq.*), bonce (*colloq.*), block (*colloq.*), nut (*colloq.*), loaf (*colloq.*). **adj.** *topmost*, top, highest, uppermost, maximal; *crowning*, climactic, supreme. **vb.** *top*, cap, crown, tip, crest; *climax*, peak, go through the roof. **adv.** *at the top of the tree*, on the top rung of the ladder.

189 BASE

See also **185** (lowness); **193** (support).
n. *base*, foot, bottom, root, underneath; *foundation*, basis, infrastructure, underlay, substratum, bedrock; *support*, plinth, pedestal, stand; *ground*, ground floor, basement, mezzanine, entresol; *minimum*, floor, lower limit, rock bottom, nadir; *starting-point*, first base, square one; *foot*, plates of meat (*colloq.*), toe, tootsie (*colloq.*).
adj. *base*, bottom, lowest, underlying, nethermost; *basic*, fundamental, rudimentary, elemental.
vb. *base*, ground, set, establish, found; *support*, underpin, underlie, maintain, uphold; *bottom out*, go through the floor, hit bedrock.
adv. *basically*, at bottom, when you get down to it.

190 VERTICALITY

See also **184** (height).
n. *verticality*, perpendicularity, uprightness, erectness; *steepness*, precipitousness, sheerness, plumbness; *vertical*, upright, pillar, column, ramrod, obelisk, stalagmite, standing-stone, menhir; *wall*, cliff, precipice, bluff, escarpment, sheer drop.
adj. *vertical*, upright, erect, perpendicular, standing, rampant; *steep*, precipitous, sheer, abrupt, plumb, vertiginous.
vb. *be vertical*, rear, stand, be upstanding; *erect*, pitch, raise, upend, cock, stick up, prick up; *plunge*, plummet, drop like a stone.
adv. *vertically*, on end, bolt upright; *from north to south*, from top to toe.

191 HORIZONTALITY

See also **292** (smoothness).
n. *horizontality*, flatness, breadth, levelness, proneness, supineness; *sweep*, vista, panorama, horizon, skyline; *plane*, level, plateau, tableland, steppe, flats, fens; *ledge*, shelf, terrace, tier, balcony; *iron*, bulldozer, steamroller, juggernaut.
adj. *horizontal*, level, plane, even, flush, flat; *prone*, prostrate, reclining, recumbent, supine, couchant.
vb. *be horizontal*, stretch, sweep, sprawl, extend; *recline*, repose, loll, lie back; *flatten*, level, even, roll, iron out, tread, trample, stamp; *raze*, floor, ground, bring down, topple.
adv. *horizontally*, widthways, from side to side, from east to west.

192 SUSPENSION

n. *suspension*, hanging, pendency, fall; *droopiness*, pendulousness, bagginess, looseness; *droop*, sag, hang, swing; *pendulum*, bob, plumbline, pendant, tassel, earring, icicle, stalactite, chandelier, hammock; *curtain*, hanging, drapery, train, skirt; *dewlap*, jowls, lobe, wattle, double chin; *hanger*, suspender, hook, spar, boom, gallows, gibbet, crane, jib.
adj. *suspended*, hanging, pendent; *pendulous*, saggy, droopy, baggy, slack; *loose*, dangling, trailing, weeping; *free-hanging*, floating, flyaway, free-floating.
vb. *suspend*, hang, drape, hitch, hook; *fall*, droop, sag, bag; *dangle*, swing, flap, trail, weep, straggle, stream, float.

193 SUPPORT

See also **189** (base).

n. *support*, underpinning, chassis, undercarriage, mounting; *reinforcement*, back-up, encouragement, sponsorship; *foundation*, base, cornerstone, mainstay, bedrock, backbone; *prop*, shore, strut, stay, buttress, pier, beam, joist, rafter, girder; *cane*, staff, walking stick, crutch, shooting stick; *stand*, tripod, trivet, easel, trestle, pedestal, plinth; *bolster*, cushion, mattress, pillow, headrest, footstool; *brace*, truss, corset, foundation garment, splint, surgical collar; *floor*, ground, pavement, terra firma, dry land; *banister*, balustrade, handrail, parapet; *bracket*, shelf, ledge, sill, platform, counter; *pivot*, fulcrum, lever, axle, spine; *supporter*, backer, sponsor, patron, ally, helpmate, tower of strength.

adj. *supporting*, structural, sustaining.

vb. *support*, sustain, maintain, carry, bear, shoulder, uphold; *prop*, shore up, underpin, buttress, brace, bolster, stay; *reinforce*, back, stand by, stick up for, sponsor, buoy up, encourage; *frame*, mount, cradle, pillow, cushion.

194 PARALLELISM

n. *parallelism*, equidistance, coextension; *correspondence*, similarity, analogy, comparison; *parallelogram*, trapezium, rectangle, tramlines, railway lines.

adj. *parallel*, equidistant, coextensive; *similar*, corresponding, analogous, comparable.

vb. *be parallel*, correspond, match, tally; *compare*, liken, equate, draw a parallel.

adv. *in parallel*, side by side, alongside, abreast.

195 OBLIQUENESS

See also **220** (angle).

n. *obliqueness*, indirectness, implicitness, ellipsis; *diagonal*, tangent, zigzag, chevron, herringbone; *deviation*, divergence, bias, slant; *slope*, incline, gradient, ramp, bank; *angle*, batter, bevel, rake, cant, list.

adj. *oblique*, indirect, implicit, elliptical, circuitous, roundabout; *angled*, squint, aslant, diagonal, transverse, sideways, sidelong.

vb. *be oblique*, lean, list, tilt, pitch, tip; *slope*, incline, shelve, bank, slant, cant, careen; *diverge*, sidestep, jink, dodge, zigzag, edge, sidle; *angle*, bevel, warp, camber, chamfer, mitre.

adv. *obliquely*, at an angle, edgeways, crabwise; *to one side*, out of true, out of plumb.

196 INVERSION

See also **126** (reversion); **129** (exchange).

n. *inversion*, transposition, substitution, swap (*colloq.*), changeover, retroversion, eversion; *anagram*, metathesis, palindrome, spoonerism; *upset*, capsizal, somersault, cartwheel, revolution; *reversal*, about-turn, U-turn, volte-face.

adj. *inverted*, inverse, topsy-turvy, upside-down.

vb. *invert*, transpose, interchange, change round, put the cart before the horse, reverse, turn the tables; *capsize*, overturn, upset, upend, stand on its head; *revolve*, somersault, turn turtle, come full circle; *tip*, tilt, keel over, topple.

adv. *inversely*, vice versa; *back to front*, inside out, upside down, head over heels, topsy turvy.

197 INTERWEAVING

See also **174** (interval); **299** (texture); **569** (materials).

n. *interweaving*, criss-crossing, network, complex, figure of eight, wickerwork, basketry; *grid*, grille, lattice, trellis, reticulation, netting, webbing; *tracery*, fretwork, filigree, honeycomb, mesh, openwork, yarn, fabric, textile; *braid*, wreath, plait, skein, cat's cradle, knot, tangle, snarl; *cross*, intersection, crossroads, crucifix, ankh, saltire, swastika.

adj. *interwoven*, interlocking, pleached, criss-cross, cruciform; *complex*, intricate, involved, tangled, ravelled, matted.

vb. *interweave*, interlace, interlock, intertwine; *plait*, braid, wreathe, pleach, twist, spin, weave, darn; *cross*, intersect, cut across, criss-cross; *enmesh*, entangle, ravel, snarl, embroil, implicate, involve.

198 EXTERIOR

See also **6** (extraneousness); **52** (exclusion).

n. *exterior*, periphery, circumference, perimeter, sidelines; *surface*, appearance, face, facade, shell, mask; *externalization*, extroversion, embodiment, concretization, materialization; *exclusion*, eviction, expulsion, ejection; *outside*, out of doors, open air, great outdoors, outdoor type, fresh-air fiend; *outside world*, parole, day release, day boy, outsider, ex-prisoner.

adj. *exterior*, external, outlying, peripheral, extraneous; *outer*, surface, superficial, prima facie, skin-deep, cosmetic, facial; *extrovert*, outward-looking, outgoing; *outside*, outdoor, out-of-house, extramural, public.

vb. *externalize*, embody, body forth, project, materialize; *expel*, eject, exclude, evict, banish; *cover*, surround, circumscribe, enclose.

adv. *on the outside*, out in the cold, in limbo; *on the face of it*, to all appearances, at first sight; *outside*, in the open, al fresco, out and about.

199 INTERIOR

See also **5** (essence); **166** (contents).

n. *interior*, inside, centre, heartland, core, hub, nub, heart, nerve centre; *pith*, marrow, quick, kernel, heartwood; *insides*, innards, inner man, vitals, viscera, entrails, guts, bowels; *introversion*, introspection, self-absorption, egotism; *insider*, inmate, internee, boarder, stay-at-home, homebody; *insertion*, injection, introduction, intromission; *absorption*, assimilation, incorporation, ingestion.

adj. *interior*, internal, inner, innermost, central; *inside*, private, intimate, domestic, home, indoor, in-house; *endemic*, deep-seated, ingrained, ingrown; *introverted*, inward-looking, introspective.

vb. *internalize*, incorporate, assimilate, absorb, ingest, inhale; *enclose*, enfold, embrace, encapsulate; *confine*, intern, imprison, shut in.

adv. *inside*, indoors, at home, en famille; *inwardly*, deep down, at heart.

200 CENTRE

See also **63** (middle).

n. *centre*, heart, nucleus, hub, epicentre, bull's eye; *middle*, waistline, midriff, diameter, watershed, parting; *pivot*, fulcrum, hinge, axis; *focus*, centre of attraction, cynosure, centrepiece; *meeting point*, junction, rallying point, node; *centrality*, importance, relevance.

adj. *central*, focal, key, crucial, vital, pivotal; *centripetal*, convergent.

vb. *centralize*, converge, concentrate, focus, home in on, zero in on; *centre on*, hinge on, turn on, pivot on.

adv. *at the heart*, at the core.

201 LINING

See also **202** (covering).

n. *lining*, liner, facing, interlining, inlay; *filling*, wadding, padding, quilting, stuffing; *insulation*, soundproofing, backing, panelling, cladding; *coating*, furring, encrustation, scale.

vb. *line*, face, interline, inlay; *fill*, stuff, wad, pad, quilt, pack; *coat*, fur, encrust.

202 COVERING

See also **175** (layer); **201** (lining); **378** (screen).

n. *covering*, surface, overlay, overlap, superimposition; *cover*, coating, topping, wrapping, packaging, lagging; *lid*, flap, shutter, trapdoor, cap, stopper, plug, bung; *envelope*, sheath, scabbard, ferule, holster; *tarpaulin*, loose cover, dustsheet, pillowcase, tea cosy; *case*, wrapper, dust jacket, boards, record sleeve, folder; *roof*, thatch, canopy, awning, tent, marquee; *hood*, umbrella, sunshade, blind, screen, curtain; *cocoon*, shroud, winding sheet, swaddling clothes, bandage; *skin*, epidermis, integument, bark, peel, rind, husk, pod, jacket; *shell*, armour, carapace, shield, crust, scab; *fur*, pelt, fleece, hair, hide, plumage; *blanket*,

sheet, mantle, robe, cloak, veil, pall, mask, disguise; *veneer*, varnish, lacquer, enamel, glaze, paint, whitewash; *flooring*, linoleum, vinyl, matting, paving, cobblestones, screed, asphalt, tarmac.
adj. *covered*, overlaid, surfaced, paved, metalled; *wrapped*, veiled, cloaked, clad, enveloped.
vb. *cover*, overlay, superimpose, layer; *coat*, spread, smear, smother; *envelop*, cloak, blanket, shroud; *wrap*, bandage, swathe, cocoon; *encase*, encapsulate, enclose, sheathe, box, pack; *roof*, thatch, tile, slate, cap, top; *surface*, floor, pave, metal, tarmac; *paint*, render, whitewash, varnish, veneer, lacquer, enamel, glaze; *mask*, hood, conceal, disguise, draw a veil over.

203 UNCOVERING
See also **205** (undress); **469** (disclosure).
n. *uncovering*, stripping, denudation, defoliation, shedding, moulting; *bareness*, undress, nakedness, baldness, alopecia; *disclosure*, unveiling, revelation, exposure; *paint-remover*, stripper, solvent, depilatory, hair-remover, defoliant; *detective*, private eye, sleuth, investigator.
adj. *uncovered*, bare, naked, stripped, denuded, threadbare; *hairless*, bald, leafless, plucked, skinned, clean-shaven, thin on top.
vb. *uncover*, divest, disrobe, strip; *skin*, flay, scalp, pluck, peel, husk, pod, shell; *shed*, cast, moult, slough; *denude*, lay bare, defoliate, devastate; *unpack*, unwrap, unfold, expose; *disclose*, divulge, reveal, unmask, unveil, take the lid off (*colloq.*).

204 DRESS
See also **202** (covering).
n. *dress*, cover, clothing, apparel, attire, garb, costume, raiment; *wardrobe*, outfit, ensemble, rig-out (*colloq.*), wear, gear, togs (*colloq.*), clobber (*colloq.*), duds (*colloq.*); *garment*, coordinates, separates, underwear, lingerie, outerwear, headgear, footwear; *dressing-up*, evening dress, white tie, finery, toilette, Sunday best, best bib and tucker, glad rags (*colloq.*), fancy dress; *uniform*, regalia, livery, subfusc, weeds, mourning, khaki, fatigues; *old clothes*, rags, hand-me-downs, cast-offs; *clothier*, tailor, costumier, outfitter, designer, couturier; *fashion*, rag trade, haute couture, high fashion.
adj. *dressed*, clad, decent, got up, overdressed, dressed up to the nines (*colloq.*), tarted up (*colloq.*), dolled up (*colloq.*); *well-dressed*, soigné, groomed, fashionable, well turned-out, smart; *tailored*, bespoke, made-to-measure, custom-made, off-the-peg, ready-to-wear.
vb. *dress*, clothe, array, robe, garb, deck out; *wear*, don, sport, try on, slip on, throw on; *dress up*, spruce up, titivate, prink, smarten up.

205 UNDRESS
See also **203** (uncovering).
n. *undress*, casual wear, civvies, plain clothes, mufti, dishabille; *nakedness*, nudity, indecent exposure, naturism, striptease, birthday suit (*colloq.*); *stripper*, ecdysiast, flasher (*colloq.*), streaker (*colloq.*), exhibitionist, nudist, naturist.
adj. *undressed*, bare, half-dressed, underdressed, barelegged, barefooted, naked, nude, starkers (*colloq.*); *décolleté*, plunging, low-necked, revealing, skimpy, mini.
vb. *undress*, strip, peel off (*colloq.*), disrobe, divest oneself; *undo*, untie, unbutton, unzip; *take off*, throw off, slip out of.
adv. *in the nude*, in the altogether (*colloq.*), in the buff (*colloq.*), in the raw (*colloq.*), without a stitch on.

206 SURROUNDINGS
See also **210** (enclosure).
n. *surroundings*, milieu, environment, background, setting, frame; *circumference*, perimeter, periphery, outskirts, boundary, environs, purlieus; *neighbourhood*, vicinity, precincts, region; *ambience*, atmosphere, mood, climate. **adj.** *surrounding*, peripheral, environmental, climatic, ambient, atmospheric.

vb. *surround*, encompass, encircle, envelop, enclose, embrace; *ring*, circumscribe, contain, cordon off, hem, circle.
adv. *on all sides*, all around, to right and to left.

207 INTERFACE
See also **176** (juxtaposition); **269** (insertion).
n. *interface*, meeting point, junction, crossroads, intersection; *boundary*, frontier, divide, watershed, parting; *midpoint*, median, midriff, diaphragm; *partition*, curtain, screen, party wall, buffer, bulkhead; *intervention*, intercession, interception, interference.
adj. *intervening*, interjacent, juxtaposed; *intermediate*, coterminous, contiguous; *interfering*, intrusive, obtrusive.
vb. *put between*, layer, sandwich, wedge, bracket; *interpose*, intercalate, introduce, interleave, interlard; *interfere*, intercede, intercept, intervene; *divide*, come between, separate, demarcate.

208 OUTLINE
See also **223** (circularity).
n. *outline*, profile, silhouette, relief, contour, shape; *frame*, border, surround, rim, edge, periphery, circumference; *sketch*, diagram, figure, delineation; *broad/rough outline*, skeleton, germ, gist, embryo.
vb. *outline*, delineate, trace, frame, silhouette, profile; *sketch*, jot, rough out, map out, block out.

209 EDGE
See also **211** (limit).
n. *edge*, verge, brink, fringe, margin, tip, corner; *lip*, rim, brim, flange, welt; *boundary*, extremity, outer limit, perimeter, confines; *coastline*, seaboard, littoral, shoreline, beach; *roadside*, kerb, verge, gutter, hard shoulder; *threshold*, sill, doorstep, porch; *edging*, frame, mounting, hem, border, frill, trim, piping.
adj. *marginal*, peripheral, borderline, fringe; *riverside*, riparian, wayside, roadside; *scalloped*, bevelled, deckle-edged.
vb. *edge*, trim, hem, fringe, border; *rim*, skirt, verge.

210 ENCLOSURE
See also **206** (surroundings).
n. *enclosure*, fold, pen, compound, paddock, stockade, corral; *arena*, pitch, ring, court, yard, rink, ground, stadium, amphitheatre; *fence*, railing, cordon, paling, barrier, palisade, hedge; *ditch*, trench, moat, ha-ha; *case*, envelope, wrapper, jacket, cover.
vb. *enclose*, pen, cage, hem in, fence in, wall up, immure, confine, corral; *encircle*, encompass, surround, besiege, picket, seal off, cordon off; *encase*, enfold, wrap, envelop.

211 LIMIT
See also **209** (edge).
n. *limit*, threshold, edge, boundary; *upper/lower limit*, ceiling, cut-off point, sticking point, saturation point; *extremity*, end, terminus, finishing line, winning post, destination; *frontier*, border, no-man's land, borderline; *dateline*, horizon, equator, skyline; *deadline*, time limit, ultimatum, final offer; *delimitation*, definition, circumscription, demarcation, restriction.
adj. *limited*, defined, demarcated, set; *bordering*, coterminous, edging.
vb. *limit*, bound, border, edge, mark out, demarcate; *delimit*, define, outline, circumscribe; *curb*, confine, restrict, contain.

212 FRONT
See also **59** (precedence).
n. *front*, fore, forefront, foreground, prominence, high profile; *anteroom*, forecourt, threshold, entrance; *frontage*, facade, fascia, facing, veneer; *vanguard*, spearhead, avant-garde, front line, firing line; *bow*, prow, nose, beak, brow, forehead; *right side*, topside, recto, heads; *face*, countenance, physionomy, kisser (*colloq.*), mush (*colloq.*), dial (*colloq.*), mug (*colloq.*); *front man*, presenter, spokesperson, figurehead, cover, decoy.

adj. *frontal*, forward, anterior, full-frontal; *facing*, opposite, oncoming, head-on; *advance*, leading, head, foremost, prominent, up-front (*colloq.*).
vb. *front*, lead, head up, spearhead; *come to the fore*, step forward, advance, forge ahead, be out in front; *face*, confront, brave, breast.
adv. *in front*, forward, downstage; *ahead*, in advance, in the forefront.

213 REAR

See also **60** (sequence).
n. *rear*, tail, stern, back end, wake, train; *rearguard*, sweeper, back, backstop; *background*, back seat, low profile, back-room boy; *backdrop*, backstage, back door, hinterland; *reverse*, verso, flipside, tails; *hindquarters*, buttocks, backside (*colloq.*), behind (*colloq.*), posterior, bum (*colloq.*), arse (*vulg.*).
adj. *rear*, back, hind, hindmost, rearmost; *reverse*, backward, back-to-front; *dorsal*, vertebral, lumbar.
vb. *back*, reverse, retrace one's steps, double back, turn tail; *bring up the rear*, lag, trail, straggle.
adv. *in the rear*, behind, upstage, aft, astern, backwards.

214 SIDE

See also **252** (deviation).
n. *side*, flank, broadside, wing, profile; *sidelines*, siding, edge, margin, fringe; *diversion*, deflection, sidestep, bypass, digression, tangent; *right*, right hand, off side, starboard; *left*, left hand, near side, on side, port, larboard, southpaw.
adj. *lateral*, side, sidelong; *oblique*, tangential, indirect, roundabout, circuitous; *right*, clockwise, ambidextrous, dextral; *left*, anticlockwise, sinistral.
vb. *flank*, edge, sidle, skirt, border; *divert*, sidetrack, deflect; *deviate*, digress, sidestep, bypass.
adv. *sideways*, crabwise; *side by side*, abreast, alongside.

215 CONTRAPOSITION

See also **14** (oppositeness).
n. *contraposition*, polarity, contrariety; *opposite*, antithesis, reverse, inverse; *polarization*, confrontation, opposition.
adj. *opposite*, contrary, counter, antithetical, opposed, adverse; *polar*, antipodean, arctic, antarctic.
vb. *be opposite*, face, confront, oppose, run counter to, challenge.
adv. *against*, contrariwise.

216 FORM

See also **149** (production); **298** (structure).
n. *form*, shape, figure, configuration; *outline*, silhouette, contour, profile; *design*, style, appearance, look, lines, format; *structure*, build, architecture, skeleton, framework, infrastructure; *pattern*, mould, template, die, stamp, prototype; *formation*, production, creation, formulation, expression.
adj. *formative*, architectural, structural; *plastic*, fictile, malleable, pliable, impressionable; *shaped*, defined, solid, three-dimensional.
vb. *form*, make, create, produce, shape, fashion, style; *outline*, sketch, design, draft; *pattern*, mould, die, stamp, coin; *model*, carve, turn, throw, sculpt, chisel, hew, cast, forge; *formulate*, express, devise, work up, lick/knock into shape (*colloq.*); *take shape*, materialize, develop, come into being.

217 SHAPELESSNESS

See also **219** (distortion).
n. *shapelessness*, amorphousness, formlessness, chaos; *indefiniteness*, indistinctness, vagueness, fuzziness, woolliness, blur; *fluidity*, liquidity, volatility, mobility, changeability; *raw material*, rough diamond, embryo, amoeba; *scribble*, scrawl, doodle, squiggle.
adj. *shapeless*, amorphous, formless, featureless, unformed, inchoate; *indefinite*, indeterminate, vague, indistinct, nebulous, blurred, fuzzy, woolly, messy, chaotic; *fluid*, liquid, volatile, mobile, unstable, protean. *raw*, rough, crude, brute, embryonic; *unfinished*, unprocessed, rough-hewn, uncut, unpolished.
vb. *deform*, warp, twist, distort, knock out of shape; *blur*, smudge, confuse,

jumble, mess up; *dissolve*, melt, thaw, liquefy.

218 SYMMETRY

See also **25** (equality).

n. *symmetry*, proportion, balance, equilibrium; *correspondence*, equivalence, analogy, parallelism; *harmony*, regularity, evenness, rhythm.

adj. *symmetrical*, proportional, balanced, equal; *corresponding*, parallel, analogous, similar; *harmonious*, regular, even, classical.

219 DISTORTION

See also **217** (shapelessness).

n. *distortion*, contortion, twistedness, convolution, tortuousness; *asymmetry*, inequality, imbalance, irregularity, disproportion, lopsidedness, squintness; *deformity*, malformation, abnormality, disfigurement, mutilation; *misrepresentation*, bias, skew, exaggeration, perversion.

adj. *distorted*, contorted, convoluted, tortuous, twisted, gnarled; *asymmetrical*, unequal, disproportionate, uneven, irregular; *askew*, awry, crooked, squint, lopsided, skew-whiff (*colloq.*); *bent*, buckled, bowed, bandy, hunchbacked, knock-kneed; *deformed*, misshapen, abnormal, stunted, crippled; *biased*, loaded, skewed, perverted.

vb. *distort*, contort, twist, screw, knot; *bend*, buckle, bow, warp, crumple, give; *grimace*, scowl, pucker, frown, pull a face; *deform*, disfigure, mangle, mutilate, cripple, stunt; *misrepresent*, misconstrue, pervert, fudge, bias, weight, skew.

220 ANGLE

See also **195** (obliqueness).

n. *angle*, crook, bend, hook, elbow, dog-leg, branch, fork, crutch; *corner*, nook, recess, niche, cranny; *triangle*, wedge, arrowhead, chevron, prism, pyramid; *square*, cube, rectangle, oblong, diamond, lozenge, rhombus, parallelogram; *polygon*, pentangle, Star of David, hexagon, octagon.

adj. *angular*, aquiline, hooked, right-angled, L-shaped; *bent*, akimbo, forked, pointed, jagged, zigzag; *triangular*, cuneiform, pyramidal, wedge-shaped; *square*, cuboid, rectangular, rhomboid; *polygonal*, hexagonal, octagonal.

vb. *angle*, point, corner, hook, bend, crook, fold, zigzag; *fork*, branch, ramify, deviate, go off at a tangent.

221 CURVE

See also **224** (convolution); **226** (convexity).

n. *curve*, flexion, arc, trajectory, parabola, sweep; *curvature*, sinuosity, concavity, convexity; *deflection*, swerve, deviation, detour; *bend*, turn, hairpin, U-turn, horseshoe, oxbow, bay, bight, cove. *loop*, endless belt, Möbius strip, oval, scallop, festoon, swag; *bow*, arch, arcade, vault, ogive, crescent, sickle, half-moon; *hump-back*, wave, undulation, S-bend, figure of eight, switchback, roller coaster.

adj. *curved*, arched, bent, ovoid, rounded, curvilinear; *semicircular*, convex, concave, domed, hemispherical; *curvy*, shapely, curvaceous, voluptuous, pear-shaped; *wavy*, undulating, rolling, sinuous; *heart-shaped*, bow-legged, bandy-legged, swan-necked; *turned-up*, retroussé, tip-tilted.

vb. *curve*, swerve, turn, bend, sweep; *bow*, flex, round, arch, vault, dome; *loop*, coil, scallop, festoon, swag; *roll*, undulate, unfold, unfurl.

222 STRAIGHTNESS

See also **190** (verticality); **191** (horizontality).

n. *straightness*, alignment, linearity, directness, verticality, horizontality, perpendicularity; *rigidity*, stiffness, tautness, inflexibility; *straight line*, beeline, direct route, short cut; *vertical*, horizontal, upright, poker, plumb, ramrod.

adj. *straight*, linear, rectilinear, true, level, horizontal; *vertical*, perpendicular, upright; *direct*, undeviating, unswerving, unbending, rigid, inflexible, stiff.

vb. *straighten*, align, level, even out, flatten, smooth, iron out; *stretch*, extend, unfold, unroll, uncurl, uncoil, unbend.

adv. *straight*, plumb, in true; *direct*, as the crow flies.

223 CIRCULARITY

See also **208** (outline); **225** (roundness); **251** (circuit); **279** (rotation).

n. *circularity*, roundness, rotundity, curvedness; *circumference*, equator, orbit, circuit, cycle; *circulation*, rotation, revolution, gyration, spin, pirouette; *circle*, ring, torus, round, disc, wheel, loop, saucer; *sphere*, orb, globe, bulb, ball; *dome*, hemisphere, boss, knob, stud; *crown*, circlet, coronet, halo, nimbus, corona, aureole; *collar*, necklace, garland, wreath, bracelet, anklet, belt, girdle.

adj. *circular*, round, discoid, toroid, annular; *spherical*, globular, tubular, cylindrical; *cyclic*, circulatory, rotatory, gyratory.

vb. *circle*, orbit, lap, wheel; *rotate*, revolve, circulate, gyrate, spin, spiral, pirouette; *encircle*, surround, loop, girdle, circumscribe.

224 CONVOLUTION

See also **221** (curve); **279** (rotation).

n. *convolution*, twist, torsion, contortion; *roll*, coil, winding, spring, spiral, screw, helix, worm, corkscrew; *curl*, wave, lock, kink, ringlet, frizz, tendril; *ripple*, swirl, whorl, vortex, whirlpool; *scroll*, flourish, curlicue, squiggle; *maze*, network, labyrinth, warren; *convolutedness*, intricacy, complexity, tortuousness, sinuousness.

adj. *convoluted*, twisted, contorted, knotted; *tortuous*, sinuous, intricate, involved, complex, labyrinthine; *spiral*, helical, loopy, coiled, serpentine, snaky, squiggly; *wavy*, corrugated, rippling, crinkly, curly, kinky, frizzy, crimped.

vb. *twist*, contort, corkscrew, writhe, squirm, wriggle, worm; *roll*, undulate, meander, loop, coil, snake; *entwine*, wreathe, enmesh, embroil; *curl*, wave, perm, crimp, crinkle, corrugate.

225 ROUNDNESS

See also **223** (circularity); **226** (convexity).

n. *roundness*, curvedness, circularity, rotundity, convexity; *sphere*, globe, balloon, bubble, ball, orb, bulb, bullet, pea, globule, bead, drop; *cylinder*, cone, tube, roller, rung, bole, trunk, drum, barrel; *paunch*, pot-belly, corporation, beer gut; *bulge*, swelling, hump, dome, hemisphere.

adj. *round*, curved, circular, beady, convex; *spherical*, globular, globose, bulbous, swollen; *cylindrical*, tubular, columnar, conical; *rotund*, rounded, paunchy, pot-bellied, barrel-chested.

vb. *round*, arch, curve, bend; *bulge*, swell, balloon, distend, inflate; *ball*, roll, coil, furl.

226 CONVEXITY

See also **221** (curve); **225** (roundness); **228** (prominence).

n. *convexity*, curvature, roundedness, tumescence, swollenness; *hemisphere*, dome, cupola, beehive, cup; *bulge*, hump, bow, arch, curve, ridge, hog's back, camber; *swelling*, excrescence, growth, tumour, nodule, lump; *pimple*, blister, boil, carbuncle, bunion; *knob*, boss, bump, nubble, bud, button; *breast*, bosom, pap, udder, dug, nipple, teat, bust, boobs (*colloq.*), bristols (*colloq.*), tits (*colloq.*), knockers (*colloq.*).

adj. *convex*, round, curved, arched, domed, hemispherical, bouffant; *swollen*, puffy, tumescent, tumid, distended, bloated; *raised*, embossed, bumpy, lumpy, nubbly, pimply; *curvaceous*, busty, buxom, bosomy, well-stacked (*colloq.*).

vb. *be convex*, arch, curve, rise, bow; *bulge*, swell, belly, billow.

227 CONCAVITY

See also **221** (curve); **231** (furrow).

n. *concavity*, hollow, depression, dip, indentation, impression; *cavity*, hole, recess, nook, alcove, burrow, cave, grotto, cavern, pothole; *basin*, pan, saucer, bowl, dish, cup; *dent*, dimple, pockmark, perforation; *pit*, crater, well, shaft, borehole, tunnel; *valley*,

gorge, gully, ravine, crevasse; *groove*, socket, channel, furrow, trench; *spoon*, scoop, ladle, trowel, bucket.
adj. *concave*, hollow, cavernous, gaping, yawning; *pitted*, dented, dimpled, pockmarked, perforated; *recessed*, indented, sunken, excavated; *grooved*, channelled, furrowed, corrugated.
vb. *make concave*, buckle, dent, stave in, cave in; *hollow*, indent, recess, depress; *gouge*, groove, channel, bore, burrow, excavate; *hole*, pit, pockmark, perforate.

228 PROMINENCE

See also **226** (convexity).
n. *prominence*, eminence, height, conspicuousness, high profile; *projection*, tongue, salient, promontory, headland, spur, point, spit; *overhang*, shelf, ledge, outcrop, crag, ridge, buttress; *protuberance*, excrescence, outgrowth, lump, bump, hump; *beak*, bill, nose, conk (*colloq.*), snout, proboscis, antenna, feeler, horn; *relief*, convexity, embossing, cameo, high relief.
adj. *prominent*, high, conspicuous, noticeable; *projecting*, salient, jutting, overhanging, beetle-browed, craggy, buck-toothed; *protuberant*, raised, convex, bulging, lumpy, humped, pop-eyed.
vb. *project*, jut, stick out, stand out, protrude, bulge; *rise*, bristle, cock, prick up, erect.

229 NOTCH

See also **296** (sharpness).
n. *notch*, serration, indentation, crenellation, scallop, zigzag, deckle edge; *nick*, V-shape, snick, cut, gash, incision; *tooth*, sprocket, ratchet, comb, saw.
adj. *notched*, serrated, jagged, ragged, saw-toothed; *stepped*, crenellated, indented, scalloped.
vb. *notch*, serrate, tooth, mill; *indent*, crimp, pink, scallop; *nick*, snick, cut, snip, clip.

230 FOLD

See also **231** (furrow).
n. *fold*, pleat, tuck, gather; *frill*, flounce, ruffle, ruche; *lapel*, cuff, turn-up, crease; *ridge*, furrow, groove, corrugation; *wrinkle*, crinkle, pucker, frown, crow's feet.
adj. *folded*, plicate, ridged, gathered, pleated, frilly; *crumpled*, creased, crushed, crinkled, dog-eared, puckered, corrugated, lined.
vb. *fold*, furl, drape, swathe, festoon; *furrow*, groove, corrugate, wrinkle, pucker, crinkle, purse, concertina; *frill*, ruffle, ruche, pleat, gather, tuck.

231 FURROW

See also **227** (concavity); **230** (fold).
n. *furrow*, groove, chase, channel, track, slot, rut; *slit*, chink, cranny, crack, crevice; *hollow*, trough, gutter, gully, ditch, trench, moat; *wave*, ripple, fluting, ribbing, corduroy; *wrinkle*, frown, corrugation, rifling, etching, incision, gash, slash.
adj. *furrowed*, wrinkled, puckered, lined, etched, incised; *grooved*, fluted, ribbed, ridged, rutted, striated.
vb. *furrow*, groove, chase, channel, chamfer, flute, rifle; *plough*, rut, rib, corrugate, wrinkle; *line*, etch, incise, score, gash, slash.

232 OPENING

See also **174** (interval).
n. *opening*, aperture, gap, hole, breach, lacuna, hiatus, break; *space*, crack, chink, interstice, cavity, pocket, orifice; *perforation*, pore, puncture, indentation, bore, pinhole, eyelet; *sieve*, strainer, colander, riddle; *mesh*, netting, fretwork, openwork, lace, filigree, broderie anglaise; *outlet*, nozzle, vent, spout, gullet, nostril, mouth, maw, gob (*colloq.*), trap (*colloq.*), cakehole (*colloq.*); *compartment*, slot, keyhole, pigeonhole, letterbox; *window*, grille, fanlight, skylight, porthole, loophole, peephole; *door*, gate, portal, entrance, hatch, trapdoor, manhole, flap; *tunnel*, shaft, bolthole, burrow, foxhole; *funnel*, chimney, flue, duct, tube; *open space*, clearing, glade, bomb site, waste ground, vista, panorama; *opener*, aperient, purgative, open sesame, password; *tin-opener*, corkscrew, key, han-

dle, knob; *punch*, bodkin, skewer, gimlet, drill, auger, bradawl; *openness*, accessibility, penetrability, permeability, porosity.
adj. *open*, ajar, agape, yawning, open-mouthed; *perforated*, riddled, honeycombed, shot through; *holey*, lacy, leaky, porous, permeable, absorbent; *accessible*, clear, unobstructed, uncluttered.
vb. *open*, unlock, unfasten, uncork, unwrap, unpack, undo; *gape*, yawn, split, rend, part, burst, explode, leak; *pierce*, puncture, perforate, gore, hole, bore, drill, punch, tattoo, riddle, pepper; *stab*, prick, skewer, nail, spear, transfix, impale; *enter*, penetrate, permeate, pervade.
adv. *openly*, out in the open, open to the four winds, al fresco.

233 CLOSURE

See also **202** (covering).
n. *closure*, occlusion, strangulation, obstruction, blockage, stoppage; *impasse*, dead end, cul de sac, road block, barricade; *impermeability*, imperviousness, staunchness, impenetrability; *stopper*, cork, bung, spigot, plug, wad, tampon; *valve*, tap, stopcock, ballcock, choke, damper; *gag*, muzzle, tourniquet, compress; *cover*, top, lid, cap, seal, shutter; *lock*, bolt, bar, latch, deadlock.
adj. *closed*, shut, barred, bolted, shuttered; *impermeable*, impenetrable, impervious, staunch, watertight, airtight, hermetically sealed; *impassable*, inaccessible, blocked, barricaded.
vb. *close*, shut, occlude, strangulate, obstruct, clog; *lock*, bar, bolt, fasten; *stop*, plug, bung, caulk, cork, seal; *block*, dam, choke, throttle, gag, muzzle.

234 MOTION

See also **236** (land travel); **239** (transfer).
n. *motion*, movement, mobility, locomotion, perambulation; *momentum*, impetus, propulsion, impulsion; *advance*, progress, headway, ascent; *retreat*, regression, withdrawal, descent; *oscillation*, fluctuation, vibration, agitation, tremor; *activity*, unrest, stir, bustle, traffic; *passage*, transit, transfer, shift, transport, conveyance; *flow*, flux, drift, current, course, run; *gait*, walk, carriage, bearing, tread, stride.
adj. *moving*, mobile, motile, locomotive, automotive, self-propelled; *transitional*, passing, shifting, fleeting; *wandering*, ambulant, peripatetic, nomadic, restless, drifting; *kinetic*, dynamic, cinematographic.
vb. *move*, go, walk, proceed, make one's way, advance, progress; *march*, tramp, stride, lope, jog, amble, saunter, stroll, waddle, shuffle; *stalk*, strut, swagger, mince; *run*, race, gallop, hare, fly, dash; *roll*, taxi, trundle, chug, wheel, coast, cruise, freewheel; *travel*, roam, wander, drift, stray; *transfer*, transport, shift, convey, dispatch; *push*, shove, budge, drive, hustle; *draw*, pull, drag, tug, haul.
adv. *in motion*, on the move, on the go, up and about; *under way*, on the road, en route, in transit.

235 MOTIONLESSNESS

See also **123** (cessation).
n. *motionlessness*, stillness, rest, immobility; *stability*, equilibrium, poise, balance, stasis; *suspension*, cessation, stagnation, inertia, deadlock, stalemate; *standstill*, stop, halt, pause, truce, lull; *stoppage*, embargo, freeze, strike; *calm*, still, quiet, hush.
adj. *motionless*, still, immobile, becalmed; *static*, stationary, stagnant, inactive, idle; *immovable*, stuck, rigid, paralysed, unbudgeable; *transfixed*, spellbound, rooted to the spot, stock-still; *sedentary*, stay-at-home, home-loving, housebound, bedridden, disabled.
vb. *be motionless*, stand still, stay put, sit tight, mark time, stagnate; *cease*, stop, come to a halt, settle, subside, die down; *pause*, rest, tarry, take a breather (*colloq.*), rest on one's oars; *immobilize*, lock, jam, stick, lodge, catch; *halt*, stop short, stop in one's tracks, brake, check, pull up.

236 LAND TRAVEL

See also **234** (motion); **242** (vehicle); **762** (recreation).

n. *land travel*, tourism, globe-trotting, sightseeing, exploration, peregrination; *journey*, voyage, odyssey, expedition, trek, safari; *trip*, jaunt, outing, excursion, spin, ride; *walk*, constitutional, stroll, ramble, hike, tramp, march, walkabout, Shank's pony; *run*, jog, race, sprint, cross-country, marathon; *route*, itinerary, stopover, terminus, destination, journey's end; *traveller*, voyager, passenger, commuter, tourist, wayfarer, sightseer, tripper; *walker*, pedestrian, hiker, rambler, jogger, runner, sprinter; *wanderer*, rover, globe-trotter, migrant, drifter, rolling stone, vagabond, vagrant, tramp, gentleman of the road.

adj. *travelling*, itinerant, peripatetic, globe-trotting, ambulant; *wandering*, migratory, nomadic, restless, vagrant, vagabond, errant.

vb. *travel*, journey, voyage, explore, tour, shuttle, commute, knock about (*colloq.*); *walk*, pace, saunter, stroll, amble; *hike*, trek, tramp, march, ramble; *trudge*, plod, slog, stump, hoof it, foot it, leg it; *run*, race, jog, sprint; *wander*, rove, roam, migrate, traipse.

adv. *by road*, overland, on foot; *on the road*, on the trail, on the beat.

237 WATER TRAVEL

See also **243** (ship); **762** (recreation).

n. *water travel*, sailing, navigation, cruising, yachting, boating; *voyage*, circumnavigation, cruise, crossing, sail; *seamanship*, seafaring, sea legs, weather eye; *navy*, fleet, merchant navy, shipping, flotilla; *water sport*, aquatics, surfing, swimming, natation, diving, windsurfing, canoeing, sculling, rowing; *seaman*, mariner, sailor, submariner, seafarer, sea dog, old salt; *captain*, crew, boatswain, master, mate, pilot, navigator; *coastguard*, lifeboatman, boatman, ferryman, Charon.

adj. *seafaring*, maritime, marine, naval, nautical, navigational, aquatic, deep-sea, ocean-going, longshore, seaworthy, waterborne.

vb. *put to sea*, set sail, embark, cast off, launch, weigh anchor; *voyage*, sail, cruise, ply, steam, ferry, run, circumnavigate; *navigate*, steer, pilot, captain; *disembark*, land, dock, berth, tie up, moor, drop anchor; *row*, scull, canoe, punt, paddle; *swim*, float, tread water, bathe, surf, windsurf, wade, paddle.

adv. *at sea*, aboard, afloat, on the high seas.

238 AIR TRAVEL

See also **244** (aircraft).

n. *air travel*, aeronautics, aerospace, aerodynamics; *flying*, aviation, gliding, hang-gliding, ballooning, parachuting, sky-diving, aerobatics; *airline*, airlift, charter, flight, airlane; *airport*, airfield, aerodrome, landing strip, runway, airstrip, terminal; *takeoff*, touchdown, landing, crash-landing, nosedive, prang (*colloq.*); *space travel*, space flight, countdown, liftoff, blastoff, orbit, docking, reentry, splashdown; *pilot*, aeronaut, aviator, aviatrix, airman/woman, flier, balloonist, parachutist, paratrooper; *astronaut*, cosmonaut, spaceman/woman, space traveller.

adj. *flying*, aeronautic, aerodynamic, aerobatic; *aerial*, airborne, in-flight, airworthy.

vb. *fly*, pilot, aviate, glide, balloon, parachute, jet; *take off*, taxi, overfly, hover, fly, drift, cruise; *come down*, touch down, land, crash, nosedive, crashland, ditch, bail out, eject; *lift off*, blast off, orbit, dock, splash down.

adv. *in flight*, in the air, in orbit, on the wing.

239 TRANSFER

See also **234** (motion); **697** (transfer of property).

n. *transfer*, relocation, shift, removal, transferal, transplantation, deportation; *transmission*, conduction, convection, transfusion, contagion; *transportation*, conveyance, dispatch, transshipment, exportation, importation, delivery; *carriage*, transport,

haulage, cartage; *freight*, consignment, shipment, cargo, container.
adj. *transferable*, movable, portable; *transmissible*, communicable, contagious, infectious.
vb. *transfer*, shift, move, convey, transmit; *dispatch*, transport, ship, tranship, export, import; *send*, consign, post, mail, forward.
adv. *in transit*, on the way, en route, under way.

240 WAY
See also **271** (passage); **315** (channel).
n. *way*, manner, method, procedure, modus operandi, measures, steps; *course*, route, direction, line, tack, short cut, detour; *approach*, access, entrance, passage, right of way; *path*, track, orbit, trajectory, channel; *trail*, footpath, bridlepath, towpath; *walk*, drive, avenue, boulevard, promenade; *road*, highway, thoroughfare, artery, trunk road, ring road, bypass, dual carriageway, motorway; *street*, terrace, crescent, circus; *sidestreet*, lane, alley, close, wynd; *railway*, railroad, main line, branch line, siding, marshalling yard; *underground*, subway, tube, funicular, monorail; *bridge*, footbridge, drawbridge, viaduct, aqueduct, flyover, cloverleaf; *causeway*, gangway, catwalk, aisle, underpass.

241 CARRIER
n. *carrier*, bearer, porter, coolie, messenger, courier, runner, postman; *common carrier*, transporter, shipper, haulier, carter, importer, exporter; *beast of burden*, packhorse, draught horse, mule, donkey; *carrier bag*, tote bag, trolley, stretcher, litter, conveyor belt.
vb. *carry*, bear, shoulder, hump, cart, heave, haul, lug, tote (*colloq.*), shlepp (*colloq.*); *convey*, post, send, forward, transport, ship, ferry.

242 VEHICLE
See also **236** (land travel).
n. *vehicle*, conveyance, transport, wheels (*colloq.*); *wagon*, dray, cart, tumbril; *carriage*, landau, brougham, hansom, buggy, gig, fly, trap; *bicycle*, tandem, pushbike, tricycle, trike, moped, scooter, motorcycle, motorbike; *car*, motor car, automobile, saloon, hatchback, convertible, coupé, shooting brake, station wagon, runabout, limousine; *van*, camper, pickup, float, pantechnicon, hearse, Black Maria, ambulance, lorry, truck, juggernaut; *bus*, coach, charabanc, double-decker, tram, trolleybus, streetcar (*US*); *stagecoach*, post chaise, hackney carriage, cab, taxi, minicab, rickshaw, trishaw; *train*, express, high-speed train, locomotive, tender, tanker, goods train, underground, subway.
adj. *vehicular*, wheeled, motorized, automotive, locomotive.

243 SHIP
See also **237** (water travel).
n. *ship*, vessel, boat, craft, tub (*colloq.*); *passenger ship*, ferry, packet, steamer, paddleboat, hovercraft, hydrofoil, liner; *freighter*, barge, tramp, tanker, collier, dredger, tug, supertanker; *launch*, lighter, painter, dinghy, wherry, lifeboat; *sailing ship*, galleon, sloop, schooner, ketch, yawl, clipper, merchantman, Indiaman; *fishing boat*, trawler, drifter, smack, whaler, factory ship; *yacht*, skiff, catamaran, junk, sampan, dhow, caique, felucca; *rowing boat*, scull, canoe, punt, coracle, gondola, kayak, pirogue; *warship*, man o' war, battleship, frigate, corvette, cruiser, destroyer, aircraft carrier.
adj. *nautical*, maritime, marine, seagoing, oceangoing, transatlantic.

244 AIRCRAFT
See also **238** (air travel).
n. *aircraft*, aeroplane, plane, flying machine, monoplane, biplane, seaplane, crate (*colloq.*); *airliner*, jet, jumbo jet, airbus, shuttle, Concorde; *helicopter*, whirlybird (*colloq.*), chopper (*colloq.*), fighter, bomber; *airship*, dirigible, balloon, glider, hang-glider; *spaceship*, satellite, rocket, capsule, module.

adj. *aviational*, aeronautical, wide-bodied, heavier-than-air, supersonic.

245 SPEED
See also **96** (immediacy); **615** (haste).
n. *speed*, velocity, rapidity, swiftness; *quickness*, alacrity, promptness, suddenness, instantaneity; *pace*, rate, tempo, momentum, rate of knots (*colloq.*), lick (*colloq.*); *haste*, hurry, rush, dispatch; *acceleration*, flying start, spurt, sprint, full throttle; *run*, race, dash, charge, gallop, stampede; *runner*, racer, speed merchant (*colloq.*), harrier, sprinter; *racehorse*, greyhound, hare, cheetah, gazelle.
adj. *speedy*, fast, swift, rapid, meteoric; *quick*, lively, snappy, quick-fire, brisk, smart; *prompt*, immediate, sudden, double-quick, alacritous, hasty, expeditious; *light-footed*, nimble, agile, fleet-footed, mercurial; *high-speed*, breakneck, headlong, precipitous, runaway.
vb. *speed*, race, flash, streak, shoot, fly; *dart*, flit, whisk, zoom, whiz (*colloq.*), zip, rush, tear, dash; *run*, gallop, hare, sprint, hot-foot it, belt, pelt, hurtle, career, stampede; *dive*, pounce, spring, swoop, lunge; *run away*, bolt, scoot, take to one's heels, scamper, scuttle, scarper (*colloq.*), skedaddle (*colloq.*); *accelerate*, hurry, hasten, quicken, hustle, step on it (*colloq.*), get a move on (*colloq.*), get weaving/cracking (*colloq.*), get one's skates on (*colloq.*), jump to it.
adv. *at full speed*, swiftly, flat out, hell for leather, post haste, helter skelter, apace; *promptly*, pronto (*colloq.*), smartish (*colloq.*), at the double, in a trice, before you can say Jack Robinson.

246 SLOWNESS
See also **616** (lack of haste).
n. *slowness*, sluggishness, lethargy, languor, inertia, slackness; *lack of haste*, patience, methodicalness, deliberation, unhurriedness, leisureliness; *hesitation*, tardiness, reluctance, unwillingness; *delay*, holdup, slowdown, work-to-rule, go-slow; *deceleration*, brake, curb, restraint, retardation; *slow motion*, snail's pace, amble, stroll, saunter, dawdle; *slow creature*, slowcoach (*colloq.*), sloth, tortoise, snail.
adj. *slow*, sluggish, lethargic, listless, languid, slack; *deliberate*, patient, painstaking, methodical, unhurried, leisurely; *hesitant*, reluctant, unwilling, tardy, dilatory, slow off the mark.
vb. *move slowly*, amble, saunter, dawdle, stroll, linger, loaf; *creep*, crawl, inch, trickle, drip, ooze; *plod*, trudge, limp, hobble, shuffle, shamble, mooch (*colloq.*); *lag*, delay, dilly-dally (*colloq.*), drag one's feet, take one's time, run out of steam, falter; *slow down*, decelerate, slacken, retard, brake, backpedal, ease off, let up.
adv. *slowly*, adagio, largo, little by little, softly softly (*colloq.*).

247 IMPULSION
See also **255** (propulsion).
n. *impulsion*, impetus, momentum, thrust, drive, propulsion, force, charge; *impact*, brunt, shock, jolt, nudge, bump, cannon, collision, crash, smash; *blow*, bang, thud, knock, rap, punch, thwack, thump; *stroke*, hit, smack, cuff, slap, clap, lash, flick, tap; *hammer*, club, cudgel, cosh, truncheon, knocker, ram, bulldozer.
vb. *impel*, thrust, drive, kick, charge; *throw*, fling, propel, launch, hurl, toss; *push*, shove, force, press, ram, bulldoze; *jerk*, jog, jolt, jar, nudge, butt, wrench, tug; *collide*, smash, crash, bang, cannon, bump, careen; *hit*, strike, clout, cuff, spank, smack, slap, rap, tap, knock; *punch*, slug, pummel, pound, bludgeon, hammer; *beat*, bash, thrash, wallop (*colloq.*), clobber (*colloq.*), belt (*colloq.*), slosh (*colloq.*), whack (*colloq.*).

248 RECOIL
See also **137** (counteraction).
n. *recoil*, rebound, bounce, spring, swing of the pendulum; *reflex*, kickback, ricochet, boomerang, cannon; *echo*, reflection, repercussion, reverberation, backlash; *reflector*, mirror, sounding board, echo chamber;

response, reply, retort, riposte, rebuff; *reaction*, double take, wince, start.
adj. *reactive*, responsive, reflexive, knee-jerk (*colloq.*); *echoey*, resonant, reverberative, repercussive; *springy*, bouncy, elastic.
vb. *recoil*, rebound, cannon, boomerang, ricochet; *spring*, bounce back, kick back, backfire; *echo*, reflect, mirror, reverberate; *react*, respond, reply, retort, rebuff.

249 DIRECTION
See also **159** (situation).
n. *direction*, bearings, situation, orientation, location, compass point, cardinal point; *trend*, tendency, drift, thrust, tack, line; *course*, route, short cut, beeline; *destination*, goal, aim, target, objective; *compass*, direction finder, signpost, map, tracking device.
adj. *directed*, headed, bound for, set.
vb. *direct*, indicate, signpost, guide, steer, level, point, aim; *orientate*, situate, take one's bearings, pinpoint, locate, track; *head for*, make for, aim for, make tracks for.
adv. *direct*, straight, point blank; *on course*, on the right track, on the right lines.

250 MIDDLE WAY
See also **63** (middle); **148** (moderation).
n. *middle way*, short cut, beeline, diameter, centre; *middle course*, median, average, happy medium, golden mean; *midpoint*, central reservation, traffic island; *middle of the road*, halfway house, compromise, moderation.
adj. *middle*, central, equidistant, direct, straight; *midway*, halfway, intermediate, medial; *neutral*, moderate, middle-of-the-road, unextreme.

251 CIRCUIT
See also **223** (circularity).
n. *circuit*, detour, bypass, loop, ring road; *digression*, deviation, way round, circumlocution.
adj. *circuitous*, roundabout, out-of-the-way; *circumlocutious*, long-winded, indirect.
vb. *circuit*, lap, loop, ring; *deviate*, digress, go out of one's way; *bypass*, skirt, avoid, give a wide berth.

252 DEVIATION
See also **214** (side); **260** (divergence).
n. *deviation*, aberration, wrong turning, disorientation; *detour*, side-step, zigzag, swerve, veer; *diversion*, shift, deflection, divergence; *digression*, aside, tangent, parenthesis.
adj. *deviant*, aberrant, off-course, off-beam, stray, wide of the mark; *digressive*, wandering, rambling, off the point, discursive.
vb. *deviate*, wander, stray, lose one's bearings, be on the wrong track; *side-step*, diverge, veer, slew, zigzag; *digress*, go off at a tangent, get side-tracked.

253 FORWARD MOTION
n. *forward motion*, progress, advance, headway; *course*, march, tide, current, flood; *step*, stride, leap, jump, spurt; *advancement*, preferment, promotion, leg-up; *development*, growth, evolution, furtherance; *improvement*, betterment, perfectibility.
adj. *forward*, progressive, advanced, up-to-date, forward-looking; *go-ahead*, enterprising, go-getting (*colloq.*); *ongoing*, continuing, inexorable, irreversible.
vb. *go forward*, proceed, progress, advance, make headway, get the go-ahead (*colloq.*); *keep on*, press on, push on, make strides, gain ground, forge ahead, get somewhere (*colloq.*); *develop*, evolve, further, bring on; *promote*, upgrade, better, improve.
adv. *forward*, onward, ahead; *progressively*, by leaps and bounds.

254 BACKWARD MOTION
See also **126** (reversion).
n. *backward motion*, recession, retraction, retreat, withdrawal, retirement, flight; *retroaction*, retrospection, regression, nostalgia; *reversion*, backward

step, relapse, backsliding; *decline*, fall off, slump, ebb; *about-turn*, volte-face, U-turn.
adj. *backward*, retrograde, retrogressive; *receding*, recessive, retreating, retractile; *retroactive*, retrospective, nostalgic.
vb. *recede*, retire, withdraw, back off, fall back; *regress*, return, revert, hark back, relapse, backslide; *reverse*, back, backtrack, backpedal, retrace one's steps, double back; *turn tail*, about-face, wheel, turn on one's heel.
adv. *backwards*, in reverse, anticlockwise, widdershins (*dial.*).

255 PROPULSION
See also **247** (impulsion).
n. *propulsion*, impulsion, drive, momentum, impetus, kick; *throw*, cast, toss, pitch, bowl; *discharge*, volley, salvo, bombardment, cannonade; *archery*, toxophily, ballistics, gunnery, artillery; *missile*, projectile, arrow, dart, bullet, shot, pellet, shell, cannonball, torpedo, rocket; *propellant*, charge, explosive, dynamite; *propeller*, pedal, oar, turbine, booster, thruster; *firearm*, shotgun, rifle, catapult, sling, bow, peashooter; *shooter*, marksman, crack shot, gunner, sniper, archer, bowler, pitcher.
adj. *propulsive*, propellent, expulsive, ballistic.
vb. *propel*, launch, project, impel, drive, thrust, kick; *throw*, cast, toss, pitch, bowl, chuck, fling, hurl, lob, bung; *fire*, catapult, pitchfork, send flying; *shoot*, discharge, loose off, volley, bombard.

256 TRACTION
See also **257** (attraction).
n. *traction*, haulage, draught, pulling, tug of war; *pull*, tug, heave, tow, trawl, haul, drag, friction; *magnetism*, attraction, charisma, drawing power; *tractor*, towrope, tugboat, windlass, dragnet, magnet.
adj. *retractive*, retractable, ductile; *magnetic*, attractive, charismatic.
vb. *draw*, pull, haul, heave, tow; *drag*, trawl, dredge, winch, reel in; *pull at*, tug, jerk, tweak, pluck, yank; *draw in*, withdraw, retract, sheathe; *attract*, magnetize, spellbind.

257 ATTRACTION
See also **256** (traction).
n. *attraction*, pull, draw, influence, gravity, magnetism; *allure*, fascination, seductiveness, charm; *lure*, bait, decoy, snare, siren, temptress; *focal point*, cynosure, centre of attraction, magnet, lodestone.
adj. *attractive*, seductive, charming, irresistible; *magnetic*, gravitational, focal, centripetal, convergent.
vb. *attract*, pull, draw, influence; *lure*, bait, ensnare, seduce; *tempt*, captivate, enthral, magnetize, mesmerize.

258 REPULSION
See also **266** (expulsion).
n. *repulsion*, rejection, rebuff, dismissal, snub, brush-off (*colloq.*); *deflection*, defence, counterstroke, parry, foil, counterattack, resistance.
adj. *repulsive*, repellent, antipathetic, offensive, off-putting; *defensive*, resistant, hostile, dismissive.
vb. *repel*, drive away, chase, dismiss; *deflect*, ward off, fend off, keep at bay, head off, parry; *reject*, rebuff, snub, cold-shoulder; *eject*, throw out, show the door, send packing (*colloq.*).

259 CONVERGENCE
n. *convergence*, confluence, concurrence, concourse, concentration; *approach*, advance, confrontation, collision course; *union*, meeting, congress, assembly, congregation; *focus*, centre, pivot, hub.
adj. *convergent*, centripetal, confluent, advancing, oncoming.
vb. *converge*, close in, approach, draw near; *come together*, assemble, congregate, concentrate, gather, cluster; *focus*, centre, home in, zero in.

260 DIVERGENCE
See also **252** (deviation).
n. *divergence*, difference, deviation, contradiction, contrariety; *radiation*, branching, ramification, bifurcation;

crossroads, fork, intersection, parting of the ways.
adj. *divergent*, radial, centrifugal; *branching*, forked, splayed, spread-eagled.
vb. *diverge*, radiate, fan out, diffuse, go one's separate ways; *branch*, ramify, fork, splay, spreadeagle.

261 ARRIVAL

n. *arrival*, advent, approach, coming, onset, advance; *entrance*, appearance, emergence, debut; *attainment*, accession, achievement, fulfilment; *landing*, disembarkation, landfall, touchdown; *destination*, goal, journey's end, terminus; *reception*, welcome, greeting, handshake, hospitality. **adj.** *arriving*, incoming, immigrant; *approaching*, impending, imminent, oncoming, advancing; *attainable*, approachable, accessible, get-at-able (*colloq.*); *welcoming*, inviting, hospitable. **vb.** *arrive*, reach, approach, draw up, gain, attain, get to, end up in, fetch up in; *land*, dismount, alight, set foot in, touch down, disembark, dock, moor; *appear*, turn up, show up, roll up (*colloq.*), drop in (*colloq.*), blow in (*colloq.*), make an entrance; *receive*, greet, welcome, kill the fatted calf.

262 DEPARTURE

n. *departure*, going, leaving, setting out; *embarkation*, takeoff, liftoff, blastoff; *emigration*, exodus, evacuation, exit, walkout; *flight*, retreat, escape, getaway, decampment, elopement, moonlight flit; *parting*, farewell, leavetaking, separation, send-off; *goodbye*, adieu, parting shot, valediction, obituary; *point of departure*, starting point, outset, springboard, jumping-off point.
adj. *departing*, farewell, valedictory; *outgoing*, outward bound, emigratory.
vb. *depart*, leave, quit, turn one's back on, vote with one's feet; *move out*, emigrate, pull out, evacuate, strike camp; *set out*, embark, set sail, take off, get under way; *escape*, flee, decamp, elope, abscond, bolt; *retire*, withdraw, retreat, bow out, sign off; *separate*, bid farewell, part company, take one's leave; *be off*, make tracks, up sticks, clear off (*colloq.*), push off (*colloq.*), slope off (*colloq.*), buzz off (*colloq.*); *rush off*, make oneself scarce (*colloq.*), beetle off (*colloq.*), vamoose (*colloq.*), skedaddle (*colloq.*), scarper (*colloq.*), beat it (*colloq.*), scram (*colloq.*).

263 ENTRY

See also **265** (admittance); **269** (insertion).
n. *entry*, admission, access, ingress; *influx*, incursion, invasion, intrusion; *inroad*, encroachment, penetration, infiltration; *enrolment*, enlistment, initiation, induction; *intake*, immigration, importation, open door, free trade; *entrance*, way in, door, gate, mouth, orifice, inlet; *entrant*, incomer, immigrant, settler, colonist; *intruder*, invader, gatecrasher, housebreaker, burglar.
adj. *incoming*, immigrant, imported; *invasive*, incursive, intrusive.
vb. *enter*, gain admittance, set foot in, cross the threshold, drop in (*colloq.*), pop in (*colloq.*); *enrol*, enlist, inscribe, induct, sign on, initiate, admit; *invade*, irrupt, trespass, encroach, gatecrash, break and enter, burgle; *penetrate*, infiltrate, permeate, percolate; *rush in*, breeze in, barge in, butt in, muscle in (*colloq.*).

264 EXIT

See also **266** (expulsion); **270** (extraction).
n. *exit*, egress, way out, fire escape; *outflow*, effluent, issue, outpouring, discharge, leak; *emanation*, emission, seepage, exudation, secretion; *eruption*, outburst, breakout, sortie, sally; *emigration*, exodus, walkout, departure; *vent*, outlet, outfall, spout, drain, overflow; *escape route*, loophole, back door, let-out.
adj. *outgoing*, emigrant, departing; *leaky*, oozy, weeping, escaping.
vb. *exit*, emerge, issue, debouch; *erupt*, sally forth, break out, escape; *emigrate*, evacuate, clear out, bale out;

emit, discharge, exude, secrete; *ooze*, weep, bleed, leak, seep; *pour*, overflow, gush, jet, spout.

265 ADMITTANCE

See also **263** (entry).

n. *admittance*, access, admission, reception, acceptance; *receptivity*, openness, accessibility, open arms, hospitality; *acceptability*, admissibility, suitability; *introduction*, initiation, rite of passage, baptism, enrolment, registration; *intake*, incorporation, absorption, ingestion.

adj. *admissible*, acceptable, suitable; *receptive*, open, accessible, welcoming, inviting, hospitable; *initiatory*, introductory, baptismal; *absorbent*, assimilative, digestive.

vb. *admit*, receive, take in, shelter; *welcome*, embrace, adopt, accept; *register*, enrol, enlist, inscribe, include; *initiate*, baptize, introduce, show the ropes (*colloq.*); *incorporate*, assimilate, internalize, absorb, digest.

266 EXPULSION

See also **161** (displacement); **258** (repulsion); **264** (exit); **270** (extraction).

n. *expulsion*, ejection, eviction, dislodgment; *dismissal*, discharge, rustication, excommunication, disbarment, the sack, the push (*colloq.*), the boot (*colloq.*), the bum's rush (*colloq.*); *deportation*, extradition, banishment, exile, repatriation, relegation; *removal*, elimination, evacuation, clearance, voidance; *ejector*, bouncer (*colloq.*), chucker-out, heavy (*colloq.*); *nausea*, vomiting, sickness, expectoration.

adj. *expulsive*, expellant, emetic, purgative, cathartic, excretory.

vb. *expel*, eject, evict, dislodge, turn out; *dismiss*, discharge, excommunicate, rusticate, send down, strike off, disbar, sack, fire; *throw out*, turf out, chuck out, drum out, root out, eradicate; *deport*, repatriate, extradite, banish, exile, relegate; *eliminate*, evacuate, void, empty, clear, purge; *emit*, disgorge, spit out, vomit, spew, retch, throw up (*colloq.*), puke (*colloq.*).

267 INGESTION

n. *ingestion*, digestion, consumption, imbibing, mastication, chewing; *nutrition*, sustenance, alimentation, dietetics, domestic science, home economics; *gluttony*, gourmandise, overeating, voraciousness; *gastronomy*, epicureanism, haute cuisine, cookery; *eater*, diner, gourmet, gastronome, connoisseur, epicure, trencherman; *provisions*, provender, foodstuffs, victuals, comestibles, rations; *food*, staff of life, ambrosia, tuck (*colloq.*), grub (*colloq.*), nosh (*colloq.*), chow (*colloq.*); *convenience food*, fast food, junk food, TV dinner, health food, wholefood; *meal*, fare, snack, titbit, morsel, bite, brunch, elevenses, tiffin; *feast*, banquet, junket, beanfeast (*colloq.*), bunfight (*colloq.*), beano (*colloq.*), slap-up meal (*colloq.*), blowout (*colloq.*); *dish*, hors d'oeuvres, starter, appetizer, entree, pudding, sweet, dessert, afters (*colloq.*); *beverage*, infusion, cocktail, brew, tipple, poison (*colloq.*); *alcohol*, spirits, hard stuff (*colloq.*), booze (*colloq.*), hooch (*colloq.*), vino (*colloq.*), plonk (*colloq.*), rotgut (*colloq.*); *drink*, draught, sip, gulp, swig (*colloq.*), dram, snort (*colloq.*), nightcap.

adj. *edible*, digestible, nutritious, drinkable, potable; *appetizing*, wholesome, tasty, palatable, moreish (*colloq.*), scrumptious (*colloq.*); *culinary*, dietary, gastronomic, cordon bleu, underdone, oven-ready, rare; *carnivorous*, herbivorous, vegetarian, omnivorous, gluttonous.

vb. *ingest*, digest, chew, masticate, consume; *eat*, feed, feast, dine, sup, put away (*colloq.*), tuck into (*colloq.*), polish off; *devour*, bolt, wolf, gorge, gobble, guzzle; *taste*, nibble, peck at, sample; *drink*, imbibe, sip, quaff, down, gulp, knock back, tipple, booze (*colloq.*); *cook*, prepare, fix (*US*), boil, simmer, poach, stew, braise, grill, roast, bake, serve up, dish up.

268 EXCRETION

n. *excretion*, secretion, exudation, discharge, expulsion, ejection, expectoration; *defecation*, evacuation, voidance;

bowel movement, constipation, dysentery, diarrhoea, runs (*colloq.*), trots (*colloq.*), Delhi belly (*colloq.*); *urination*, micturation, call of nature, incontinence, weak bladder, enuresis; *excreta*, excrement, faeces, stool, turd (*vulg.*), dung, muck, shit (*vulg.*), crap (*vulg.*), manure, droppings, guano; *urine*, water, pee (*colloq.*), piddle (*colloq.*), wee (*colloq.*), piss (*vulg.*); *saliva*, mucus, catarrh, spittle, sweat, perspiration.
adj. *excretory*, diuretic, laxative, purgative, cathartic; *faecal*, urinary, excremental, shitty (*vulg.*), crappy (*vulg.*); *continent*, toilet-trained, housetrained.
vb. *excrete*, evacuate, discharge, expel, eject, pass; *defecate*, foul, soil, be caught short, shit (*vulg.*), crap (*vulg.*); *urinate*, relieve oneself, micturate, spend a penny (*colloq.*), pee (*colloq.*), piddle (*colloq.*), widdle (*colloq.*), piss (*vulg.*); *secrete*, exude, perspire, sweat; *expectorate*, spit, salivate, drool, slobber, hawk.

269 INSERTION

See also **207** (interface); **263** (entry).
n. *insertion*, introduction, interjection, interpolation, intercalation; *injection*, inoculation, vaccination, transfusion, implantation, impregnation; *insert*, inlay, inclusion, filling, stuffing.
adj. *inserted*, included, interjectional, parenthetical, by-the-by (*colloq.*).
vb. *insert*, introduce, interject, interpolate, intercalate, include, drag in (*colloq.*); *infuse*, instil, imbue, impregnate; *inject*, inoculate, vaccinate, transfuse, implant; *inset*, inlay, embed, encapsulate, sheathe, encase; *immerse*, plunge, bury, steep, souse, dunk.

270 EXTRACTION

See also **264** (exit); **266** (expulsion).
n. *extraction*, removal, withdrawal, excision; *displacement*, dislodgment, excavation, extrication, suction, aspiration; *extortion*, squeezing, expression, wringing out; *distillation*, separation, refinement, condensation; *extract*, essence, distillate, sublimate; *extractor*, excavator, dredger, digger, scoop; *forceps*, tweezers, pliers, wrench, syringe, siphon, pump.
vb. *extract*, remove, withdraw, excise; *displace*, dislodge, extricate, winkle out; *extort*, elicit, squeeze, force, express, wring out, get blood out of a stone; *excavate*, mine, quarry, dredge, dig up; *pump*, suck, vacuum, aspirate, siphon off, tap, milk; *distil*, refine, separate, condense, cream off.

271 PASSAGE

See also **240** (way).
n. *passage*, movement, transit, crossing, journey, voyage; *access*, right of way, thoroughfare, traffic, circulation; *entrance*, infiltration, penetration, permeation, percolation, osmosis; *crossing point*, bridge, ford, zebra crossing, frontier post, checkpoint; *passport*, visa, safe-conduct, laissez-passer, ID.
vb. *pass*, proceed, move through, circulate, journey, voyage, patrol, do the rounds (*colloq.*); *cross*, traverse, negotiate, transit, overfly; *enter*, penetrate, permeate, osmose, percolate, infiltrate; *bridge*, ford, straddle, span.

272 OVERSTEPPING

See also **575** (excess); **820** (lack of entitlement).
n. *overstepping*, trespass, entrenchment, encroachment, intrusion, invasion; *transgression*, violation, infringement, infraction, breach; *excessiveness*, exaggeration, overestimation, hyperbole.
adj. *excessive*, undue, unwarranted, uncalled-for; *intrusive*, invasive, encroaching; *exaggerated*, overdone, far-fetched, over the top (*colloq.*).
vb. *overstep*, go too far, overshoot, overrun, overreach; *trespass*, entrench, encroach, impinge, intrude, invade, poach, muscle in on; *transgress*, violate, infringe, usurp, breach; *exceed*, surpass, outdo, excel, transcend; *exaggerate*, overdo, overrate, overestimate.

273 SHORTFALL

See also **574** (insufficiency).
n. *shortfall*, insufficiency, short measure, shortage, deficit; *lack*, want, dearth, scarcity, famine; *shortcoming*,

inadequacy, imperfection, defect, deficiency; *incompleteness*, half measures, perfunctoriness, cursoriness.
adj. *short*, deficient, minus, wanting, lacking, missing; *defective*, imperfect, inadequate, substandard; *incomplete*, half-done, perfunctory, cursory.
vb. *fall short*, miss, lack, want, need, require, cry out for; *fail*, fall through, disappoint, leave something to be desired, not come up to scratch (*colloq.*).

274 ASCENT

See also **184** (height); **276** (raising).
n. *ascent*, climb, rise, ascension, levitation, liftoff, takeoff; *upturn*, upsurge, upswing, increase, spiral, quantum jump; *jump*, leap, vault, spring, bound, hop, skip, high jump; *mountaineering*, climbing, alpinism; *gradient*, incline, slope, hill, ramp; *stairway*, ladder, steps, escalator, lift; *climber*, mountaineer, alpinist, steeplejack, high-jumper, hurdler, steeplechaser.
adj. *ascending*, upward, uphill; *rising*, mounting, buoyant, bullish.
vb. *ascend*, climb, rise, mount, soar, spiral; *take off*, lift off, rocket, surge; *jump*, spring, leap, vault, bound, hop, skip; *scale*, top, breast, clear, hurdle, shin up.
adv. *upwards*, in the ascendant, on the up and up (*colloq.*).

275 DESCENT

See also **185** (lowness); **277** (lowering).
n. *descent*, plunge, dive, swoop, slide, dip, landing, touchdown; *decline*, fall, drop, slump, downturn, tumble, spill; *collapse*, failure, comedown, demotion, downfall, débâcle; *avalanche*, subsidence, cascade, waterfall, chute, precipice; *caving*, potholing, mining, speleology; *diver*, submariner, caver, potholer, speleologist.
adj. *descending*, downward, downhill; *falling*, sinking, declining, bearish; *sagging*, droopy, depressed, down in the mouth (*colloq.*).
vb. *descend*, plunge, dive, swoop, settle, subside, dip; *land*, touch down, alight, dismount, get down; *decline*, fall, drop, plummet, crash, slump, tumble, spill; *cascade*, overflow, pour, shower; *sink*, submerge, drown, go under; *trip*, stumble, lurch, totter, stagger, collapse, nosedive, bite the dust (*colloq.*).

276 RAISING

See also **184** (height); **274** (ascent).
n. *raising*, erection, elevation, uplift, levitation; *boost*, promotion, upgrading, leg-up (*colloq.*); *height*, eminence, loftiness, sublimity; *raising agent*, leaven, yeast, fermentation; *lifter*, crane, derrick, lever, hoist, jack, lift, escalator, dumb waiter, springboard.
adj. *raised*, erect, upstanding, vertical; *elevated*, sky-high, lofty, eminent, high-flown, sublime.
vb. *raise*, erect, build, put up; *lift*, uplift, hoist, lever, jack up, prop up, shoulder; *send up*, lob, loft, flight; *elevate*, enhance, exalt, put on a pedestal; *arise*, rear, jump up, be upstanding, jump to one's feet.

277 LOWERING

See also **185** (lowness); **186** (depth); **275** (descent).
n. *lowering*, depression, deflation, levelling, demolition; *debasement*, demotion, downgrading, humilation; *overthrow*, overturn, upset, toppling; *crouch*, hunch, duck, bend, stoop, bob, curtsy, genuflection.
adj. *lowered*, depressed, deflated, flattened; *lowering*, humiliating, debasing, demeaning.
vb. *lower*, depress, deflate, squash; *flatten*, level, raze, demolish, fell, ground; *bring down*, topple, floor, overthrow, undermine, torpedo, scuttle; *demote*, downgrade, debase, humble, cashier; *crouch*, stoop, bend, hunch, duck, curtsy, bob, kneel, genuflect.

278 ORBITAL MOTION

See also **279** (rotation).
n. *orbital motion*, rotation, revolution, circulation, circumnavigation; *orbit*, lap, circuit, tour, round trip; *circle*, wheel, spiral, gyre; *satellite*, moon,

planet, spaceship, sputnik; *ring road*, orbital, bypass.
adj. *orbital*, roundabout, circular, circuitous.
vb. *orbit*, turn, lap, circuit, revolve, rotate, spiral, wheel; *ring*, circle, circumscribe, gird, loop.

279 ROTATION

See also **223** (circularity); **224** (convolution); **278** (orbital motion).
n. *rotation*, revolution, orbit, cycle; *turn*, roll, spiral, gyration, twirl, corkscrew, pirouette, whirl; *swirl*, eddy, whirlpool, vortex, maelstrom, whirlwind, cyclone, tornado; *roundabout*, merry-go-round, carousel, turntable; *rotor*, propeller, screw, turbine, windmill; *spindle*, axle, lathe, shaft, pivot.
adj. *rotary*, gyratory, spinning, revolving, cyclic.
vb. *rotate*, revolve, orbit, circuit; *turn*, spiral, corkscrew, pirouette, twirl, whirl, swirl; *roll*, wind, reel, spin; *pivot*, swivel, hinge.

280 OSCILLATION

See also **119** (regularity); **281** (agitation).
n. *oscillation*, fluctuation, alternation, reciprocation, undulation, ebb and flow; *vibration*, flutter, tremor, agitation, shake, quiver; *palpitation*, pulse, throb, beat; *pendulum*, bob, oscillator, vibrator, metronome; *rocker*, seesaw, cradle, shuttle, swing; *vacillation*, wavering, indecision, hesitation.
adj. *oscillating*, fluctuating, alternating, reciprocating; *vibrating*, pulsating, throbbing, rhythmical; *vacillating*, hesitant, indecisive, irresolute.
vb. *oscillate*, swing, alternate, fluctuate, reciprocate, undulate; *vibrate*, quake, tremble, quiver, flutter, palpitate; *pulsate*, throb, beat, pound, tick; *rock*, sway, seesaw, zigzag, teeter, reel, stagger; *vacillate*, waver, hesitate, falter.
adv. *to and fro*, from side to side, back and forth.

281 AGITATION

See also **280** (oscillation).
n. *agitation*, vibration, jerkiness, unsteadiness, tremulousness, palpitation; *tumult*, turmoil, commotion, confusion, stir, bustle; *fuss*, bother, song and dance (*colloq.*), fluster, flap (*colloq.*), tizz (*colloq.*); *turbulence*, ferment, effervescence, seethe, swell, squall; *disturbance*, perturbation, nervousness, jumpiness, edginess, butterflies (*colloq.*), jitters (*colloq.*), heebie-jeebies (*colloq.*), collywobbles (*colloq.*); *restlessness*, feverishness, itchiness, fidgetiness, twitchiness; *tremor*, quiver, shiver, shudder, judder, throb; *convulsion*, paroxysm, spasm, fit, throes, seizure; *jolt*, jar, shock, start, jerk, twitch.
adj. *agitated*, troubled, disturbed, confused, shaken, shocked; *restless*, feverish, fidgety, itchy, twitchy; *nervous*, anxious, perturbed, jumpy, edgy, jittery (*colloq.*), nervy, like a cat on hot bricks (*colloq.*); *flustered*, fussing, fluttery, hot and bothered (*colloq.*); *convulsive*, jerky, fitful, spasmodic, paroxysmic; *turbulent*, stormy, tempestuous, seething, effervescent; *tremulous*, shaky, wobbly, quaking, quivering, trembling.
vb. *be agitated*, boil, churn, heave, seethe, ferment, bubble, effervesce; *convulse*, writhe, squirm, thresh, toss and turn; *vibrate*, quake, throb, palpitate, tremble, flutter, quiver, shiver, shake; *shudder*, judder, jolt, jar, jerk, twitch; *disturb*, rumple, ruffle, muddy, stir, whisk, beat; *flicker*, twinkle, sparkle, glimmer, gutter, sputter.

282 MATERIAL WORLD

See also **3** (reality).
n. *material world*, matter, mass, substance, stuff, body, material, fabric; *embodiment*, incarnation, materialization, solid object, flesh and blood; *concreteness*, corporeality, solidity, tangibility, palpability; *thing*, object, article, gadget, thingamajig (*colloq.*); *ingredient*, element, constituent, component, particle, atom, molecule.
adj. *material*, real, physical, actual, objective; *concrete*, solid, palpable, tangible, sensible; *corporeal*, bodily, fleshly, carnal, worldly, materialistic.

vb. *materialize*, embody, body forth, objectify, incarnate.

283 NONMATERIAL WORLD

See also **396** (intellect).

n. *nonmaterial world*, unreality, insubstantiality, incorporeality, intangibility, impalpability; *spirituality*, otherworldliness, idealism, transcendence, unearthliness; *occultism*, spiritualism, mysticism, paranormal, extra-sensory perception; *psyche*, mind, intellect, soul, spirit, subjectivity, self.

adj. *immaterial*, incorporeal, intangible, ideal, abstract, nonphysical, insubstantial; *disembodied*, shadowy, ghostly, ethereal, unreal; *spiritual*, otherworldly, transcendent, unearthly; *occult*, mystical, psychic, spiritualist.

vb. *dematerialize*, disembody, disintegrate; *idealize*, intellectualize, conceptualize, spiritualize.

284 UNIVERSE

n. *universe*, world, creation, cosmos, macrocosm, space, outer space, galaxy; *earth*, globe, sphere, planet earth, spaceship earth; *heavens*, firmament, empyrean, primum mobile, ether, atmosphere; *celestial body*, planet, star, constellation, comet, meteor, asteroid, satellite, quasar, pulsar, black hole, nova, nebula, falling/shooting star, meteorite; *zodiac*, horoscope, house, ascendant, astrological sign; *sun*, solar system, eye of heaven, daystar, midnight sun; *astronomy*, stargazing, astrophysics, cosmology, cosmography; *earth sciences*, geology, geography, orography, hydrography, cartography.

adj. *universal*, cosmic, macrocosmic, galactic, interstellar; *earthly*, global, worldly, terrestrial, earthbound, tellurian; *celestial*, heavenly, extraterrestrial, ethereal, empyreal, alien; *starry*, stellar, astral, sidereal; *solar*, lunar, nebular, planetary, asteroidal; *astronomical*, cosmological, astrophysical; *geological*, geographical, orographic, cartographic.

285 HEAVINESS

See also **287** (density).

n. *heaviness*, gravity, weight, bulk; *mass*, force, pressure, density; *load*, burden, encumbrance, cargo, freight, ballast, counterweight, counterpoise; *heavy object*, paperweight, sandbag, millstone, lead, stone, plumb, sinker, lead balloon, ton of bricks (*colloq.*); *weighing machine*, scales, balance, weighbridge; *weightiness*, ponderousness, gravitas, seriousness.

adj. *heavy*, bulky, massive, solid, dense; *overweight*, top-heavy, laden, charged; *burdensome*, onerous, cumbersome, unwieldy, clumsy, awkward; *leaden*, oppressive, crushing, insupportable; *weighty*, ponderous, grave, serious, heavyweight (*colloq.*).

vb. *weigh*, balance, outweigh, tip the scales; *pressurize*, lean on, weigh on, encumber, oppress; *burden*, saddle, weigh down, load, overload, weight.

286 LIGHTNESS

See also **306** (air).

n. *lightness*, weightlessness, buoyancy, portability; *airiness*, thinness, transparency, translucence, flimsiness, delicacy, fluffiness; *light object*, cork, float, bob, buoy, inflatable; *air*, foam, froth, bubble, fluff, gauze, gossamer, feather, thistledown; *raising agent*, leaven, yeast, aerator, lightener, thinner.

adj. *light*, buoyant, weightless, portable; *lightweight*, underweight, flyweight, bantamweight; *insubstantial*, flimsy, floaty, feathery, fluffy, frothy; *thin*, gauzy, diaphanous, transparent, translucent.

vb. *be light*, levitate, rise, surface, float, hover, waft, soar; *lighten*, leaven, thin, reduce; *unload*, disencumber, throw overboard, jettison, discard.

287 DENSITY

See also **182** (thickness); **285** (heaviness).

n. *density*, solidity, compactness, concreteness; *mass*, bulk, body, thickness, consistency; *consolidation*, concretization, crystallization, solidification, coagulation; *condensation*, concentration, congestion, saturation; *impenetrability*, impermeability, imperviousness,

incompressibility; *solid*, block, lump, nugget, clot, cake.
adj. *dense*, solid, compact, concrete, hard, stiff; *bulky*, massive, substantial, thick; *clotted*, curdled, caked, matted; *condensed*, packed, serried, concentrated, thick on the ground; *impenetrable*, impermeable, nonporous, incompressible.
vb. *become dense*, crystallize, harden, stiffen, set, freeze; *solidify*, congeal, coagulate, thicken, clot, curdle, cake; *make dense*, pack, compress, condense, concentrate; *crowd*, mass, throng, accumulate.

288 SPARSENESS

See also **183** (thinness).
n. *sparseness*, thinness, fineness, wispiness; *rarefaction*, dilution, attenuation, adulteration; *rarity*, infrequency, smattering, sprinkling.
adj. *sparse*, thin, fine, wispy, straggly; *rare*, infrequent, intermittent; *scattered*, dotted, strung out, thin on the ground.
vb. *rarefy*, thin, reduce, adulterate, attenuate, dilute; *scatter*, dot, sprinkle, strew.

289 HARDNESS

See also **294** (toughness).
n. *hardness*, toughness, resilience, resistance, firmness, resoluteness; *stiffness*, rigidity, inflexibility, intractability; *petrification*, ossification, fossilization, sclerosis; *hard-heartedness*, unyieldingness, harshness, callousness, insensitivity; *hard substance*, stone, grit, flint, rock, granite, cement, brick, marble, diamond, steel, iron; *hardwood*, oak, teak, board, bone, horn, shell, armour, carapace.
adj. *hard*, tough, resilient, resistant, firm, unyielding; *rock-hard*, unbreakable, shatterproof, adamantine; *stiff*, rigid, inflexible, intractable, unbending; *stony*, gritty, flinty, steely, rocky; *bony*, horny, woody, crystalline, glassy, vitreous; *hardened*, reinforced, tempered, case-hardened, vitrified; *hard-hearted*, callous, harsh, insensitive.
vb. *harden*, toughen, reinforce, temper; *stiffen*, starch, freeze, solidify; *petrify*, ossify, fossilize, crystallize, vitrify.

290 SOFTNESS

See also **293** (elasticity); **317** (semiliquid).
n. *softness*, suppleness, springiness, elasticity, give; *pliancy*, flexibility, plasticity, malleability, tractability, ductility; *flaccidity*, limpness, flabbiness, floppiness, slackness, sponginess, doughiness; *tenderness*, gentleness, mildness, mellowness; *pulp*, mud, clay, dough, putty, butter, wax; *down*, velvet, cushion, pillow, feather bed, padding, wadding.
adj. *soft*, yielding, springy, supple, elastic; *pliant*, flexible, plastic, malleable, tractable, ductile; *flaccid*, limp, flabby, floppy, slack; *spongy*, doughy, soggy, pulpy, mushy; *downy*, velvety, cushiony, feathery; *tender*, gentle, mellow, mild.
vb. *soften*, tenderize, mash, pulp, squash, dissolve, melt; *yield*, give, bend, flex; *relax*, ease, sag, flop, slacken; *cushion*, pillow, pad, buffer; *mellow*, relent, temper, sweeten.

291 ROUGHNESS

See also **301** (friction).
n. *roughness*, asperity, harshness, coarseness, crudity; *hairiness*, shagginess, scaliness, scratchiness; *ruggedness*, cragginess, unevenness, jaggedness, knobbliness, brokenness; *rough object*, file, sandpaper, emery board; *bristle*, prickle, tweed, sackcloth, scab, scale, encrustation.
adj. *rough*, harsh, grating, coarse, grainy, gravelly; *uneven*, rutted, pitted, ridged, bumpy, knobbly; *crude*, unfinished, roughcast, rough-hewn; *rugged*, gnarled, craggy, jagged, serrated; *hairy*, hirsute, shaggy, unshaven, dishevelled, unkempt, tousled; *bristly*, scratchy, prickly, tweedy, scaly, scabby, encrusted.
vb. *roughen*, coarsen, harshen; *ridge*, corrugate, serrate, notch; *ruffle*, ripple, dishevel, tousle; *bristle*, prickle, chafe, grate, abrade.

292 SMOOTHNESS

See also **191** (horizontality); **302** (lubrication).

n. *smoothness*, evenness, flatness, levelness; *continuity*, unbrokenness, uninterruptedness; *softness*, silkiness, shininess, glassiness; *slipperiness*, slitheriness, oiliness, greasiness; *suavity*, urbanity, polish, sleekness; *finish*, glaze, lustre, sheen, gloss, shine, varnish; *velvet*, satin, glass, marble, mirror, millpond; *roller*, iron, sandpaper, file.

adj. *smooth*, even, flat, level; *continuous*, uninterrupted, unbroken, smooth-running, streamlined; *soft*, silky, satiny, velvety, clean-shaven; *shiny*, glassy, glossy, lustrous; *sleek*, suave, urbane, polished; *slippery*, slithery, greasy, oily.

vb. *smooth*, even, plane, level, flatten, roll, iron out; *shine*, gloss, polish, buff, glaze, finish; *oil*, grease, slick, lubricate; *slide*, slip, glide, skate, coast.

293 ELASTICITY

See also **290** (softness).

n. *elasticity*, pliability, flexibility, ductility; *expandibility*, extensibility, stretch, give; *spring*, bounce, recoil; *rubberiness*, resilience, buoyancy; *elastic band*, indiarubber, spring, coil.

adj. *elastic*, pliable, flexible, ductile, tensile; *expandable*, extensible, stretchy; *springy*, bouncy, rubbery, resilient, buoyant.

vb. *be elastic*, stretch, expand, give, extend, flex; *bounce*, recoil, spring, rebound.

294 TOUGHNESS

See also **289** (hardness).

n. *toughness*, hardness, strength, durability; *resistance*, tenacity, resilience, stamina; *leatheriness*, chewiness, rubberiness, elasticity; *fibre*, sinew, cartilage, gristle.

adj. *tough*, hard, strong, unbreakable; *durable*, hard-wearing, long-lasting, imperishable; *resistant*, tenacious, unflagging, indefatigable; *leathery*, chewy, rubbery, gristly, cartilaginous; *fibrous*, woody, stringy, sinewy.

vb. *be tough*, wear, outlast, survive, stay the course; *toughen*, harden, strengthen, temper.

295 BRITTLENESS

n. *brittleness*, breakability, frangibility, fragility; *frailty*, flimsiness, delicateness, fineness; *sharpness*, crispness, crunchiness, flakiness, crumbliness, friability; *brittle substance*, glass, eggshell, matchwood, thin ice.

adj. *brittle*, breakable, frangible, fragile; *frail*, flimsy, insubstantial, delicate, papery, wafer-thin; *sharp*, crisp, crunchy, crispy, flaky, crumbly, friable, powdery.

vb. *be brittle*, snap, crack, split, chip, break; *fragment*, fracture, splinter, disintegrate, flake, crumble.

296 SHARPNESS

See also **229** (notch).

n. *sharpness*, pointedness, jaggedness, prickliness, serratedness; *incisiveness*, acuteness, keenness, acuity, mordancy, trenchancy; *sting*, bite, prick, cut, stab; *needle*, pin, nail, barb, point, prong, spur, spike, tine; *spine*, prickle, thorn, tooth, fang, tusk, incisor; *cutting edge*, blade, razor, knife, scissors, shears, secateurs, scalpel, cleaver, guillotine; *sharpener*, file, whetstone, grindstone, carborundum, steel.

adj. *sharp*, pointed, jagged, toothed, serrated, notched; *prickly*, spiny, thorny, barbed, spiky; *razor-sharp*, cutting, keen, trenchant, biting, acute, incisive, trenchant, mordant.

vb. *sharpen*, grind, hone, file, whet, edge; *point*, taper, barb, spur; *prick*, sting, bite, pierce, stab, lance.

297 BLUNTNESS

n. *bluntness*, smoothness, roundedness, stubbiness, flatness; *dullness*, obtuseness, insensitivity; *outspokenness*, frankness, directness, straightforwardness.

adj. *blunt*, smooth, rounded, stubby, snub, flat; *dull*, obtuse, insensitive; *outspoken*, frank, direct, straightforward.

vb. *blunt*, dull, bate, take the edge off, flatten, round.

298 STRUCTURE

See also **216** (form).

n. *structure*, organization, arrangement, pattern, plan; *form*, shape, architecture, make-up, composition, constitution; *framework*, fabric, bodywork, skeleton, anatomy, infrastructure; *construction*, building, edifice, erection, superstructure, elevation.

adj. *structural*, organizational, constructional, architectural, tectonic; *organic*, anatomical, formal, skeletal.

vb. *structure*, organize, plan, pattern, arrange; *shape*, form, construct, build, erect, raise, assemble.

299 TEXTURE

See also **197** (interweaving).

n. *texture*, structure, tissue, web, network; *finish*, surface, feel, touch, sensation; *weave*, grain, warp, weft, woof, nap, pile; *fibre*, filament, yarn, thread, string, tow; *textile*, cloth, material, fabric.

adj. *textural*, textile, woven, spun; *rough*, ribbed, hairy, woolly, tweedy, fibrous, coarse-grained, granulated; *smooth*, finespun, delicate, silky, satiny, cottony.

300 POWDERINESS

n. *powderiness*, dustiness, frosting, efflorescence, bloom; *crumbliness*, flakiness, friability, looseness; *pulverization*, grinding, pounding, erosion, abrasion, attrition; *powder*, dust, sand, pollen, flour, grit, talc, ash, chalk; *granule*, grain, speck, mote, particle, flake, crumb; *grinder*, crusher, mill, hammer, pestle.

adj. *powdery*, dusty, sandy, floury, farinaceous, chalky; *crumbly*, flaky, friable, loose; *ground*, granulated, pulverized, gritty, grainy.

vb. *powder*, dust, sand, flour, sprinkle; *pulverize*, pound, grind, bruise, crush, mill; *crumble*, flake, granulate, chip.

301 FRICTION

See also **291** (roughness).

n. *friction*, drag, resistance, roughness; *rubbing*, abrasion, erosion, corrosion, attrition; *rub*, scrape, graze, polish, elbow grease; *irritation*, grating, tension, irascibility, prickliness; *rubber*, eraser, scraper, sander, emery paper, pumice, sandpaper, file, rasp.

adj. *frictional*, abrasive, irritant; *rough*, rasping, grating.

vb. *rub*, smooth, burnish, scour, polish, buff; *abrade*, scrape, scuff, bark, graze, scratch; *erode*, corrode, wear away, fray; *grind*, rasp, file, plane; *irritate*, chafe, grate, fret, rub up the wrong way.

302 LUBRICATION

See also **292** (smoothness); **319** (oiliness).

n. *lubrication*, nonfriction, smoothness, slipperiness; *oiliness*, greasiness, unctuousness, waxiness; *lubricant*, oil, wax, grease, tallow; *ointment*, salve, balm, cream, lotion, emollient.

adj. *lubricated*, oiled, smooth-running; *oily*, greasy, waxy, slippery.

vb. *lubricate*, oil, grease, wax; *smear*, anoint, cream, daub; *ease*, smooth over, oil the wheels, pour oil on troubled waters.

303 FLUID

n. *fluid*, liquid, gas, condensation, water; *juice*, sap, liquor, gravy, stock, whey; *body fluid*, blood, rheum, pus, saliva, lymph, mucus, plasma, serum; *solution*, infusion, suspension, decoction; *fluidity*, liquidity, juiciness, wateriness, runniness; *liquefaction*, liquidization, dissolution, deliquescence, thaw; *flow*, flux, haemorrhage, suppuration, secretion; *solvent*, liquidizer, blender, liquefier.

adj. *fluid*, liquid, gaseous, soluble; *watery*, runny, juicy, sappy, moist; *molten*, liquefied, dissolved, deliquescent; *rheumy*, weeping, bleeding, pussy, suppurating.

vb. *make fluid*, liquefy, dissolve, deliquesce, condense; *liquidize*, melt, thaw, defrost, render, melt down, smelt; *flow*, run, pour, stream, well up.

304 GAS

n. *gas*, air, ether, atmosphere, exhalation; *smoke*, steam, fumes, reek, cloud, miasma; *vaporization*, distillation, evaporation, atomization; *vaporizer*, atomizer, spray, aerosol, condenser; *gaseousness*, volatility, effervescence, fermentation, fizziness.

adj. *gaseous*, vaporous, volatile, airy, atmospheric, ethereal; *smoky*, steamy, cloudy, misty; *gassy*, fizzy, effervescent, carbonated, sparkling, bubbly.

vb. *gasify*, evaporate, vaporize, volatilize, atomize, distil; *aerate*, fumigate, oxygenate, carbonate; *smoke*, steam, fume, reek, exhale, give off.

305 WATER

See also **308** (moisture).

n. *water*, H_2O, fluid, liquid, wet; *moisture*, steam, vapour, condensation; *sweat*, perspiration, exudate, tears, saliva, spittle; *wateriness*, wetness, dampness, runniness; *dilution*, solution, saturation, hydration; *rainwater*, sea water, fresh water, meltwater, ice, salt water, brine; *shower*, douche, bath, dip, wash, hydrotherapy, irrigation; *irrigator*, well, oasis, hydrant, tap, standpipe, sprinkler.

adj. *watery*, fluid, aqueous, liquid, aquatic; *dilute*, hydrated, saturated, watered down; *wet*, soaked, drenched, streaming, dripping, wringing, sopping, waterlogged, awash.

vb. *water*, moisten, sprinkle, irrigate, hydrate; *water down*, dilute, thin, adulterate, dissolve; *wet*, soak, souse, douse, steep, immerse, wash, bathe, rinse, sluice, hose down; *drench*, flood, inundate, saturate, waterlog, deluge, swamp.

306 AIR

See also **286** (lightness); **316** (wind).

n. *air*, gas, ether, atmosphere, oxygen, ozone; *wind*, breeze, blast, gust; *open air*, open, fresh air, great outdoors; *ventilation*, air-conditioning, airing, exposure; *airiness*, lightness, buoyancy, weightlessness; *air bubble*, froth, foam, suds, lather, spray, spindrift, mousse, soufflé, meringue; *aeration*, fermentation, leavening, yeast, raising agent.

adj. *airy*, gaseous, ethereal, weightless; *aerial*, buoyant, inflated, lighter-than-air, pneumatic; *bubbly*, foamy, frothy, aerated, yeasty, fizzy; *breezy*, windy, blowy, fresh, gusty; *open-air*, outdoor, al fresco.

vb. *aerate*, inflate, oxygenate, air, ventilate, expose; *blow*, blast, gust, puff, huff; *bubble*, froth, foam, sparkle, fizz, gurgle, simmer, ferment.

307 WEATHER

See also **308** (moisture); **316** (wind).

n. *weather*, elements, weather conditions, climate; *high*, anticyclone, blue skies, heatwave, scorcher (*colloq.*), dry spell, drought; *low*, depression, cyclone, precipitation; *rainfall*, rain, drizzle, shower, downpour, cloudburst, deluge, monsoon, rainy season, rains; *fog*, mist, haze, smog, pea-souper (*colloq.*); *snow*, sleet, hail, snowfall, snowstorm, blizzard, black ice, frost, cold snap; *storm*, high wind, squall, gale, hurricane, typhoon, whirlwind, tornado; *cloud*, cloud cover, cumulus, cirrus, nimbus, stratus, mackerel sky; *barometer*, glass, weather vane, weathercock, windsock, weather forecast, weatherman, meteorologist, climatologist.

adj. *meteorological*, climatic, atmospheric, barometric; *windy*, stormy, squally, blustery; *rainy*, showery, drizzly, snowy, freezing, wintry; *cloudy*, overcast, misty, hazy, foggy; *fair*, clear, sunny, bright, hot, baking, scorching, boiling, sweltering.

vb. *rain*, pour, sleet, hail, snow, freeze; *clear up*, change, brighten up, shine, break through; *blow*, gust, blow up, brew.

308 MOISTURE

See also **305** (water); **307** (weather).

n. *moisture*, dampness, humidity, dankness, wetness; *vapour*, steam, condensation, rising damp, seepage; *perspiration*, sweat, dew, drizzle, spray, precipitation, mist; *mud*, wet, slime, mire, ooze, sludge; *marsh*, swamp,

bog, quicksand, quagmire, wetlands, fen, floodplain.
adj. *moist*, humid, damp, dank, clammy, muggy, close; *wet*, tear-stained, dewy, sweaty, misty, drizzly; *marshy*, swampy, boggy, oozy, soggy, squelchy, muddy, sodden, sludgy, waterlogged, splashy, slushy.
vb. *moisten*, dampen, humidify; *sprinkle*, spatter, spray, dabble, splash, slosh (*colloq.*); *be moist*, perspire, sweat, ooze, leak, seep, trickle, dribble.

309 DRYNESS

n. *dryness*, aridity, parchedness, thirst, drought; *dehydration*, drainage, evaporation, desiccation; *desert*, sand dune, dustbowl, wasteland, Sahara; *dryer*, absorbent, blotter, sponge, mop, towel, wringer, spin-dryer, tumble-dryer.
adj. *dry*, bone-dry, parched, thirsty; *desert*, arid, rainless, sandy, dusty, barren; *dehydrated*, desiccated, sun-dried, baked; *waterproof*, dampproof, rainproof, showerproof, watertight; *dried-up*, withered, shrivelled, sere.
vb. *dry*, freeze-dry, drain, dehydrate, evaporate, desiccate; *absorb*, blot, mop up, wipe, sponge, towel; *dry up*, parch, wither, shrivel, bake, toast; *drip-dry*, spin-dry, tumble-dry, wring.

310 OCEAN

See also **314** (running water).
n. *ocean*, sea, briny, the deep, the blue, drink (*colloq.*); *high seas*, open sea, seven seas, main, waters; *seaboard*, coastline, littoral, inshore waters; *channel*, sound, strait, fiord, sea loch, inlet; *estuary*, mouth, delta, firth; *gulf*, bay, bight, cove, lagoon, creek; *wave*, billow, breaker, roller, surf, white horses; *oceanography*, hydrography, hydrology.
adj. *oceanic*, pelagic, deep-sea, marine, maritime, underwater, submarine; *coastal*, littoral, inshore, offshore, seagoing, oceangoing.

311 LAND

See also **313** (plain); **321** (mineral).
n. *land*, ground, terrain, dry land, terra firma; *mainland*, continent, inland, interior, hinterland; *island*, isle, islet, atoll, reef, sandbank, archipelago; *peninsula*, promontory, headland, isthmus, spit; *plain*, desert, steppe, tundra, polder, highland, lowland; *shore*, strand, beach, seaside, riverbank, floodplain; *earth*, soil, topsoil, alluvium, clay, loam, gravel; *rock*, stone, boulder, pebble, scree; *crag*, outcrop, cliff, escarpment; *limestone*, sandstone, granite, shale, schist, chalk.
adj. *terrestrial*, mainland, inland, continental, overland; *coastal*, onshore, riparian, riverine; *rocky*, stony, pebbly, gritty, gravelly, sandy; *clayey*, alluvial, loamy, chalky, flinty, slaty; *insular*, peninsular, sea-girt, marooned, high and dry, cast away.

312 LAKE

n. *lake*, loch, lough, lagoon, inland sea, sea loch, fiord; *creek*, basin, mudflat, wash, fen, marsh; *pool*, pond, tarn, mere, millpond, reservoir, dam; *waterhole*, oasis, puddle, wallow, well.

313 PLAIN

See also **311** (land).
n. *plain*, expanse, open country, downs, wold, champaign, plateau, tableland; *lowland*, flats, valley, basin, delta; *desert*, tundra, heath, moorland; *grassland*, prairie, steppe, savannah, pampas, veld; *pasture*, field, meadow, lea, park, grounds, green belt, greensward, common.

314 RUNNING WATER

See also **310** (ocean); **315** (channel).
n. *running water*, flow, tide, bore, current, undertow; *river*, waterway, watercourse, canal; *stream*, tributary, feeder, rivulet, brook, burn, beck, rill, runnel; *torrent*, freshet, rapids, white water; *waterfall*, cataract, cascade, falls, weir, Niagara; *flood*, spate, flash flood, tidal wave, tsunami; *spring*, fountain, jet, geyser, waterspout; *wash*, backwash, wake, eddy, swirl, millrace, whirlpool.
adj. *running*, flowing, tidal, fluvial; *choppy*, broken, rough, gurgling, babbling; *smooth*, calm, glassy, meandering, sluggish.

vb. *run*, flow, pour, stream, course, race, rush; *tumble*, surge, roll, dash, swirl, eddy; *gush*, spout, squirt, well up, bubble up; *splash*, lap, swash, wash, slosh (*colloq.*), plash; *trickle*, dribble, ooze, leak, seep. *flow gently*, murmur, babble, gurgle, meander, wind, glide, slide; *flood*, cascade, overflow, spill, inundate, deluge.

315 CHANNEL

See also **240** (way); **314** (running water).

n. *channel*, conduit, course, canal, waterway; *ditch*, trench, moat, riverbed, gutter, pipeline, aqueduct; *lock*, sluice, floodgate, watergate, weir, barrier; *drain*, gully, overflow, culvert, outfall, waterspout, sewer, downpipe, drainpipe.

316 WIND

See also **306** (air); **307** (weather).

n. *wind*, air, draught, downdraught, current, thermal; *blast*, headwind, crosswind, airstream, slipstream, jetstream, tailwind; *trade wind*, sirocco, chinook, föhn, mistral, harmattan; *breeze*, zephyr, whiff, waft, puff, breath; *squall*, flurry, storm, tempest, hurricane, typhoon, whirlwind, tornado; *bellows*, windbag, air pipe, airway, lung, gill, nostril, blowhole; *respiration*, breathing, inhalation, exhalation, expiration, flatulence, belch, burp (*colloq.*), hiccup, fart (*vulg.*); *pant*, gasp, sigh, sniff, wheeze, cough, sneeze, asthma.

adj. *windy*, airy, draughty, exposed, windswept; *breezy*, blowy, gusty, squally, blustery, stormy; *panting*, out of breath, snuffly, wheezy, chesty, asthmatic.

vb. *blow*, waft, sigh, sough, stir; *blast*, gust, buffet, bluster, blow up, freshen, storm, rage; *air*, fan, ventilate, air-condition; *breathe*, inhale, exhale, expire; *pant*, gasp, puff, wheeze, sniff, snuffle, snort; *belch*, burp (*colloq.*), hiccup, break wind, fart (*vulg.*).

317 SEMILIQUID

See also **182** (thickness); **290** (softness).

n. *semiliquid*, semifluid, emulsion, paste, colloid; *soup*, stew, gruel, porridge, slops; *mud*, slush, ooze, slime, silt, sludge, lava; *pulp*, puree, pap, mush, stodge, curd, batter; *pulpiness*, sponginess, squelchiness, sogginess, squashiness, runniness; *juiciness*, succulence, sappiness, overripeness.

adj. *semiliquid*, semifluid, runny, watery; *juicy*, sappy, succulent, overripe; *thick*, clotted, curdled, coagulated; *pulpy*, soupy, mushy, squashy, spongy, squelchy, soggy, sloppy, sludgy.

vb. *pulp*, puree, mash, liquidize, stew; *thicken*, curdle, clot, congeal, emulsify.

318 VISCOSITY

n. *viscosity*, viscidity, stickiness, clamminess, glutinousness, adhesiveness, tackiness; *adhesive*, glue, gum, resin, paste, size, birdlime, tar; *mucus*, phlegm, albumen, pus, matter; *glaze*, gelatine, syrup, honey, treacle, jelly, slime, goo (*colloq.*), gunge (*colloq.*).

adj. *viscous*, viscid, sticky, tacky, clammy; *adhesive*, gluey, gummy, resinous, tarry; *slimy*, mucous, syrupy, treacly, gooey (*colloq.*), gungy (*colloq.*).

319 OILINESS

See also **302** (lubrication).

n. *oiliness*, unctuousness, greasiness, fattiness, soapiness; *oil*, lubricant, petroleum, paraffin, kerosene; *fat*, grease, soap, tallow, lanolin, blubber, suet, lard, dripping, butter, cream; *ointment*, unguent, salve, liniment, embrocation, pomade, brilliantine.

adj. *oily*, unctuous, oleaginous, slippery, lubricated; *fatty*, soapy, greasy, adipose, pinguid, blubbery, waxy, buttery, creamy.

vb. *oil*, lubricate, grease, wax, soap; *smear*, spread, anoint, baste, butter, cream.

320 ORGANISM

See also **322** (life).

n. *organism*, microorganism, bacterium, virus, germ; *cell*, protoplasm, enzyme, protein, gene, chromosome, DNA; *animal*, plant, flora, fauna, creature, being; *life sciences*, biology, biochemistry, ecology, botany, zoology; *evolution*, development, natural selection, Darwinism, genetics, biotechnology, genetic engineering.

adj. *organic*, bacterial, viral, microscopic; *cellular*, single-celled, chromosomal, genetic; *biological*, ecological, zoological, biochemical, botanical.

321 MINERAL

See also **311** (land).

n. *mineral*, rock, ore, gemstone, metal, precious metal, alloy; *petrification*, fossil, fossil fuel, coal, lignite; *deposit*, vein, stratum, layer, coal measures; *quartz*, topaz, beryl, corundum, feldspar, basalt, obsidian; *mineralogy*, geology, metallurgy.

adj. *mineral*, inorganic, inanimate; *fossilized*, crystalline, glassy, hard, metallic; *mineralogical*, geological, metallurgical.

322 LIFE

See also **1** (existence); **152** (fertility); **320** (organism).

n. *life*, living, being, animation, growth, vital force; *creation*, propagation, birth, nativity, procreation; *existence*, lifetime, one's born days, life history, life cycle, longevity; *soul*, spirit, heart, lifeblood, breath, wind; *creature*, being, mortal, individual, human, organism; *mortality*, way of all flesh, human condition, man's estate, life expectancy, quality of life; *resuscitation*, survival, artificial respiration, kiss of life, lifesaver, life-support system; *vitality*, vigour, vivaciousness, liveliness, verve, energy.

adj. *living*, live, alive and kicking, breathing, quick, viable; *vital*, lively, animated, vivacious, spirited, vigorous; *human*, mortal, finite, ephemeral; *existing*, surviving, long-lived.

vb. *live*, exist, breathe, draw breath; *survive*, outlive, be spared, keep body and soul together, have nine lives, be in the land of the living; *be born*, hatch, come into the world, arrive, see the light of day; *revitalize*, revive, resuscitate, breathe new life into, give a new lease of life; *animate*, enliven, liven up, invigorate, energize.

323 DEATH

See also **2** (nonexistence); **62** (end); **324** (killing); **325** (burial).

n. *death*, mortality, fatality, casualty, losses, death toll; *extinction*, decease, departure, exit, demise, release; *natural death*, accidental death, brain death, stillbirth, miscarriage, abortion; *unnatural death*, murder, foul play, suicide, mercy killing, euthanasia; *deathbed*, death knell, dying day, last hour, dying breath, death rattle, death throes, last words, last rites, last will and testament; *afterlife*, eternity, other side, next world, heaven, hell, happy hunting grounds (*colloq.*), underworld, Hades, Valhalla; *the dead*, ancestors, forefathers, spirits, shades; *death notice*, death certificate, obituary, post mortem, autopsy, inquest; *bereavement*, loss, mourning, widowhood, orphanage.

adj. *dying*, moribund, half-dead, not long for this world, done for, slipping away, in extremis; *dead*, deceased, departed, stone dead, dead and gone, dead as a doornail, extinct, defunct, kaput (*colloq.*); *lifeless*, inert, inanimate, stillborn; *deathly*, fatal, mortal, lethal, deadly; *surviving*, bereaved, widowed, orphaned; *late*, lamented, sainted, posthumous.

vb. *die*, perish, expire, pass over/away, fall asleep, give up the ghost, depart this life, croak (*colloq.*), snuff it (*colloq.*), peg out (*colloq.*), pop one's clogs (*colloq.*), kick the bucket (*colloq.*), push up daisies (*colloq.*); *die out*, wither, fade, go west, go the way of all flesh, go for a burton (*colloq.*); *be dying*, have one foot in the grave (*colloq.*), be on one's last legs (*colloq.*), be at death's door, be a goner (*colloq.*); *drop dead*, die in harness, fall, lay down one's life, be slain.

324 KILLING

See also **150** (destruction); **323** (death).

n. *killing*, destruction, bloodshed, bloodletting, bloodsports, cull; *murder*, homicide, manslaughter, suicide, self-slaughter, hara kiri, felo de se; *execution*, capital punishment, decapitation, hanging, the rope, the gallows, electrocution, garrotte, the stake, auto-da-fe; *assassination*, liquidation, extermination, annihilation, genocide; *carnage*, massacre, bloodbath, butchery, slaughter, holocaust, pogrom, night of the long knives; *killer*, murderer, butcher, assassin, hitman (*colloq.*), executioner, hangman, lynch mob, cutthroat, axeman; *corpse*, body, remains, cadaver, stiff (*colloq.*), mummy, carcass.

adj. *deadly*, destructive, lethal, fatal, toxic, malignant; *murderous*, homicidal, bloodthirsty, psychopathic; *suicidal*, self-destructive, kamikaze; *cadaverous*, corpselike, deathly.

vb. *kill*, slaughter, destroy, put down, butcher, massacre, exterminate, liquidate, annihilate, decimate; *murder*, assassinate, do in (*colloq.*), lynch, bump off (*colloq.*), rub out (*colloq.*); *slay*, dispatch, bring down, shoot, stab, run through, string up, strangle, smother, suffocate; *execute*, hang, decapitate, behead, guillotine, electrocute, gas, garrotte; *kill oneself*, take one's life, commit suicide, do oneself in (*colloq.*).

325 BURIAL

See also **323** (death).

n. *burial*, interment, entombment, cremation; *funeral*, obsequies, last rites, lying-in-state, mourning, wake, cortege; *cemetery*, graveyard, crematorium, churchyard, Calvary, golgotha, catacombs; *grave*, tomb, shrine, sepulchre, mausoleum, vault, crypt; *funeral parlour*, mortuary, morgue; *coffin*, sarcophagus, catafalque, bier, pyre, hearse, pall, shroud, winding sheet; *requiem*, dead march, dirge, lament, elegy, epitaph, obituary.

adj. *buried*, interred, dead and buried, six feet under; *funeral*, funerary, mortuary, elegiac, sepulchral.

vb. *bury*, inter, lay to rest, entomb, enshrine, cremate, embalm, mummify; *mourn*, lament, regret, keen, pay one's last respects; *disinter*, exhume, dig up, unearth.

326 ANIMAL

See also **328** (agriculture).

n. *animal*, beast, dumb animal, creature, wildlife, fauna; *quadruped*, biped, invertebrate, vertebrate, omnivore, herbivore, carnivore; *mammal*, amphibian, reptile, marsupial, ruminant, rodent, crustacean, fish; *domestic animal*, livestock, pet, vermin; *wild animal*, game, endangered species; *bird*, fowl, poultry, bird of prey, hen, cock, chick, fledgling; *cow*, cattle, heifer, bull, calf, bullock, ox, milch cow; *horse*, mare, stallion, foal, filly, colt, pony, nag (*colloq.*), hack, hunter, gee-gee (*colloq.*); *sheep*, ewe, ram, lamb, wether; *pig*, swine, sow, boar, piglet, hog; *dog*, bitch, pup, mongrel, cur, hound, tyke (*colloq.*), mutt (*colloq.*), pooch (*colloq.*), bow-wow (*colloq.*), man's best friend; *cat*, tabby, tom, kitten, pussy (*colloq.*), moggy (*colloq.*), big cat, wildcat; *insect*, larva, grub, pupa, imago, creepy-crawly (*colloq.*); *zoo*, menagerie, safari park, game reserve, aviary, apiary, aquarium.

adj. *animal*, bestial, brutish, feral, wild; *domestic*, tame, house-trained, broken in; *mammalian*, reptilian, amphibian, bovine, equine, ovine, porcine, canine, feline; *omnivorous*, herbivorous, carnivorous, insectivorous.

327 PLANT

See also **329** (horticulture).

n. *plant*, flower, vegetable, weed, herb, shrub, bush, tree, sapling; *plant life*, flora, vegetation, biomass, greenery, verdure; *wood*, forest, jungle, greenwood, woodland, heath, scrub, undergrowth; *copse*, thicket, spinney, plantation, orchard, grove; *branch*, bough, twig, shoot, leaf, foliation, stem, stalk, trunk, bole; *root*, tuber, bulb, corm, rhizome, seed; *flowerhead*, bloom, flo-

ret, bud, petal, inflorescence, raceme, panicle; *grass*, pasture, sward, lawn, turf, sod, divot.
adj. *vegetal*, floral, botanical, horticultural; *evergreen*, deciduous, coniferous, hardy, annual, biennial, perennial; *verdant*, leafy, grassy, herbaceous, lush, overgrown, rank; *woody*, sylvan, arboreal, bosky, scrubby, shrubby, jungly.
vb. *plant*, afforest, cultivate, garden, botanize; *grow*, germinate, sprout, shoot, take root, strike.

328 AGRICULTURE

See also **326** (animal).
n. *agriculture*, farming, stockbreeding, factory farming, animal husbandry, agronomy, veterinary science; *farm*, ranch, hatchery, stud farm, battery, piggery; *stable*, byre, cowshed, sheepfold, pen, coop, sty, hutch; *farmstead*, collective farm, kolkhoz, kibbutz, estate, smallholding, croft; *farmer*, agronomist, tenant farmer, peasant, yeoman, smallholder, crofter, shepherd, farmhand, serf; *crop*, produce, yield, harvest, glut.
adj. *agricultural*, agronomic, agrarian; *arable*, pastoral, bucolic, rustic, rural; *purebred*, thoroughbred, crossbred, hybrid, domesticated.
vb. *farm*, ranch, raise, rear, breed, grow; *dig*, till, plough, cultivate, rotivate, drain, reclaim; *irrigate*, fertilize, manure, rake, harrow, hoe; *sow*, broadcast, drill, mow, reap, harvest, gather in, thresh, winnow.

329 HORTICULTURE

See also **327** (plant).
n. *horticulture*, arboriculture, viticulture, market gardening, landscape gardening, topiary; *nursery*, garden centre, orchard, plantation, vineyard; *garden*, allotment, kitchen garden, cabbage patch, herbaceous border, shrubbery, rockery; *park*, arboretum, botanical gardens, herbarium; *hothouse*, greenhouse, glasshouse, orangery, conservatory, cold frame, cloche; *gardener*, horticulturalist, nurseryman, seedsman, market gardener, planter.
adj. *horticultural*, floral, herbal, herbaceous, alpine, hardy, exotic.
vb. *cultivate*, garden, grow, propagate, force, graft; *sow*, plant out, harden off, prick out, transplant; *fertilize*, manure, topdress, mulch.

330 HUMANKIND

n. *humankind*, humanity, human race, mankind, womankind; *human being*, creature, homo sapiens, android, humanoid; *hominid*, apeman, Neanderthal man, troglodyte, savage, barbarian; *person*, individual, mortal, soul, body, personage, figure; *fellow*, character (*colloq.*), customer (*colloq.*), card (*colloq.*), cove (*colloq.*); *family*, house, tribe, clan, sept, line, dynasty; *community*, public, society, masses, tribalism, herd instinct; *population*, populace, people, nation, civilization, culture.
adj. *human*, humanoid, anthropoid, hominoid; *anthropological*, sociological, cultural, ethnological; *interpersonal*, familial, tribal, social, communal, collective, public, civic.

331 NATIONALITY

n. *nationality*, ethnicity, nationhood, statehood; *nationalism*, patriotism, chauvinism, jingoism, racism, antisemitism; *nation*, state, commonwealth, republic, people, ethnic minority; *native*, Brit (*colloq.*), Pommie (*colloq.*), Sassenach (*derog.*), Jock (*colloq.*), Paddy (*colloq.*), Mick (*derog.*), Taffy (*colloq.*); *foreigner*, outsider, immigrant, wop (*derog.*), wog (*derog.*), black, coloured, darkie (*derog.*), coon (*derog.*), nigger (*derog.*), Asian, Pakki (*derog.*); *Latin*, Continental, Frog (*derog.*), Kraut (*derog.*), Eyetie (*derog.*), dago (*derog.*), Polack (*derog.*), Yid (*derog.*), Argie (*derog.*), Yank (*colloq.*).
adj. *national*, racial, ethnic; *nationalistic*, patriotic, jingoistic, chauvinist, racist.

332 MALE

n. *male*, he, man, boy, youth, lad, stripling, Adam, spear side; *masculinity*, manliness, virility, manhood, mannishness, patriarchy, machismo; *gen-*

tleman, lord, master, sir, mister; *fellow*, chap (*colloq.*), bloke (*colloq.*), geezer (*colloq.*), codger (*colloq.*), buffer (*colloq.*), guy (*colloq.*), mate (*colloq.*), buddy (*colloq.*), squire (*colloq.*), governor (*colloq.*); *he-man*, beefcake (*colloq.*), stud, male chauvinist, MCP, misogynist; *bachelor*, homosexual, boyfriend, escort, husband, bridegroom, family man, househusband, paterfamilias, widower, patriarch; *male animal*, cock, drake, gander, capon, jack, buck, stag, dog, stallion, bull, ox, colt, boar, ram, billy, tom.
adj. *male*, masculine, manly, virile, mannish, butch (*colloq.*), macho; *unmanly*, womanish, effeminate, androgynous.

333 FEMALE

n. *female*, she, woman, Eve, fair sex, weaker sex, distaff side; *femininity*, womanhood, womanliness, motherliness; *feminism*, sisterhood, Women's Movement, Women's Lib/Liberation, matriarchy, misandry, lesbianism; *girl*, lass, wench, damsel, maiden, colleen, nymphet, dolly bird; *bachelor girl*, career woman, spinster, old maid, girlfriend, bride, wife, homemaker, housewife, widow, dowager; *lady*, madam, ma'am, dame (*colloq.*), chick (*colloq.*), doll (*colloq.*), bird (*colloq.*), skirt (*colloq.*), crumpet (*colloq.*), cheesecake (*colloq.*); *female animal*, hen, goose, duck, bitch, vixen, heifer, mare, ewe, filly, nanny, doe, hind.
adj. *female*, feminine, gynaecological, obstetric; *womanly*, ladylike, matronly, maternal; *feminist*, liberated, sisterly, lesbian.

334 SENSATION

See also **729** (feeling); **730** (sensitivity).
n. *sensation*, feeling, sensitivity, sensibility; *hypersensitivity*, allergy, soreness, tenderness, rawness; *sense*, feel, touch, perception, awareness; *response*, reaction, reflex, impression; *physicality*, sensuality, body language.
adj. *sentient*, sensible, sensory; *sensitive*, responsive, perceptive, aware, impressionable, susceptible; *sore*, tender, raw, exposed, hypersensitive, allergic; *physical*, bodily, sensuous.
vb. *sense*, feel, see, hear, touch, taste, smell; *respond*, react, register, realize; *awaken*, arouse, sensitize, impress.

335 INSENSIBILITY

See also **731** (insensitivity).
n. *insensibility*, deadness, numbness, dullness, anaesthesia; *insensitivity*, indifference, callousness; *inertness*, paralysis, catalepsy, catatonia, stupor; *unconsciousness*, coma, trance, faint, swoon, blackout; *anaesthetic*, analgesic, painkiller, sedative, tranquillizer, narcotic.
adj. *insensible*, numb, dead, dull, anaesthetized; *inert*, paralysed, catatonic, cataleptic; *unconscious*, comatose, stupefied, punch-drunk; *insensitive*, unfeeling, callous, thick-skinned.
adj. *desensitize*, deaden, numb, dull, anaesthetize; *drug*, dope, put under, knock out, sedate, tranquillize; *lose consciousness*, swoon, faint, pass out, black out.

336 PHYSICAL PLEASURE

See also **734** (joy).
n. *physical pleasure*, enjoyment, satisfaction, gratification; *pleasure-seeking*, sensuality, debauchery, dissipation, hedonism; *excitement*, arousal, kick (*colloq.*), thrill, turn-on (*colloq.*), orgasm, ecstasy; *ease*, comfort, contentment, wellbeing, euphoria, creature comforts, bed of roses, lap of luxury.
adj. *pleasurable*, agreeable, enjoyable, gratifying, titillating; *comfortable*, easy, luxurious, cosseted, pampered, cushy (*colloq.*); *sensual*, voluptuous, rakish, debauched, hedonistic, dissipated.
vb. *enjoy*, relish, savour, revel, wallow, bask, luxuriate; *excite*, titillate, arouse, thrill, turn on (*colloq.*); *thrive*, prosper, be in clover, live the life of Riley (*colloq.*).

337 PHYSICAL PAIN

See also **735** (sorrow).
n. *physical pain*, illness, suffering, dis-

tress, discomfort; *hurt*, injury, wound, trauma, shock, anguish, agony; *wound*, cut, gash, abrasion, bruise, contusion, sprain, fracture; *pang*, twinge, stab, sting, cramp, stitch, gripe, colic.
adj. *painful*, sore, aching, tender, raw, uncomfortable; *distressing*, agonizing, excruciating, exquisite; *injured*, wounded, hurt, traumatized; *stinging*, itchy, smarting, throbbing, stabbing, shooting.
vb. *cause pain*, distress, agonize, torment; *injure*, wound, cut, gash, lacerate, sprain, wrench; *hurt*, ache, smart, burn, gnaw, sting, throb; *wince*, flinch, writhe, squirm.

338 TOUCH

n. *touch*, feel, contact, friction, pressure, squeeze; *handling*, manipulation, massage, reflexology; *light touch*, graze, brush, stroke, caress, pat, flick, tap; *sensation*, itch, scratch, tickle, tingle, prickly heat, pins and needles.
adj. *tactile*, touchable, tangible, palpable; *deft*, delicate, gentle, nimble, feathery; *firm*, tight, clumsy, heavy-handed, rough.
vb. *touch*, feel, finger, sense, fumble, grope, scrabble; *brush*, graze, skim, stroke, caress, pat, dab, paw, nuzzle; *handle*, manhandle, manipulate, massage, knead.

339 HEAT

n. *heat*, warmth, tepidness, lukewarmness, white heat, incandescence; *fever*, flush, glow, sweat, lather; *temperature*, boiling point, flashpoint, overheating, fever pitch; *fire*, flame, spark, blaze, bonfire, conflagration, inferno, holocaust; *heating*, burning, cauterization, combustion, ignition, incineration, cremation; *burn*, scald, scorch, brand, sunburn; *heater*, radiator, solar panel, space heater, geyser, boiler; *cooker*, stove, oven, hob, range, grate, fireplace, hearth; *furnace*, kiln, forge, incinerator, oasthouse.
adj. *hot*, red-hot, white-hot, incandescent, glowing; *feverish*, boiling, sweltering, baking, scorching, torrid, tropical, sultry; *warm*, tepid, lukewarm, temperate, mild, balmy; *burning*, fiery, flaming, ablaze, aflame, afire, alight; *flammable*, inflammable, combustible, incendiary.
vb. *heat*, warm, boil, bake, scald, toast, scorch, fry, roast, grill; *burn*, kindle, flame, catch fire, flare up, blaze.

340 COLD

n. *cold*, coolness, chilliness, coldness, frostiness, iciness; *chill*, hypothermia, chilblains, frostbite; *wintriness*, snow, sleet, hail, frost, ice, black ice, hoarfrost, rime, icicle; *refrigeration*, glaciation, congelation, freezing; *refrigerator*, cooler, icebox, fridge, deep-freeze, freezer, cold storage.
adj. *cold*, stone-cold, ice-cold, frigid, chilly, parky (*colloq.*); *wintry*, icy, frosty, arctic, Siberian; *keen*, biting, piercing, raw, bitter, cutting; *frozen*, glacé, frappé, on the rocks.
vb. *chill*, cool, freeze, refrigerate, deep-freeze; *frost*, ice, ice up, sleet, hail, snow.

341 FUEL

n. *fuel*, kindling, firewood, tinder, faggot, log; *fossil fuel*, peat, coal, charcoal, coke, lignite, anthracite, petroleum, kerosene, paraffin, natural gas; *nuclear power*, solar energy, electricity, hydroelectricity; *lighter*, flint, firelighter, taper, spill, match, fuse, touchpaper.
adj. *combustible*, flammable, inflammable, incendiary, explosive.
vb. *fuel*, feed, stoke, power, add fuel to the flames; *light*, kindle, fire, catch.

342 TASTE

n. *taste*, flavour, savour, tang, bite, aftertaste, body, richness, tastiness; *sharpness*, sweetness, bitterness, saltiness, brackishness, piquancy, tanginess, spiciness; *appetite*, gusto, relish, zest, heartiness; *palate*, tongue, tastebuds, sweet tooth; *delicacy*, titbit, ambrosia, nectar, caviar.
adj. *tasty*, savoury, wholesome, flavourful, flavoursome; *sharp*, tangy, piquant, bitter, salty, peppery, spicy, sweet; *rich*, full-bodied, mellow, fruity.

delicious, tempting, appetizing, mouthwatering, delectable, palatable, moreish (*colloq.*), scrumptious (*colloq.*), yummy (*colloq.*).
vb. *taste*, sample, try, sip, lick; *savour*, relish, smack one's lips, come back for more, enjoy; *taste of*, savour of, smack of.

343 TASTELESSNESS

n. *tastelessness*, insipidness, blandness, staleness, flatness; *unwholesomeness*, unsavouriness, rankness, rottenness, rancidness; *gruel*, porridge, bread and water, slops, sawdust, dishwater, junk food.
adj. *tasteless*, flavourless, insipid, bland, thin, watery, wishy-washy, diluted; *unappetizing*, unwholesome, unpalatable, stale, overcooked, underdone, inedible; *unsavoury*, bitter, sour, rancid, rank, off, rotten, sickly, cloying, yukky (*colloq.*).
vb. *pall*, cloy, sicken, nauseate, repel, disgust, turn one's stomach.

344 PIQUANCY

n. *piquancy*, pungency, tastiness, bite, zest, tang, nip; *savouriness*, sharpness, tartness, sourness, saltiness, pepperiness, spiciness; *seasoning*, condiment, flavouring, additive, aromatic, herb, relish, spice, dressing; *ginger*, pepper, chilli, cayenne, curry, marinade.
adj. *piquant*, pungent, tasty, hot, tangy; *savoury*, salty, peppery, gingery, spicy, bitter, sour, tart, bittersweet, sweet-and-sour.
vb. *flavour*, season, spice, curry, ginger up, marinade.

345 SWEETNESS

n. *sweetness*, sugariness, saccharinity, sickliness; *sweetener*, sugar, saccharin, honey, nectar, mead, syrup, treacle, molasses; *confectionery*, candy, fudge, bonbon, sweetmeat, fondant, icing, frosting.
adj. *sweet*, sugary, sticky, saccharin, sickly, cloying, syrupy, treacly; *sugared*, honeyed, candied, crystallized, iced, glacé, frosted.
vb. *sweeten*, sugar, sugar-coat, candy, crystallize, ice, frost.

346 SOURNESS

n. *sourness*, tartness, astringency, acidity, acerbity, bitterness, sharpness; *acid*, vinegar, lemon, bitters, gall, alum, wormwood, acid drop.
adj. *sour*, sourish, unsweetened, tart, acid, astringent, acerbic, bitter; *green*, unripe, vinegary, sharp, unsweetened, dry.
vb. *sour*, turn, curdle, acidulate, set one's teeth on edge.

347 ODOUR

See also **349** (fragrance); **350** (stench).
n. *odour*, smell, aroma, scent, fragrance, bouquet, perfume; *stink*, stench, pong (*colloq.*), pollution; *exhalation*, breath, whiff, fumes, reek, vapour, effluvium; *redolence*, headiness, pungency, acridness.
adj. *odorous*, odoriferous, redolent, smelly; *scented*, perfumed, fragrant, heady, sweet-smelling; *foul*, stale, noxious, polluted, pungent, rank; *olfactory*, nasal.
vb. *smell*, exhale, give off, emit, stink, reek; *inhale*, sniff, nose, breathe in.

348 ODOURLESSNESS

n. *odourlessness*, lack of smell, freshness, sweetness, fresh air, unpollutedness, smokeless zone; *deodorization*, purification, fumigation, ventilation; *deodorant*, fumigant, disinfectant, air freshener.
adj. *odourless*, unscented, unperfumed, scentless; *deodorized*, pure, fresh, unpolluted, sweet-smelling.
vb. *deodorize*, freshen, clean, purify, ventilate, air, fumigate.

349 FRAGRANCE

See also **347** (odour).
n. *fragrance*, sweet smell, scent, bouquet, odour, aroma; *perfume*, toilet water, eau de cologne, aftershave, pomade; *pomander*, pot pourri, joss stick, air freshener; *essential oil*, fixative, civet, musk, ambergris, attar;

balm, spice, incense, sandalwood, camphor, honeysuckle, lavender, rose.
adj. *fragrant*, odorous, aromatic, redolent; *sweet-smelling*, perfumed, musky, flowery, spicy, fruity.
vb. *scent*, perfume, spice, sweeten.

350 STENCH
See also **347** (odour).
n. *stench*, stink, pong (*colloq.*), niff (*colloq.*), fetor, bad breath, halitosis, B.O.; *foulness*, rankness, putrefaction, rancidness, staleness, mustiness, fustiness; *atmospheric pollution*, fumes, smog, reek, miasma, fug, frowst; *stinker*, stinkbomb, skunk, bad egg, ammonia, sulphur.
adj. *smelly*, stinking, fetid, foul, offensive, noxious, pongy (*colloq.*), niffy (*colloq.*); *high*, gamy, off, putrid, rancid, rank, pungent, foxy; *stale*, stuffy, fuggy, frowsty, polluted, acrid, smoky.
vb. *stink*, reek, fume, smell, pong (*colloq.*), hum (*colloq.*), stink to high heaven.

351 HEARING
See also **353** (sound).
n. *hearing*, audition, auscultation, acoustics; *audibility*, distinctness, loudness, earshot, hearing distance; *overhearing*, eavesdropping, bugging, wiretapping; *listener*, auditor, hearer, audience; *headphones*, stethoscope, earpiece, hearing aid.
adj. *aural*, audiovisual, auditory, acoustic; *audible*, loud, distinct, clear.
vb. *hear*, listen, catch, be all ears (*colloq.*), hearken, heed, lend an ear, prick up one's ears; *overhear*, eavesdrop, listen in on, bug, wire-tap.

352 DEAFNESS
n. *deafness*, hardness of hearing, tone-deafness, deaf-mutism; *inaudibility*, indistinctness, faintness, softness; *lip-reading*, sign language, deaf aid, ear trumpet.
adj. *deaf*, hard of hearing, deaf-mute, deaf and dumb, stone-deaf, deaf as a post; *inaudible*, indistinct, faint, muted; *tone-deaf*, tin-eared (*colloq.*), cloth-eared (*colloq.*); *deafening*, ear-splitting, earshattering.
vb. *deafen*, make one's ears ring; *go unheard*, fall on deaf ears, go unheeded; *not listen*, turn a deaf ear, ignore.

353 SOUND
See also **351** (hearing); **355** (loudness); **526** (voice).
n. *sound*, noise, utterance, speech-sound; *resonance*, reverberation, sonority, loudness; *sound effect*, soundtrack, sound wave, voiceover; *tone*, pitch, level, timbre, intonation, cadence, lilt; *audibility*, distinctness, clarity; *record-player*, gramophone, hi-fi, stereo, sound system, music centre; *acoustics*, dynamics, phonetics.
adj. *sounding*, sonic, acoustic, dynamic, radiophonic; *audio*, mono, stereophonic, binaural, quadraphonic; *audible*, distinct, loud, clear, noisy, sonorous.
vb. *sound*, resound, ring out, reverberate, carry; *utter*, emit, speak, vocalize, voice.

354 SILENCE
See also **527** (voicelessness).
n. *silence*, noiselessness, soundlessness, stillness, hush, lull, peace and quiet; *muteness*, voicelessness, speechlessness, taciturnity; *silencer*, gag, muzzle, blackout.
adj. *silent*, noiseless, soundless, soundproof, hushed, still, quiet, peaceful; *mute*, unspoken, voiceless, speechless, tongue-tied, lost for words, monosyllabic, taciturn.
vb. *silence*, still, hush, quieten, lull; *mute*, tone down, subdue, quell; *muffle*, gag, muzzle, drown out.

355 LOUDNESS
See also **353** (sound); **357** (sudden sound); **359** (resonance).
n. *loudness*, distinctness, clarity, audibility; *volume*, crescendo, decibels, sonority; *noise*, report, bang, roar, crash, boom, reverberation; *stridency*, shrillness, vociferousness, noisiness, clamourousness; *shout*, yell, bellow, guffaw, cry, shriek, scream, screech,

blare, bray, catcall, boo; *din*, row, racket, clamour, outcry, hullabaloo, hubbub, caterwauling; *amplifier*, loud pedal, megaphone, loudhailer, loudspeaker, microphone, public-address system; *siren*, alarm, klaxon, foghorn, gong, trumpet.
adj. *loud*, audible, distinct, clear; *noisy*, clamorous, lusty, strident, vociferous, stentorian, loud-mouthed; *resonant*, sonorous, ringing, plangent; *shrill*, high-pitched, piercing, earsplitting, deafening.
vb. *be loud*, reverberate, resound, peal, swell, ring out, clang, blare, crash, thunder; *shout*, yell, bellow, roar, guffaw, cry out, screech, scream, shriek; *be noisy*, clamour, deafen, raise Cain, raise the roof (*colloq.*), make the rafters ring.
adv. *loudly*, at the top of one's voice, fortissimo.

356 FAINTNESS
See also **360** (mutedness).
n. *faintness*, softness, lowness, mutedness, indistinctness, inaudibility; *low sound*, whisper, undertone, sigh, murmur, mutter, mumble, hum, moan, groan, squeak; *tinkle*, rustle, swish, whirr, purr, lap, pad, patter.
adj. *faint*, soft, low, muted, murmured, soft-spoken, indistinct, inaudible; *quiet*, hushed, subdued, muffled, distant, far-off.
vb. *be faint*, die away, fade, weaken; *whisper*, murmur, croon, mutter, moan, groan, sigh; *tinkle*, chirr, whirr, purr, lap, swish, rustle, sough.
adv. *faintly*, under one's breath, sotto voce, piano, out of earshot.

357 SUDDEN SOUND
See also **355** (loudness).
n. *sudden sound*, report, pistol shot, gunfire, backfire, explosion, sonic boom, thunderclap; *bang*, crash, crack, peal, blast, burst, volley, salvo; *knock*, rap, tap, clap, rat-at-tat; *shout*, yell, whoop, hoot, screech, scream, shriek.
vb. *bang*, crash, thunder, crack, burst out; *explode*, backfire, erupt, go off, ring out, peal; *cry out*, shout, scream, yelp, whoop, hoot.

358 REPEATED SOUND
n. *repeated sound*, reverberation, echo, roll, rumble; *rattle*, clatter, racket, chatter, babble, rhubarb, background noise; *drumming*, tattoo, thrumming, strumming, throbbing, pulse; *trill*, tremolo, vibrato, quaver; *buzz*, whirr, chirr, hum, drone.
vb. *roll*, rumble, grumble, reverberate, echo; *drum*, thrum, strum, beat, tick, throb; *trill*, vibrate, tremble, quaver; *rattle*, clatter, chatter, drone, hum, whirr.

359 RESONANCE
See also **355** (loudness).
n. *resonance*, reverberation, plangency, sonorousness, hollowness; *echo*, overtone, ring, ping, clang, twang, peal, chime; *tinkle*, clink, chink, clank, jangle, jingle; *bell*, gong, chimes, cymbals, tubular bells, glockenspiel, echo chamber.
adj. *resonant*, reverberant, plangent, sonorous, hollow, echoey, lingering, vibrant; *metallic*, tinkly, jingling, ringing, clanking.
vb. *resonate*, vibrate, carry, reverberate, echo; *peal*, chime, ring, ting, ping, twang, jingle, jangle; *clink*, clank, chink, tinkle.

360 MUTEDNESS
See also **356** (faintness).
n. *mutedness*, nonresonance, deadness, dullness, muffledness, indistinctness; *thud*, thump, thwack, clump, plonk, clonk, plop; *mute*, silencer, damper, soft pedal.
adj. *muted*, dead, dull, muffled, subdued, indistinct.
vb. *mute*, deaden, dull, soften; *subdue*, damp, stifle, muffle, tone down, lower; *thud*, thump, pound, clump, clonk, plonk, plop.

361 HISSING SOUND
adj. *hissing*, sibilant, fizzy, wheezy, splashy, sploshy.
vb. *hiss*, whisper, splash, swish, swash,

sigh, sough; *rustle*, rasp, whistle, wheeze; *buzz*, fizz, sizzle, spit, sputter.

362 HARSH SOUND

See also **366** (dissonance).

n. *harsh sound*, screech, squawk, croak, caw, skirl, shriek; *rasp*, cough, hawk, grate, scrape, scratch; *roughness*, hoarseness, huskiness, gruffness; *stridency*, shrillness, raucousness, braying; *discord*, dissonance, cacophony, jangle, clash.

adj. *harsh*, strident, shrill, raucous, brassy, tinny; *hoarse*, husky, gruff, throaty, growly, guttural; *rough*, rasping, grating, scratchy, rusty, creaky; *discordant*, jarring, cacophonous, dissonant, jangly, clashing.

vb. *shriek*, screech, squawk, croak, caw, bray, skirl, blare, clang; *scrape*, scratch, grate, rasp, saw, grind, creak; *jar*, clash, jangle, set one's teeth on edge.

363 HUMAN CRY

See also **355** (loudness).

n. *human cry*, shout, call, exclamation, ejaculation; *outcry*, clamour, raised voices, noise, din, hubbub; *yell*, yelp, whoop, hoot, halloo; *cheer*, hurrah, boo, catcall; *howl*, wail, roar, guffaw, bellow; *shriek*, scream, screech, squeal; *moan*, groan, grunt, whimper, gasp.

adj. *loud*, high-pitched, clamorous, noisy, vocal, vociferous, lusty, full-throated.

vb. *cry out*, call out, exclaim, ejaculate; *shout*, clamour, yell, bawl, holler (*colloq.*), howl, yowl, wail, caterwaul; *shriek*, screech, squeal, yelp; *chant*, chorus, cheer, whoop, boo, yodel; *roar*, rant, bellow, guffaw, hoot; *moan*, groan, whinge (*colloq.*), whimper, sob, gasp, grunt.

364 ANIMAL CRY

n. *animal cry*, call, birdcall, note, song.

vb. *cry*, call, caw, coo, quack, cluck, crow, cackle, honk, croak, gobble; *cheep*, peep, chirrup, tweet, whistle, warble, twitter, chatter; *squawk*, screech, squeal, scream; *bark*, yap, yelp, bay, bell, howl, whine; *grunt*, growl, snarl, roar; *neigh*, bray, whinny, whicker, snort, snicker; *miaow*, mew, purr, hiss, spit; *bleat*, baa, moo, low, bellow; *hum*, drone, buzz, chirr.

365 MELODY

See also **367** (music).

n. *melody*, harmony, euphony, concord, tonality, consonance; *melodiousness*, tunefulness, musicality, mellifluousness, sweetness; *tune*, air, song, strain, refrain, ditty; *pitch*, intonation, register, key.

adj. *melodic*, tuneful, musical, true, in tune; *melodious*, harmonious, euphonious, sweet, mellifluous, dulcet, silvery, bell-like; *catchy*, lilting, memorable, singable, hummable.

vb. *be melodious*, harmonize, blend, chime in, chorus.

366 DISSONANCE

See also **362** (harsh sound).

n. *dissonance*, discord, disharmony, tone-deafness, atonality; *harshness*, raucousness, tonelessness, monotony; *cacophony*, caterwauling, Babel, row, racket, din.

adj. *dissonant*, discordant, atonal, out-of-tune, off-key, tone-deaf, flat, sharp; *inharmonious*, untuneful, unmusical, toneless, monotonous, singsong; *cacophonous*, raucous, harsh, jarring, jangling, grating.

vb. *be dissonant*, jangle, jar, grate, clash.

367 MUSIC

See also **365** (melody); **368** (musician).

n. *music*, harmony, melody, music-making, musicianship; *classical music*, chamber music, light music, Muzak (*tdmk.*); *pop music*, rock, blues, soul, disco, country and western, reggae, folk, punk, new wave, jazz, swing, trad, bop, jazz-rock; *performance*, recital, concert, gig (*colloq.*), jam session, recording session; *tune*, theme, signature, tune, backing, incidental music; *score*, libretto, lyrics, songbook, sheet music; *piece*, composition, work, opus, arrangement, setting, orchestration,

improvisation; *song*, ballad, hymn, psalm, spiritual, aria, madrigal; *opera*, operetta, oratorio, chorale, mass, musical; *overture*, sonata, fugue, suite, concerto, symphony; *dance music*, jig, minuet, gavotte, mazurka, polka, waltz, foxtrot; *prelude*, intermezzo, impromptu, nocturne, scherzo, serenade, requiem, rondo.
adj. *musical*, tuneful, melodic, polyphonic, contrapuntal; *classical*, highbrow, straight, romantic, baroque; *popular*, lowbrow, middlebrow, bluesy, jazzy, hot (*colloq.*), cool (*colloq.*), funky (*colloq.*); *vocal*, operatic, choral, unaccompanied; *instrumental*, orchestral, symphonic, solo.

368 MUSICIAN
See also **367** (music).
n. *musician*, player, performer, soloist, accompanist, instrumentalist, artiste, virtuoso; *minstrel*, bard, troubadour, busker, one-man band; *singer*, vocalist, songster, chorister, prima donna, diva; *soprano*, mezzosoprano, contralto, treble, alto, countertenor, tenor, baritone, bass; *composer*, arranger, librettist, songwriter; *conductor*, maestro, leader, bandmaster, bandleader; *orchestra*, chamber orchestra, ensemble, group, band; *duo*, trio, quartet, quintet, sextet, octet.
vb. *play*, perform, execute, interpret, play by ear, sight-read, accompany; *sound*, pluck, bow, blow, beat, finger, tickle the ivories (*colloq.*); *sing*, vocalize, intone, carol, trill, chant, chorus; *arrange*, score, orchestrate, compose, set to music, transpose.

369 MUSICAL INSTRUMENT
n. *musical instrument*, synthesizer, record-player, tape-recorder, cassette deck, music centre, sound system; *record*, disc, album, cassette, tape, LP., EP., single, compact disc, digital record; *wind instrument*, brass, trumpet, trombone, bugle, flugelhorn, saxophone, French horn, tuba, euphonium, bagpipes; *woodwind*, oboe, bassoon, flute, clarinet; *stringed instrument*, double bass, cello, violin, fiddle (*colloq.*), viola, harp; *guitar*, mandolin, lute, banjo, ukelele, cithar, zither, dulcimer; *keyboard instrument*, piano, grand, baby grand, upright, harpsichord, virginals, spinet, harmonium, organ, accordion; *percussion*, timpani, kettledrum, cymbal, triangle, tambourine, drum, vibraphone, marimba, xylophone, gong, chimes, glockenspiel, maracas, castanets.

370 VISION
See also **372** (visibility).
n. *vision*, seeing, sight, eyesight; *perception*, recognition, insight, imagination, mind's eye; *visual defect*, short-sightedness, myopia, long-sightedness, presbyopia, astigmatism, squint, strabismus, cast, colour blindness, cataract; *eye*, naked eye, peepers (*colloq.*), orbs (*colloq.*), glad eye (*colloq.*), sheep's eyes, evil eye; *look*, gaze, stare, glance, eye contact, glimpse, peek, peep, butcher's (*colloq.*), dekko (*colloq.*), once-over (*colloq.*), look-see (*colloq.*); *inspection*, scrutiny, reconnaissance, surveillance, watch, observation, lookout; *view*, sight, spectacle, eyesore, eyeful (*colloq.*), sight for sore eyes (*colloq.*); *survey*, perspective, overview, bird's eye view, outlook; *viewer*, spectator, observer, watcher, eye witness, onlooker, bystander, audience; *optical device*, telescope, binoculars, field glasses, microscope, magnifying glass; *spectacles*, glasses, specs (*colloq.*), goggles, contact lens, pince-nez, monocle, bifocals; *optical illusion*, mirage, will o' the wisp, ignis fatuus, trick photography, phantom.
adj. *visual*, ocular, optical, ophthalmic; *perceptive*, observant, clear-sighted, perspicacious; *sharp-eyed*, watchful, eagle-eyed, hawk-eyed, lynx-eyed; *short-sighted*, myopic, purblind, long-sighted, presbyopic, colour-blind, cross-eyed, wall-eyed, astigmatic.
vb. *see*, behold, perceive, discern, make out, recognize; *glimpse*, catch sight of, spot, espy, clap eyes on; *look*, gaze, stare, gape, glare, peer, focus, fix, eye; *glance*, peek, peep, peer, wink, blink, squint, leer, ogle; *inspect*, scrutinize,

scan, peruse, look up and down, pore over; *watch*, observe, look out for, keep a weather eye open, keep one's eyes skinned/peeled (*colloq.*).

371 BLINDNESS

n. *blindness*, sightlessness, night-blindness, snow-blindness, colour-blindness, word-blindness, dyslexia; *blind spot*, blind side, tunnel vision; *blinkers*, blindfold, eye patch.
adj. *blind*, visually handicapped, blind as a bat, sightless, eyeless, unseeing; *blinded*, blindfold, blinkered, benighted; *blinding*, dazzling, flashing.
vb. *blind*, dazzle, blinker, blindfold, hoodwink; *go blind*, lose one's sight, be in the dark (*colloq.*), not see the wood for the trees.

372 VISIBILITY

See also **370** (vision).
n. *visibility*, conspicuousness, obviousness, prominence; *distinctness*, clarity, plainness, discernibility, perceptibility; *seeing distance*, field of vision, eyeshot, view.
adj. *visible*, discernible, perceptible, observable, detectable; *noticeable*, conspicuous, eye-catching, prominent; *apparent*, evident, obvious, plain, clear, crystal-clear, distinct, definite, clear-cut; *unmistakable*, glaring, blatant, flagrant, egregious.
vb. *be visible*, stand out, show up, leap to the eye, stick out like a sore thumb (*colloq.*); *appear*, come into view, loom, materialize.
adv. *visibly*, in full view, before one's very eyes, under one's nose.

373 INVISIBILITY

See also **376** (dimness); **469** (concealment).
n. *invisibility*, imperceptibility, indistinctness, vagueness, dimness; *poor visibility*, mistiness, haziness, fogginess; *concealment*, disguise, smokescreen, veil, curtain.
adj. *invisible*, unseen, imperceptible, indiscernible, unrecognizable; *inconspicuous*, microscopic, minute, faint; *indistinct*, unclear, vague, blurred, hazy, misty, foggy; *hidden*, obscured, submerged, latent.
vb. *be invisible*, hide, lurk, escape notice, be lost to view; *disappear*, fade, vanish, submerge; *conceal*, veil, screen, curtain.
adv. *out of sight*, out of focus.

374 LIGHT

See also **377** (light source).
n. *light*, first light, dawn, broad daylight, sunlight, twilight, dusk, half-light, moonlight, starlight; *illumination*, lamplight, candlelight, artificial light; *brightness*, radiance, brilliance, luminosity; *shine*, lustre, gloss, sheen, iridescence, highlight; *ray*, beam, shaft, pencil, streak, chink; *flash*, glint, glitter, twinkle, sparkle, flicker; *gleam*, glimmer, shimmer, glow, nimbus, halo; *dazzle*, glare, blaze, flare; *luminescence*, fluorescence, phosphorescence, northern lights, aurora borealis; *play of light*, light and shade, dappling, chiaroscuro; *radiation*, X-ray, laser, hologram; *reflection*, refraction, diffraction.
adj. *light*, lit, floodlit, spotlit; *bright*, radiant, brilliant, effulgent; *gleaming*, lambent, flickering, shimmery; *sparkly*, glittery, glinting, twinkly, flashing, coruscating; *shiny*, lustrous, glossy, wet-look; *incandescent*, glowing, luminescent, phosphorescent, fluorescent, Dayglo (*tdmk.*).
vb. *shine*, blaze, dazzle, flash, sparkle, glitter, glint; *gleam*, glow, shimmer, flicker, twinkle; *radiate*, beam, reflect, refract, emit; *illuminate*, irradiate, light up, brighten.

375 DARKNESS

See also **376** (dimness); **384** (black).
n. *darkness*, blackness, murkiness, gloominess, night, nightfall; *dusk*, gloom, murk, shadow, silhouette; *blackout*, eclipse, fadeout, lights out.
adj. *dark*, black, inky, pitch-black, coal-black; *gloomy*, sombre, murky, shadowy, dingy; *nocturnal*, night-time, benighted, unlit, starless, moonless.
vb. *darken*, blacken, dim, fade out; *extinguish*, douse, switch off, snuff out;

befog, obscure, obfuscate, eclipse, overshadow.

376 DIMNESS

See also **373** (invisibility); **380** (opaqueness).

n. *dimness*, faintness, indistinctness, vagueness, fuzziness; *cloudiness*, mistiness, smokiness, haziness, opacity; *twilight*, half-light, gloaming, dusk, bad light; *murk*, gloom, shade, penumbra, shadow; *mist*, fog, haze, blur, film, cloud.

adj. *dim*, faint, indistinct, bleary, blurred, fuzzy; *vague*, nebulous, confused, grey; *filmy*, cloudy, opaque, obscured; *hazy*, misty, foggy, smoky; *shadowy*, twilit, gloomy, murky, dingy.

vb. *dim*, fade, wane, die away; *obscure*, bedim, befog, mist up, cloud, muddy; *blur*, smear, dirty, besmirch.

377 LIGHT SOURCE

See also **374** (light).

n. *light source*, naked light, flare, torch, bonfire; *fire*, coal, ember, brand, flame; *match*, lighter, taper, spill, candle; *lamp*, flashlight, lantern, headlamp, searchlight, floodlight; *light bulb*, fluorescent tube, strip lighting, strobe light, neon light, spotlight; *warning light*, sidelight, indicator, tail light, traffic light, lighthouse, beacon; *light fitting*, chandelier, electrolier, pendant, standard lamp.

adj. *luminous*, flaming, glowing, incandescent, dazzling, well-lit.

378 SCREEN

See also **202** (covering).

n. *screen*, shield, shelter, covering, shade; *awning*, canopy, windbreak, safety curtain; *sunscreen*, visor, sunglasses, eyeshade, parasol, umbrella; *blind*, shutter, jalousie, curtain, netting; *veil*, hood, mask, cloak, blindfold, blinkers.

adj. *screened*, shaded, protected, shuttered, blinkered; *shady*, sheltered, secluded.

vb. *screen*, shield, protect, shelter, shade; *conceal*, curtain, veil, cloak, blanket, hood, mask, shroud.

379 TRANSPARENCY

n. *transparency*, clearness, limpidity, pellucidity; *translucence*, thinness, fineness, gauziness, diaphanousness; *glass*, ice, water, crystal, cellophane, Perspex (*tdmk.*); *gauze*, lace, chiffon, gossamer.

adj. *transparent*, clear, limpid, pellucid, sheer, see-through; *translucent*, thin, fine, filmy, gauzy, lacy, diaphanous, revealing; *glassy*, crystalline, vitreous, crystal-clear.

380 OPAQUENESS

See also **376** (dimness).

n. *opaqueness*, opacity, filminess, cloudiness, muddiness, turbidity, murkiness; *opalescence*, milkiness, pearliness, frosting; *fog*, mist, film, smokescreen, smoked glass; *mattness*, thickness, density.

adj. *opaque*, filmy, cloudy, muddy, turbid, unclear, murky; *opalescent*, milky, pearly, matt, frosted; *foggy*, misty, smoky, hazy.

vb. *make opaque*, cloud, film, frost, smoke, darken, muddy, dim.

381 COLOUR

See also **490** (painting).

n. *colour*, hue, saturation, tone, brilliance, intensity; *chromaticism*, primary/secondary/complementary colour; *shade*, tint, tincture, dash, touch, tinge; *coloration*, colouring, pigmentation, colour scheme; *spectrum*, prism, rainbow, palette; *pigment*, paint, dye, stain, watercolour, wash, distemper; *colourfulness*, vividness, gaudiness, garishness.

adj. *coloured*, chromatic, tinted, dyed, colourfast; *colourful*, multicoloured, polychrome, variegated, technicoloured, psychedelic; *gaudy*, bright, vivid, garish, harsh, shocking, clashing, lurid, loud; *pale*, subdued, soft, subtle, pastel, muted; *deep*, rich, glowing, intense, brilliant.

vb. *colour*, tint, shade, tinge; *dye*, stain, wash, distemper, rouge; *paint*, pigment, enamel, crayon, daub.

382 COLOURLESSNESS

See also **383** (white).

383 WHITE

n. *colourlessness*, achromatism, neutrality, monochrome; *discoloration*, fading, bleaching, whitening; *pallor*, paleness, whiteness, bloodlessness, pastiness, sallowness, anaemia; *greyness*, drabness, insipidness, dullness, dinginess; *decolorant*, bleach, peroxide, whitener.
adj. *colourless*, achromatic, neutral, monochromatic; *natural*, undyed, bleached, faded, discoloured; *pale*, pallid, wan, pasty, sallow, washed out, anaemic, etiolated, livid, ashen; *fair*, ash-blond, mousy, albino; *grey*, dull, drab, dingy, insipid, lacklustre.
vb. *lose colour*, fade, run, discolour, pale; *decolorize*, bleach, whiten, blanch, etiolate.

383 WHITE

See also **382** (colourlessness).
n. *white*, ivory, magnolia, off white, broken white, ecru, cream; *whiteness*, paleness, creaminess, blondness, fairness; *milkiness*, pearliness, silverness, snowiness; *white heat*, incandescence, white light, white water, white horses, spume; *snow*, alabaster, milk, moonstone, hoarfrost, rime; *whitener*, whitewash, blanco, pipeclay, chalk; *white metal*, white gold, platinum, nickel.
adj. *white*, light, bright, dazzling; *pure white*, snow-white, lily-white, milk-white; *fair*, blond, ash-blond, flaxen, platinum-blond, albino; *white-haired*, hoary, silvery, snowy, grizzled; *whitish*, creamy, milky, pearly, chalky, floury, mealy, frosted; *white-skinned*, Caucasian, pale, ashen, waxen.
vb. *whiten*, lighten, fade, pale; *silver*, frost, rime, grizzle; *blanch*, bleach, whitewash.

384 BLACK

See also **375** (darkness).
n. *black*, ebony, sable, jet, ink, soot, carbon, coal, pitch; *blackness*, swarthiness, inkiness, sootiness; *Negro*, coloured, nigger (*derog.*), blackamoor.
adj. *black*, blackish, dirty, inky, sooty, fuliginous; *jet-black*, blue-black, pitch-black, coal-black, black as the ace of spades; *black-haired*, brunette, raven-haired; *dark-skinned*, swarthy, dusky, Negroid; *dark*, sombre, murky, gloomy, Stygian.
vb. *blacken*, darken, singe, char; *dirty*, smudge, tarnish, besmirch.

385 GREY

n. *grey*, taupe, pewter, lead, slate, gunmetal; *greyness*, dullness, drabness, colourlessness.
adj. *grey*, pearl-grey, dapple-grey, silver-grey, dove-grey, oyster; *dark grey*, blue-grey, slaty, steely, leaden; *opalescent*, pearly, silvery, frosted; *grey-haired*, greying, grizzled, pepper-and-salt, hoary; *greyish*, neutral, drab, smoky, hazy.

386 BROWN

n. *brown*, ochre, sepia, raw sienna, burnt umber, bistre; *bronze*, amber, copper, cinnamon, coffee, caramel, mocha, chocolate, mahogany; *brunette*, redhead, bay, roan, sorrel.
adj. *brown*, brownish, hazel, dun, nut-brown, tan, tawny, khaki; *light brown*, fawn, biscuit, beige, buff, oatmeal, café-au-lait; *reddish-brown*, coppery, chestnut, russet, liverish, auburn, peaty; *dark brown*, nigger-brown, swarthy, bronzed, tanned, sunburnt.
vb. *brown*, burn, scorch, toast, tan, bronze.

387 RED

n. *red*, carmine, vermilion, crimson lake, cochineal, rouge, henna; *redness*, rosiness, floridness, ruddiness, blush, flush, glow, high colour; *ruby*, garnet, coral, flame, blood, gore; *rose*, poppy, cherry, lobster, beetroot; *wine*, port, burgundy, claret.
adj. *red*, reddish, ruddy, rosy, apple-cheeked, rubicund, florid, sanguine; *blood-red*, bloody, gory, bloodshot; *red-hot*, glowing, flaming, warm; *bright red*, scarlet, crimson, pillarbox-red, brick-red, terracotta; *reddish-brown*, russet, rufous, oxblood; *red-gold*, titian, redheaded, strawberry blond; *light red*, pink, salmon-pink, shell pink, peachy, flesh-coloured, old rose; *dark red*, purplish, cerise, magenta, rose.

vb. *redden*, rouge, henna, raddle; *blush*, flush, glow, crimson, mantle, colour.

388 ORANGE

n. *orange*, amber, burnt orange, gamboge; *copper*, rust, bronze, ginger, henna; *tangerine*, apricot, peach, marmalade, marigold.
adj. *orange*, orangey, tan, russet; *coppery*, auburn, gingery, carroty.

389 YELLOW

n. *yellow*, chrome yellow, ochre, saffron, turmeric; *yellowness*, sallowness, biliousness, jaundice; *yellow metal*, gold, brass, ormolu; *lemon*, mustard, egg yolk, cream, butter; *primrose*, jonquil, daffodil, jasmine, mimosa, buttercup.
adj. *yellow*, yellowy, golden, blond, flaxen· *pale yellow*, creamy, honey-coloured, corn-coloured; *bright yellow*, lemon-yellow, primrose-yellow, canary-yellow, sulphur-yellow; *dark yellow*, old gold, mustardy, tawny, sandy, sallow.

390 GREEN

n. *green*, viridian, bice, verdigris, chlorophyll; *greenness*, greenery, verdure, leafiness, green belt, grass, turf; *emerald*, jade, aquamarine, beryl; *lime*, greengage, avocado, olive.
adj. *green*, greenish, glaucous, viridescent; *grassy*, leafy, mossy, verdant; *bright green*, grass-green, apple-green, pea-green, chartreuse, lime-green; *dark green*, sage-green, sea-green, celadon, moss-green, bottle-green, olive-green, khaki; *greenish-blue*, eau-de-Nil, turquoise.

391 BLUE

n. *blue*, cyan, cobalt blue, Prussian blue, ultramarine, indigo, woad; *sapphire*, lapis lazuli, turquoise, aquamarine; *forget-me-not*, cornflower, harebell, gentian, delphinium.
adj. *blue*, bluish, cerulean, sky-blue, azure; *light blue*, powder blue, duck-egg blue, Cambridge blue, Wedgwood blue; *bluey-green*, turquoise, kingfisher blue, peacock blue, electric blue; *bluey-grey*, slaty, steely, gunmetal; *dark blue*, Oxford blue, royal blue, midnight blue, blue-black, navy.

392 PURPLE

n. *purple*, amethyst, gentian violet, Tyrian purple; *plum*, aubergine, mulberry, damson, cherry; *lilac*, heather, violet, lavender, heliotrope, fuchsia; *wine*, burgundy, claret, grape.
adj. *purple*, purplish, mauve, maroon, puce, magenta, cerise.

393 VARIEGATION

n. *variegation*, diversity, variety, nonuniformity, colourfulness; *patchwork*, motley, tartan, mosaic, chequerboard, marquetry; *kaleidoscope*, spectrum, rainbow, prism, coat of many colours; *iridescence*, shot silk, mother of pearl, tiger's eye, watered silk; *jasper*, agate, tortoiseshell, marble; *patch*, blotch, splotch, spot, dot, fleck, speck, freckle, speckle.
adj. *variegated*, multicoloured, polychromatic, colourful; *iridescent*, chatoyant, opalescent, pearly, nacreous, moiré; *patchy*, mottled, chequered, particoloured; *striped*, barred, marbled, veined, streaky; *pied*, grizzled, brindled, pepper-and-salt, piebald, skewbald; *spotted*, speckled, stippled, dotted, studded.
vb. *variegate*, diversify, chequer, patch, counterchange; *sprinkle*, pepper, dot, spangle, speckle, dapple; *stripe*, bar, vein, marble, streak, striate; *stain*, splash, blotch, mottle.

394 APPEARANCE

See also **464** (display).
n. *appearance*, phenomenon, manifestation, realization, materialization, embodiment; *aspect*, exterior, outside, externals, appearances; *front*, veneer, image, facade, pose, semblance, guise, first impressions; *look*, expression, countenance, mien, demeanour, air, bearing; *sight*, spectacle, panorama, display, exhibition; *apparition*, vision, mirage, hallucination, phantom, will o' the wisp.
adj. *apparent*, outward, external, super-

ficial, visible, manifest; *seeming*, ostensible, specious, plausible, deceptive, meretricious.
vb. *appear*, seem, look, come over as; *show*, exhibit, display, manifest; *arise*, materialize, come into being, emerge, come to light, surface; *arrive*, turn up, show up, put in an appearance, pop up (*colloq.*), crop up.
adv. *apparently*, ostensibly, on the face of it, to all appearances; *superficially*, at face value, at first sight, prima facie; *on view*, on show, on display.

395 DISAPPEARANCE

See also **373** (invisibility).
n. *disappearance*, departure, flight, escape, elopement; *loss*, shrinkage, diminution, evaporation, dissolution; *extinction*, obliteration, erasure, cancellation, dispersal; *eclipse*, fadeout, blackout, disappearing trick; *evanescence*, transience, transitoriness, elusiveness.
adj. *disappearing*, vanishing, evanescent, transient, fleeting; *vanished*, missing, absentee, gone, lost to view, invisible.
vb. *disappear*, vanish, dematerialize, melt into thin air, sink without trace; *evaporate*, dissolve, dispel, disperse, scatter; *fade*, pale, shrink, dwindle; *depart*, escape, flee, elope, decamp, absent oneself, do a bunk (*colloq.*), play truant, go AWOL; *hide*, lurk, lie low, hide out; *obliterate*, erase, expunge, wipe out; *withdraw*, remove from the scene, carry off, kidnap, spirit away.

396 INTELLECT

See also **283** (nonmaterial world); **398** (thought).
n. *intellect*, mind, psyche, consciousness, awareness, self; *perception*, cognition, intuition, imagination, insight; *rationality*, reason, sense, understanding, comprehension, judgment, discernment, acumen; *intelligence*, I.Q., wits, senses, brains, grey matter, head, loaf (*colloq.*); *common sense*, nous (*colloq.*), savvy (*colloq.*), gumption, horse sense; *cleverness*, brilliance, braininess, high I.Q., genius; *intellectual*, egghead (*colloq.*), blue stocking, highbrow, genius, brainbox (*colloq.*); *psychologist*, psychiatrist, psychoanalyst, psychotherapist, shrink (*colloq.*), trick cyclist (*colloq.*).
adj. *intellectual*, mental, conceptual, abstract, cerebral, theoretical; *cognitive*, perceptual, conscious, aware, intuitive, imaginative; *intelligent*, clever, brilliant, bright, gifted, forward, quick-witted, brainy (*colloq.*); *sensible*, rational, commonsensical, logical, reasoned; *psychic*, psychological, psychosomatic, subliminal, subconscious.
vb. *think*, conceive, imagine, reason, intellectualize, theorize, conceptualize; *perceive*, realize, understand, comprehend, discern, sense; *be intelligent*, use one's head, have one's wits about one, know a thing or two (*colloq.*).

397 LACK OF INTELLECT

See also **399** (lack of thought).
n. *lack of intellect*, instinct, intuition, unreason, unintellectuality; *unintelligence*, brainlessness, mindlessness, inanity, vacuity; *stupidity*, dullness, slowness, obtuseness, low I.Q.; *backwardness*, retardation, arrested development, mental deficiency, cretinism, imbecility, feeble-mindedness; *stupid person*, dullard, dunderhead, dunce, blockhead (*colloq.*), thicko (*colloq.*); *mental defective*, cretin, moron, idiot, half-wit, cabbage.
adj. *unintellectual*, intuitive, instinctive, animal, brute; *irrational*, unreasoning, illogical; *mindless*, brainless, vacuous, empty-headed, inane, scatterbrained; *unintelligent*, stupid, slow-witted, dim (*colloq.*), dull, obtuse, thick (*colloq.*), dense, boneheaded (*colloq.*), slow on the uptake; *mentally deficient*, backward, retarded, subnormal, feeble-minded, wanting, not all there, cretinous, moronic.

398 THOUGHT

See also **396** (intellect); **400** (reason).
n. *thought*, thinking, cogitation, concentration, cerebration, speculation, brainwork, intellectual exercise;

thoughtfulness, pensiveness, abstractedness, preoccupation, absorption, daydreaming, brown study; *consideration*, contemplation, deliberation, rumination, introspection, meditation, soul-searching; *reflection*, hindsight, afterthought, second thoughts; *forethought*, prudence, foresight, forward planning.

adj. *thinking*, deliberative, speculative, imaginative, cerebral, intellectual; *thoughtful*, pensive, studious, abstracted, preoccupied, engrossed, dreamy; *reflective*, meditative, introspective, contemplative.

vb. *think*, conceive, imagine, fancy; *cogitate*, ruminate, cerebrate, deliberate, rack one's brains; *consider*, contemplate, reflect, meditate, muse, brood, introspect, mull over, chew over; *think of*, invent, devise, dream up, think up; *speculate*, theorize, hypothesize, fantasize; *reconsider*, review, think again, have second thoughts; *preoccupy*, engross, absorb, obsess; *strike one*, come to mind, occur, cross one's mind.

adv. *on reflection*, on consideration, on second thoughts, with hindsight; *in mind*, on one's mind, on the brain.

399 LACK OF THOUGHT

See also **397** (lack of intellect); **401** (intuition).

n. *lack of thought*, intuition, spontaneity, instinct, flair, gut reaction, reflex, knee-jerk response; *thoughtlessness*, mindlessness, senselessness, irrationality, illogicality; *ignorance*, stupidity, empty-headedness, fatuousness, inanity.

adj. *unthinking*, unreflective, unimaginative, unoriginal; *intuitive*, spontaneous, instinctive, automatic, reflexive; *mindless*, thoughtless, ill-considered, senseless, irrational, illogical, half-baked (*colloq.*); *ignorant*, stupid, empty-headed, fatuous, inane, vacuous, blank.

vb. *not think about*, ignore, disregard, put out of one's mind, dismiss, laugh off, not give a second thought; *intuit*, sense, feel in one's bones.

400 REASON

See also **398** (thought).

n. *reason*, rationality, logic, ratiocination; *argumentation*, disputation, analysis, speculation, abstraction, rationalization; *induction*, deduction, lateral thinking, implication, inference; *premise*, hypothesis, postulate, assumption, supposition, thesis, theorem.

adj. *rational*, logical, conceptual, abstract, academic; *reasonable*, sensible, cogent, coherent, objective; *hypothetical*, theoretical, suppositional, putative, speculative; *analytical*, deductive, a priori, inductive, a posteriori.

vb. *reason*, argue, dispute, rationalize, intellectualize, philosophize; *theorize*, speculate, hypothesize, assume, presuppose; *infer*, deduce, conclude, imply, work out, put two and two together; *be logical*, follow, cohere, hang together, stand to reason, add up (*colloq.*), hold water, make sense.

401 INTUITION

See also **397** (lack of intellect); **455** (prediction).

n. *intuition*, instinct, feeling, insight, spontaneity, gut reaction; *irrationality*, illogicality, incoherence, unreason; *hypersensitivity*, sixth sense, extra-sensory perception, telepathy, second sight, clairvoyance; *presentiment*, hunch, guess, foreboding, premonition.

adj. *intuitive*, instinctive, visceral, spontaneous, impulsive; *irrational*, illogical, incoherent, subjective, impressionistic; *involuntary*, subconscious, subliminal, reflex, automatic, Pavlovian, mechanical, knee-jerk; *psychic*, clairvoyant, telepathic.

vb. *intuit*, guess, divine, sense, feel in one's bones; *use guesswork*, feel one's way, play it by ear (*colloq.*), follow one's nose (*colloq.*).

402 CURIOSITY

See also **414** (question).

n. *curiosity*, interest, concern, eagerness, inquiring mind; *inquisitiveness*, prying, officiousness, nosiness (*colloq.*); *morbid curiosity*, prurience, salaciousness, voyeurism, ghoulishness; *interro-*

gation, cross-examination, detection, quizzing, grilling, third degree (*colloq.*); *spy*, eavesdropper, voyeur, peeping Tom, ghoul, snooper (*colloq.*), rubberneck (*colloq.*), nosy parker (*colloq.*); *gossip*, scandalmonger, newsmonger, newshound, busybody.
adj. *curious*, interested, inquisitive, eager, agog; *prurient*, salacious, voyeuristic, ghoulish; *meddlesome*, interfering, officious, nosy (*colloq.*); *inquisitorial*, questioning, interrogatory.
vb. *be curious*, eavesdrop, listen in on, spy, snoop (*colloq*); *question*, interrogate, cross-examine, quiz; *enquire*, ask, seek to know; *meddle*, interfere, pry, poke/stick one's nose in.

403 LACK OF CURIOSITY

See also **405** (inattention); **756** (indifference).
n. *lack of curiosity*, unconcern, detachment, aloofness; *indifference*, nonchalance, insouciance, impassivity; *apathy*, inertia, boredom, listlessness.
adj. *incurious*, uninterested, unconcerned, detached, aloof; *indifferent*, nonchalant, insouciant, phlegmatic, impassive; *apathetic*, unenthusiastic, bored, blasé, listless.

404 ATTENTION

See also **406** (carefulness).
n. *attention*, notice, regard, heed; *mindfulness*, thoughtfulness, solicitude, consideration; *attentiveness*, concentration, alertness, watchfulness, vigilance; *observation*, inspection, scrutiny, surveillance; *preoccupation*, absorption, raptness, intentness, undivided attention; *studiousness*, application, diligence, assiduousness; *attention to detail*, meticulousness, scrupulousness, punctiliousness, conscientiousness.
adj. *attentive*, mindful, solicitous, considerate, thoughtful; *diligent*, studious, sedulous, assiduous; *meticulous*, scrupulous, punctilious, painstaking; *alert*, aware, conscious, watchful, observant, vigilant; *preoccupied*, absorbed, intent, rapt, engrossed, wrapped up in, riveted; *fixated*, obsessed, single-minded, brooding.
vb. *pay attention*, attend, heed, be on the ball (*colloq.*); *notice*, register, spot, take note, sit up and take notice, prick up one's ears; *observe*, watch, scrutinize, inspect, peruse; *concentrate*, drink in, lap up, hang on someone's words, be all ears (*colloq.*); *preoccupy*, engross, absorb, captivate; *draw attention to*, point out, mention, alert to.

405 INATTENTION

See also **403** (lack of curiosity); **407** (negligence).
n. *inattention*, negligence, carelessness, unawareness; *forgetfulness*, obliviousness, oversight, lapse, disregard; *thoughtlessness*, heedlessness, inconsiderateness, unconcern; *casualness*, offhandedness, desultoriness, cursoriness, vagueness; *absent-mindedness*, distractedness, abstraction, daydreaming, wool-gathering; *dreamer*, scatterbrain, butterfly mind.
adj. *inattentive*, negligent, careless, unmindful; *forgetful*, oblivious, absent-minded, unaware, unobservant; *thoughtless*, heedless, inconsiderate, cavalier; *casual*, offhand, desultory, cursory, superficial; *abstracted*, vague, pensive, dreamy, lost in thought, distracted; *flighty*, dizzy, mercurial, featherbrained, scatty (*colloq.*).
vb. *be inattentive*, overlook, neglect, disregard, miss, let slip; *forget*, lose track of, digress, lose the thread, wander; *daydream*, muse, moon, build castles in Spain; *distract*, disconcert, bewilder, put off.

406 CAREFULNESS

See also **404** (attention); **754** (caution).
n. *carefulness*, mindfulness, solicitude, consideration, attentiveness; *prudence*, circumspection, judiciousness, caution, vigilance; *care*, heed, concern, regard; *conscientiousness*, thoroughness, meticulousness, trouble, pains; *methodicalness*, orderliness, tidiness, neatness, fastidiousness; *accuracy*, precision, exactitude, rigour, perfectionism.
adj. *careful*, mindful, thoughtful, considerate, attentive, solicitous; *prudent*,

cautious, circumspect, judicious, wary; *conscientious*, thorough, meticulous, scrupulous, painstaking; *methodical*, orderly, neat, tidy, fastidious, fussy; *exacting*, accurate, rigorous, perfectionist, pedantic.
vb. *be careful*, mind, heed, take into consideration; *watch out*, tread warily, mind one's step, mind one's P's and Q's; *beware of*, look out for, give a wide berth, steer clear of; *check up on*, keep tabs on, keep under surveillance.

407 NEGLIGENCE

See also **405** (inattention).
n. *negligence*, carelessness, forgetfulness, inattentiveness; *neglect*, oversight, dereliction, omission, lapse; *imprudence*, recklessness, impetuosity, indiscretion; *inexactitude*, inaccuracy, looseness, loose ends; *laxity*, slackness, sloppiness, untidiness, slovenliness.
adj. *negligent*, careless, forgetful, inattentive, remiss, neglectful; *casual*, lax, lackadaisical, slack, sloppy, slovenly, slipshod; *neglected*, untidy, unkempt, uncared-for; *reckless*, imprudent, indiscreet, off one's guard, impetuous.
vb. *neglect*, omit, miss, forget; *disregard*, ignore, overlook, turn a blind eye to; *discount*, dismiss, pooh-pooh (*colloq.*), laugh off; *avoid*, dodge, shirk, let slide, leave in the lurch; *gloss over*, scamp, skate over, skip; *procrastinate*, drift, freewheel, let the grass grow under one's feet.

408 IDEA

n. *idea*, notion, concept, abstraction, thought; *imagination*, fancy, invention, brainchild, wheeze (*colloq.*), wrinkle (*colloq.*); *theory*, hypothesis, conjecture, supposition, conception; *attitude*, opinion, viewpoint, stance; *fixed idea*, idée fixe, obsession, fixation, one-track mind.
adj. *ideal*, abstract, notional, conceptual; *theoretical*, hypothetical, conjectural, suppositional; *fanciful*, whimsical, imaginary, all in the mind.

409 TOPIC

n. *topic*, subject, concern, matter, food for thought; *theme*, message, burden, gist, content; *question*, problem, issue, thesis, point, argument, case; *proposal*, suggestion, motion, resolution; *news*, rumour, gossip, current events, current affairs.
adj. *topical*, current, actual, up-to-the-minute; *newsworthy*, thought-provoking, controversial, debatable.
adv. *on the agenda*, under discussion; *in the air*, on everyone's lips.

410 ARGUMENT

See also **635** (disagreement).
n. *argument*, discussion, dialogue, debate, exchange of views; *dispute*, quarrel, altercation, war of words, slanging match (*colloq.*); *controversy*, disputation, polemics, argumentation, dissension; *case*, thesis, grounds, premise, point at issue, pros and cons; *argumentativeness*, contentiousness, quarrelsomeness, combativeness.
adj. *argumentative*, disputatious, quarrelsome, litigious; *controversial*, contentious, polemical, provocative; *arguable*, debatable, questionable, controvertible, moot; *heated*, stormy, violent, ding-dong (*colloq.*); *well-argued*, cogent, coherent, logical, analytical, rational.
vb. *argue*, debate, discuss, bandy words; *quibble*, split hairs, chop logic, nit-pick, argue the toss; *quarrel*, dispute, wrangle, bicker, cross swords, have words, *attack*, pick holes in, outargue, shoot down in flames, demolish; *defend*, plead for, support, make out a case for.

411 SOPHISTRY

n. *sophistry*, false logic, illogicality, circularity; *casuistry*, speciousness, rationalization, doublethink; *ambiguity*, equivocation, mystification, obscurantism, woolliness; *quibbling*, hair-splitting, chicanery, choplogic; *fallacy*, contradiction in terms, non sequitur, inconsistency; *distortion*, perversion, newspeak, doubletalk.
adj. *sophistical*, casuistical, Jesuitical; *illogical*, unsound, circular, specious; *ambiguous*, equivocal, woolly, flimsy, waffly (*colloq.*); *fallacious*, contradic-

tory, inconsistent, misleading; *captious*, hair-splitting, pettifogging, nit-picking.
vb. *reason falsely*, equivocate, quibble, cavil, split hairs; *mislead*, pervert, distort, mystify, bamboozle (*colloq.*), blind someone with science; *avoid the issue*, beat about the bush, miss the point, digress.

412 DEMONSTRATION

See also **417** (verification); **420** (evidence).
n. *demonstration*, proof, justification, validation, vindication, affirmation; *argument*, exposition, explanation, elucidation, illustration, clarification.
adj. *demonstrable*, arguable, justifiable, verifiable; *expository*, explanatory, elucidatory, illustrative; *affirmative*, conclusive, corroborative, irrefutable, incontrovertible, unanswerable.
vb. *demonstrate*, show, prove, establish, make out a case for, prove one's point; *affirm*, justify, vindicate, validate, substantiate, corroborate; *explain*, expound, illustrate, elucidate.

413 REFUTATION

See also **415** (answer); **421** (counter-evidence).
n. *refutation*, confutation, disproof, rebuttal; *challenge*, disputation, contention, calling in question; *contradiction*, negation, denial, repudiation; *exposure*, invalidation, denunciation, criticism, hatchet job (*colloq.*).
adj. *refuted*, disproved, invalidated, demolished; *negatory*, contradictory, condemnatory, denunciatory.
vb. *refute*, rebut, invalidate, prove wrong, disprove; *contradict*, negate, deny, repudiate, gainsay, give the lie to; *challenge*, pick someone up on, take issue with, contend, disagree with; *expose*, show up, explode, denounce, condemn; *outargue*, puncture, deflate, squash, crush, shoot down in flames.

414 QUESTION

See also **402** (curiosity).
n. *question*, enquiry, query, request, petition; *interrogation*, examination, investigation, inquisition, quiz; *exploration*, quest, probe, search, inquest, survey, fact-finding mission; *questionnaire*, poll, interview, canvass, vox pop; *review*, scrutiny, study, inspection, cross-examination, analysis; *riddle*, enigma, problem, brainteaser (*colloq.*), poser, 64 000 dollar question.
adj. *questioning*, enquiring, inquisitive, searching, quizzical, interrogative; *exploratory*, preliminary, investigative, detective; *problematical*, knotty, enigmatic, baffling, puzzling.
vb. *question*, ask, enquire, request; *probe*, look into, investigate, delve into, leave no stone unturned; *explore*, try out, test, put out feelers, take the temperature of; *survey*, scrutinize, inspect, screen, canvass, poll; *challenge*, badger, pester, heckle, lobby.

415 ANSWER

See also **413** (refutation).
n. *answer*, reply, reaction, response, acknowledgment, feedback; *retort*, rejoinder, riposte, comeback; *repartee*, backchat, lip (*colloq.*), badinage; *rebuttal*, countercharge, right of reply, counterblast, retaliation.
adj. *answering*, responsive, affirmative, positive; *negative*, contradictory, defensive, retaliatory.
vb. *answer*, reply, respond, take one's cue, acknowledge; *retort*, riposte, rebut, come back on; *react*, counter, parry, retaliate; *contradict*, negate, deny, disclaim.

416 EXPERIMENT

n. *experiment*, attempt, try-out, test, trial, dry run, practice shot, pilot scheme, rehearsal, audition, run-through; *experimentation*, research, verification, proving; *speculation*, guesswork, trial and error, gamble, long shot, shot in the dark; *testing agent*, litmus test, benchmark, yardstick, criterion, touchstone; *subject*, guinea pig, control sample, sounding board.
adj. *experimental*, empirical, practical; *provisional*, tentative, probationary, unproven; *speculative*, hypothetical,

exploratory, open-ended, hit-or-miss, random.

vb. *experiment*, test, sample, try out, research; *practise*, rehearse, audition, run through; *speculate*, hypothesize, gamble, fly a kite; *improvise*, feel one's way, play it by ear (*colloq.*), muddle through.

417 VERIFICATION

See also **412** (demonstration); **427** (certainty).

n. *verification*, demonstration, affirmation, validation, substantiation, authentication; *confirmation*, attestation, certification, corroboration, justification, vindication, proof; *check*, audit, inquest, post mortem, autopsy.

adj. *verified*, certified, attested, proven, tried and tested, authentic, genuine; *verifiable*, demonstrable, ascertainable, provable.

vb. *verify*, establish, prove, demonstrate, affirm, substantiate; *validate*, authenticate, attest, certify; *vindicate*, justify, confirm, corroborate, bear out; *check*, go over, cross-check, double check.

418 DISCRIMINATION

See also **18** (dissimilarity); **429** (judgment).

n. *discrimination*, discernment, circumspection, judgment, acumen; *distinction*, differentiation, nuance, nicety, shade of meaning; *perspicacity*, penetration, astuteness, shrewdness, insight, sensitivity; *appreciation*, refinement, connoisseurship, taste, flair, subtlety; *selectivity*, choosiness (*colloq.*), fussiness, fastidiousness.

adj. *discriminating*, perspicacious, judicious, circumspect, discerning; *fastidious*, selective, fussy, choosy (*colloq.*), picky (*colloq.*), difficult; *subtle*, delicate, fine, nice, nuanced; *critical*, exacting, rigorous, careful.

vb. *discriminate*, distinguish, differentiate, discern; *sort*, sift, tell apart, separate the sheep from the goats; *appraise*, judge, evaluate; *select*, choose, pick out, single out.

419 LACK OF DISCRIMINATION

n. *lack of discrimination*, unperceptiveness, insensitivity, coarseness; *crudeness*, randomness, inexactness, haphazardness; *confusion*, jumble, hotchpotch, muddle, mixed bag, grist to the mill.

adj. *undiscriminating*, unselective, uncritical, unperceptive, insensitive; *unrefined*, crude, rough and ready, coarse, unpolished, unsubtle; *indiscriminate*, random, haphazard, hit-or-miss; *broad*, generalized, wholesale, blanket.

vb. *not discriminate*, lump together, roll into one, jumble, muddle, confuse, blur.

420 EVIDENCE

See also **412** (demonstration).

n. *evidence*, indication, sign, symptom; *data*, facts, information, dossier, documentation, file; *proof*, corroboration, verification, support, foundation, backing; *testimony*, witness, exhibit, statement, affidavit, attestation, deposition, allegation; *recommendation*, endorsement, reference, testimonial, credentials, warranty, seal of approval.

adj. *evidential*, indicative, symptomatic, suggestive, telling; *factual*, documentary, first-hand, straight from the horse's mouth; *corroborative*, reliable, affirmative, conclusive, irrefutable.

vb. *evidence*, show, indicate, reveal, suggest, betoken, evince; *give evidence*, attest, testify, bear witness; *recommend*, vouch for, guarantee, endorse; *support*, ratify, corroborate, confirm, bear out, verify.

421 COUNTEREVIDENCE

See also **413** (refutation).

n. *counterevidence*, contradiction, counterclaim; *rebuttal*, refutation, negation, denial; *conflicting evidence*, disproof, hostile witness, discrepancy.

adj. *contradictory*, negatory, conflicting, damaging.

vb. *contraindicate*, run counter to, point in the other direction, give the lie to, disprove; *refute*, rebut, contradict, negate, go against; *weaken*, damage, undermine, expose.

422 QUALIFICATION

n. *qualification*, reservation, proviso, condition, stipulation, prerequisite; *limitation*, specification, exception, restriction, modification; *exemption*, concession, allowance, mitigation, extenuation; *loophole*, escape clause, let-out, get-out.
adj. *qualifying*, restrictive, conditional, provisional, contingent, dependent; *mitigating*, extenuating, concessionary.
vb. *qualify*, modify, limit, restrict; *stipulate*, specify, lay down, insist on; *concede*, exempt, make allowance for, take into account; *mitigate*, moderate, extenuate, play down.

423 POSSIBILITY

See also **425** (probability).
n. *possibility*, eventuality, contingency, chance, off-chance, opportunity, likelihood; *potentiality*, virtuality, makings, possibilities, promise; *feasibility*, practicability, viability, capability.
adj. *possible*, potential, virtual, hypothetical; *attainable*, realizable, doable, achievable, obtainable; *practicable*, workable, viable, feasible; *credible*, reasonable, plausible, conceivable, likely, arguable.
vb. *make possible*, enable, facilitate, bring about; *have possibilities*, show promise, have the makings of, have potential.
adv. *possibly*, perhaps, maybe; *arguably*, potentially.

424 IMPOSSIBILITY

See also **426** (improbability).
n. *impossibility*, impracticability, hopelessness, absurdity; *impasse*, deadlock, dead end, blank wall, hopeless case, no-no (*colloq.*).
adj. *impossible*, impracticable, unworkable, not on (*colloq.*); *inconceivable*, unthinkable, unimaginable, implausible, unlikely, unreasonable; *insuperable*, insurmountable, insoluble, incurable, incorrigible; *unobtainable*, unavailable, unattainable, inaccessible.
vb. *be impossible*, be out of the question, be beyond the bounds of possibility; *make impossible*, rule out, prohibit, disallow, exclude; *attempt the impossible*, wish for the moon, find a needle in a haystack, get blood out of a stone, square the circle.

425 PROBABILITY

See also **423** (possibility).
n. *probability*, likelihood, expectation, prospect, promise; *predictability*, reliability, liability, fair chance, sporting chance; *conjecture*, assumption, educated guess, safe bet.
adj. *probable*, likely, foreseeable, predictable, liable, expected; *plausible*, reasonable, convincing, credible; *prospective*, hopeful, promising, rising.
vb. *be probable*, be on the cards, be in the offing; *foresee*, expect, predict, look forward to; *assume*, conjecture, guess, suppose.
adv. *probably*, in all likelihood, ten to one.

426 IMPROBABILITY

See also **424** (impossibility).
n. *improbability*, unlikelihood, doubtfulness, remote/outside/slim chance, long odds; *implausibility*, inconceivability, absurdity, ludicrousness; *forlorn hope*, pious hope, long shot, shot in the dark.
adj. *improbable*, unlikely, doubtful, dubious, uncertain; *implausible*, unconvincing, unbelievable, far-fetched, absurd.

427 CERTAINTY

See also **417** (verification); **434** (belief).
n. *certainty*, certitude, likelihood, inevitability, inexorability; *reliability*, dependability, infallibility, trustworthiness, unimpeachability; *assurance*, conviction, confidence, blind faith; *predictability*, definiteness, foregone conclusion, safe bet, dead cert (*colloq.*), sure thing (*colloq.*).
adj. *certain*, definite, sure, categorical; *unmistakable*, unequivocal, unambiguous, conclusive; *inevitable*, unavoida-

ble, inexorable, ineluctable; *uncontrovertible*, undeniable, unquestionable, unimpeachable; *assured*, confident, convinced, unshakable; *reliable*, trustworthy, dependable, rock-solid; *infallible*, foolproof, failsafe, low-risk, gilt-edged.
vb. *know for certain*, feel sure of, put one's shirt on, bet one's bottom dollar; *rely on*, depend on, bank on, trust in; *make certain*, ensure, guarantee, confirm, check, double check; *finalize*, settle, firm up (*colloq.*), decide, clinch, wrap up (*colloq.*).
adv. *certainly*, doubtless, definitely, come rain or shine, no matter what, come hell or high water.

428 UNCERTAINTY

See also **435** (disbelief).
n. *uncertainty*, indefiniteness, doubtfulness, dubiousness; *ambiguity*, ambivalence, vagueness, borderline case, grey area; *indecision*, diffidence, hesitation, vacillation, irresolution; *unreliability*, fallibility, untrustworthiness, unpredictability, volatility, capriciousness; *doubt*, query, question mark, misgivings; *conjecture*, gamble, guess, toss-up (*colloq.*), unknown quantity, pig in a poke.
adj. *uncertain*, unsure, doubtful, dubious; *precarious*, chancy, risky, dodgy (*colloq.*), touch and go; *unpredictable*, unforeseeable, unknowable, fickle, volatile, capricious; *fallible*, untrustworthy, unreliable; *indefinite*, vague, ambivalent, ambiguous, undecided; *hesitant*, indecisive, diffident, unconfident, irresolute; *questionable*, arguable, debatable, moot.
vb. *be uncertain*, be in two minds, hesitate, waver, vacillate, shilly-shally (*colloq.*), dither (*colloq.*); *doubt*, disbelieve, wonder, suspect, challenge, query; *grope*, fumble, flounder, not know which way to turn; *hinge*, depend, hang in the balance, be in the lap of the gods.

429 JUDGMENT

See also **418** (discrimination).
n. *judgment*, discretion, discernment, discrimination, acumen; *adjudication*, arbitration, umpirage, refereeing; *estimation*, evaluation, appraisal, assessment; *criticism*, opinion, comment, review, critique; *verdict*, ruling, decree, award, decision, settlement; *impartiality*, objectivity, fairness, justice; *judge*, umpire, referee, arbitrator, adjudicator, assessor.
adj. *judicial*, discretionary, judicatory; *judicious*, discerning, circumspect, shrewd; *judgmental*, critical, censorious, condemnatory; *approving*, appreciative, favourable, lenient; *impartial*, unbiased, objective, fair, just, broad-minded.
vb. *judge*, referee, umpire, adjudicate, arbitrate, decide, settle; *estimate*, appraise, assess, evaluate, size up, weigh up; *criticize*, review, pass judgment on, rule on; *pronounce*, decree, conclude, sum up.

430 MISJUDGMENT

See also **140** (tendency); **441** (error).
n. *misjudgment*, miscalculation, error, mistake, misconception; *wrongheadedness*, obstinacy, foolishness, fallibility; *partiality*, bias, partisanship, favouritism, one-sidedness, prejudice, bigotry; *injustice*, unfairness, discrimination, intolerance; *narrow-mindedness*, racism, chauvinism, sexism, colour prejudice, apartheid, segregation; *insularity*, parochialism, provincialism, closed mind.
adj. *mistaken*, misguided, wrong-headed, fallible; *partial*, biased, partisan, one-sided, unfair, unjust; *prejudiced*, bigoted, opinionated, dogmatic; *discriminatory*, sexist, racist, chauvinist; *insular*, parochial, provincial, narrow-minded, intolerant, hidebound, petty.
vb. *misjudge*, miscalculate, mistake, misconceive; *prejudice*, preconceive, presuppose, jump to conclusions; *bias*, predispose, warp, load, slant, skew, distort; *favour*, take sides, discriminate.

431 OVERESTIMATION

See also **482** (exaggeration).
n. *overestimation*, overvaluation, exces-

siveness, exorbitancy; *overstatement*, exaggeration, hyperbole, puff (*colloq.*), hype (*colloq.*), ballyhoo (*colloq.*); *overconfidence*, overoptimism, presumption, arrogance.
adj. *overrated*, overpraised, disappointing, not up to expectation; *overvalued*, overpriced, exorbitant, excessive; *overstated*, overdone, overemphasized, hyperbolic, over the top (*colloq.*); *overconfident*, overoptimistic, overenthusiastic, overambitious.
vb. *overestimate*, overshoot, overrate, overvalue; *overemphasize*, overpraise, exaggerate, hype (*colloq.*), build up, talk up (*colloq.*), lay it on with a shovel/trowel (*colloq.*); *maximize*, make much of, make a mountain out of a molehill.

432 UNDERESTIMATION
See also **483** (understatement).
n. *underestimation*, undervaluation, understatement, conservative estimate; *self-deprecation*, modesty, reticence, humility; *pessimism*, defeatism, despondency; *depreciation*, disparagement, belittlement.
adj. *underrated*, undervalued, neglected, overlooked, unsung; *modest*, self-effacing, self-deprecating, retiring; *pessimistic*, defeatist, despondent, gloomy; *disparaging*, derogatory, depreciative.
vb. *underestimate*, undervalue, underrate, underprice; *neglect*, overlook, do less than justice to, pass over; *minimize*, understate, play down, soft-pedal (*colloq.*); *disparage*, belittle, slight, pooh-pooh (*colloq.*), run down.

433 DISCOVERY
n. *discovery*, exploration, research, experimentation, excavation, prospecting; *encounter*, meeting, happening, coincidence; *realization*, revelation, inspiration, flash of insight; *invention*, find, results, findings, strike; *location*, identification, sighting, detection.
adj. *exploratory*, experimental, fact-finding; *probing*, investigative, detective.
vb. *discover*, invent, come up with, find out, learn; *happen on*, come across, hit upon, light upon, stumble across, encounter; *realize*, tumble to, see the light, catch on (*colloq.*), twig (*colloq.*); *unearth*, uncover, disinter, dig up, bring to light, ferret/nose out, detect; *find*, track down, locate, spot, sight, identify; *explore*, excavate, probe, investigate.

434 BELIEF
See also **427** (certainty); **868** (religion).
n. *belief*, credence, acceptance, conviction, assurance, certainty; *confidence*, faith, trust, reliance, expectation; *opinion*, persuasion, view, sentiment; *credo*, tenet, principle, creed, dogma, profession, ideology, doctrine, article of faith; *attitude*, position, viewpoint, standpoint, outlook, world-view; *prejudice*, dogmatism, bigotry, fanaticism; *credulity*, blind faith, superstition, naivety, gullibility; *credibility*, plausibility, likelihood.
adj. *believable*, credible, plausible, convincing, persuasive; *trustworthy*, dependable, reliable, trusty; *confident*, certain, sure, positive, convinced, assured; *opinionated*, dogmatic, doctrinaire, bigoted, fanatical; *credulous*, naive, gullible, superstitious, trusting, confiding.
vb. *believe*, maintain, hold, profess, avow; *trust*, rely, depend, count, bank, swear by, give credence; *adopt*, embrace, espouse, believe in; *think*, deem, allow, grant, be of the opinion; *be credulous*, fall for, take on trust, swallow (*colloq.*), buy (*colloq.*); *convince*, persuade, assure, win over, convert.

435 DISBELIEF
See also **428** (uncertainty); **869** (unbelief).
n. *disbelief*, incredulity, scepticism, cynicism; *doubt*, uncertainty, dubiety, unsureness; *unbelief*, agnosticism, atheism, heresy; *distrust*, mistrust, suspicion, wariness, misgiving, doubts, qualms, scruples; *recantation*, retrac-

tion, renunciation, disclaimer, apostasy; *derision*, scorn, mockery, ridicule.
adj. *disbelieving*, incredulous, sceptical, cynical, unconvinced; *doubtful*, dubious, unsure, uncertain; *unbelieving*, agnostic, atheistic, heretical, lapsed; *distrustful*, mistrustful, suspicious, wary, hesitant; *incredible*, unbelievable, inconceivable, implausible, unlikely; *untrustworthy*, unreliable, suspect, questionable; *derisive*, mocking, scornful.
vb. *disbelieve*, reject, call in question, challenge, discredit; *mock*, deride, scorn, laugh in the face of, laugh out of court; *mistrust*, distrust, suspect, have one's doubts about, hesitate; *recant*, retract, disclaim, renounce, change one's mind.

436 ASSENT

See also **19** (accord).
n. *assent*, agreement, concurrence, consent; *acceptance*, acknowledgment, acquiescence, submission, compliance; *sanction*, ratification, green light, go-ahead (*colloq.*); *approval*, approbation, thumbs-up (*colloq.*), endorsement, backing, support; *cooperation*, collaboration, unanimity, harmony, unison.
adj. *assenting*, consenting, agreeable, favourable, sympathetic; *accepting*, acquiescent, compliant, submissive; *cooperative*, collaborative, unanimous, likeminded; *approved*, unopposed, signed, carried.
vb. *assent*, consent, concur, agree, see eye to eye; *accept*, abide by, acquiesce, submit, comply, accede; *cooperate*, collaborate, meet half-way, fall in with; *admit*, concede, grant, allow, acknowledge; *sanction*, ratify, approve, welcome, applaud, okay (*colloq.*); *endorse*, support, back, second, go along with, sympathize with.

437 DISSENT

n. *dissent*, disagreement, discord, dissension; *dispute*, argument, quarrel, wrangle, controversy, difference of opinion; *negation*, contradiction, denial, repudiation, opposition, defiance; *disapproval*, dissatisfaction, discontent, disaffection, secession; *protest*, remonstration, objection, demurral, rejection, refusal; *disinclination*, reluctance, unwillingness, recalcitrance, disobedience.

adj. *dissenting*, dissident, recusant, disaffected, dissatisfied, discontented; *disinclined*, reluctant, unwilling, opposed, defiant, disobedient, bolshie (*colloq.*).

vb. *dissent*, disagree, agree to differ; *quarrel*, argue, fall out, wrangle, bicker; *dispute*, challenge, resist, oppose, defy, disobey; *refuse*, negate, reject, repudiate, deny; *object*, protest, demur, cavil, expostulate, remonstrate; *disapprove*, look askance at, frown on, hold no brief for.

438 KNOWLEDGE

See also **444** (wisdom); **624** (skill).
n. *knowledge*, wisdom, learning, erudition, scholarliness, pedantry; *awareness*, cognizance, understanding, comprehension, grasp, ken; *familiarity*, acquaintance, experience, dealings; *education*, schooling, instruction, enlightenment, information, illumination; *literacy*, numeracy, three Rs, rote-learning, book-learning; *skill*, accomplishment, expertise, proficiency, mastery, savvy (*colloq.*), know-how (*colloq*); *scholar*, student, intellectual, pedant, bookworm, polymath, Renaissance man, know-all (*colloq.*).

adj. *knowing*, wise, all-knowing, omniscient; *knowledgeable*, informed, well up on, au courant, au fait; *educated*, literate, numerate, well-read, lettered, enlightened, cultivated; *scholarly*, learned, bookish, erudite, donnish, academic, pedantic; *aware*, cognizant, conscious, familiar with, conversant, versed; *proficient*, skilful, accomplished, experienced.

vb. *know*, understand, comprehend, grasp; *get to know*, familiarize oneself with, acquaint oneself with, experience; *learn*, study, memorize, master; *know thoroughly*, know off pat, have at one's fingertips, know inside out, know backwards; *educate*, instruct, inform, enlighten.

439 IGNORANCE

See also **625** (unskilfulness).

n. *ignorance*, unknowingness, unawareness, incomprehension; *unfamiliarity*, inexperience, greenness, rawness; *inexpertness*, amateurishness, clumsiness, awkwardness, unskilfulness; *benightedness*, superstition, philistinism, illiteracy, stupidity, folly; *ignoramus*, dunce, booby, philistine, moron.

adj. *ignorant*, unknowing, uncomprehending, unwitting, unaware, unconscious; *unfamiliar*, inexperienced, raw, green, uninitiated; *uneducated*, uninformed, unenlightened, illiterate, philistine, crass, stupid; *inexpert*, unskilful, amateurish, clumsy, clueless (*colloq.*); *unknown*, uncharted, undiscovered, mysterious, enigmatic.

vb. *be ignorant*, not know, not have the foggiest idea, not have a clue (*colloq.*), not have an inkling; *mystify*, keep in the dark, baffle, perplex.

440 ACCURACY

See also **478** (truth).

n. *accuracy*, exactness, precision, exactitude; *correctness*, rightness, aptness, appropriateness; *meticulousness*, punctiliousness, rigour, pedantry, perfectionism; *fidelity*, truth, realism, authenticity, verisimilitude.

adj. *accurate*, precise, exact, spot on (*colloq.*), dead on (*colloq.*), bang on (*colloq.*); *correct*, right, apt, appropriate; *meticulous*, punctilious, rigorous, pedantic, perfectionist; *faithful*, true-to-life, factual, documentary, historical.

vb. *be accurate*, ring true, hit the nail on the head (*colloq.*); *prove accurate*, corroborate, substantiate, validate, bear out.

adv. *literally*, to the letter, verbatim, word for word.

441 ERROR

See also **430** (misjudgment); **479** (untruth).

n. *error*, mistake, miscalculation, misjudgment; *misunderstanding*, misconception, fallacy, misconstruction, misrepresentation, delusion; *inaccuracy*, imprecision, inexactness, carelessness, sloppiness; *wrongness*, unsoundness, falseness, misguidedness; *blunder*, oversight, gaffe, faux pas, lapse, howler (*colloq.*), bloomer (*colloq.*), clanger (*colloq.*); *misprint*, literal, erratum, corrigendum.

adj. *erroneous*, wrong, false, fallacious, delusory; *inaccurate*, incorrect, imprecise, inexact, wide of the mark; *misleading*, untrue, apocryphal, unfounded; *mistaken*, misguided, misinformed, misled; *erring*, fallible, wrong-headed, gone astray, off the rails (*colloq.*).

vb. *err*, be in the wrong, misjudge, miscalculate, blot one's copybook; *misunderstand*, misconceive, misinterpret, be at cross-purposes, bark up the wrong tree (*colloq.*); *blunder*, slip up, put one's foot in it (*colloq.*), boob (*colloq.*), make a balls-up/cockup (*vulg.*); *mislead*, misinform, deceive, delude, lead astray.

442 MAXIM

n. *maxim*, proverb, saying, adage, byword, saw, dictum; *epigram*, aphorism, apophthegm, witticism; *watchword*, slogan, catch phrase, motto; *moral*, golden rule, object lesson, cautionary tale; *truism*, cliché, platitude, bromide, chestnut (*colloq.*).

adj. *proverbial*, gnomic, aphoristic, epigrammatic; *pithy*, terse, witty, cryptic; *trite*, banal, hackneyed, commonplace, platitudinous, corny (*colloq.*).

443 NONSENSE

See also **445** (folly); **459** (lack of meaning); **772** (ridiculousness).

n. *nonsense*, silliness, foolishness, ridiculousness, absurdity; *senselessness*, meaninglessness, fatuousness, inanity; *rubbish*, drivel, gibberish, twaddle (*colloq.*), crap (*vulg.*), bullshit (*vulg.*), codswallop (*colloq.*).

adj. *nonsensical*, ridiculous, silly, foolish, laughable, ludicrous, absurd; *senseless*, meaningless, fatuous, asinine, inane; *crazy*, mad, preposterous, harebrained, crackpot (*colloq.*).

vb. *be absurd*, fool around, make a fool of oneself, act the fool; *rant*, rave, talk rot (*colloq.*), talk through a hole in one's head (*colloq.*).

444 WISDOM

See also **396** (intellect); **438** (knowledge).

n. *wisdom*, sagacity, sapience, profundity; *discernment*, perspicacity, penetration, acumen, insight; *understanding*, awareness, enlightenment, far-sightedness; *knowledge*, experience, learning, erudition, scholarliness; *common sense*, horse sense, level-headedness, sanity, realism, shrewdness, astuteness; *wise man*, sage, guru, mentor, pundit, thinker, Solomon.

adj. *wise*, sagacious, sapient, profound, deep; *perspicacious*, discerning, insightful, penetrating; *enlightened*, aware, understanding, far-sighted, long-headed; *knowledgeable*, experienced, learned, erudite, scholarly; *commonsensical*, realistic, level-headed, shrewd, astute.

vb. *be wise*, know the ways of the world, know what's what, have one's feet on the ground, have one's head screwed on (*colloq.*).

445 FOLLY

See also **397** (lack of intellect); **443** (nonsense); **447** (insanity).

n. *folly*, foolishness, silliness, stupidity; *futility*, pointlessness, fatuousness, meaninglessness, senselessness, absurdity; *imprudence*, indiscretion, recklessness, wildness; *lunacy*, madness, craziness, insanity, infatuation; *shallowness*, frivolity, levity, light-headedness, giddiness; *fool*, dolt, idiot, imbecile, moron, cretin, donkey, ass, goose (*colloq.*); *clown*, buffoon, simpleton, ninny, booby, sap, twit (*colloq.*), twerp (*colloq.*), berk (*colloq.*), prat (*colloq.*).

adj. *foolish*, stupid, silly, idiotic, asinine; *futile*, pointless, senseless, meaningless, absurd; *lunatic*, mad, crazy, insane; *unwise*, imprudent, indiscreet, irresponsible, reckless, wild; *shallow*, frivolous, light-headed, scatterbrained, giddy, scatty (*colloq.*); *puerile*, infantile, brainless, moronic, soft in the head.

vb. *be foolish*, look an idiot, make a fool of oneself, get one's fingers burned, never learn; *ramble*, burble, drivel, gibber, maunder, rabbit (*colloq.*); *go mad*, take leave of one's senses, be out of one's mind.

446 SANITY

n. *sanity*, saneness, rationality, coherence, reasonableness; *normality*, balance, stability, equilibrium; *common sense*, sobriety, lucidity, composure, clear-headedness, level-headedness.

adj. *sane*, rational, reasonable, coherent, sound; *normal*, balanced, stable, on an even keel; *lucid*, compos mentis, clear-headed, sober, calm, level-headed.

vb. *be sane*, be in one's right mind, be in possession of one's faculties; *see reason*, come to one's senses, calm down, compose oneself.

447 INSANITY

See also **58** (disturbance); **445** (folly).

n. *insanity*, mental illness, madness, lunacy, derangement; *maladjustment*, psychosis, neurosis, psychopathy, senility; *schizophrenia*, paranoia, hysteria, senile dementia, catatonia; *mania*, compulsion, obsession, phobia, fixation, complex, hangup (*colloq.*); *delusion*, hallucination, split personality, delirium, frenzy; *nervous breakdown*, neurasthenia, depression, baby blues (*colloq.*), melancholia; *eccentricity*, oddness, queerness, crankiness, weirdness; *lunatic*, madman, psychopath, schizophrenic, paranoiac, maniac, nutcase (*colloq.*), nut (*colloq.*), loony (*colloq.*); *eccentric*, crank, nutter (*colloq.*), oddball (*colloq.*), weirdo (*colloq.*).

adj. *insane*, mentally ill, mad, lunatic, disturbed, deranged, unbalanced, unhinged, senile, gaga (*colloq.*); *maladjusted*, autistic, neurotic, psychotic, schizoid, paranoid, hysterical, neurasthenic; *maniacal*, obsessive, fixated, compulsive, phobic, depressive, melancholic, manic-depressive; *crazed*, frenzied, delirious, raving, incoherent, demented, non compos mentis; *frantic*,

distraught, possessed, wild, berserk; *crazy* (*colloq.*), screwy (*colloq.*), loony (*colloq.*), nuts (*colloq.*), bonkers (*colloq.*), crackers (*colloq.*), bananas (*colloq.*), cuckoo (*colloq.*); *touched*, wanting, barmy (*colloq.*), batty (*colloq.*), daft (*colloq.*), potty (*colloq.*), dotty (*colloq.*), not all there, not right in the head, certifiable; *eccentric*, odd, queer, weird, cranky; *perverted*, twisted, warped, sick, kinky (*colloq.*).
vb. *be insane*, rave, ramble, wander, see things, have a screw loose (*colloq.*); *go mad*, go out of one's mind, break down (*colloq.*), crack up (*colloq.*), flip one's lid (*colloq.*), lose one's marbles (*colloq.*), go off one's rocker (*colloq.*); *madden*, craze, unhinge, unbalance, drive up the wall/round the bend (*colloq.*).

448 MEMORY

See also **486** (record).
n. *memory*, recollection, reminiscence, remembrance, recall, evocation; *good memory*, retention, total recall, photographic memory; *nostalgia*, retrospection, hindsight, flashback, blast from the past (*colloq.*), golden oldie (*colloq.*); *souvenir*, memento, keepsake, reminder, memorial, monument, relic; *memorandum*, memo, aide-memoire, mnemonic, cue.
adj. *remembered*, fresh, vivid, distinct; *memorable*, unforgettable, indelible, haunting; *reminiscent*, evocative, redolent, nostalgic, retrospective, commemorative.
vb. *remember*, recollect, recall, bring to mind, evoke; *retain*, not forget, stamp/fix on one's memory; *reminisce*, recapture, relive, go down memory lane, hark back, cast one's mind back, dredge up, dig up; *remind*, prompt, jog the memory, refresh one's memory, call up, bring back, ring a bell; *memorize*, commit to memory, learn by heart, get off pat.

449 OBLIVION

See also **405** (inattention).
n. *oblivion*, unconsciousness, unawareness, blankness, limbo; *forgetfulness*, absent-mindedness, inattention, abstractedness; *loss of memory*, amnesia, mental block, blank; *obliteration*, effacement, erasure.
adj. *oblivious*, unconscious, unaware, heedless, unmindful; *forgetful*, absent-minded, abstracted, inattentive, amnesiac; *forgotten*, half-remembered, dim, hazy, indistinct.
vb. *forget*, misremember, clean forget, have a memory like a sieve; *be forgotten*, slip one's mind, go in one ear and out the other; *half-remember*, have on the tip of one's tongue, have at the back of one's mind; *efface*, obliterate, wipe out, erase; *forgive*, amnesty, bury the hatchet, let bygones be bygones.

450 EXPECTATION

See also **104** (future time); **453** (foresight).
n. *expectation*, expectancy, anticipation, suspense, curiosity; *optimism*, confidence, hope, trust, certainty; *pessimism*, apprehension, dread, anxiety; *forecast*, outlook, prospect, lookout.
adj. *expectant*, waiting, ready, prepared, forewarned; *eager*, curious, agog, itching; *optimistic*, hopeful, confident, sanguine; *pessimistic*, apprehensive, gloomy, anxious; *expected*, foreseen, hoped for, longed for; *prospective*, future, impending.
vb. *expect*, contemplate, foresee, forecast, predict, see coming, bargain for; *await*, stand by, be at the ready, be on the edge of one's seat, be on tenterhooks; *anticipate*, look forward to, hope for, long for; *rely on*, count on, bank on, have confidence in; *dread*, fear, have qualms/misgivings; *be expected*, be in store, loom, be on the cards.
adv. *expectantly*, with bated breath, in suspense.

451 SURPRISE

See also **454** (lack of foresight); **759** (wonder).
n. *surprise*, shock, astonishment, amazement, wonderment; *revelation*, eye-opener (*colloq.*), bombshell, bolt from the blue, windfall, stunner (*col-*

loq.); *unexpectedness*, suddenness, unpredictability, uncertainty.
adj. *surprised*, astonished, astounded, startled, stunned, thunderstruck, dumbfounded; *off-guard*, taken aback, caught unawares, caught napping/on the hop (*colloq.*); *unexpected*, unforeseen, unannounced, sudden, abrupt; *surprising*, amazing, shocking, staggering (*colloq.*).
vb. *not expect*, not suspect, be caught out, be wrong-footed; *ambush*, spring, pounce, trap; *amaze*, astound, astonish, startle, bowl over (*colloq.*), stun; *jolt*, electrify, galvanize, shock.
adv. *unexpectedly*, all of a sudden, out of the blue.

452 DISAPPOINTMENT

n. *disappointment*, disillusionment, disenchantment, false dawn, anticlimax, letdown, comedown (*colloq.*); *failure*, flash in the pan, damp squib, washout (*colloq.*); *setback*, blow, hitch, snag, hiccup (*colloq.*); *frustration*, dissatisfaction, disgruntlement, discontent; *discouragement*, despondency, gloom, chagrin, regret.
adj. *disappointed*, dissatisfied, disgruntled, discontented; *disillusioned*, disenchanted, disabused, jaundiced, embittered, soured; *foiled*, thwarted, baffled, frustrated; *discouraged*, despondent, regretful, let down, crestfallen, sick as a parrot (*colloq.*); *disappointing*, unsatisfactory, anticlimactic, not up to expectation, overrated.
vb. *disappoint*, fall short, leave something to be desired; *frustrate*, thwart, foil, get the better of; *disillusion*, disenchant, disabuse, bring down to earth with a bang; *betray*, let down (*colloq.*), jilt, leave in the lurch (*colloq.*); *be disappointed*, learn one's lesson, learn the hard way, find out to one's cost, have one's fingers burned.

453 FORESIGHT

See also **450** (expectation); **455** (prediction).
n. *foresight*, anticipation, forethought, premeditation, far-sightedness, vision; *preparedness*, readiness, provision, contingency plan; *foreknowledge*, forewarning, presentiment, foreboding, prediction; *prescience*, second sight, clairvoyance, precognition.
adj. *foresighted*, prescient, clairvoyant, prophetic, visionary; *far-sighted*, provident, prudent, prepared, ready; *anticipatory*, preemptive, premeditated.
vb. *foresee*, forecast, predict, prophesy, forewarn; *anticipate*, expect, preempt, forestall; *make provision*, prepare, premeditate, provide for, take precautions, plan ahead.

454 LACK OF FORESIGHT

See also **451** (surprise).
n. *lack of foresight*, unpreparedness, unreadiness, improvidence; *shortsightedness*, blindness, thoughtlessness, imprudence; *improvisation*, spontaneity, extemporization.
adj. *unprepared*, unready, unsuspecting, caught unawares; *improvident*, shiftless, thoughtless, imprudent, prodigal, happy-go-lucky; *improvised*, makeshift, extempore, unpremeditated, off-the-cuff.
vb. *lack foresight*, muddle through, live from day to day, live from hand to mouth; *improvise*, extemporize, think on one's feet.

455 PREDICTION

See also **453** (foresight); **877** (occultism).
n. *prediction*, prophesy, forecast, prognosis; *omen*, warning, sign, presage, portent; *ominousness*, portentousness, auspiciousness; *clairvoyance*, extra-sensory perception, prescience, precognition, foreknowledge; *astrology*, palmistry, divination, augury, fortune-telling; *horoscope*, I Ching, tarot, crystal ball; *prophet*, oracle, soothsayer, seer, astrologer, medium, clairvoyant, palmist; *forecaster*, futurologist, Cassandra, doom merchant.
adj. *predictive*, prophetic, apocalyptic, revelatory; *ominous*, portentous, oracular, auspicious; *clairvoyant*, prescient, psychic.
vb. *predict*, foresee, prophesy, foretell, forewarn; *forecast*, read the future,

prognosticate; *foreshadow*, presage, prefigure, augur, spell, portend.

456 SUPPOSITION

See also **408** (idea).

n. *supposition*, assumption, premise, postulate; *idea*, suggestion, proposition, notion, fancy, conception; *theory*, hypothesis, conjecture, surmise, guess, inkling, hunch; *speculation*, guesswork, long shot, gamble.

adj. *suppositional*, hypothetical, conjectural, notional; *theoretical*, speculative, academic, armchair; *supposed*, alleged, so-called, putative.

vb. *suppose*, assume, presume, postulate, posit; *conjecture*, surmise, guess, divine, hazard a guess; *theorize*, hypothesize, speculate, imagine; *suggest*, propose, moot, put forward.

457 IMAGINATION

See also **4** (unreality); **479** (untruth).

n. *imagination*, creativity, inventiveness, originality, ingenuity; *mental image*, conception, visualization, projection, figment; *vision*, mind's eye, insight, empathy; *notion*, idea, whim, vagary, flight of fancy; *delusion*, hallucination, mirage, phantom; *fantasy*, fiction, escapism, make-believe, romance, daydreaming, wishful thinking, pipe dream, cloud-cuckoo-land.

adj. *imaginative*, creative, inventive, original, ingenious; *imaginary*, unreal, fictitious, make-believe, fabulous, legendary, mythological; *fanciful*, whimsical, fantastical, escapist, romantic, quixotic, idealistic.

vb. *imagine*, invent, create, devise, dream up, make up; *conceive*, think of, conjure up, visualize; *fantasize*, idealize, romanticize; *pretend*, make believe, daydream, build castles in Spain.

458 MEANING

See also **460** (intelligibility); **503** (clarity).

n. *meaning*, substance, essence, content, pith, matter; *sense*, import, force, tenor, drift, gist; *significance*, meaningfulness, point; *hidden meaning*, connotation, association, implication, suggestion, allusion; *figure of speech*, metaphor, simile, hyperbole; *symbolism*, allegory, parable, double meaning, ambiguity.

adj. *meaningful*, significant, pithy, meaty; *pointed*, telling, pregnant, revealing; *suggestive*, allusive, elliptical, implicit; *figurative*, metaphorical, allegorical, symbolic, connotative; *equivocal*, ambiguous, nebulous; *literal*, unambiguous, unequivocal, denotative; *synonymous*, equivalent, tautologous, tantamount; *semantic*, linguistic, philological.

vb. *mean*, denote, signify, designate; *symbolize*, stand for, connote, imply, suggest; *refer*, allude, mention, drive at, get at (*colloq.*); *convey*, express, communicate.

adv. *in a sense*, so to speak, as it were, that is to say.

459 LACK OF MEANING

See also **443** (nonsense); **461** (unintelligibility).

n. *lack of meaning*, meaninglessness, senselessness; *irrelevance*, insignificance, unimportance; *hollowness*, emptiness, triteness, banality, flatness; *unintelligibility*, illegibility, indecipherability, opaqueness; *nonsense*, gibberish, jargon, doubletalk, double Dutch (*colloq.*), gobbledygook (*colloq.*); *rubbish*, verbiage, twaddle (*colloq.*), claptrap (*colloq.*), piffle (*colloq.*), bunk (*colloq.*), flannel, hot air, eyewash (*colloq.*), guff (*colloq.*), waffle (*colloq.*).

adj. *meaningless*, senseless, expressionless, inscrutable, blank; *incomprehensible*, incoherent, unintelligible, opaque; *irrelevant*, insignificant, unimportant; *hollow*, empty, trivial, banal, trite; *nonsensical*, absurd, inane, fatuous; *verbose*, long-winded, waffly (*colloq.*).

vb. *mean nothing*, make no sense, not add up (*colloq.*); *talk nonsense*, prattle, babble, prate, rattle on, rabbit on (*colloq.*), blather; *jabber*, gibber, gabble, drivel, rant, rave.

460 INTELLIGIBILITY

See also **458** (meaning); **503** (clarity).

n. *intelligibility*, comprehensibility, legibility, readability, audibility; *clarity*, lucidity, limpidity, coherence; *simplicity*, straightforwardness, unambiguousness, explicitness; *simplification*, translation, explanation, demystification, popularization, vulgarization.

adj. *intelligible*, comprehensible, understandable, legible, readable, audible, decipherable; *clear*, lucid, limpid, coherent, transparent; *recognizable*, discernible, distinguishable, visible; *simple*, straight-forward, plain, explicit, unambiguous, forthright; *self-evident*, self-explanatory, obvious.

vb. *be intelligible*, make sense, add up (*colloq.*), speak for itself; *understand*, comprehend, penetrate, fathom; *take in*, take on board, cotton on, tumble to, twig (*colloq.*); *recognize*, discern, distinguish, make out; *clarify*, simplify, elucidate, decode, decipher, translate.

461 UNINTELLIGIBILITY

See also **459** (lack of meaning); **504** (obscurity).

n. *unintelligibility*, incomprehensibility, meaninglessness, incoherence; *difficulty*, obscurity, impenetrability, opaqueness; *illegibility*, indecipherability, unreadability, inaudibility, indistinctness; *jargon*, gibberish, mumbo-jumbo (*colloq.*), hocus-pocus (*colloq.*), double Dutch (*colloq.*); *equivocation*, pun, double entendre, weasel word, newspeak; *puzzlement*, perplexity, bafflement.

adj. *unintelligible*, incomprehensible, meaningless, incoherent; *impenetrable*, unfathomable, inscrutable, opaque; *obscure*, abstruse, esoteric, recondite, obfuscatory; *illegible*, indecipherable, unreadable, inaudible; *puzzling*, mysterious, enigmatic, cryptic; *ambiguous*, equivocal, paradoxical, evasive; *puzzled*, baffled, perplexed, nonplussed, flummoxed (*colloq.*), stumped (*colloq.*).

vb. *not understand*, make nothing of, not make head or tail of (*colloq.*), be at sea (*colloq.*); *be unintelligible*, baffle, perplex, puzzle, go over one's head, be beyond one; *equivocate*, prevaricate, fudge, obscure, obfuscate, complicate.

462 INTERPRETATION

n. *interpretation*, explanation, elucidation, clarification, illustration, exemplification; *account*, commentary, exposition, exegesis, explication, critique; *rendition*, version, paraphrase, adaptation; *annotation*, gloss, crib, translation, transcription; *application*, reading, construction, diagnosis, analysis.

adj. *interpretative*, explanatory, explicatory, elucidatory, illustrative; *critical*, analytical, diagnostic, evaluative.

vb. *interpret*, explain, expound, elucidate; *illuminate*, clarify, throw light on, account for; *read*, construe, understand, analyse, diagnose; *render*, reword, paraphrase, translate, transcribe, adapt; *comment on*, criticize, annotate, edit, gloss; *decipher*, decode, explain, solve, puzzle out, read between the lines.

adv. *namely*, to wit, that is, viz.

463 MISINTERPRETATION

n. *misinterpretation*, misunderstanding, misreading, misconstruction; *mistake*, misconception, misapprehension, error, delusion; *misrepresentation*, distortion, perversion, falsification; *travesty*, parody, caricature, mockery.

vb. *misinterpret*, misunderstand, misread, misconstrue, read into; *mistake*, confuse, get hold of the wrong end of the stick, get one's wires crossed; *falsify*, distort, twist, pervert, garble, scramble; *misrepresent*, travesty, parody, caricature.

464 DISPLAY

See also **394** (appearance); **785** (showiness).

n. *display*, presentation, demonstration, exhibition; *manifestation*, appearance, materialization, realization; *revelation*, disclosure, publication, exposure; *visibility*, prominence, conspicuousness, obviousness; *exhibit*, specimen, evidence, showpiece, collector's item; *show*, fair, exposition, market, parade,

pageant; *showroom*, showcase, shop window, market place.
adj. *displayed*, conspicuous, prominent, noticeable, striking; *visible*, apparent, manifest, plain; *marked*, pronounced, evident, obvious, patent; *glaring*, flagrant, overt, eye-catching, blatant, public; *open*, candid, frank, above board.
vb. *display*, present, demonstrate, exhibit; *manifest*, show, evince, give signs of; *unfold*, reveal, unveil, divulge, disclose; *expose*, lay bare, unearth, unfurl, unsheathe; *emphasize*, highlight, spotlight, feature, throw into prominence/relief, foreground; *advertise*, publicize, proclaim, announce; *flaunt*, parade, show off, brandish, flourish.
adv. *on display*, on view, on show; *in public*, openly, for all to see.

465 LATENCY

See also **373** (invisibility); **467** (secret); **469** (concealment).
n. *latency*, dormancy, imperceptibility, invisibility; *concealment*, secrecy, hiddenness, obscurity; *insidiousness*, treacherousness, stealthiness, underhandedness; *undercurrent*, undertone, insinuation, hint, innuendo; *enigma*, unknown quantity, snake in the grass, nigger in the woodpile, mole (*colloq.*), secret agent.
adj. *latent*, dormant, quiescent, hidden, imperceptible; *invisible*, concealed, submerged, subterranean, underground; *inconspicuous*, unseen, obscure, unsung, backroom; *unspoken*, unsaid, tacit, implicit; *secret*, clandestine, covert, undercover; *insidious*, treacherous, underhand, stealthy; *indirect*, veiled, suggestive, allusive.
vb. *be latent*, hide, keep a low profile, lie low, lie doggo (*colloq.*); *steal*, creep, slink, lurk; *hint*, imply, suggest, insinuate.

466 INFORMATION

See also **470** (publication); **471** (news).
n. *information*, knowledge, intelligence, news, facts, data, statistics, info (*colloq.*), gen (*colloq.*), dope (*colloq.*), lowdown (*colloq.*); *communication*, report, message, statement, bulletin, communiqué, dispatch, press release, handout, update; *dissemination*, diffusion, transmission, broadcast, distribution, circulation; *announcement*, notification, intimation, warning, instruction, briefing; *hint*, clue, advice, tip-off (*colloq.*), word in one's ear; *informant*, reporter, messenger, spokesman, courier; *informer*, source, channel, grapevine (*colloq.*), little bird (*colloq.*), supergrass, mole (*colloq.*), nark (*colloq.*), stool pigeon, sneak, telltale.
adj. *informative*, instructive, helpful, enlightening; *communicative*, forthcoming, chatty, newsy, gossipy; *informed*, briefed, posted, apprised, primed, clued up (*colloq.*), genned up (*colloq.*), au courant.
vb. *inform*, apprise, acquaint, enlighten, fill someone in, put in the picture, wise up (*colloq.*); *instruct*, brief, notify, warn, advise, tip off (*colloq.*); *communicate*, convey, put across/over, transmit, diffuse, broadcast, circulate, put about; *be informed*, know the score (*colloq.*), be in the know (*colloq.*), know the state of play; *impart*, reveal, tell, leak, blab (*colloq.*), blow the gaff (*colloq.*), let the cat out of the bag (*colloq.*); *inform on*, betray, denounce, tell tales on, squeal (*colloq.*), rat (*colloq.*), shop (*colloq.*).

467 SECRET

See also **465** (latency).
n. *secret*, mystery, riddle, puzzle, enigma, code, cipher; *suppression*, concealment, censorship, misinformation, blackout, cover-up; *secrecy*, privacy, confidence, discretion, reticence; *secretiveness*, furtiveness, shiftiness, stealth.
adj. *secret*, top-secret, hush-hush (*colloq.*), confidential, classified; *covert*, clandestine, undercover, behind-the-scenes, anonymous, incognito; *underhand*, hole-and-corner, furtive, shifty, stealthy; *secretive*, unforthcoming, uncommunicative, buttoned-up, tight-lipped, close; *private*, discreet, reticent, cagey (*colloq.*).

vb. *keep secret*, keep under wraps, not let on, not breathe a word, hold one's tongue, clam up, keep one's counsel; *suppress*, gag, censor, whitewash; *conceal*, cover up, hush up, sweep under the carpet.
adv. *in secret*, in private, in camera, behind closed doors; *confidentially*, privately, between ourselves; *secretly*, on the sly, on the quiet.

468 DISCLOSURE

See also **203** (uncovering); **470** (publication).
n. *disclosure*, exposure, revelation, discovery, exposé; *publication*, announcement, proclamation, promulgation; *betrayal*, indiscretion, leak, give-away (*colloq.*); *confession*, admission, avowal, acknowledgment.
adj. *disclosed*, revealed, exposed, out, public; *revealing*, indiscreet, tell-tale, informative; *candid*, frank, open, forthcoming.
vb. *disclose*, divulge, reveal, uncover; *expose*, unveil, lay bare, unmask, blow someone's cover; *publish*, air, ventilate, take the lid off (*colloq.*); *announce*, declare, proclaim, promulgate; *confess*, admit, own up, come clean (*colloq.*), make a clean breast of it; *confide*, open up, bare one's soul, unburden oneself, tell all; *betray*, let slip, leak, give the game away, spill the beans (*colloq.*), let the cat out of the bag (*colloq.*).

469 CONCEALMENT

See also **465** (latency).
n. *concealment*, hiding, dissimulation, pretence, masquerade; *conspiracy*, intrigue, machinations, plotting; *disguise*, camouflage, subterfuge, smokescreen, anonymity, pseudonym; *mask*, cloak, veil, cover; *hiding-place*, hideout, hidey-hole (*colloq.*), cache, den, lair, retreat, refuge.
adj. *concealed*, latent, hidden, buried, gone to ground/earth; *disguised*, masked, anonymous, incognito; *clandestine*, secret, furtive, hole-and-corner; *conspiratorial*, cloak-and-dagger, backdoor, surreptitious, Machiavellian.
vb. *conceal*, hide, stow away, secrete, stash (*colloq.*), bury; *disguise*, dissimulate, camouflage, mask, cloak, veil, cover up; *hide*, lurk, skulk, lie low, steal, slink, creep; *ambush*, creep up on, lie in wait, waylay; *conspire*, intrigue, plot, contrive.

470 PUBLICATION

See also **466** (information); **468** (disclosure); **471** (news).
n. *publication*, proclamation, announcement, disclosure; *circulation*, dissemination, diffusion, broadcasting; *publicity*, promotion, advertising, hype (*colloq.*), ballyhoo (*colloq.*), media coverage; *public relations*, PR, image-making, soft sell, showmanship; *public place*, forum, arena, theatre, platform, rostrum, pulpit, soapbox; *public*, audience, readership, market, admass; *notice*, advertisement, placard, poster, puff (*colloq.*), blurb (*colloq.*); *slogan*, commercial, plug (*colloq.*), trailer; *publicist*, promoter, advertiser, adman, PR man; *herald*, announcer, messenger, town crier, barker, tout; *common knowledge*, open secret, public property, household name.
adj. *published*, broadcast, current, circulating, available; *public*, notorious, infamous, celebrated.
vb. *publish*, announce, proclaim, disclose; *distribute*, circulate, put about, disseminate, diffuse; *broadcast*, relay, pass on, spread the word, noise abroad, shout from the rooftops; *herald*, trumpet, blaze aboard, beat the drum; *publicize*, promote, sell, advertise, hype (*colloq.*), plug (*colloq.*), trail.

471 NEWS

See also **466** (information); **470** (publication).
n. *news*, current affairs, tidings, intelligence, word; *report*, story, newsflash, headlines, stop press, scoop, exclusive; *press*, fourth estate, journalism, Fleet Street; *newspaper*, daily, broadsheet, quality, heavy (*colloq.*), tabloid, rag (*colloq.*), gutter press, yellow press, underground press; *organ*, journal, periodical, weekly, gazette, magazine,

glossy; *rumour*, hearsay, buzz, canard, gossip, tittle-tattle, scandal, sensationalism; *reporter*, journalist, correspondent, newsman, newshound, gossip, scandal-monger, grapevine, bush telegraph.

adj. *newsworthy*, scandalous, sensational; *current*, abroad, topical, going round, rumoured, rife; *newsy*, chatty, gossipy, informative.

vb. *report*, publish, spread, noise abroad; *be newsworthy*, make news, hit the headlines, cause a sensation, make a splash.

472 COMMUNICATIONS

n. *communications*, signalling, semaphore, Morse code, telegraphy, telephony; *telecommunications*, telegram, cable, wire, walkie-talkie, intercom, bleeper, telephone, videophone, answering machine; *post*, mail, pigeon post, parcel post, recorded delivery, registered post; *media*, broadcasting, television, small screen, telly (*colloq.*), gogglebox (*colloq.*), videorecorder; *radio*, wireless, transmitter, crystal set, steam radio, transistor; *station*, channel, network, wavelength, frequency, airwaves; *broadcast*, transmission, relay, telecast, simulcast, outside broadcast; *programme*, recording, repeat, sitcom, docudrama, soap opera, chat show, quiz, phone-in, telethon; *broadcaster*, newsreader, presenter, announcer, commentator, anchorman.

473 AFFIRMATION

See also **436** (assent).

n. *affirmation*, declaration, assertion, pronouncement, statement; *profession*, admission, confession, avowal; *allegation*, claim, accusation, charge; *assurance*, confirmation, corroboration, support, endorsement, backing; *pledge*, promise, commitment, guarantee; *insistence*, emphasis, stress, vehemence.

adj. *affirmative*, positive, declarative; *definite*, categorical, unequivocal, express; *assertive*, peremptory, emphatic, insistent; *pledged*, committed, sworn, fully paid-up; *plain*, blunt, round, outspoken.

vb. *affirm*, state, express, declare, assert, pronounce; *profess*, admit, confess, avow, own up to; *allege*, claim, maintain, hold; *confirm*, assure, corroborate, second, endorse, support, back; *emphasize*, stress, reiterate, insist on, urge; *promise*, pledge, swear, engage, commit.

474 NEGATION

See also **437** (dissent).

n. *negation*, nay, negative, veto, refusal, rejection; *denial*, disavowal, repudiation, disclaimer, dissociation; *rebuttal*, refutation, challenge, contradiction; *renunciation*, abnegation, abjuration, retraction; *revocation*, repeal, cancellation, abrogation, annulment.

adj. *negative*, negatory, contrary, contradictory; *opposed*, antagonistic, dissident, recusant.

vb. *negate*, negative, veto, deny, refuse; *refute*, rebut, gainsay, contradict, reject; *repudiate*, disavow, disown, disclaim, dissociate oneself; *renounce*, forswear, abjure, abnegate; *revoke*, abrogate, cancel, annul, repeal.

475 TEACHING

See also **477** (school).

n. *teaching*, pedagogy, schooling, education, edification, enlightenment; *guidance*, instruction, tuition, coaching; *induction*, initiation, training, preparation; *inculcation*, indoctrination, brainwashing, propaganda; *lesson*, class, seminar, tutorial, clinic, workshop; *course*, curriculum, syllabus, timetable; *adult education*, night school, evening classes, day release, sandwich course, block release; *teacher*, instructor, coach, trainer, tutor, educationalist, pedagogue, master, mistress, mentor, guru.

adj. *educational*, pedagogic, scholastic, academic; *educative*, didactic, instructive; *extramural*, extracurricular, recreational; *vocational*, liberal, technical, practical.

vb. *teach*, instruct, tutor, lecture; *coach*, train, school, drill, exercise;

educate, guide, cultivate, edify, enlighten; *initiate*, induct, prepare, break in, show the ropes (*colloq.*); *instil*, inculcate, indoctrinate, din in, hammer in.

476 LEARNING

See also **438** (knowledge).

n. *learning*, lore, knowledge, skill; *wisdom*, erudition, scholarliness, learnedness; *apprenticeship*, tutelage, pupillage, novitiate, training; *self-improvement*, study, application, industry; *lesson*, assignment, project, homework, prep (*colloq.*), revision; *learner*, apprentice, disciple, beginner, recruit, tyro, novice, probationer; *scholar*, pupil, autodidact, student, tutee, undergraduate, swot (*colloq.*), bookworm.

adj. *studious*, industrious, diligent, motivated; *learned*, scholarly, lettered, academic, erudite, knowledgeable, wise.

vb. *learn*, find out, study, apply oneself; *train*, practise, get the hang of (*colloq.*), acquire the knack; *revise*, learn up, swot (*colloq.*), brush up (*colloq.*), burn the midnight oil, mug up (*colloq.*), bone up (*colloq.*).

477 SCHOOL

See also **476** (learning).

n. *school*, academy, institute, seminary, conservatoire; *primary school*, infant school, nursery, creche, kindergarten; *secondary school*, blackboard jungle, grammar/comprehensive/public/state/prep/boarding school, crammer, finishing school, sixth-form college; *further education*, college, campus, university, varsity (*colloq.*), polytechnic, poly (*colloq.*), Oxbridge, redbrick/plate-glass university, groves of academe, alma mater; *schoolroom*, classroom, lecture hall, amphitheatre, auditorium.

478 TRUTH

See also **440** (accuracy).

n. *truth*, plain/honest truth, facts of life, home truths; *truthfulness*, veracity, honesty, integrity, probity; *candour*, sincerity, openness, frankness; *straightforwardness*, forthrightness, downrightness, bluntness; *ingenuousness*, naivety, artlessness, guilelessness.

adj. *truthful*, veracious, honest, upright; *reliable*, trustworthy, bona fide, honest-to-goodness, genuine; *candid*, sincere, open, frank, above board; *straightforward*, forthright, blunt, direct, bald, downright; *ingenuous*, naive, artless, guiless.

vb. *be truthful*, tell the truth, stick to the facts, give the true story; *speak one's mind*, speak up, make no bones about, call a spade a spade; *confess*, own up, open one's heart, make a clean breast of it.

479 UNTRUTH

See also **441** (error); **457** (imagination).

n. *untruth*, inaccuracy, falsehood, exaggeration, misrepresentation, distortion, perversion; *invention*, fabrication, fiction, romance, faction; *half-truth*, evasion, equivocation, ambiguity, white lie; *dishonesty*, disingenuousness, insincerity, falseness, duplicity, mendaciousness; *lie*, fib, whopper (*colloq.*), hoax, tall story, yarn (*colloq.*), cock and bull story, fairy tale, old wives' tale, superstition, fantasy.

adj. *untrue*, false, fictitious, unreal, imaginary; *fictional*, made-up, make-believe, fairy-tale, fabulous, legendary; *dishonest*, disingenuous, insincere, duplicitous, mendacious, lying; *evasive*, equivocal, ambiguous, hypocritical, two-faced; *spurious*, bogus, phoney, so-called.

vb. *lie*, pretend, dissemble, make believe; *invent*, fabricate, spin, weave, cook up; *exaggerate*, embellish, embroider, dress up.

480 DECEPTION

n. *deception*, dishonesty, duplicity, double-dealing, fraudulence; *deceitfulness*, artfulness, guile, craftiness, cunning; *treachery*, betrayal, perfidy, treason; *deceptiveness*, illusoriness, speciousness, meretriciousness; *trickery*, chicanery, sharp practice, sleight of hand, skulduggery (*colloq.*), hanky-panky (*colloq.*), jiggery-pokery (*colloq.*); *fraud*, racket, dodge, swindle, fiddle (*colloq.*), cheat, swiz (*colloq.*), rip-off (*colloq.*), con (*colloq.*); *trick*, ruse, stratagem, contrivance, wheeze (*colloq.*); *deceiver*, hypocrite, liar, impostor, traitor; *trickster*, cheat, fake, charlatan, quack, mountebank, rogue, swindler, con man (*colloq.*), shyster, wide boy (*colloq.*), spiv (*colloq.*), cowboy; *dupe*, fool, gull, soft touch, patsy (*colloq.*), mug (*colloq.*), fall guy (*colloq.*), sucker (*colloq.*).

adj. *deceitful*, dishonest, lying, duplicitous, treacherous, perfidious; *tricky*, artful, crafty, sly, wily, cunning; *fraudulent*, underhand, shifty, furtive; *deceptive*, illusory, specious, meretricious; *duped*, taken in, gulled, hoodwinked, taken for a ride (*colloq.*).

vb. *deceive*, defraud, cheat, fiddle (*colloq.*), wangle (*colloq.*), con (*colloq.*), swindle, fleece, diddle (*colloq.*), rip off (*colloq.*); *beguile*, delude, mislead, dupe, hoodwink, gull, bamboozle (*colloq.*), double-cross, put one over on (*colloq.*), lead up the garden path (*colloq.*); *be deceived*, be had (*colloq.*), fall for, get taken for a ride (*colloq.*).

481 FALSEHOOD

See also **479** (untruth).

n. *falsehood*, dishonesty, disingenuousness, insincerity, bad faith, mendaciousness; *hypocrisy*, cant, lip-service, cupboard love, crocodile tears; *deceitfulness*, duplicity, fraudulence, perjury, treason; *pretence*, dissimulation, play-acting, trickery; *front*, facade, show, semblance, sham, bluff, simulation; *falsification*, counterfeiting, forgery, faking.

adj. *false*, dishonest, untrue, mendacious, lying; *hypocritical*, insincere, two-faced, disingenuous, mealy-mouthed; *deceitful*, shifty, sly, double-dealing, duplicitous, treacherous, perfidious; *falsified*, unfounded, trumped-up, rigged, framed, fixed; *seeming*, feigned, put on, assumed, pretended; *fake*, bogus, sham, phoney, counterfeit, simulated, fraudulent.

vb. *be false*, lie, fib, lie through one's teeth, perjure oneself, bear false witness; *falsify*, doctor, fiddle (*colloq.*), cook (*colloq.*), fix, rig, frame, nobble (*colloq.*); *fake*, forge, counterfeit, simulate; *pretend*, feign, dissimulate, dissemble, play-act, pass oneself off as.

482 EXAGGERATION

See also **431** (overestimation).

n. *exaggeration*, overemphasis, overstatement, overkill, overexposure; *extravagance*, excessiveness, exorbitance, outrageousness, flamboyance; *inflatedness*, bombast, pomposity, hyperbole, hot air (*colloq.*); *fuss*, to-do, ballyhoo (*colloq.*), storm in a teacup; *melodrama*, purple patch, sensationalism, hype (*colloq.*); *yarn* (*colloq.*), tall story (*colloq.*), fisherman's tale, flight of fancy.

adj. *exaggerated*, overstated, overdone, over the top (*colloq.*); *extravagant*, outrageous, flamboyant, preposterous; *excessive*, exorbitant, inordinate, disproportionate, astronomical; *inflated*, bombastic, pompous, high-flown, overblown; *melodramatic*, histrionic, sensational, highly coloured, overwritten, hyperbolic.

vb. *exaggerate*, overemphasize, overstate, overexpose, overdo, go too far, go to extremes; *inflate*, magnify, talk up, blow up, make mountains out of molehills; *dramatize*, embroider, play up, hype (*colloq.*), pile on the agony, lay it on thick (*colloq.*).

483 UNDERSTATEMENT

See also **432** (underestimation).

n. *understatement*, underemphasis, minimization, underestimation; *subtlety*, delicacy, restraint, refinement; *simplicity*, plainness, bareness, austereness; *reserve*, reticence, diffidence, modesty; *suggestion*, trace, suspicion, soupçon; *insipidness*, pallidness, tastelessness, wishy-washiness (*colloq.*).

adj. *understated*, underemphasized, underestimated, underrated; *simple*, plain, bare, stark, unadorned; *delicate*, subtle, restrained, pastel, watercolour; *insipid*, pallid, diluted, wishy-washy (*colloq.*); *reserved*, reticent, diffident,

modest, unassuming; *imperceptible*, inconspicuous, unimpressive, underwhelming (*colloq.*).
vb. *understate*, underemphasize, underplay, underestimate, underrate; *moderate*, tone down, play down, water down, dilute; *deflate*, puncture, cut down to size, bring down to earth.

484 SIGN

n. *sign*, indication, mark, evidence, symptom; *image*, symbol, emblem, token; *hint*, pointer, clue, indicator, signpost, omen; *marker*, milestone, landmark, monument, memorial; *signal*, semaphore, tick-tack, warning sign, siren, alarm, beacon; *sign language*, mime, dumb show, charades, body language; *gesture*, nod, wink, shrug, nudge, wave; *applause*, clap, cheer, big hand (*colloq.*); *hiss*, boo, catcall, V-sign, raspberry, slow handclap; *badge*, insignia, coat of arms, crest, bearings, blazon; *uniform*, livery, dress, colours, tartan, old school tie; *flag*, ensign, standard, banner, pennant, tricolour, Union Jack/Flag, Blue Peter, skull and crossbones, Stars and Stripes.
adj. *indicative*, symptomatic, revealing, telling, significant; *symbolic*, token, emblematic, representational; *expressive*, suggestive, redolent.
vb. *indicate*, show, point to, signal, signpost; *reveal*, manifest, betoken, betray, attest to, evince; *symbolize*, stand for, represent, signify; *mark out*, designate, delimit, demarcate; *gesticulate*, mimic, act out, mime, copy; *gesture*, motion, wave, beckon, nod, shrug, point; *frown*, scowl, grimace, pout, smile.

485 IDENTIFICATION

n. *identification*, classification, designation, naming; *identity*, individuality, selfhood, particularity, idiosyncrasy; *identifying sign*, name, signature, autograph, fingerprint, initials, monogram; *proof of identity*, passport, I.D. card, visiting card; *trademark*, hallmark, brand name, imprint, logo, colophon; *marking*, track, spoor, footprint; *password*, watchword, shibboleth; *label*, nameplate, ticket, tag, docket, sticker; *seal*, stamp, counterfoil, stub, duplicate.
adj. *identifying*, classificatory, designatory; *characteristic*, typical, individual, idiosyncratic, quirky; *identifiable*, recognizable, distinguishable, discernable; *identified*, named, known, branded, earmarked.
vb. *identify*, name, classify, categorize, pin down, pigeonhole; *label*, ticket, tag, docket, stamp, number, letter; *sign*, seal, autograph, countersign, initial, brand, tattoo, earmark.

486 RECORD

See also **448** (memory).
n. *record*, register, roll, catalogue, inventory; *documentation*, file, dossier, case history, curriculum vitae; *account*, report, minutes, notes, jottings, memo; *diary*, journal, scrapbook, album, log, chronicle, archive, annals; *index card*, filing system, microfiche, tape recording, videotape, data bank; *monument*, statue, memorial, cairn, obelisk; *trace*, vestige, relic, remains; *trail*, track, path, swath, wake, wash, tidemark; *recorder*, registrar, clerk, amanuensis, scribe, secretary; *chronicler*, historian, diarist, archivist.
vb. *record*, register, document, catalogue, index, list, file; *report*, document, chronicle, set down, film, tape-record, photograph, video; *note*, minute, jot down, table, log; *score*, chalk up, mark up, notch up, tick off.
adv. *on record*, in black and white, on tape, in the can (*colloq.*).

487 OBLITERATION

See also **449** (oblivion).
n. *obliteration*, erasure, effacement, deletion; *cancellation*, annulment, revocation, repeal; *suppression*, censorship, blackout; *abolition*, elimination, liquidation, annihilation; *blank*, void, tabula rasa, clean slate; *rubber*, eraser, sponge, Snopake (*tdmk.*).
vb. *obliterate*, erase, efface, rub out, wipe out, blot out, snopake; *delete*, cross out, score out, strike out, scrub

(*colloq.*); *cancel*, annul, revoke, repeal; *suppress*, quash, censor, blue-pencil, black out; *expunge*, eliminate, liquidate, annihilate; *bury*, submerge, cover up.

488 REPRESENTATION

n. *representation*, depiction, description, delineation; *enactment*, performance, rendering; *personification*, imitation, impersonation, characterization; *illustration*, exemplification, typification, symbolization, figuration; *impression*, likeness, portrayal, image; *portrait*, icon, effigy, statue, waxwork, dummy, photograph, painting, hologram; *reproduction*, facsimile, duplicate, copy; *design*, blueprint, sketch, outline, diagram; *plan*, map, chart, projection; *ornamental art*, fine arts, performing arts, photography, cinematography.

adj. *representative*, typical, exemplary, symbolic, emblematic, figurative; *descriptive*, graphic, vivid, evocative, impressionistic; *representational*, illustrative, pictorial, realistic, naturalistic, true-to-life.

vb. *represent*, stand for, symbolize, connote, mean, signify; *typify*, characterize, illustrate, exemplify; *personify*, epitomize, embody, incarnate; *enact*, perform, mimic, impersonate, imitate; *depict*, describe, delineate, draw; *portray*, picture, figure, image, capture, evoke; *design*, sketch, draft, block out, map, chart, outline.

489 MISREPRESENTATION

n. *misrepresentation*, distortion, exaggeration, perversion, falsification; *travesty*, caricature, parody, mockery; *poor likeness*, daub, scrawl, botch, pale imitation, mere shadow; *misinterpretation*, misconstruction, misreading.

adj. *misrepresented*, falsified, distorted, inaccurate, misleading; *flat*, cardboard, unrealistic, infelicitous, inept.

vb. *misrepresent*, distort, exaggerate, pervert, falsify, mislead; *travesty*, caricature, parody, make a mockery of.

490 PAINTING

n. *painting*, art, fine art, graphics, illustration; *artistry*, composition, technique, draughtsmanship, brushwork, palette; *representation*, treatment, handling, rendering, depiction, portrayal; *artistic medium*, watercolour, oil, pastel, crayon, charcoal, tempera, gouache, acrylic; *picture*, mural, fresco, poster, canvas; *sketch*, line drawing, model, cartoon, maquette; *work of art*, old master, chef d'oeuvre, masterpiece; *studio*, atelier, gallery, museum; *portrait*, still life, collage, miniature, landscape, seascape, interior; *artist*, painter, draughtsman, designer, colourist.

adj. *artistic*, painterly, pictorial, picturesque, scenic, graphic; *representational*, realistic, figurative, Impressionist; *abstract*, nonrepresentational, nonobjective, Expressionist, Cubist, minimalist.

vb. *paint*, portray, depict, illustrate, limn, daub; *draw*, sketch, crayon, pencil; *colour*, shade, tint, wash, ink.

491 PHOTOGRAPHY

See also **525** (cinema).

n. *photography*, photojournalism, cinematography, radiography, holography; *photograph*, photo, X-ray, hologram, snapshot, snap, still, frame; *slide*, diapositive, transparency, print; *negative*, exposure, enlargement, blow-up, shot; *film*, filmstrip, microfilm, spool, reel, cassette, cartridge; *camera*, lens, viewfinder, flash, enlarger, projector, viewer, epidiascope, carousel.

adj. *photographic*, cinematographic, radiographic, holographic; *photogenic*, camera-shy, snap-happy (*colloq.*); *overexposed*, underexposed, fuzzy, grainy.

vb. *photograph*, take, snap, photostat, X-ray; *expose*, develop, print, process, enlarge, reproduce.

492 SCULPTURE

n. *sculpture*, plastic arts, modelling, carving, origami; *relief*, cameo, embossing, bas-relief, low relief, mezzo-relievo, high relief; *statue*, statuary, figurine, statuette, bust, head, torso, construction, mobile, stabile; *model*, maquette, death mask, cast, mould; *bronze*, stone, marble, clay, papier-mâché.

adj. *sculptured*, sculpted, graven, moulded, glyptic; *plastic*, mouldable, fictile, malleable; *embossed*, raised, repoussé.

vb. *sculpt*, sculpture, carve, hew, cut, chisel; *model*, fashion, mould, shape, cast; *raise*, emboss, undercut.

493 ENGRAVING

n. *engraving*, etching, intaglio, drypoint, line engraving, photogravure; *mezzotint*, aquatint, woodcut, linocut; *chasing*, fluting, chamfering, groove, line, channel, incision, glyph; *chisel*, burin, graver, needle.

adj. *engraved*, graven, etched; *incised*, carved, grooved, chased, sunk, recessed, fluted, chamfered.

vb. *engrave*, etch, chase, chamfer, chisel, incise; *impress*, stamp, recess.

494 LANGUAGE

See also **496** (word).

n. *language*, speech, tongue, talk, communication, body language, sign language; *style*, diction, parlance, vocabulary, idiom, phraseology, terminology, lingo (*colloq.*), patter, jargon; *natural language*, mother tongue, lingua franca, pidgin, creole, franglais; *artificial language*, Esperanto, Volapuk, computer language, BASIC, FORTRAN, COBOL; *usage*, Standard English, Queen's English, Received Pronunciation; *dialect*, vernacular, patois, Scouse, Brummie, Geordie, Mummerset; *regionalism*, accent, brogue, burr; *slang*, colloquialism, argot, cant, back slang, pig Latin, rhyming slang; *linguistics*, philology, grammar, semantics, phonetics.

adj. *linguistic*, philological, grammatical, semantic, phonetic; *idiomatic*, colloquial, slangy, racy, vulgar, demotic, common; *dialectal*, regional, local, broad, thick; *bilingual*, fluent, polyglot, multilingual.

495 LETTER

See also **513** (writing).

n. *letter*, character, sign, symbol, alphabet, ABC, syllabary; *picture writing*, ideogram, pictogram, hieroglyphic, cuneiform, rune; *lettering*, italic, copperplate, cursive, minuscule, capital, majuscule, uncial; *initial*, monogram, abbreviation, contraction, acronym, acrostic; *speech sound*, vowel, consonant, phoneme, syllable; *spelling*, orthography, transliteration, misspelling, cacography, dyslexia.

adj. *alphabetical*, hieroglyphic, runic, Cyrillic; *syllabic*, consonantal, vocalic; *capital*, upper-case, small, lower-case, italic, roman.

vb. *alphabetize*, syllabify, transliterate, spell; *initial*, letter, sign.

496 WORD

See also **494** (language).

n. *word*, expression, term, name, locution, phrase; *synonym*, antonym, homonym, homophone; *abbreviation*, contraction, acronym, portmanteau word, blend; *word origin*, etymology, root, derivative, folk etymology; *word-play*, pun, spoonerism, anagram, nonce word, neologism, coinage, weasel word; *slogan*, catch phrase, watchword, vogue word, buzzword, cliché; *swearword*, four-letter word, obscenity, oath, billingsgate, bad language; *long word*, polysyllable, mouthful, tongue twister; *barbarism*, corruption, malapropism, solecism; *word list*, glossary, vocabulary, lexicon, dictionary, thesaurus, index, concordance.

adj. *verbal*, lexical, terminological; *literal*, verbatim, word for word; *articulate*, fluent, expressive; *wordy*, verbose, sesquipedalian.

vb. *word*, state, formulate, phrase; *articulate*, express, put into words, verbalize.

497 NAME

n. *name*, designation, appellation, denomination; *epithet*, handle (*colloq.*), moniker (*colloq.*), nickname, pet name, sobriquet, pseudonym, pen name; *forename*, first/Christian/given name, middle name, surname, maiden name, last/family name, patronymic, metronymic; *place name*, toponym, eponym, namesake; *nomenclature*, terminology, classification, identification; *naming*, roll call, dubbing ceremony, christening, baptism; *title*, style, form of address, signature, label.

adj. *named*, titled, nee, alias, a.k.a., so-called; *nominal*, titular, in name only, named after, eponymous.

vb. *name*, call, term, designate, denominate; *title*, style, christen, baptize, dub, nickname; *classify*, identify, label, tag.

498 MISNOMER

n. *misnomer*, wrong name, pseudonym, pen name, nom de plume, alias, false name, nom de guerre; *nickname*, pet name, sobriquet, assumed name, stage name; *false identity*, impersonation, imposture, mistaken identity; *misnaming*, miscalling, malapropism, solecism; *anonymity*, namelessness, facelessness, no name, anon, so-and-so, A.N. Other, Mr X; *unnamed thing*, what's-its-name, thingummy (*colloq.*), thingamajig (*colloq.*), thingamabob (*colloq.*), thingie (*colloq.*).

adj. *misnamed*, pseudonymous, professed, so-called, self-styled, would-be; *anonymous*, nameless, faceless, unknown, unidentified, unnamed, incognito.

vb. *misname*, miscall, mistake; *impersonate*, pass oneself off as, go under the name of.

499 PHRASE

n. *phrase*, expression, turn of phrase, locution, construction, collocation, idiom; *set phrase*, saying, formula, proverb, catch phrase, cliché, motto; *inscription*, phrasing, wording, diction, parlance; *rephrasing*, rewording, restatement, paraphase, circumlocution.

vb. *phrase*, word, express, state, formulate, put into words; *rephrase*, reword, restate, paraphrase.

500 GRAMMAR

n. *grammar*, usage, syntax, word order, morphology, word formation; *declension*, inflection, conjugation, case, person, number, tense, voice, mood, agreement; *word class*, part of speech, noun, pronoun, adjective, modifier, verb, adverb, conjunction, article, determiner, preposition, interjection; *subject*, predicate, object, complement, apposition; *affix*, prefix, suffix, infix.

adj. *grammatical*, syntactic, morphological, correct, well-formed, standard, acceptable; *nominal*, adjectival, verbal, adverbial, prepositional, interjectional; *comparative*, superlative, absolute; *active*, passive, subjunctive.

vb. *parse*, analyse, construe, conjugate, inflect, decline; *qualify*, modify, govern, take, agree.

501 GRAMMATICAL ERROR

n. *grammatical error*, solecism, misusage, barbarism; *mistake*, slip of the tongue/pen, split infinitive, double negative, dangling participle; *ungrammaticality*, misconstruction, hypercorrection.

adj. *ungrammatical*, incorrect, hypercorrect, unacceptable; *nonstandard*, substandard, loose, sloppy, careless.

502 STYLE

n. *style*, mode, fashion, manner, idiom, vein, strain; *phraseology*, vocabulary, wording, diction, register, level, tone; *fluency*, mastery, articulacy, eloquence, word power, command, rhetoric, oratory; *elegance*, power, vigour, raciness; *inelegance*, awkwardness, clumsiness, stiltedness.

adj. *stylistic*, literary, rhetorical, oratorical; *mannered*, stylized, idiosyncratic, quirky; *elegant*, well crafted, well turned, fluent, articulate, eloquent; *inelegant*, infelicitous, stilted, clumsy, awkward, ponderous, flat, prosaic.

503 CLARITY

See also **460** (intelligibility).

n. *clarity*, clearness, lucidity, limpidity, transparency; *intelligibility*, perspicuity,

straightforwardness, unambiguousness; *exactness*, preciseness, explicitness, directness; *simplicity*, plainness, unadornedness, baldness.
adj. *clear*, lucid, limpid, transparent; *intelligible*, perspicuous, understandable, straightforward, uncomplicated, unambiguous; *simple*, plain, uncluttered, unadorned; *exact*, precise, clear-cut, explicit, direct, spelt out, in words of one syllable.

504 OBSCURITY

See also **461** (unintelligibility).
n. *obscurity*, unintelligibility, abstruseness, opaqueness; *complexity*, convolutedness, denseness, overcompression; *vagueness*, indefiniteness, ambiguity, obfuscation, obscurantism; *inexactness*, impreciseness, looseness, diffuseness, sloppiness; *wordiness*, verbosity, bombast, waffle (*colloq.*).
adj. *obscure*, unclear, unintelligible, opaque; *abstruse*, esoteric, recondite, recherché; *vague*, indefinite, ambiguous, obscurantist, obfuscatory; *complex*, involved, intricate, dense, compressed; *inexact*, imprecise, loose, woolly, sloppy, diffuse; *wordy*, verbose, overwritten, bombastic.

505 CONCISENESS

See also **179** (shortness); **520** (summary).
n. *conciseness*, concision, succinctness, brevity, pithiness; *terseness*, curtness, compression, economy, laconicism; *shorthand*, telegraphese, ellipsis; *condensation*, abridgment, summary, résumé.
adj. *concise*, succinct, brief, economical, short and sweet; *terse*, curt, monosyllabic, laconic, lapidary; *pithy*, epigrammatic, aphoristic, sententious; *compressed*, dense, compact, condensed, summarized; *crisp*, clipped, trenchant, incisive.
vb. *be concise*, come straight to the point, cut a long story short, not beat about the bush, cut the cackle (*colloq.*); *abbreviate*, contract, abridge, summarize; *compress*, condense, boil down, telescope.
adv. *in brief*, in a word, in a nutshell.

506 DIFFUSENESS

See also **530** (talkativeness).
n. *diffuseness*, wordiness, verbosity, long-windedness, prolixity; *discursiveness*, repetitiveness, filibustering, padding, waffle (*colloq.*); *digression*, excursus, disquisition, peroration, harangue, tirade; *pleonasm*, tautology, redundancy, circumlocution.
adj. *diffuse*, verbose, wordy, long-winded, prosy, prolix; *repetitive*, redundant, tautologous, pleonastic, circumlocutious, roundabout; *protracted*, lengthy, tedious, long-drawn-out; *discursive*, digressive, rambling, off the point.
vb. *be diffuse*, enlarge, expand, dilate, amplify, elaborate, expatiate; *draw out*, spin out, pad, protract, filibuster; *discourse*, hold forth, harangue, perorate; *digress*, wander, ramble, rabbit (*colloq.*), blather (*colloq.*), gush, waffle (*colloq.*).
adv. *at length*, ad nauseam, on and on.

507 EMPHASIS

n. *emphasis*, stress, reiteration, insistence, vehemence; *force*, strength, power, vigour, punch (*colloq.*); *vividness*, raciness, verve, sparkle; *incisiveness*, trenchancy, pointedness, bite, edge, mordancy; *conviction*, fervour, passion, eloquence, cogency; *grandiloquence*, solemnity, weight, gravitas.
adj. *emphatic*, reiterative, insistent, vehement; *forceful*, powerful, cogent, vigorous, strongly worded, hard-hitting, punchy (*colloq.*); *vivid*, lively, sparkling, graphic, racy; *incisive*, trenchant, pointed, biting, cutting, mordant; *passionate*, fervent, convincing, persuasive, eloquent, effective; *serious*, weighty, measured, solemn, grave; *grandiloquent*, inspired, lofty, sublime.
vb. *emphasize*, stress, insist on, reiterate, underline, underscore, spell out, ram home, say in no uncertain terms; *persuade*, convince, carry weight, hit home.

508 LACK OF EMPHASIS

n. *lack of emphasis*, insipidness, vapidness, flatness; *prosiness*, turgidity, stiltedness, ponderousness; *dullness*, dryness, tediousness, jejuneness; *ineffectiveness*, feebleness, limpness, understatedness; *sentimentality*, mawkishness, schmaltz (*colloq.*).
adj. *unemphatic*, weak, insipid, colourless, flat; *prosy*, turgid, stilted, ponderous; *dull*, dry, thin, impoverished, jejune; *ineffective*, feeble, limp, understated; *prosaic*, pedestrian, clichéd, hackneyed, trite; *sentimental*, mawkish, novelettish, schmaltzy (*colloq.*), corny (*colloq.*).

509 SIMPLICITY

n. *simplicity*, straightforwardness, clarity, directness; *plainness*, naturalness, restraint, no frills, austerity, starkness, baldness; *unaffectedness*, unpretentiousness, homeliness, unsophistication, artlessness, naivety; *frankness*, candour, matter-of-factness, downrightness, bluntness.
adj. *simple*, straightforward, direct, uncomplicated, easy; *plain*, unadorned, unvarnished, uncluttered, natural, homespun; *austere*, restrained, stark, bare, bald; *unpretentious*, unaffected, unassuming, down-to-earth, no-nonsense, matter-of-fact; *unsophisticated*, artless, naive, innocent; *everyday*, workaday, homely, commonplace, humdrum.
vb. *speak plainly*, not mince one's words, spell it out, call a spade a spade, get down to brass tacks.
adv. *simply*, in plain English, in words of one syllable, not to put too fine a point on it.

510 ORNAMENT

See also **766** (decoration).
n. *ornament*, adornment, embellishment, enhancement; *ornamentation*, decoration, embroidery, frills, fuss, clutter; *ornateness*, preciousness, tweeness, floweriness, floridness, purple passage; *rhetoric*, bombast, fustian, pomposity, turgidity; *extravagance*, flamboyance, showiness, flashiness; *pretentiousness*, affectation, sententiousness, grandioseness.
adj. *ornate*, elaborate, decorative, rich, lavish; *fussy*, frilly, cluttered, busy; *precious*, twee, flowery, florid; *extravagant*, flamboyant, showy, flashy; *rhetorical*, orotund, resonant, high-flown, grandiloquent; *inflated*, pompous, turgid, bombastic, pretentious, sententious.
vb. *decorate*, embellish, enhance, embroider, lay it on with a shovel/trowel (*colloq.*).

511 ELEGANCE

n. *elegance*, taste, style, refinement, beauty, gracefulness; *restraint*, simplicity, classicism, proportion; *symmetry*, balance, flow, rhythm, harmony, smoothness, ease; *poise*, decorum, distinction, stateliness, dignity; *correctness*, propriety, appropriateness, felicity; *stylishness*, sophistication, smartness, polish, flair.
adj. *elegant*, tasteful, stylish, beautiful, graceful, refined; *restrained*, simple, understated, classical, symmetrical; *harmonious*, balanced, well-proportioned, flowing, rhythmic, smooth; *felicitous*, appropriate, well-put, correct, proper; *distinguished*, stately, dignified, poised, decorous; *sophisticated*, smart, polished, soigné, well-groomed.
vb. *make elegant*, beautify, refine, polish, finish, smarten up.

512 INELEGANCE

n. *inelegance*, gracelessness, ugliness, unsightliness, unshapeliness, lumpishness; *gaucheness*, awkwardness, clumsiness, ungainliness, unwieldiness; *artificiality*, stiffness, stiltedness, woodenness; *tastelessness*, vulgarity, impropriety, incorrectness, inappropriateness; *crudeness*, boorishness, uncouthness, coarseness.
adj. *inelegant*, graceless, gauche, awkward, clumsy, ungainly; *ugly*, unsightly, unshapely, lumpy; *artificial*, forced, contrived, laboured, stiff, stilted, wooden; *inappropriate*, infelicitous, jarring, grating, incorrect, improper; *tasteless*, vulgar, unrefined,

common; *crude*, coarse, boorish, uncouth.

513 WRITING

See also **495** (letter); **515** (correspondence).

n. *writing*, composition, authorship, journalism, hackwork, Grub Street; *correspondence*, paperwork, documentation, bumf (*colloq.*), notes; *written matter*, script, copy, manuscript, typescript, transcript, minutes; *caption*, heading, legend, epigraph, inscription, rubric; *handwriting*, longhand, scribble, scrawl, cacography; *shorthand*, stenography, speedwriting, typewriting; *calligraphy*, penmanship, copperplate, pothook, flourish; *alphabet*, braille, code, cipher, hieroglyphics, pictogram, ideogram, cryptogram; *stationery*, vellum, parchment, papyrus, scroll.
adj. *written*, graphic, handwritten, manuscript, autograph, holograph; *italic*, roman, cursive, uncial; *bold*, round, flowing, spidery, cramped, crabbed.
vb. *write*, pen, trace, print, type, scribble, scrawl; *compose*, draft, put into writing, set down in black and white, put pen to paper; *copy*, transcribe, take down, jot, note, minute.

514 PRINT

n. *print*, type, newsprint, copy, text, printout; *publication*, impression, edition, offprint, reprint, print run; *printing*, lithography, offset, letterpress; *typesetting*, filmsetting, photocomposition, cold type, Monotype (*tdmk.*), Linotype (*tdmk.*), hot metal; *typography*, typeface, fount, upper/lower case, boldface, lightface, serif, sansserif; *page*, folio, proof, galley, revise, bromide; *printer's error*, correction, literal, typo; *printer*, typesetter, compositor, proofreader, copy editor, subeditor.
adj. *printed*, typographic, typeset, in/out of print.
vb. *print*, print off, run off, publish; *typeset*, photocompose, filmset.

515 CORRESPONDENCE

See also **513** (writing).

n. *correspondence*, communication, exchange, acknowledgment, reply, answer; *post*, mail, letters, postbag, delivery, dispatch; *letter*, epistle, missive, circular, chain letter, round robin, junk mail (*colloq.*); *greetings card*, postcard, love letter, Valentine, billet doux, poison pen letter; *correspondent*, addressee, sender, recipient, penfriend, penpal; *envelope*, s.a.e., cover, stamp, seal, postcode.
adj. *epistolary*, postal, air-mail.
vb. *correspond*, write, communicate, acknowledge, reply, drop a line to (*colloq.*); *post*, forward, mail, send; *address*, stamp, frank, seal.

516 BOOK

See also **518** (literature).

n. *book*, volume, tome, manuscript, MS, title; *bestseller*, classic, remainder, potboiler; *publication*, edition, impression, reprint, reissue; *text*, libretto, screenplay, scenario, lyrics; *library*, set, collection, anthology, series, compendium; *booklet*, pamphlet, leaflet, tract, brochure, prospectus; *bibliography*, catalogue, reading list, index; *cover*, dust jacket, binding, spine, boards; *page*, recto, verso, flyleaf, endpaper, frontispiece, appendix; *reader*, bookworm, bibliophile, librarian, bookseller.
adj. *hardback*, cased, softback, bound, looseleaf, paperback.

517 DESCRIPTION

See also **488** (representation).

n. *description*, account, exposition, delineation, portrayal, profile; *narration*, report, recital, tale, anecdote; *nonfiction*, reportage, documentary, biography, travelogue; *story*, narrative, plot, subplot, scenario, storyline; *history*, chronicle, annals, memoirs, case history, life story; *summary*, thumbnail sketch, cameo, vignette; *narrator*, story-teller, raconteur, historian, chronicler.
adj. *descriptive*, expository, narrative, graphic; *colourful*, vivid, scenic, picturesque; *true-to-life*, naturalistic, realistic, photographic; *expressive*, evocative, suggestive, impressionistic.

vb. *describe*, depict, delineate, characterize, represent; *draw*, paint, sketch, outline; *narrate*, recount, relate, tell, report, chronicle.

518 LITERATURE

See also **516** (book); **521** (poetry); **522** (prose).

n. *literature*, prose, poetry, classics, criticism, lit. crit; *novel*, drama, short story, novella; *nonfiction*, autobiography, biography, memoirs; *fiction*, romance, science fiction, sci-fi, detective story, thriller, whodunnit (*colloq.*); *pulp fiction*, trash, pap, novelette, penny dreadful, instant book, novelization; *bestseller*, blockbuster (*colloq.*), potboiler, classic; *writer*, author, dramatist, poet, novelist, litterateur, ghostwriter, wordsmith.

adj. *literary*, poetic, epic, heroic, mock-heroic, picaresque; *fictional*, romantic, cloak-and-dagger.

vb. *write*, author, compose, ghostwrite, compile, edit; *fictionalize*, dramatize, novelize, adapt.

519 DISSERTATION

n. *dissertation*, discourse, essay, treatise, thesis, monograph, paper; *exposition*, disquisition, examination, enquiry, survey, study, commentary, analysis, critique; *review*, notice, article, piece, write-up, editorial, leader.

adj. *discursive*, expository, critical, analytical.

vb. *dissertate*, treat, handle, discuss, examine; *develop*, amplify, go into, expatiate on, discourse on; *criticize*, comment, review, survey, write up.

520 SUMMARY

See also **505** (conciseness).

n. *summary*, résumé, precis, abstract, synopsis; *contents*, substance, gist, the long and short of it; *outline*, sketch, rundown, digest; *selection*, condensation, anthology, compilation, miscellany.

adj. *summarized*, abridged, condensed, potted; *concise*, brief, succinct, sketchy.

vb. *summarize*, sum up, precis, abstract; *condense*, conflate, abridge, boil down.

521 POETRY

See also **518** (literature).

n. *poetry*, poesy, verse, rhyme, alliteration, assonance; *poem*, verses, lines, epic, ode, hymn, elegy, lay; *light verse*, ballad, jingle, doggerel, limerick, clerihew, ditty; *verse form*, sonnet, haiku, couplet, triplet, quatrain, sestina, stanza, blank verse; *prosody*, versification, scansion, metrics; *metre*, foot, accent, beat, stress, rhythm, cadence; *poet*, bard, poet laureate, versifier, poetaster, rhymester, troubadour, minstrel.

adj. *poetic*, lyric, rhapsodic, epic, bardic, heroic, elegiac; *metrical*, prosodic, rhythmical, accented.

vb. *versify*, compose, scan, rhyme, elegize.

522 PROSE

See also **518** (literature).

n. *prose*, writing, running text, chapter, paragraph; *nonfiction*, history, biography, memoirs, reportage; *fiction*, novel, short story, essay, prose poem, stream of consciousness; *prosaicness*, plainness, prosiness, dullness, matter-of-factness; *speech*, address, talk, discourse, anecdote.

adj. *prosaic*, prosy, pedestrian, dull; *unaccented*, flat, unrelieved, uninspired; *historical*, factual, biographical.

523 DRAMA

n. *drama*, play, production, revival, spectacle, vehicle; *tragedy*, comedy, farce, melodrama, pantomime, revue skit; *vaudeville*, music hall, variety, musical comedy, cabaret, floor show; *theatre*, stage, footlights, West End, Broadway, theatreland, show business; *premiere*, opening night, preview, first night, sell-out, smash hit; *performance*, act, turn, role, part, bit/walk-on part, cameo, audition, rehearsal; *theatricals*, mime, charade, masque, dumb show; *stage directions*, exit, entrance, cue, prompt; *prologue*, epilogue, finale, final curtain, encore; *scenery*, set, props,

costume, wardrobe, greasepaint, make-up; *auditorium*, front of house, proscenium, apron, wings, flies, theatre-in-the-round; *balcony*, stalls, circle, gods (*colloq.*), stage door; *actor*, actress, leading lady/man, understudy, extra, trouper, thespian, entertainer, performer; *theatricality*, histrionics, staginess, ham (*colloq.*); *cast*, dramatis personae, company, troupe, chorus line.
adj. *dramatic*, theatrical, histrionic, stagy; *tragic*, straight, legitimate, melodramatic, blood-and-thunder, kitchen-sink; *comic*, farcical, burlesque, slapstick, knockabout (*colloq.*).
vb. *dramatize*, stage, present, put on, produce, direct; *perform*, play, act, enact, mime, tread the boards, go on stage, audition, rehearse; *overact*, play to the gallery, ham it up (*colloq.*), upstage, steal the limelight; *underact*, miss one's cue, fluff one's lines, dry (*colloq.*), corpse (*colloq.*), ad-lib.

524 DANCE
n. *dance*, ballet, tap dance, modern dance, folk dance; *choreography*, solo, pirouette, pas de deux, set; *minuet*, gavotte, mazurka, polka, polonaise; *ballroom dancing*, old-time dancing, waltz, foxtrot, quickstep, tango, bossa nova, rumba, cha-cha; *country dance*, jig, reel, hornpipe, morris dance, barn dance, square dance; *rock'n roll*, twist, jive, disco, Charleston, black bottom, boogie (*colloq.*); *ball*, hop, thé dansant, knees-up (*colloq.*); *dancer*, ballerina, corps de ballet, chorus girl, hoofer (*colloq.*).
adj. *balletic*, graceful, stately, rhythmic, lively.
vb. *dance*, take the floor, shuffle, trip the light fantastic; *leap*, skip, spin, pirouette, cavort, cut a caper; *twist*, jive, bop (*colloq.*), disco, stomp (*colloq.*), jitterbug (*colloq.*), boogie (*colloq.*).

525 CINEMA
See also **491** (photography).
n. *cinema*, motion pictures, celluloid, silver/big screen, Hollywood; *cinematography*, animation, cartoon, montage, soundtrack, Technicolor (*tdmk.*), Sensurround (*tdmk.*), Cinerama (*tdmk.*); *camerawork*, shot, still, tracking shot, special effects, close-up, fade-out, freeze-frame; *script*, screenplay, scenario, shooting script, continuity; *film*, movie, remake, silent, talkie, newsreel, trailer, short; *feature film*, B-movie, western, horse opera, spaghetti western, biopic, blue movie, skinflick (*colloq.*), blockbuster (*colloq.*), weepie (*colloq.*), tearjerker (*colloq.*); *studio*, picture house, picture palace, fleapit (*colloq.*), box office; *director*, star, co-star, screen idol, starlet.
adj. *cinematic*, cinematographic, photogenic, star-studded, bankable.
vb. *film*, shoot, roll, pan, track; *show*, project, screen, release; *script*, edit, produce, direct, cast, bankroll (*colloq.*).

526 VOICE
See also **353** (sound); **528** (speech).
n. *voice*, speech, utterance, tongue, exclamation, ejaculation; *articulation*, enunciation, delivery, pronunciation, elocution; *intonation*, modulation, inflection, pitch, tone, timbre; *accent*, burr, twang, drawl, lisp; *loud voice*, roar, shout, bellow, yell; *soft voice*, murmur, whisper, hiss.
adj. *vocal*, oral, phonetic, vocalic; *distinct*, aloud, clear, bell-like, fluting, sing-song; *loud*, shrill, strident, booming.
vb. *voice*, speak, utter, verbalize, vocalize, give voice/tongue, exclaim, ejaculate; *articulate*, enunciate, pronounce, elocute; *modulate*, inflect, intone, drone, drawl; *flute*, carol, warble, trill; *raise one's voice*, speak up, shout, boom, roar, bellow; *lower one's voice*, pipe down (*colloq.*), whisper, breathe, hiss.

527 VOICELESSNESS
See also **354** (silence); **531** (taciturnity).
n. *voicelessness*, silence, muteness, dumbness, speechlessness, inarticulacy; *hoarseness*, huskiness, gruffness, croakiness, breathiness, wheeziness.
adj. *voiceless*, speechless, silent, mute,

dumb; *inarticulate*, tongue-tied, dumbstruck, taciturn, mum; *hoarse*, husky, cracked, croaky, breathy, wheezy.
vb. *lose one's voice*, be mute, be struck dumb, be at a loss for words; *say nothing*, hold one's tongue (*colloq.*), shut up (*colloq.*), stick in one's throat, choke on; *silence*, gag, muffle, stifle, cut short, break in on.

528 SPEECH
See also **526** (voice); **532** (address).
n. *speech*, language, utterance, tongue, word of mouth; *articulacy*, fluency, eloquence, way with words, gift of the gab (*colloq.*); *discourse*, talk, conversation, dialogue, monologue, spiel, patter (*colloq.*); *rhetoric*, public speaking, oration, peroration, declamation, earful (*colloq.*); *comment*, remark, observation, aside, a word in edgeways; *speaker*, talker, lecturer, orator, spokesperson, mouthpiece.
adj. *spoken*, oral, verbal, vocal; *articulate*, fluent, eloquent, bilingual, polyglot; *rhetorical*, oratorical, declamatory, tub-thumping.
vb. *speak*, vocalize, voice, utter, say, articulate, verbalize; *speak up*, break one's silence, pipe up, find one's tongue, open one's mouth; *declare*, declaim, speak out, sound off, say one's piece, have one's say; *lecture*, orate, sermonize, pontificate, speechify, spout; *dictate*, trot out, reel off, recite.

529 SPEECH DEFECT
n. *speech defect*, aphasia, speech impediment, stammer, stutter, lisp, cleft palate; *inarticulacy*, indistinctness, mumbling, slur, drawl, twang.
adj. *inarticulate*, indistinct, thick, slurred; *nasal*, adenoidal, twangy, sibilant.
vb. *speak badly*, stammer, stutter, falter, hem and haw, hesitate; *mutter*, mumble, swallow one's words, gabble; *slur*, drawl, lisp, nasalize, speak with a plum in one's mouth.

530 TALKATIVENESS
See also **506** (diffuseness).
n. *talkativeness*, loquacity, garrulity, chattiness, fluency, volubility; *verbosity*, wordiness, prolixity, logorrhoea, verbal diarrhoea; *chatter*, prattle, jaw (*colloq.*), gossip, tittle-tattle, blather, gush, waffle (*colloq.*), gas (*colloq.*), hot air (*colloq.*); *chatterer*, chatterbox (*colloq.*), blatherskite (*colloq.*), windbag (*colloq.*), gasbag (*colloq.*).
adj. *talkative*, loquacious, voluble, garrulous; *verbose*, prolix, wordy, long-winded; *fluent*, glib, effusive, gushing, fulsome; *chatty*, gossipy, gabby (*colloq.*), gassy (*colloq.*).
vb. *be talkative*, chatter, prattle, run on, talk nineteen to the dozen, talk the hind leg off a donkey, rabbit on (*colloq.*), yak (*colloq.*); *jabber*, gabble, prate, blather, yap (*colloq.*); *digress*, ramble, wander, maunder, drone on, monopolize/hog the conversation; *expatiate*, sound off, spout (*colloq.*), outtalk, filibuster.

531 TACITURNITY
n. *taciturnity*, muteness, speechlessness, silence, quietness; *reserve*, reticence, uncommunicativeness, discretion; *curtness*, brusqueness, gruffness, terseness, laconism.
adj. *taciturn*, silent, mum, mute, speechless, tongue-tied; *reserved*, reticent, unforthcoming, uncommunicative, discreet, tight-lipped, close; *curt*, gruff, brusque, terse, laconic, monosyllabic.
vb. *be taciturn*, give nothing away, keep one's counsel, hold one's peace, hold one's tongue (*colloq.*), keep one's mouth shut, save one's breath, dry up, shut up (*colloq.*).

532 ADDRESS
See also **528** (speech).
n. *address*, apostrophe, aside, salutation, greeting; *speech*, public address, lecture, talk, oration, peroration, toast; *invocation*, appeal, interpellation, exhortation, pep talk (*colloq.*); *sermon*, homily, harangue, tirade; *addressee*, audience, captive audience, listener.
vb. *address*, apostrophize, greet, hail, salute, accost, buttonhole (*colloq.*); *orate*, perorate, speechify, pontificate;

invoke, appeal, exhort, interpellate; *preach*, sermonize, harangue, lecture.

533 CONVERSATION

n. *conversation*, talk, dialogue, communication; *exchange*, banter, badinage, repartee, slanging match (*colloq.*); *chat*, tête à tête, heart-to-heart, natter (*colloq.*), confab (*colloq.*), chinwag (*colloq.*); *gossip*, chitchat, tittle-tattle, small talk; *conference*, parley, colloquy, symposium, summit, convention, pow-wow (*colloq.*); *consultation*, interview, audience; *discussion*, debate, talking shop (*colloq.*).
adj. *conversational*, chatty, newsy, forthcoming, communicative; *animated*, heated, quick-fire, ding-dong (*colloq.*).
vb. *converse*, talk, chat, pass the time of day, bandy words; *gossip*, tittle-tattle, natter (*colloq.*), chew the fat (*colloq.*); *confer*, parley, talk over, discuss, debate, go into a huddle.

534 SOLILOQUY

n. *soliloquy*, monologue, monody, aside, apostrophe; *solo*, one-man show, one-man band, one-hander.
vb. *soliloquize*, talk to oneself, think aloud, talk to a brick wall (*colloq.*), waste one's breath.

535 WILL

See also **537** (willingness); **539** (resolution).
n. *will*, volition, intention, purpose; *wish*, desire, inclination, preference, mind, disposition; *resolution*, determination, wilfulness, obstinacy; *will power*, assertiveness, self-control, self-determination, autonomy; *free will*, choice, option, discretion, free hand.
adj. *willing*, desirous, inclined, disposed, agreeable; *spontaneous*, unasked, unprompted, ready; *voluntary*, optional, discretionary, arbitrary; *autonomous*, independent, unconstrained, assertive, autocratic; *wilful*, self-willed, single-minded, determined; *intentional*, volitional, deliberate, willed, designed.
vb. *will*, wish, desire, want; *intend*, determine, purpose, plan; *be independent*, know one's own mind, be one's own man, go one's own way; *assert oneself*, impose one's will, have one's own way; *choose*, opt for, plump for, favour.
adv. *at will*, ad libitum, as one pleases; *willingly*, voluntarily, of one's own accord, off one's own bat.

536 NECESSITY

See also **547** (predetermination).
n. *necessity*, compulsion, obligation, Hobson's choice, last resort; *determinism*, fatalism, force of circumstances, act of God; *inevitability*, unavoidability, destiny, fate, karma, lot; *prerequisite*, precondition, requirement, imperative, must; *instinct*, compulsion, reflex, Pavlovian reaction, knee-jerk reaction.
adj. *necessary*, required, requisite, imperative, indispensable; *compulsory*, obligatory, binding, mandatory, unavoidable, inescapable; *inevitable*, inexorable, ineluctable, preordained, fateful; *involuntary*, automatic, instinctive, mechanical.
vb. *necessitate*, oblige, dictate, compel; *require*, demand, insist, stipulate; *have no alternative/option*, bow to fate, take it or leave it, make a virtue of necessity; *preordain*, destine, doom, predetermine.

537 WILLINGNESS

See also **535** (will).
n. *willingness*, readiness, promptness, alacrity, zeal, eagerness; *inclination*, disposition, tendency, propensity, penchant; *goodwill*, cooperation, collaboration, helpfulness, spontaneity; *consent*, compliance, acquiescence, receptiveness; *obedience*, docility, tractability, pliability.
adj. *willing*, agreeable, acquiescent, compliant; *cooperative*, helpful, spontaneous, voluntary, unprompted; *prompt*, ready, eager, keen, zealous, enthusiastic; *inclined*, favourable, amenable, receptive, game; *obedient*, submissive, tractable, docile, manageable.
vb. *be willing*, feel like, have a mind to, desire to; *agree*, acquiesce, comply,

consent; *cooperate*, collaborate, show willing, go along with, bend over backwards; *volunteer*, jump at, leap at, not hesitate.
adv. *willingly*, readily, gladly, voluntarily, with good grace, at the drop of a hat, like a shot.

538 UNWILLINGNESS

See also **542** (obstinacy).
n. *unwillingness*, reluctance, disinclination, hesitation; *doubt*, scruple, qualm, reservation; *disagreement*, disfavour, objection, demurral; *aversion*, repugnance, dislike, avoidance; *recalcitrance*, refractoriness, obstinacy, sullenness; *indifference*, apathy, abstention, dissociation.
adj. *unwilling*, reluctant, disinclined, loath; *half-hearted*, begrudging, forced, lukewarm; *averse*, opposed, unfavourable, hostile; *uncooperative*, unhelpful, sullen, bolshie (*colloq.*); *recalcitrant*, refractory, obstinate, awkward, disaffected; *hesitant*, tentative, cautious, unenthusiastic; *indifferent*, apathetic, uninterested, negligent.
vb. *be unwilling*, force oneself, not have the heart to, stick at, jib, balk, dig in one's heels; *object*, demur, cavil, protest; *hesitate*, scruple, hold off, hang back, drag one's feet; *recoil*, fight shy of, duck, shirk, slack, not pull one's weight.
adv. *unwillingly*, with bad grace, with heavy heart, under protest.

539 RESOLUTION

See also **43** (adhesion); **535** (will).
n. *resolution*, determination, resolve, firmness; *tenacity*, perseverance, staunchness, constancy; *will power*, relentlessness, ruthlessness, iron will; *drive*, energy, vigour, forcefulness; *commitment*, single-mindedness, devotion, dedication; *fortitude*, character, backbone, moral fibre; *spirit*, mettle, pluck, guts (*colloq.*).
adj. *resolute*, resolved, determined, single-minded, intent, set, bent on; *tenacious*, persevering, staunch, firm; *forceful*, energetic, driving, strong-willed; *uncompromising*, committed, whole-hearted, diehard; *ruthless*, grim, steely, implacable, indomitable; *intransigent*, inflexible, unbending, immovable, unshakable.
vb. *be resolute*, stand firm, stand one's ground, not budge, not give an inch; *resolve*, determine, make up one's mind, decide, will; *commit oneself*, set one's heart on, go all out for, not take no for an answer, put one's foot down (*colloq.*).

540 PERSEVERANCE

See also **43** (adhesion); **542** (obstinacy).
n. *perseverance*, persistence, tenacity, firmness; *steadfastness*, staunchness, constancy, dedication, devotion; *stamina*, staying power, patience, endurance; *tirelessness*, indefatigability, stalwartness, doggedness; *application*, assiduousness, sedulousness, diligence.
adj. *persevering*, persistent, tenacious, stubborn; *steadfast*, staunch, firm, stalwart, doughty; *constant*, devoted, dedicated, unwavering; *patient*, long-suffering, dogged, plodding; *undaunted*, unflagging, unfailing, tireless, indefatigable; *assiduous*, sedulous, industrious, diligent.
vb. *persevere*, persist, keep on, keep at it, never say die; *hold out*, hang on, stick it out, stay the course; *plod*, slog, beaver (*colloq.*), plug away (*colloq.*), peg away (*colloq.*).
adv. *to the bitter end*, come hell or high water, through thick and thin, come what may.

541 VACILLATION

See also **44** (nonadhesion); **544** (caprice).
n. *vacillation*, irresolution, indecision, uncertainty; *hesitation*, doubt, half-heartedness, apathy; *weakness*, faint-heartedness, gutlessness, spinelessness; *capriciousness*, fickleness, inconstancy, unpredictability; *suggestibility*, impressionability, malleability, pliancy.
adj. *vacillating*, indecisive, hesitant, wavering, changeable; *irresolute*, unresolved, uncertain, undecided; *capricious*, unstable, unpredictable,

inconstant, fickle; *weak*, spineless, weak-kneed, faint-hearted, pusillanimous; *suggestible*, impressionable, malleable, pliable; *apathetic*, lukewarm, tepid, unenthusiastic.
vb. *vacillate*, fluctuate, waver, seesaw, blow hot and cold, shilly-shally (*colloq.*), dither; *hesitate*, falter, be in two minds, have second thoughts, hem and haw.

542 OBSTINACY

See also **538** (unwillingness); **540** (perseverence).
n. *obstinacy*, determination, perseverence, doggedness; *stubbornness*, obduracy, mulishness, pig-headedness; *intransigence*, inflexibility, toughness, hard line; *intractability*, incorrigibility, sullenness, dourness; *perverseness*, contrariness, bloody-mindedness (*colloq.*), cussedness (*colloq.*).
adj. *obstinate*, tenacious, persevering, dogged; *stubborn*, obdurate, self-willed, stiff-necked, pig-headed, mulish, dour; *intransigent*, tough, adamant, unyielding, inflexible, hard-line, immovable, unshakable; *dogmatic*, diehard, hidebound, opinionated, set in one's ways; *perverse*, contrary, cussed (*colloq.*), bloody-minded (*colloq.*); *intractable*, incorrigible, headstrong, wilful, unmanageable.
vb. *be obstinate*, persevere, persist, stick to one's guns; *resist*, hold out, dig in one's heels, put one's foot down.
adv. *over one's dead body* (*colloq.*), no way (*colloq.*).

543 EQUIVOCATION

n. *equivocation*, evasiveness, ambiguity, slipperiness, shiftiness; *uncertainty*, unpredictability, unreliability, untrustworthiness; *opportunism*, timeserving, hypocrisy, double-dealing; *infidelity*, disloyalty, treachery, perfidy; *defection*, desertion, apostasy, recantation; *reversal*, about-turn, U-turn, second thoughts, volte-face.
adj. *equivocal*, evasive, ambiguous, deceptive; *untrustworthy*, unreliable, shifty, slippery; *duplicitous*, hypocritical, two-faced, timeserving; *capricious*, fickle, changeable, mercurial; *disloyal*, disaffected, apostate.
vb. *equivocate*, face both ways, say one thing and mean another, run with the hare and hunt with the hounds, have it both ways; *change one's mind/tune*, get cold feet, back out; *recant*, retract, go back on one's word, backtrack, backpedal; *desert*, defect, cross the floor, change sides.

544 CAPRICE

See also **541** (vacillation).
n. *caprice*, whim, fancy, impulse, notion; *humour*, mood, fad, craze, nine days' wonder; *capriciousness*, whimsicality, changeability, inconstancy, instability; *unreliability*, unpredictability, inconsistency, arbitrariness.
adj. *capricious*, whimsical, fanciful, irrational; *temperamental*, moody, changeable, mercurial; *fickle*, unpredictable, inconstant, volatile; *erratic*, wayward, irresponsible, feckless.
vb. *be capricious*, chop and change, blow hot and cold, act on impulse, take it into one's head.

545 SELECTION

n. *selection*, choice, option, alternative; *selectiveness*, eclecticism, choosiness, discrimination; *preference*, predilection, fancy, pick, favourite; *discretion*, first refusal, casting vote, veto; *vote*, ballot, poll, plebiscite, referendum.
adj. *selective*, eclectic, discriminating, fastidious, choosy (*colloq.*), particular; *optional*, discretionary, preferential, à la carte; *select*, choice, hand-picked, recherché.
vb. *select*, choose, pick, opt for, plump, settle on; *prefer*, fancy, favour, earmark, single out, reserve; *discriminate*, shop around, pick and choose, make up one's mind; *cull*, glean, sift, winnow, cream off.

546 REJECTION

n. *rejection*, dismissal, exclusion, veto; *disapproval*, dissatisfaction, fault-finding, captiousness; *refusal*, rebuff, disclaimer, denial, repudiation; *reject*,

discard, seconds, cast-off; *undesirability*, unsuitability, ineligibility, inadmissibility.
adj. *rejected*, unwanted, discarded, excluded; *undesirable*, unsuitable, ineligible, inadmissible.
vb. *reject*, turn down, decline, pass over; *refuse*, spurn, disdain, look a gift horse in the mouth; *discard*, scrap, ditch, junk (*colloq.*), throw out; *deny*, rebuff, repudiate, disown, disclaim; *dismiss*, rule out of court, give short shrift to, show the door; *exclude*, veto, blackball, cold-shoulder, give the brush-off (*colloq.*).

547 PREDETERMINATION
See also **536** (necessity); **559** (preparation).
n. *predetermination*, preordination, predestination, necessity; *preparation*, premeditation, prearrangement, rehearsal, forward planning; *agenda*, plan, order of the day, timetable, schedule; *foregone conclusion*, fix (*colloq.*), dead cert (*colloq.*), put-up job, frame-up (*colloq.*).
adj. *predetermined*, foreordained, premeditated, prearranged; *planned*, deliberate, preconceived, intentional, appointed.
vb. *predetermine*, predestine, foreordain, appoint; *premeditate*, preconceive, prepare, prearrange; *plan*, rehearse, schedule, timetable; *rig*, engineer, stage-manage, fix (*colloq.*).

548 IMPROVISATION
See also **560** (lack of preparation).
n. *improvisation*, extemporization, ad-libbing, makeshift; *spontaneity*, impetuosity, impulsiveness, instinctiveness; *reflex*, impulse, snap decision, flash of inspiration, brainwave (*colloq.*).
adj. *improvised*, extempore, impromptu, makeshift, ad hoc; *spontaneous*, impulsive, impetuous, instinctive; *sudden*, unpremeditated, involuntary, automatic, unthinking, knee-jerk.
vb. *improvise*, act on impulse, extemporize, ad-lib, vamp, think on one's feet, play it by ear.
adv. *on the spur of the moment*, off-hand, off the cuff (*colloq.*), off the top of one's head (*colloq.*).

549 HABIT
See also **71** (rule); **72** (conformity).
n. *habit*, disposition, custom, wont, tendency, second nature; *familiarity*, force of habit, routine, regularity, daily round, groove, rut; *tradition*, precedent, orthodoxy, convention, mores, practice, usage; *protocol*, ritual, done thing, received wisdom; *habituation*, acclimatization, adjustment, conditioning.
adj. *habitual*, customary, regular, wonted, usual; *familiar*, conversant, known, accustomed, commonplace; *traditional*, orthodox, conventional, accepted; *long-standing*, time-honoured, hallowed, venerable; *ingrained*, deep-seated, deep-rooted, dyed-in-the-wool; *seasoned*, practised, inured, hardened, set in one's ways.
vb. *be in the habit of*, make a habit of, tend to; *adjust to*, accustom oneself to, get used to, get the hang/feel of; *habituate*, acclimatize, naturalize, condition.

550 UNACCUSTOMEDNESS
n. *unaccustomedness*, unwontedness, unfamiliarity, strangeness, novelty; *unconventionality*, unorthodoxy, nonconformity, irregularity; *neglect*, decay, rustiness, disuse.
adj. *unaccustomed*, unused, unfamiliar, novel, new, strange; *unusual*, unwonted, unprecedented, irregular; *unconventional*, unorthodox, nonconformist, radical; *neglected*, disused, rusty, decaying.
vb. *discontinue*, leave off, break with tradition, break the mould, turn over a new leaf; *wean*, cure, break the habit.

551 PERSUASION
See also **134** (motive); **139** (influence); **434** (belief).
n. *persuasion*, advertising, salesmanship, spiel (*colloq.*), honeyed words; *inducement*, incitement, pressure, carrot (*colloq.*); *persuadability*, credulity,

credulousness, gullibility, susceptibility; *temptation*, bribery, enticement, encouragement; *persuader*, salesman, tempter; *pretext*, justification, plea, defence, pretence, allegation; *conviction*, conversion; *submission*, compliance; *concession*, agreement.

adj. *persuasive*, convincing, seductive, honey-tongued, plausible; *tempting*, enticing, seductive; *persuadable*, credulous, gullible, susceptible, easily swayed, submissive, compliant.

vb. *persuade*, advertise, get s.o. to do sth.; *goad*, cajole, wheedle, bully into, egg on (*colloq.*); *coerce*, push into, induce, brainwash, twist round one's little finger (*colloq.*); *incite*, stimulate, prick, prompt; *tempt*, bribe, entice, encourage; *plead*, claim, pretend, allege; *convince*, convert; *be persuaded*, succumb, yield, submit, comply; *concede*, agree.

552 DISSUASION

n. dissuasion, discouragement, no encouragement; *deterrence*, disincentive, intimidation; *deterrent*, killjoy, wet blanket (*colloq.*).

adj. *dissuasive*, discouraging; *deterrent*, intimidating, daunting; *cautionary*.

vb. *dissuade*, discourage, talk out of, advise against, put off, pour cold water on; *deter*, deflect, intimidate, daunt; *caution/warn against*.

553 INTENTION

See also **539** (resolution); **557** (plan); **755** (desire).

n. *intention*, intent, resolve, resolution, determination, threat; *project*, plan, design, calculation, meaning; *aim*, goal, objective, target, end; *destination*, terminus, station, port, airport.

adj. *intent/hell-bent on*; intentional, deliberate, voluntary, conscious.

vb. *intend*, resolve, decide, determine, threaten, look; *plan*, project, purpose, propose, undertake, mean, earmark; *aim*, go for; *hope*, expect, aspire, reckon on, calculate; *consider*, contemplate.

554 CHANCE

See also **135** (lack of motive).

n. *chance*, accident, fluke, coincidence, luck, luck of the draw, fate, the way the cookie crumbles (*colloq.*), toss-up (*colloq.*); *good luck*, bad luck, fortune, misfortune; *risk*, hazard, speculation, flutter, pig in a poke; *gambling*, gamble, bet, wager, stake; *horse-/greyhound-racing*, tote, football pools; *casino*, bingo, roulette, one-armed bandit; *lottery*, raffle, tombola, draw, premium bond; *stock exchange*, bear, bull, stag; *gambler*, speculator, punter, backer; *bookmaker*, bookie, turf accountant.

adj. *chance*, accidental, coincidental, lucky, fortuitous; *unintentional*, inadvertent, involuntary, unconscious; haphazard, random, happy-go-lucky; *risky*, hazardous, speculative, chancy.

vb. *gamble*, bet, wager, stake, game, punt, back; *risk*, hazard, speculate, have a flutter, run a risk, take risks, venture; *draw straws*, pick the short straw, spin a coin, toss for it.

adv. *by chance*, accidentally, coincidentally, as it happens, oddly enough; *on the off chance*.

555 PURSUIT

See also **414** (question); **761** (recreation).

n. *pursuit*, chase, prosecution, search, frisking, quest, enquiry; *exploration*, excavation, dig; *hunt*, stalk, trap, snare; *fishing*, ferretting, rabbitting, mousing; *pursuer*, seeker, searcher, search party, explorer; *hunter*, huntsman, fisherman, poacher, trapper, beater, stalker, tracker; *ratter*, rabbitter, mouser; *trawler*, drifter, whaler; *quarry*, prey; *steeplechase*, paperchase, treasure hunt.

adj. *pursuant*, in pursuit, on one's tail; *searching*, exploratory.

vb. *pursue*, follow, chase, seek, search, quest, look for, be after, enquire; *forage*, rummage, ferret, leave no stone unturned, sniff out (*colloq.*); *explore*, excavate, dig; *hunt*, stalk, beat, trail, track, poach, shoot, fish, trawl; *harry*, dog, shadow, tail.

556 AVOIDANCE

See also **605** (escape).

n. *avoidance*, sidestep, evasive action, dodge; *escape*, evasion; *forbearance*, moderation, abstinence; *refusal*, rejection, boycott; *nonparticipation*, noninvolvement, noncooperation; *avoider*, dodger, abstainer; *shirker*, idler, deserter, truant, coward.

adj. *avoiding*, evasive, shy, reluctant, elusive; *forbearing*, abstemious; *uncooperative*, reluctant, unwilling, reticent, unforthcoming; *avoidable*, unavoidable, inescapable.

vb. *avoid*, sidestep, dodge; *escape*, evade; *prevent*, avert; *eschew*, shun, fight shy of, give a miss, not go near, leave, let alone; *steer clear of*, give a wide berth to, not touch with a bargepole (*colloq.*); *refuse*, reject, black (*colloq.*); *forbear*, refrain, abstain, forswear, hold back, do without; *shirk*, duck, cop out (*colloq.*), chicken out (*colloq.*).

557 PLAN

See also **488** (representation).

n. *plan*, project, proposal, suggestion, scheme, intention; *programme*, layout, design, blueprint, outline, recipe, organization; *diagram*, pattern, model, map, sketch, cartography; *strategy*, approach, course of action, agenda, schedule; *plot*, intrigue, conspiracy, (little) game (*colloq.*); *planner*, proposer, originator; *designer*, layout artist, map-maker, cartographer; *strategist*, plotter, conspirator.

adj. *planned*, projected, proposed; *schematic*, strategic; *plotting*, conspiratorial, scheming.

vb. *plan*, project, propose, suggest; *lay out*, draft, design, model, draw up, set out; *conceive*, hatch, dream up (*colloq.*); *organize*, schedule, approach, think ahead, orchestrate, engineer; *map*, sketch; *plot*, scheme, conspire, intrigue.

558 REQUIREMENT

See also **536** (necessity).

n. *requirement*, need, must, necessary, requisite; *necessity*, prerequisite, essential, sine qua non, stipulation; *want*, lack, demand, call for, shortage; *compulsion*, obligation.

adj. *required*, necessary, needed, indispensable; *essential*, vital; *wanted*, lacking, called for, in demand; *needy*, in need, deprived, destitute; *compulsory*, obligatory. **vb.** *require*, need, stand in need of, necessitate, stipulate; *want*, lack, call for, feel the lack of; *compel*, oblige, must.

adv. *in need*, in want; *of necessity*, necessarily.

559 PREPARATION

See also **57** (arrangement); **547** (predetermination).

n. *preparation*, making ready, getting ready, groundwork; *preliminaries*, tuning, priming, loading, approach, run-up; *acclimatization*, seasoning, hardening (off); *trial*, trial run, pilot (scheme), practice, rehearsal, dress rehearsal; *study*, prep, homework; *arrangement*, prearrangement, premeditation; *precaution*, provision, allowance, nest egg; *provisioning*, provisions, equipment; *preparedness*, readiness, fitness; *preparer*, trainer, pioneer, trailblazer, répétiteur, coach.

adj. *preparatory*, precautionary, preliminary, in preparation; *prepared*, ready (and waiting), standing by, fit, rehearsed, keyed up, primed, tuned, equipped, in readiness; *acclimatized*, seasoned, weathered, hardened (off); *ready-made*, off-the-peg, cooked, processed, oven-ready, ready to eat, instant.

vb. *prepare*, make ready, pave the way, lay the foundations, blaze a trail, prepare the ground, clear the decks, stand by, arrange (for); *prime*, load, tune, warm up, soften up, dig (over); *provide*, provision, equip, fit out; *acclimatize*, season, weather, harden (off); *rehearse*, practise, coach, train, groom, do one's homework, study; *allow for*, make provision for, put by (for a rainy day).

560 LACK OF PREPARATION

See also **111** (youth); **451** (surprise); **548** (improvisation).

n. *lack of preparation*, unpreparedness, unreadiness; *lack of rehearsal/training/practice*; *rush*, haste; *improvisation*; *surprise*.

adj. *unprepared*, unready, caught napping/unawares/off one's guard, caught on the hop (*colloq.*), caught with one's pants/trousers down (*colloq.*); *unrehearsed*, untrained, unpractised; *rushed*, ill-equipped, disorganized, half-baked; *improvised*, impromptu, snap, extempore, extemporized, ad hoc; *unseasoned*, not weathered, not hardened (off); *raw*, uncooked.

vb. *be unprepared*, *unready*, etc., not prepare, plan, etc., live from day to day, cross that bridge when one comes to it, make no provision for; *improvise*, extemporize.

adv. *extempore*, off the cuff, off the top of one's head (*colloq.*).

561 ATTEMPT

n. *attempt*, try, essay, bid; *endeavour*, effort; *go* (*colloq.*), shot (*colloq.*), stab (*colloq.*), bash (*colloq.*), jab (*colloq.*), crack (*colloq.*).

adj. *game*, venturesome, tenacious, obstinate; *successful*, futile, desperate.

vb. *attempt*, try, essay, bid, seek; *endeavour*, make an effort, lift a finger; *strain*, struggle, strive, go all out, do one's best; *give it/have a go/shot/stab/bash/jab/crack* (*colloq.*), give it a whirl (*colloq.*).

562 UNDERTAKING

See also **61** (beginning); **683** (promise).

n. *undertaking*, enterprise, business, task, job; *exercise*, operation, project, matter in hand, concern; *adventure*, quest, cause; *promise*, contract, agreement, obligation, commitment.

adj. *enterprising*, daring, adventurous, venturesome; *contracted*, obliged, committed.

vb. *undertake*, go in for, tackle, address oneself to; *take part in*, participate in, engage in, busy oneself with; *embark on*, launch into, take up, assume, take on (oneself), get involved in, let oneself in for, get to grips with, get one's teeth into (*colloq.*); *promise*, contract, agree, commit oneself.

563 RELINQUISHMENT

See also **543** (equivocation); **696** (disposal).

n. relinquishment, giving up, abdication, renunciation, abandonment, castaway; *departure*, leaving, defection, desertion, walk-out, secession, retirement; *surrender*, handing over, ceding, cession, waiver.

adj. *relinquished*, abandoned, marooned, cast off.

vb. relinquish, give up, abdicate, renounce, forswear; *abandon*, maroon, cast away, forsake, ditch (*colloq.*); *depart*, leave, quit, defect, desert, withdraw, walk out, secede, retire, drop out; *surrender*, hand over, cede, waive, forgo; *resign*, give in, drop, chuck (*colloq.*).

564 USE

See also **566** (misuse); **578** (usefulness).

n. *use*, employment, utilization, exploitation; *application*, appliance, exercise, adoption, practice, usage; *consumption*, wear, wear and tear; *usefulness*, applicability, benefit, practicality, purpose, point, pragmatism.

adj. *used*, in use, employed, utilized, applied, accepted, adopted; *worn*, used up, worn out, second-hand, nearly new (*colloq.*); *useful*, practical, pragmatic; *usable*, available, disposable.

vb. *use*, employ, put to use, put into service, utilize, make use of, avail oneself of, resort to; *exploit*, harness, capitalize on, take advantage of, cash in on (*colloq.*); *apply*, exercise, practise, put into practice, adopt; *consume*, expend, use up, wear, wear away/down/out; *reuse*, recycle; *requisition*, commandeer, deploy.

565 NONUSE

See also **62** (end); **563** (relinquishment); **579** (uselessness).

n. nonuse, abeyance, unemployment; *discontinuance*, disuse, withdrawal, suspension, abolition; *rejection*, abandonment, scrapping; *abstinence*, avoidance; *store*, storage; *uselessness*.
adj. *unused*, unutilized, in abeyance, not in use, out of order; *new*, brand-new, pristine; *unemployed*, resting, idle; *discontinued*, withdrawn, suspended, abolished; *disused*, derelict, neglected, laid up, left to rot, in mothballs, mothballed; *extra*, spare, in hand, in reserve, surplus, superfluous; *useless*, impractical, pointless, senseless; *unusable*, unavailable.
vb. *not use*, etc, avoid, do without; *discontinue*, withdraw, suspend, abolish, dispense with; *reject*, abandon, scrap, ditch, drop, dump; *shelve*, lay/put aside, put in mothballs, mothball, put on a back burner.

566 MISUSE
See also **564** (use); **572** (waste).
n. *misuse*, abuse, maltreatment, mishandling, rough handling, malpractice, misapplication; *perversion*, prostitution, desecration; *wrong*, hurt; *overuse*, extravagance; *waste*.
vb. *misuse*, abuse, maltreat, mishandle, handle roughly, force, misapply; *pervert*, prostitute, desecrate; *wrong*, hurt; *misappropriate*, embezzle; *overuse*, overwork; *waste*, squander.

567 MEANS
See also **136** (operation); **568** (tool); **569** (materials).
n. *means*, method, way, device, medium; *ability*, knowledge, skill; *equipment*, wherewithal, materiel, provisions, facilities, tools, resources, channel; *money*, capital, necessary, credit; *manpower*.
vb. *enable*, provide the means, equip, resource; *finance*, back, raise the money; *be able*, manage, find a way.

568 TOOL
See also **138** (instrumentality); **567** (means).
n. *tool*, implement, utensil, gadget, instrument; *knife*, fork, spoon, tin-opener, bottle-opener, corkscrew, nutcracker; *nail*, hammer, screw, screwdriver; *drill*, bit, auger, brace, punch; *pliers*, pincers, tweezers, wrench, spanner, jemmy, crowbar, lever; *cutter*, chisel, plane, spokeshave, saw, router; *machine*, machinery, device, apparatus, mechanism, appliance; *wheel*, pulley, handle, block and tackle, clockwork, gears; *motor*, engine, petrol/diesel engine, internal combustion engine, steam engine, jet engine, rocket motor; *generator*, dynamo, turbine; *computer*, robot, calculator; *press*, mill.
adj. *mechanical*, mechanized, automatic.

569 MATERIALS
See also **197** (interweaving); **202** (covering); **567** (means).
n. *materials*, raw materials, building blocks; *mineral*, ore, sand, asbestos, clay, stone, marble, flint, masonry; *metal*, iron, gold, silver, copper, tin, nickel, lead, zinc; *alloy*, (stainless) steel, brass, bronze, gunmetal; *brick*, breeze block, glass, plaster, plasterboard, cement, (reinforced) concrete, mortar; *paving*, tarmac, asphalt, chippings, gravel, cobbles, flagstones; *tile*, slate, thatch, roofing felt; *wood*, timber, board, plank, rafter, joist, lath, plywood, chipboard, hardboard; *leather*, skin, hide; *paper*, rag, esparto grass, pulp, (card)board, millboard, pasteboard, strawboard, papier mâché; *bank*, bond, wove, laid; *cartridge paper*, art paper, (super)calendered paper, notepaper, carbon paper; *tissue paper*, tracing paper, crepe paper, newsprint; *plastic*, polythene, polystyrene, Perspex, PVC (polyvinyl chloride), Celluloid, Cellophane, fibreglass; *textile*, cloth, material, fabric, stuff; *cotton*, calico, poplin, shirting, towelling, terry, denim, gingham; *wool*, jersey, cashmere, angora; *suiting*, tweed, worsted, serge, mohair, felt, baize; *linen*, lawn, cambric, holland; *silk*, satin, taffeta, cheesecloth, chiffon, crêpe de chine, muslin, voile; *velvet*, corduroy, cord, velour, twill, flannelette; *nylon*, rayon, polyester,

polycotton, Crimplene, Terylene, Dacron; *chintz*, damask, candlewick; *jute*, hessian, sacking, ticking, sailcloth, canvas, tapestry, mull.

570 STORE

See also **66** (assembly); **603** (preservation).

n. *store*, provision, stock, stock-in-trade, stockpile, backlog; *supply*, source, fount; *heap*, pile, load, mass, mound, collection, abundance, profusion, wine lake (*colloq.*), butter mountain (*colloq.*); *collection*, file, dictionary, thesaurus; *quarry*, mine, deposit, field, lode, vein, seam; *funds*, assets, reserves, nest egg, investment, holding; *horde*, treasure, cache; *bank*, account, deposit, savings, balance, credit; *dowry*, trousseau, bottom drawer; *storage*, warehousing, safekeeping; *warehouse*, stockroom, depot, garage, depository, repository, vault, magazine, arsenal; *battery*, accumulator; *cellar*, pantry, larder, storeroom, cupboard, loft, attic; *barn*, silo, granary, haystack, hayrick; *reservoir*, water tower, gasholder, gasometer, septic tank, cesspit; *refrigerator*, fridge, freezer; *trunk*, chest, safe; *computer*, microcomputer, microprocessor, word processor; *computing*, electronic data processing, DP, information retrieval; *hardware*, keyboard, terminal, VDU (visual display unit), disk drive, tape reader, CPU (central processing unit), printer; *software*, program, computer language, machine code/language, data, bit, byte, input, output, interface; *memory*, data base, data bank, punched cards, magnetic tape, (floppy) disk, disk pack, printout.

adj. *stored*, etc., in store; *in hand*, in reserve, in stock; *spare*.

vb. *store*, pile up, heap up, load up, stack (up); *store away*, put away, file (away), stash away (*colloq.*); *stock up*, stockpile, amass, accumulate, buy in, buy up, lay in, fuel (up); *save*, bank, invest, deposit; *save up*, hoard, squirrel away, put by for a rainy day; *garage*, warehouse, put in store; *lay up*, cocoon, put in mothballs, mothball; *preserve*, pickle, bottle, preserve, salt, dry, refrigerate, freeze; *keep in reserve/hand*, put aside.

571 PROVISION

See also **453** (foresight); **559** (preparation); **685** (negotiation).

n. *provision*, supply, furnishing, delivery, purveying, fitting out, provisioning, catering; *provisions*, food, rations, supplies, stores, reserves, equipment; *budget*, management; *maintenance*, alimony, assistance; *provider*, supplier, purveyor, caterer; *storekeeper*, butler, quartermaster, housekeeper, cook; *shopkeeper*, merchant, grocer; *lender*, manager, purser, bursar, steward.

adj. *provided*, supplied, furnished, catered, all found, available, well-equipped.

vb. *provide*, supply, furnish, deliver, procure, purvey, fit out, arm, provision, cater; *feed*, serve, afford, give; *maintain*, board, put up (*colloq.*); *budget*, make provision, stock up, manage.

572 WASTE

See also **566** (misuse); **727** (extravagance).

n. *waste*, profligacy, wastefulness; *extravagance*, overspending, unnecessary expense; *consumption*, wear, attrition, erosion, atrophy, exhaustion, depletion; *leakage*, loss, escape, pollution; *overproduction*, superfluity, excess, misuse; *rubbish*, scrap, waste product, effluent.

adj. *wasteful*, profligate, extravagant, unnecessary; *superfluous*, disposable; *wasted*, lost, exhausted, misspent, futile, down the drain (*colloq.*).

vb. *waste*, squander, throw away, blow (*colloq.*); *misuse*, overwork; *consume*, wear, erode, deplete, exhaust; *leak*, escape, dissipate, pollute; *come to nothing*, go down the drain (*colloq.*).

573 SUFFICIENCY

See also **49** (completeness); **738** (satisfaction).

n. *sufficiency*, adequacy, acceptability, competence; *enough*, (bare) minimum,

right amount, pass mark, quorum, what is acceptable, breadline, subsistence; *plenty*, abundance, copiousness; *a lot*, lashings (*colloq.*), bags (*colloq.*), oodles (*colloq.*); *profusion*, riot, feast; *lushness*, luxuriance.
adj. *sufficient*, adequate, enough, minimal, quorate; *satisfactory*, acceptable, competent, just right; *plentiful*, plenteous, abundant, copious; *wealthy*, affluent, generous, liberal; *profuse*, lush, luxuriant.
vb. *suffice*, be sufficient/enough; *satisfy*, fill the bill, do, pass muster, qualify; *be plentiful*, abound, swarm, proliferate; *teem/bristle with*, crawl with (*colloq.*).

574 INSUFFICIENCY

See also **50** (incompleteness); **273** (shortfall); **739** (dissatisfaction).
n. *insufficiency*, inadequacy, incompetence, failure; *not enough*, too little, too few, lack; *deficit*, shortfall, insufficient funds; *poverty*, need, starvation diet; *famine*, starvation, drought; *scarcity*, dearth, shortfall.
adj. *insufficient*, inadequate, not enough, too little, too few; *unsatisfactory*, unacceptable, incompetent; *poor*, disadvantaged, underprivileged, on supplementary benefit; *scarce*, in short supply, rare; *lacking*, deficient, light on (*colloq.*), thin, scant; *miserly*, mingy.
vb. *not suffice*, etc., be insufficient, etc., fall short, not come up to; *fail*, lack, want, require.

575 EXCESS

See also **272** (overstepping); **727** (extravagance); **844** (self-indulgence).
n. *excess*, too many, too much, overabundance, enough and to spare; *redundance*, redundancy, superfluity, glut, plethora, duplication, overkill; *flood*, inundation, saturation, congestion; *extra*, bonus, spare, surplus, balance; *overdoing it*, officiousness, ostentation, extravagance, obtrusiveness; *overindulgence*, too much of a good thing, overdose, overeating; *fat*, obesity, flab (*colloq.*); *satiety*, engorgement, surfeit.
adj. *excessive*, too many, too much, overmuch, inordinate; *redundant*, superfluous, unnecessary; *flooded*, overflowing, saturated, stuffed; *extra*, spare, surplus; *officious*, ostentatious, extravagant, exorbitant, over the top (*colloq.*); *fat*, obese; *satiated*, sated, jaded, gorged.
vb. *be excessive*, etc., overstep, overdo it, go over the top (*colloq.*); *flood*, saturate, overflow; *overindulge*, overeat; *duplicate*, go begging; *satiate*, sate, jade, pall, gorge.

576 IMPORTANCE

See also **5** (essence); **31** (superiority); **774** (repute).
n. *importance*, significance, consequence; *substance*, matter, consideration, weight, value, moment, import, big deal (*colloq.*); *seriousness*, solemnity, gravity, no laughing matter; *prominence*, eminence; *heart of the matter*, cornerstone, linchpin, be-all and end-all; *urgency*, priority, emergency, matter of life and death; *VIP*, notable, personality, personage, magnate, tycoon, big gun (*colloq.*), bigwig (*colloq.*), big noise (*colloq.*).
adj. *important*, significant, big; *substantial*, considerable, weighty, urgent, momentous, eventful, earth-shattering; *serious*, solemn, grave; *leading*, notable, foremost, conspicuous; *central*, chief, basic, essential, major, main, fundamental, primary, principal; *influential*, formidable, illustrious, powerful; *exceptional*, imposing, outstanding, eminent, august, distinguished; *famous*, prominent, well-known.
vb. *be important*, etc., matter, count, carry weight, deserve attention; *make important*, promote, put on a pedestal; *stress*, underline, highlight, emphasize; *glorify*, honour, value, think a lot of, celebrate.

577 UNIMPORTANCE

See also **32** (inferiority); **187** (shallowness); **780** (humility).
n. *unimportance*, insignificance, trivial-

ity, frivolity, pettiness; *irrelevance*, immateriality, red herring; *the little man*, nonentity, figurehead, pawn, second fiddle; *trifle*, storm in a teacup, nothing to speak/write home about, technicality, small beer, pinprick.
adj. *unimportant*, ordinary, insignificant, inconsequential; *little*, negligible, wretched, paltry, measly (*colloq.*); *irrelevant*, immaterial, obscure, contemptible; *inessential*, unnecessary, fringe, peripheral.
vb. *be unimportant*, etc., not matter, not count, cut no ice, play second fiddle; *make light of*, think unimportant, play down.

578 USEFULNESS

See also **152** (fertility); **564** (use); **580** (convenience).
n. *usefulness*, utility, handiness, practicality; *adaptability*, suitability, applicability, efficacy; *convenience*, serviceability, availability, helpfulness; *value*, worth, advantage, profitability, productivity, mileage (*colloq.*).
adj. *useful*, handy, practical, functional; *adaptable*, suitable, applicable, efficacious, effective; *convenient*, multipurpose, versatile, serviceable, available, helpful; *valuable*, invaluable, worthwhile, profitable, productive, economic; *pragmatic*.
vb. *be useful*, etc., be of use, come in handy (*colloq.*); *function*, work, serve, help.

579 USELESSNESS

See also **153** (infertility); **565** (nonuse); **581** (inconvenience).
n. *uselessness*, inutility; *unsuitability*, inefficacy, inadequacy, inconvenience, unavailability; *pointlessness*, futility, disadvantage, waste of time, wild-goose chase; *worthlessness*, waste, rubbish, dead duck.
adj. *useless*, unusable, unpractical; *unadaptable*, unsuitable, unemployable; *inconvenient*, unserviceable, unavailable, unhelpful, out of order, broken down; *pointless*, futile, vain; *worthless*, good-for-nothing, unprofitable, unrewarding; *ineffectual*, feckless.
vb. *be useless*, etc., not work, not function, not help, come to nothing; *flog a dead horse*, tilt at windmills; *make useless*, etc., sabotage, cripple, disable, spike.

580 CONVENIENCE

See also **115** (timeliness); **578** (usefulness); **629** (easiness).
n. *convenience*, ease, ease of use, easiness, facilitation, straightforwardness; *accessibility*, ease of access, closeness; *suitability*, pragmatism, expediency; *opportunism*, timeserving, utilitarianism, profit, advantage; *opportunity*, spare time, leisure; *freedom*, comfort, service, speed.
adj. *convenient*, easy to use, user-friendly; *accessible*, close, nearby, easy to reach, get-at-able (*colloq.*); *practical*, suitable, workable, pragmatic; *auspicious*, opportune, profitable, advantageous; *opportunist*, timeserving, utilitarian; *comfortable*, fast.
vb. *be convenient*, etc., not clash, suit, do work, fit; *benefit*, help, pay.

581 INCONVENIENCE

See also **116** (untimeliness); **579** (uselessness); **628** (difficulty).
n. *inconvenience*, difficulty, hindrance, drawback, handicap; *unsuitability*, previous engagement, awkwardness, unpleasantness; *discomfort*, disadvantage, inadvisability.
adj. *inconvenient*, difficult to use, cumbersome, unwieldy; *unsuitable*, unsatisfactory, inappropriate, awkward, unhappy; *inopportune*, untimely; *inadvisable*, disadvantageous, inexpedient.
vb. *be inconvenient*, etc., not do, not work, not help, not benefit; *inconvenience*, put out, incommode, bother, disrupt.

582 WORTH

See also **721** (price); **584** (perfection); **837** (virtue).
n. *worth*, goodness, excellence, greatness, quality, merit, virtue; *good quality*, redeeming feature, good point, saving grace; *value*, price; *pick*, élite, elect, chosen few, cream, crème de la

crème; *superman*, superwoman, genius, ace, champion, paragon, cat's whiskers (*colloq.*), bee's knees (*colloq.*); *masterpiece*, plum, pièce de résistance, flagship; *hit*, knockout, blockbuster, best thing since sliced bread (*colloq.*); *classic*, all-time great.

adj. *good*, excellent, outstanding, fine, great, quality; *worthy*, commendable, creditable, admirable, praiseworthy; *choice*, handpicked, select; *superb*, wonderful, magnificent, fantastic, fabulous, glorious, marvellous, splendid, terrific, top-notch (*colloq.*); *super*, brill (*colloq.*), magic (*colloq.*), ace (*colloq.*), out of this world (*colloq.*); *best*, prime, premium, A-1, first-class, blue-chip, supreme; *classic*, vintage; *wholesome*, healthy, sound; *valuable*, priceless, good value; *not bad*, passable, tolerable, satisfactory, decent, acceptable, OK;

vb. *have value*, be worth it, rate, count; *do good*, improve, enhance, benefit.

583 WORTHLESSNESS

See also **604** (harm).

n. *worthlessness*, poor/low quality, shoddiness, mediocrity; *unworthiness*, wickedness, baseness, vileness, nastiness; *corruption*, depravity, obscenity, indecency, vulgarity.

adj. *worthless*, poor-/low-quality, second-rate, mediocre, indifferent; *shoddy*, low-grade, cheap, tacky, cheap and nasty, trashy; *lousy* (*colloq.*), rotten (*colloq.*), crummy (*colloq.*), ropy (*colloq.*); *awful*, dreadful, ghastly, wretched, horrid, horrible, terrible, beastly, grotty (*colloq.*); *wicked*, evil, base, vile, nasty, mean, shabby, vicious, villainous; *corrupt*, depraved, obscene, indecent, vulgar, sordid; *unworthy*, despicable, disgraceful, shameful, deplorable.

vb. *make worthless*, devalue, debase, cheapen, degrade; *do no good*, make things worse, be of no value.

584 PERFECTION

See also **49** (completeness); **188** (summit); **582** (worth); **653** (completion).

n. *perfection*, faultlessness, flawlessness, impeccability; *correctness*, irreproachability, infallibility, integrity; *ideal*, sanspareil, paragon, model; *summit*, height, acme, peak; *example*, standard, pattern, showpiece.

adj. *perfect*, ideal, faultless, flawless, impeccable; *unbeatable*, unrivalled, beyond compare, matchless, peerless, supreme; *correct*, irreproachable, infallible; *immaculate*, pristine, spotless, stainless; *pure*, unadulterated, whole, entire, complete, one hundred per cent, sound.

vb. *perfect*, hone, polish, refine; *consummate*, crown, cap, seal, round off.

585 IMPERFECTION

See also **50** (incompleteness); **767** (blemish).

n. *imperfection*, faultiness, unsoundness; *immaturity*, underdevelopment, incompleteness, inadequacy, deficiency; *deformity*, disfigurement, discoloration, distortion, damage; *unevenness*, patchiness; *flaw*, fault, mistake, failing, defect, shortfall; *catch*, snag, drawback; *blemish*, mark, chip, crack, scratch, impurity.

adj. *imperfect*, faulty, unsound, flawed, defective; *immature*, underdeveloped, incomplete, inadequate, deficient, missing; *deformed*, disfigured, discoloured, distorted, damaged; *uneven*, patchy; *fair*, middling, could do better (*colloq.*); *blemished*, impure, marked, chipped, cracked, scratched, shopsoiled.

vb. *fall short*, not make the grade, be found wanting; *flaw*, mar, spoil.

586 CLEANNESS

See also **39** (purity); **590** (hygiene); **850** (morality).

n. *cleanness*, spotlessness, whiteness, shine, polish; *cleaning* (up), cleansing, washing (down/off/out/up), wiping (down/off/up), mopping up, scouring, scrubbing; *purge*, flush, dialysis, purification, filtration; *decontamination*, sterilization, delousing; *hygiene*, sanitation; *bath* (tub), public baths, shower, sauna, Turkish bath, jacuzzi, (wash)basin, bidet; *washing machine*, launderette, laundry, dishwasher; *soap* (flakes), shampoo, toothpaste, pumice (stone); *washing powder*, detergent, biological powder; *disinfectant*, bleach, antiseptic, cleanser; *polish*, shoe polish, wax, whitewash, blacking, blanco; *brush*, scrubbing brush, toothbrush, nailbrush, broom, mop, sponge, duster; *vacuum cleaner*, filter, mat; *cleaner*, washerwoman, launderer, char(lady), roadsweeper, dustman.

adj. *clean*, spotless, fresh, shiny, polished, neat, tidy; *sterile*, aseptic, antiseptic; *hygienic*, sanitary, disinfectant, detergent.

vb. *clean*, freshen, whiten, shine, polish; *cleanse*, wash (down/off/out/up), wipe (down/off/up), rinse, sluice, mop up, scour, scrub, sponge; *flush*, purify, dialyse, filter; *launder*, bleach, dry-clean; *bath*, bathe, shower; *sweep* (up), brush, dust, vacuum, spring-clean; *sanitize*, sterilize, disinfect, deodorize.

587 DIRTINESS

See also **591** (lack of hygiene); **851** (immorality).

n. *dirtiness*, uncleanness, uncleanliness, squalor; *contamination*, adulteration, pollution; *dirt*, filth, muck, mess; *mud*, slime, grease, dust, grime, oil, gunge (*colloq.*); *stain*, smear, patch, ring, mark, smudge, tarnish; *pigsty*, tip, slum, gutter, sewer; *slut*, pig (*colloq.*), mucky pup (*colloq.*).

adj. *dirty*, unclean, foul, squalid, filthy, mucky, messy, grotty (*colloq.*); *muddy*, slimy, greasy, dusty, grimy, oily, gungy (*colloq.*); *stained*, smeared, marked, smudged, tarnished; *contaminated*, adulterated, polluted.

vb. *dirty*, mess up, begrime, soil, muddy; *stain*, smear, mark, smudge, tarnish; *contaminate*, adulterate, pollute, foul.

588 HEALTH

See also **145** (vigour); **590** (hygiene).

n. *health*, healthiness, good condition, good health, convalescence, recovery; *fitness*, wellbeing, vitality, soundness; *salubrity*, wholesomeness, health food, fresh air, nonsmoker, health freak (*colloq.*).

adj. *healthy*, in good health, well; *convalescent*, on the mend, up and about, fully recovered; *fit* (as a fiddle), sound, robust, strapping, hale and hearty; *health-giving*, wholesome, nutritious, salubrious, nonsmoking, invigorating, beneficial, good for, therapeutic.

vb. *enjoy good health*, keep well, have a clean bill of health, feel fit, be in the pink (*colloq.*).

589 ILL HEALTH

See also **146** (inertness); **591** (lack of hygiene).

n. *ill health*, poor health, infirmity, indisposition; *illness*, sickness, disease, disorder, ailment, complaint, affliction, condition; *lack of fitness*, weakness, debility; *attack*, seizure, fit, stroke, breakdown; *infection*, epidemic, contagion, inflammation, fever, virus, bug (*colloq.*); *cold*, influenza, flu, fever, sore throat, headache, cough; *measles*, German measles, chicken pox, smallpox; *polio*(*myelitis*), multiple sclerosis, muscular dystrophy, rheumatism, arthritis, ulcer, gangrene; *whooping cough*, pneumonia, tuberculosis, bronchitis, tonsillitis; *malaria*, typhoid, cholera, scarlet fever, hepatitis, leprosy; *diarrhoea*, dysentery, gastroenteritis, stomach upset; *heart disease*, allergy, anaemia; *cancer*, tumour, leukaemia; *diphtheria*, tetanus, rabies, venereal disease.

adj. *unhealthy*, in poor health, poorly, sickly, infirm, off colour (*colloq.*), under the weather (*colloq.*); *ill*, sick, diseased, ailing, indisposed, down with, laid up; *unfit*, weak, out of condition; *unwholesome*, poisonous, toxic, bad for, debilitating; *infectious*, contagious, catching, endemic, epidemic.

vb. *be unhealthy*, etc., not feel well, etc.; *suffer from*, ail, complain of; *sicken*, fall ill, catch, contract, go down with.

590 HYGIENE
See also **586** (cleanness); **588** (health).
n. *hygiene*, sanitation, cleanliness, public health, preventive medicine; *quarantine*, vaccination, inoculation, immunization; *disinfection*, sterilization, purification, pasteurization, chlorination, antisepsis; *hygienist*, sanitary inspector, sanitary engineer.
adj. *hygienic*, sanitary, germ-free; *disinfected*, sterilized, sterile, purified, pasteurized, chlorinated, antiseptic.
vb. *sanitize*, disinfect, sterilize, purify, boil, pasteurize, chlorinate; *vaccinate*, inoculate, immunize.

591 LACK OF HYGIENE
See also **587** (dirtiness); **589** (ill health).
n. *lack of hygiene*, lack of sanitation, no proper drainage, dirtiness; *epidemic*, outbreak, infestation, pollution, miasma.
adj. *unhygienic*, insanitary, dirty, germ-ridden, infected; *infested*, polluted, unfit for human habitation, condemned.
vb. *infect*, infest, pollute, condemn.

592 IMPROVEMENT
See also **253** (forward motion); **594** (repair).
n. *improvement*, amelioration, betterment; *development*, progress, advance; *reform*, modernization, new broom; *refinement*, enrichment, polish, enhancement; *advancement*, promotion; *upturn*, recovery, boom; *correction*, amendment, revision, editing, proofreading; *improver*, reformer, refiner, reviser, editor, proofreader.
adj. *improved*, better, reformed, amended, revised, edited; *developed*, advanced; *reforming*, reformatory, progressive.
vb. *improve*, get better; *better oneself*, turn over a new leaf, mend one's ways, pull one's socks up (*colloq.*); *develop*, progress, make progress, make advances; *improve upon*, elaborate on, go one better; *reform*, modernize, streamline, upgrade; *refine*, enrich, polish, enhance; *advance*, promote; *correct*, amend, revise, edit, proofread, rewrite.

593 DETERIORATION
See also **46** (disintegration); **142** (powerlessness); **150** (destruction); **254** (backward motion); **597** (blight).
n. *deterioration*, detriment, impairment, impoverishment, degeneration; *decline*, retrogression, slide, downturn, slump; *dilapidation*, disrepair, ruin; *decay*, rot, rotting, rust, erosion, corrosion, decomposition; *damage*, injury, wound, blemish, mark.
adj. *deteriorated*, impaired, impoverished, degenerate; *in decline*, retrogressive, failing; *dilapidated*, tumbledown, ruined; *decayed*, rotten, rusty, eroded, corroded, decomposed; *damaged*, injured, wounded, blemished, marked.
vb. *deteriorate*, worsen, get worse, degenerate, go downhill, go to the dogs (*colloq.*), go to pot (*colloq.*), *decline*, fall off, retrogress, slump, fail; *decay*, rot, rust, erode, eat away, corrode, decompose; *impair*, degrade, lower, coarsen, spoil; *damage*, injure, wound, blemish, mark.

594 REPAIR
See also **592** (improvement); **596** (remedy).
n. *repair*, mend, mending, remedy; *restoration*, renovation, refurbishment, reconditioning, refit, overhaul; *darn*, patch; *recuperation*, convalescence, recovery, healing; *cure*, refreshment, tonic, pick-me-up; *repairer*, mender, restorer, refurbisher, renovator, healer.
adj. *repaired*, mended, remedied, rectified; *restored*, renovated, refurbished, reconditioned, overhauled; *healed*, cured; *reparable*, mendable, restorable; *restorative*, curative, therapeutic, remedial, corrective.
vb. *repair*, mend, put right, fix, remedy, rectify; *restore*, renovate, refurbish, recondition, refit, overhaul; *heel*, sole, darn, patch; *heal*, cure; *recuperate*, convalesce, recover, get better.

595 DAMAGE

See also **604** (harm); **828** (disparagement).

n. *damage*, disrepair, injury, impairment, hurt, harm; *stain*, blemish, mark, foxing, discoloration, smudge; *tear*, dent, rip, scratch, disfigurement, scar; *corrosion*, rust, tarnish, rot, decay; *erosion*, weathering, wear and tear, battering; *wound*, cut, gash, bruise, sprain, strain.

adj. *damaged*, injured, impaired; *stained*, blemished, marked, foxed, discoloured, smudged; *torn*, scratched, scarred, disfigured, ravaged; *corroded*, rusty, tarnished, rotten, decayed; *eroded*, weathered, worn, frayed, battered; *wounded*, hurt, bruised, sprained, strained.

vb. *damage*, injure, impair, harm, spoil; *stain*, blemish, mark, discolour, smudge; *tear*, scratch, dent, rip, disfigure, deface; *corrode*, rust, tarnish, rot, decay; *erode*, eat away, weather, wear, batter; *wound*, hurt, cut, gash, bruise, sprain, strain.

596 REMEDY

See also **137** (counteraction); **594** (repair).

n. *remedy*, correction, corrective measure, cure, therapy; *help*, aid, first aid, relief; *atonement*, amends, redress; *medicine*, homeopathy, surgery, dentistry; *medicament*, medication, treatment, drug; *placebo*, panacea, quack remedy, patent medicine; *pill*, tablet, suppository, lozenge, capsule; *mixture*, linctus, ointment, balm; *antidote*, antacid, emetic, laxative; *plaster*, splint, dressing, bandage, poultice; *injection*, inoculation, vaccination, vaccine, jab (*colloq.*); *doctor*, physician, dentist, surgeon, nurse, therapist, healer.

adj. *remedial*, corrective, curative, healing, therapeutic; *soothing*, calming, emollient, anaesthetic; *medicinal*, medical, homeopathic, surgical.

vb. *remedy*, correct, cure, put right, fix, heal; *help*, aid, relieve, treat, tend, nurse; *soothe*, calm, drug, anaesthetize; *atone*, make amends, redress; *dress*, bathe, operate, set, inject.

597 BLIGHT

See also **593** (deterioration).

n. *blight*, rot, mould, mildew, fungus, rust; *infestation*, plague, pest, vermin, woodworm; *cancer*, canker, gangrene, necrosis; *bane*, curse, scourge, bugbear, cross, affliction; *nuisance*, annoyance, irritant, thorn in the flesh, pain (*colloq.*), pest (*colloq.*), pain in the arse/neck (*colloq.*); *poison*, toxin, carcinogen.

adj. *blighted*, rotten, mouldy, mildewed, wormeaten; *accursed*, afflicted, wretched; *pestilential*, infuriating, pesky (*colloq.*); *cancerous*, gangrenous, diseased; *poisonous*, toxic, carcinogenic.

598 SAFETY

See also **600** (refuge); **687** (security).

n. *safety*, preservation, security; *guarantee*, surety, warranty, insurance, failsafe; *protection*, shelter, defence, harbour, sanctuary, asylum; *immunity*, safe conduct, invulnerability, impregnability; *safekeeping*, custody, quarantine; *safety net*, lifebelt, lifeline, lifesaver; *precaution*, preventive measure, prophylaxis, immunization; *protector*, guardian, defender, security forces, police, vigilante; *guard*, gaoler, warder, patrol, watchman, bodyguard, minder, lifeguard; *warden*, curator, custodian, keeper, gamekeeper.

adj. *safe*, secure, sure; *guaranteed*, under warranty, insured; *immune*, invulnerable, impregnable; *hygienic*, non-toxic, childproof, unbreakable; *prophylactic*, preventive, protective; *unharmed*, safe and sound, in one piece, unscathed; *guarded*, locked up, under lock and key, behind bars, in quarantine.

vb. *be safe*, keep out of harm's way, keep a safe distance, give a wide berth, take precautions, be prepared; *safeguard*, immunize, protect, preserve; *defend*, shelter, shield, harbour, guard; *patrol*, police, watch over, have charge of, keep under surveillance.

599 DANGER
See also **425** (probability); **601** (trap).

n. *danger*, peril, hazard, black spot; *crisis*, flashpoint, trouble spot; *menace*, threat, sword of Damocles; *danger signal*, warning, red light, alarm; *danger zone*, no-go area, firing line, no man's land; *insecurity*, jeopardy, risk, precariousness.

adj. *dangerous*, perilous, hazardous, risky; *menacing*, threatening; *unsafe*, insecure, in jeopardy, precarious, dodgy (*colloq.*); *critical*, delicate; treacherous, slippery.

vb. *endanger*, put at risk, imperil, jeopardize; *menace*, threaten, loom; *hazard*, risk, expose, play with fire, tempt fate; *court danger*, skate on thin ice, sail too near the wind, enter the lions' den, run the gauntlet.

600 REFUGE
See also **469** (concealment); **598** (safety); **640** (defence).

n. *refuge*, retreat, asylum, sanctuary, haven, shelter, safe house; *air-raid shelter*, fallout shelter, bunker, dugout, trench, foxhole, bolthole; *central refuge*, central reservation, traffic island, emergency lane; *earth*, lair, den, burrow, nest; *fort*, castle, fortress, stockade, keep, stronghold, bastion; *screen*, cover, shield, windbreak; *refugee*, evacuee, displaced person, DP camp.

vb. *seek refuge*, run for cover, take shelter, make port.

601 TRAP
See also **242** (vehicle); **599** (danger); **668** (restraint).

n. *trap*, pitfall, snare, ambush; *mantrap*, gin, pit, noose, booby trap, mine; *decoy*, bait, blind, lure, diversion; *reef*, bar, sandbank, shoal, submerged rock, undertow, crevasse, quicksand.

vb. *trap*, ensnare, ambush, lie in wait.

602 WARNING
See also **484** (sign); **623** (advice); **678** (veto).

n. *warning*, caution, notice, lesson; *information*, nod, wink, word; *early warning*, advance notice, clue, hint, deterrent, warning shot; *admonishment*, rebuke, reprimand, telling-off, yellow card; *premonition*, presage, foreboding; *omen*, writing on the wall, harbinger of doom; *danger signal*, red flag, red light, fire alarm, foghorn; *horn*, hooter, klaxon, siren, tocsin; *alarm clock*, warning light, alarm bell, beacon; *SOS*, mayday, flare, distress signal.

adj. *cautionary*, warning, deterrent; *ominous*, symptomatic.

vb. *warn*, caution, give notice; *inform*, advise, notify, tip off, tip the wink (*colloq.*); *admonish*, reprove, rebuke, reprimand, tell off; *give/raise/sound the alarm*, dial 999, alert; *look out!*, watch your step!

603 PRESERVATION
See also **570** (store).

n. *preservation*, saving, safekeeping, maintenance; *conservation*, conservancy, protection; *game reserve*, bird sanctuary, nature reserve; *conservation area*, ancient monument, listed building; *refrigeration*, freezing, cold storage, drying, freeze-drying, canning, preserving, bottling; *embalming*, mummification, taxidermy; *preservative*, sugar, salt, brine, spice, pickle, water glass, ice, dry ice, formaldehyde.

adj. *preservative*, protective, preserving; *preserved*, salted, pickled, iced, frozen, dried, smoked, canned, tinned, potted, bottled; *well-preserved*, fresh, intact.

vb. *preserve*, save, maintain; *conserve*, protect, list; *paint*, varnish, creosote; *cure*, smoke, refrigerate, freeze, dry, can, bottle; *embalm*, mummify, stuff.

604 HARM
See also **583** (worthlessness); **595** (damage); **737** (unpleasantness).

n. *harm*, ill, hurt, damage, injury, detriment; *bad luck*, misfortune, disaster, destruction, ruin; *cruelty*, malevolence, viciousness, wrong, evil, persecution; *hurtfulness*, malice, spite, scandal, libel, slander, defamation; *unwholesomeness*, noxiousness, poison, toxin, pollution, radioactivity.

adj. *harmful*, damaging, injurious, per-

nicious, insidious, deleterious, detrimental; *disastrous*, destructive, ruinous; *harsh*, savage, fierce; *cruel*, malevolent, vicious, wrong, hurtful; *malicious*, spiteful, bitchy, libellous, slanderous, defamatory; *fatal*, lethal, deadly, poisonous, malignant, terminal; *toxic*, noxious, polluting, radioactive; *unwholesome*, infectious, unhygienic.
vb. *harm*, hurt, damage, injure, impair; *destroy*, ruin, wreck, undermine, play havoc with; *abuse*, ill-treat, wrong, persecute, victimize; *libel*, slander, defamate; *poison*, intoxicate, pollute, irradiate.

605 ESCAPE

See also **556** (avoidance); **606** (deliverance); **822** (exemption).
n. *escape*, flight, getaway, breakout, departure; *evasion*, avoidance, truancy, desertion, (moonlight) flit (*colloq.*); *rescue*, deliverance, freeing, letting off, reprieve; *withdrawal*, retreat, decampment, elopement; *get-out*, let-out, escape clause, loophole; *leak*, discharge, burst, seepage; *narrow escape*, close/near thing, close shave (*colloq.*); *way out*, (emergency) exit, egress, escape hatch, bolthole, fire escape, ejector seat; *escapee*, fugitive, runaway, deserter, truant.
adj. *escaped*, free, at large, truant, flown, AWOL.
vb. *escape*, flee, depart, take flight, break out; *evade*, elude, avoid, give the slip; *desert*, abscond, play truant, do a (moonlight) flit (*colloq.*); *rescue*, deliver, save, free, reprieve; *withdraw*, retreat, decamp, elope; *leak*, discharge, burst forth.

606 DELIVERANCE

See also **598** (safety); **605** (escape).
n. *deliverance*, rescue, saving, salvage; *extrication*, salvation, redemption, cure; *reprieve*, discharge, acquittal, pardon, liberation; *respite*, cease-fire, truce, stay of execution, remission, breather (*colloq.*); *rescuer*, deliverer, saviour, redeemer, liberator.
vb. *deliver*, rescue, free, save; *be the saving of*, salvage, retrieve, extricate, redeem, cure; *reprieve*, discharge, acquit, let off, pardon, liberate.

607 ACTION

See also **523** (drama); **609** (activity); **645** (war); **856** (litigation).
n. *action*, doing, commission, perpetration, execution, performance; *step*, move, manoeuvre, initiative, measure, act, deed; *feat*, exploit, achievement, accomplishment; *activity*, work, job, task, occupation; *perpetrator*, executor, performer, doer, worker, activist.
adj. *acting*, active, in operation, operational, at work, employed, in the act, occupational.
vb. *do*, act, commit, conduct, perpetrate, execute, prosecute, perform, ply; *undertake*, put into effect, implement, enact, carry out; *accomplish*, achieve, bring about/off; *work*, function, be in operation, occupy oneself.

608 INACTION

See also **146** (inertness); **610** (inactivity).
n. *inaction*, inertness, passivity, failure/inability to act, abstention; *immobility*, paralysis, stasis; *rest*, idleness, unemployment, leisure; *suspension*, abeyance.
adj. *out of action*, inoperative, inert, passive; *immobile*, paralysed, static; *resting*, idle, unemployed; *suspended*, in abeyance.
vb. *do nothing*, fail to act, refrain, abstain, stay neutral, opt out, pass the buck; *shelve*, put on ice, mothball; *not act*, let sleeping dogs lie, wait and see, bide one's time, mark time, tick over, stand (idly) by, not lift a finger; *twiddle one's thumbs*, kick one's heels, be at a loose end.

609 ACTIVITY

See also **607** (action).
n. *activity*, movement; *nimbleness*, agility, liveliness, briskness; *life*, energy, vigour, get-up-and-go (*colloq.*); *business*, dealing, trading; *stir*, burst, fit, flurry; *bustle*, fuss, agitation, ado, bother, to-do, commotion; *readiness*,

keenness, willingness, eagerness, alacrity; *enterprise*, enthusiasm, dynamism; *concentration*, diligence, industry; *determination*, tirelessness, perseverance; *hard worker*, slogger, busy bee (*colloq.*), eager beaver (*colloq.*); *enthusiast*, fanatic, militant, zealot.
adj. *active*, on the go, moving, in motion, working; *nimble*, agile, lively, brisk, busy; *keen*, willing, eager, enterprising, enthusiastic; *diligent*, industrious, energetic, vigorous, dynamic; *determined*, tireless, dogged, unflagging.
vb. *be active*, etc.; *rouse oneself*, make an effort, exert oneself, gird one's loins; *bustle*, hurry, get a move on, not hang about (*colloq.*), go for it (*colloq.*).

610 INACTIVITY

See also **146** (inertness); **608** (inaction); **619** (fatigue).
n. *inactivity*, inertia, torpor, listlessness; *quiet*, peace, calm, stillness; *laziness*, sloth, lethargy, apathy, indolence; *sleep*, rest, repose, nap, siesta, snooze, shut-eye (*colloq.*), kip (*colloq.*); *hibernation*, aestivation; *unconsciousness*, trance, coma, stupor; *strike*, lockout, shutdown; *laggard*, lazy-bones, slacker, loafer, passenger, sleeping partner; *layabout*, scrounger, good-for-nothing; *idle rich*, leisured classes.
adj. *inactive*, still, motionless, peaceful, calm; *slow-moving*, listless, sluggish, torpid; *idle*, slothful, indolent, lazy, leisured; *unenterprising*, apathetic, indifferent; *unconscious*, comatose, asleep; *tired*, weary, dopey, groggy, sleepy, somnolent.
vb. *be inactive*, etc., stagnate, drift, let things slide; *delay*, stall, drag one's feet, loiter, dawdle; *laze about*, lounge, loaf, idle, shirk, skive; *sleep*, doze, nap, slumber, rest; *hibernate*, aestivate.

611 WORK

See also **149** (production).
n. *work*, task, job, assignment, mission, undertaking, venture; *employment*, gainful employment, service; *post*, position, function, situation; *appointment*, vacancy, opening, headhunting; *profession*, occupation, line of work, career, trade, craft; *industry*, commerce, business, dealings, trade, affairs; *worker*, breadwinner, wage-earner, white-/blue-collar worker, professional (person), artisan, labourer.
adj. *working*, workaday, employed, self-employed, freelance, busy (with); *professional*, businesslike, efficient; *occupational*, industrial, commercial.
vb. *work*, do a job, work for, be engaged on, engage in, earn one's living; *apply for*, take a job; *employ*, take on, hire, appoint, engage, recruit, select, headhunt; *trade*, do/conduct/transact business, deal, negotiate.

612 LEISURE

See also **618** (ease); **761** (recreation).
n. *leisure*, free time, spare time, one's own time, time off, break, recess, retirement; *leisure activities*, recreation, relaxation, rest, sport, leisure centre; *holiday*, vacation, furlough, leave, leave of absence, R & R, sabbatical.
adj. *leisured*, unoccupied, retired, resting; *sabbatical*, on holiday.
vb. *take time off*, take a break, holiday, go on holiday; *relax*, take one's time, have all the time in the world; *retire*, give up work, drop out.
adv. *in one's own time*, at one's own pace, at one's leisure, at one's convenience.

613 WORKER

See also **149** (production).
n. *worker*, employee, self-employed person, freelance(r); *slave*, bondsman, menial, fag, coolie, bearer; *dogsbody*, skivvy, drudge, hewer of wood and drawer of water, chief cook and bottle-washer, factotum; *servant*, domestic (servant), maid, valet, tweeny, cook, chambermaid, housekeeper, butler, footman, groom, ostler; *dustman*, cleaner, char(lady), daily, help; *farmer*, farmhand, farm labourer, dairyman, shepherd; *forester*, nurseryman, gardener; *workman*, artisan, blue-collar worker, tradesman, craftsman, handy-

man, odd-job man, apprentice, (casual) labourer; *mechanic*, repairman, fitter; *factory worker*, steelworker, docker; *builder*, bricklayer, mason, plasterer, decorator, painter, electrician, glazier, tiler, slater, plumber; *carpenter*, cabinetmaker, joiner; *smith*, blacksmith, welder; *miner*, coalminer, collier; *jeweller*, goldsmith, silversmith, watchmaker, clockmaker; *tailor*, dressmaker; *author*, writer, journalist, photographer, editor, printer, proofreader, bookbinder; *businessman*, businesswoman, dealer, trader, merchant, middleman, wholesaler; *retailer*, shopkeeper, shop assistant, check-out girl; *employer*, industrialist, manufacturer; *manager*, supervisor, director, executive; *staff*, personnel, workforce, labour force, manpower, payroll; *office worker*, white-collar worker, clerk, secretary, shorthand typist, personal assistant, girl Friday, tealady, teaboy; *banker*, stockbroker, jobber; *lawyer*, solicitor, barrister; *engineer*, electrical/mechanical/civil engineer, architect, draughtsman, designer, town planner; *functionary*, operative, officer, executant, practitioner.

614 WORKSHOP

n. *workshop*, workplace, place of work; *workroom*, study, library, studio, atelier; *office*, bureau, shop, establishment, laboratory; *factory*, works, plant, installation; *yard*, site, industrial estate, depot, station, branch, dock; *shop floor*, production/assembly line; *mine*, quarry, foundry, refinery, laundry, kitchen, farm.

615 HASTE

See also **245** (speed); **753** (rashness).

n. *haste*, hurry, rush, bustle, scurry, scramble; *urgency*, pressure, deadline, rush job; *acceleration*, hastening, precipitation, recklessness, impatience; *dash*, burst of speed, push, spurt, sprint, race (against time).

adj. *hasty*, hurried, in a rush, fast, hustling; *urgent*, top-priority, hot off the press; *pressurized*, hard-pressed, hard-pushed; *rushed*, eleventh-hour, last-minute, skimped; *rash*, reckless, precipitate, impatient.

vb. *hurry*, rush, hustle, scurry, scramble, not waste time, lose no time; *throw together*, cobble together, whip up, hack out; *speed up*, hasten, dispatch, precipitate, expedite, railroad (*colloq.*); *hurry up*, goad, put a bomb under; *dash*, push, spurt, sprint, race, tear, zoom, whizz, bomb along (*colloq.*).

616 LACK OF HASTE

See also **246** (slowness); **406** (carefulness).

n. *lack of haste*, slowness, steadiness, deliberation; *leisure*, time to spare, no hurry; *dilatoriness*, hesitation, lack of enthusiasm, caution; *laziness*, procrastination, no sense of time, unpunctuality, mañana; *dawdle*, amble, saunter, stroll, trot, jog; *crawl*, snail's pace; *conscientiousness*, attention (to detail), thoroughness, accuracy; *consideration*, thoughtfulness; *dawdler*, crawler, plodder, slowcoach, Sunday-afternoon driver, late riser, lie-abed.

adj. *unhurried*, slow, steady, deliberate; *dilatory*, unenthusiastic, hesitant, cautious; *leisurely*, easygoing, phlegmatic, plodding; *lazy*, sluggish, slothful, languid; *late*, tardy, unpunctual; *painstaking*, conscientious, thorough, accurate; *considered*, thoughtout.

vb. *have all the time in the world*, take no note of time; *hesitate*, drawl, spin out, drag out; *not be hurried*, think over, weigh up, ponder, not rush into things, sleep on it; *dawdle*, amble, saunter, shamble, stroll, trot, jog; *crawl*, creep, inch; *linger*, loiter, (dilly-) dally.

617 EXERTION

n. *exertion*, effort, strain, muscle, elbow grease (*colloq.*); *force*, pressure, thrust, pull, tug, tension; *labour*, work, toil, hard graft, application; *hard work*, slog, fag (*colloq.*), grind; *trouble*, pains, sweat, bother, pain (*colloq.*); *exercise*, physical education, PE, physical training, PT, drill; *keep-fit*, jogging, aerobics, sport, games.

adj. *laborious*, gruelling, backbreaking, exhausting, arduous, uphill, killing; *industrious*, hard-working, dogged; *strenuous*, demanding, energetic.
vb. *exert oneself*, strive, try, make an/the effort, endeavour, strain; *labour*, toil, sweat, work, hump; *grind*, plod, slog away, make heavy weather of; *apply oneself*, buckle down, knuckle down, set to, pull one's finger out; *go to great trouble*, bend over backwards, put oneself to a lot of bother, put oneself out, bust a gut (*colloq.*); *spare no effort*, do one's utmost, pull out all the stops.
adv. *laboriously*, with brute force, by the sweat of one's brow, the hard way; *with a vengeance*, all out, flat out, hammer and tongs (*colloq.*), tooth and nail (*colloq.*).

618 EASE
See also **612** (leisure); **629** (easiness); **740** (relief).
n. *ease*, repose, rest, relaxation; *comfort*, restfulness, peace and quiet, calm, tranquillity; *pause*, break, coffee/tea/lunch-break, lunch hour, recreation period; *holiday*, vacation, leave, furlough, day off, weekend, bank holiday.
adj. *at ease*, relaxed,, casual, laid back (*colloq.*); *restful*, relaxing, comfortable, peaceful, quiet, calm, tranquil.
vb. *be at ease*, etc., take one's ease, rest, take it easy, relax, put one's feet up, lounge; *stop*, take a break, slow down, take time off; *take a holiday*, get away from it all, go on leave.

619 FATIGUE
See also **144** (weakness); **610** (inactivity).
n. *fatigue*, tiredness, weariness; *sleepiness*, somnolence, drowsiness, doziness; *weakness*, faintness, feebleness; *exhaustion*, prostration, collapse.
adj. *fatigued*, tired, weary; *sleepy*, somnolent, drowsy, dozy; *weak*, faint, feeble, drained; *exhausted*, worn out, all in, dead beat, dropping (*colloq.*), pooped (*colloq.*), whacked (*colloq.*), fagged out (*colloq.*), knackered (*colloq.*), shattered (*colloq.*); *fatiguing*, tiring, punishing, knackering (*colloq.*), shattering (*colloq.*).
vb. *be tired*, etc.; *tire*, flag, wilt, droop; *fall asleep*, nod off, drop off, conk out (*colloq.*), flake out (*colloq.*), crash out (*colloq.*), go out like a light (*colloq.*); *collapse*, drop; *fatigue*, tire, weary, exhaust, wear out, tax, flog.

620 REFRESHMENT
See also **145** (vigour); **267** (ingestion); **740** (relief).
n. *refreshment*, recreation, renewal, recuperation, revival, recovery, restoration, relief; *invigoration*, stimulation, fillip; *food*, drink, stimulant, tonic.
adj. *refreshing*, reviving, restoring, restorative, recuperative; *cool*, invigorating, stimulating, bracing; *refreshed*, recovered.
vb. *refresh*, freshen, revive, restore; *reinvigorate*, stimulate, perk up, enliven; *be refreshed*, recover, recuperate, get one's second wind, get one's breath back; *take a breather*, cool off, stretch one's legs, freshen up, recharge one's batteries.

621 CONDUCT
See also **607** (action); **622** (management).
n. *conduct*, behaviour, comportment, actions; *customs*, way of life, moves; *style*, manner, air, attitude, demeanour; *way of speaking*, tone of voice, presentation; *good behaviour*, (good) manners, (good) breeding; *bad behaviour*, misbehaviour, misconduct, misdemeanours, rudeness; *past* (behaviour/history), background, (track) record; *practice*, methods, system, procedure, common practice, organization; *control*, guidance, supervision; *strategy*, plan, tactics, policy, programme.
adj. *behavioural*; *strategic*, tactical, planned.
vb. *behave*, conduct oneself/one's affairs, act, acquit oneself; *behave well*, be on one's best behaviour, behave oneself, set an example, mind one's P's and Q's; *behave badly*, misbehave,

play up; *carry on*, run, manage, control, run, supervise.

622 MANAGEMENT

See also **57** (arrangement); **621** (conduct); **651** (success); **657** (authority); **665** (master).

n. *management*, direction, handling, running, administration, bureaucracy, organization, order; *authority*, command, charge, control, supervision, leadership; *government*, legislation, jurisdiction, power, regulation, politics, dictatorship, tyranny; *manager*, administrator, controller, coordinator, organizer, official, bureaucrat, executive, chairman, boss; *housekeeper*, steward, agent, deputy; *director*, inspector, chief, overseer, foreman, supervisor, board of directors; *legislator*, leader, politician, (prime) minister, premier, secretary of state, governor, statesman, prefect; *officer*, commander, captain; *chancellor*, vice-chancellor, governing body, warden, master, dean.

adj. *administrative*, organizational, bureaucratic, political; *managerial*, directorial, governmental, supervisory, legislative, governing, guiding; *authoritative*, in charge, commanding, leading, statesmanlike; *dictatorial*, tyrannical, despotic.

vb. *manage*, direct, handle, run, administer, organize, coordinate, order; *command*, be in charge of, head up, control, steer, supervise, lead, guide, be in the driving seat; *govern*, legislate, regulate, police.

623 ADVICE

See also **442** (maxim); **602** (warning).

n. *advice*, counsel, counselling, guidance; *recommendation*, tip, suggestion, hint, intimation, word in one's ear; *persuasion*, dissuasion, support, encouragement; *precept*, tenet, (golden) rule, guidelines; *instruction*, direction, ordinance, injunction, regulation, ruling, prescription; *warning*, caution, notice, criticism, admonition, admonishment; *adviser*, counsellor, guide, tutor, confidant(e), mentor; *consultant*, lawyer, counsel, steering committee; *busybody*, back-seat driver.

adj. *advisory*, consultative, guiding, steering; *persuasive*, dissuasive, encouraging, supportive, cautionary; *prescriptive*, mandatory, statutory, binding.

vb. *advise*, counsel, advocate, recommend; *suggest*, submit, propose, hint, intimate; *persuade*, dissuade, encourage, enjoin, warn, guide; *consult*, call in, seek/take advice, consult counsel, see one's solicitor; *instruct*, prescribe, lay down.

624 SKILL

See also **141** (power); **438** (knowledge).

n. *skill*, facility, mastery, adeptness, adroitness, deftness; *ability*, competence, capability, capacity; *talent*, gift, genius, forte, flair, bent; *training*, experience, accomplishment, know-how; *expertise*, knack, touch, grip, technique; *skilled person*, man of many parts, master, veteran, old hand; *specialist*, professional, authority, expert; *genius*, talent; *craftsman*, artist, technician.

adj. *skilful*, skilled, apt, adept, adroit, deft, good at; *able*, competent, capable, talented, gifted; *professional*, authoritative, expert, businesslike; *trained*, experienced, accomplished, practised.

vb. *be skilful*, etc., excel, shine, play one's cards well, have a gift/talent, know the ropes, know one's way around.

625 UNSKILFULNESS

See also **142** (powerlessness); **439** (ignorance).

n. *unskilfulness*, clumsiness, awkwardness; *inexperience*, lack of experience/practice, rustiness; *inability*, incapacity, ineptitude, incompetence, inefficiency; *mismanagement*, mishandling, bungling, tactlessness, thoughtlessness; *mess*, hash, shambles, faux pas, pig's ear (*colloq.*), cockup (*colloq.*); *bungler*, bodger, amateur, jack of all trades and master of none, butterfingers.

adj. *unskilful*, clumsy, awkward, ham-

fisted, bumbling; *inexperienced*, unqualified, unpractised, rusty; *inept*, incapable, incompetent, ineffectual, failed; *inefficient*, impractical, inexpert, unprofessional, unbusinesslike; *amateurish*, scratch, home-made, Heath Robinson, slapdash; *thoughtless*, tactless, ill-considered, foolish.
vb. *be unskilful*, etc., not have the knack, be no good at, bumble, fumble, flounder; *botch*, spoil, fluff, make a mess/hash of, bungle, mess up (*colloq.*), cock up (*colloq.*), make a pig's ear of (*colloq.*), fuck up (*vulg.*); *mismanage*, mishandle, blunder, blow it (*colloq.*).

626 CUNNING

See also **444** (wisdom); **480** (deception).
n. *cunning*, craft, craftiness, guile, slyness, artfulness, dishonesty, deceit, stealth, sleight of hand; *ingenuity*, resourcefulness, wisdom, shrewdness, cleverness; *ruse*, plot, intrigue, scheme, trick, deception, dodge, wiles, wrinkle, chicanery; *artful dodger*, snake in the grass, slyboots, plotter, schemer, cheat, trickster, con-man (*colloq.*), wide boy.
adj. *cunning*, crafty, sly, artful, wily, disingenuous, deceitful, scheming, shady; *ingenious*, resourceful, shrewd, clever, canny, sharp, smart (*colloq.*), not born yesterday (*colloq.*).
vb. *be cunning*, etc., plot, intrigue, scheme; *trick*, deceive, cheat, hoax, con (*colloq.*), put one over on (*colloq.*); *outwit*, outsmart, get the better of.

627 NAIVETY

See also **434** (belief); **439** (ignorance).
n. *naivety*, artlessness, innocence, simplicity, ingenuousness; *naturalness*, unsophistication, unaffectedness; *sincerity*, straightforwardness, frankness, candour, openness; *innocent*, child, ingénue, greenhorn, beginner, yokel, simpleton.
adj. *naive*, artless, green, innocent, wide-eyed, simple, ingenuous, unstudied; *natural*, unsophisticated, unaffected, childlike, unlearned; *sincere*, straightforward, frank, candid, open.
vb. *be naive*, etc., rush in where angels fear to tread, say what one thinks, speak one's mind, not mince one's words.

628 DIFFICULTY

See also **581** (inconvenience); **630** (hindrance).
n. *difficulty*, arduousness, laboriousness, awkwardness, inconvenience; *ordeal*, tall order, handful, uphill struggle, hard going, labours of Hercules, no picnic (*colloq.*); *trouble*, bother, hole (*colloq.*), scrape (*colloq.*), pickle (*colloq.*); *predicament*, dilemma, problem, fix; *puzzle*, teaser, poser, headache (*colloq.*); *obstacle*, impediment, stumbling block, complication, handicap.
adj. *difficult*, hard, arduous, laborious, tough, uphill, demanding; *awkward*, inconvenient, unmanageable, unwieldy; *troublesome*, bothersome; *problematic*, complex, complicated, involved, puzzling; *stubborn*, cussed, hard to shift, obstinate; *delicate*, ticklish, tricky, knotty.
vb. *be difficult*, etc., make things difficult, make difficulties for, plague; *trouble*, put to trouble/inconvenience, inconvenience, put out, perplex, bother, irk; *puzzle*, perplex, give one a headache, complicate matters; *hinder*, hamper, obstruct; *be in difficulty*, get into difficulties, run into trouble, flounder, get out of one's depth, come unstuck.
adv. *with difficulty*, uphill, the hard way, against the stream.

629 EASINESS

See also **580** (convenience); **631** (help).
n. *easiness*, ease, facility; *straightforwardness*, simplicity, convenience, feasibility; *facilitation*, simplification, deregulation; *sinecure*, cushy number (*colloq.*), soft option, easy way out, line of least resistance; *easy target*, easy meat, sitting duck; *no problem*, open-and-shut case, plain sailing, dod-

dle (*colloq.*), picnic (*colloq.*), piece of cake (*colloq.*), money for jam/old rope (*colloq.*), child's play (*colloq.*), kid's stuff (*colloq.*), cinch (*colloq.*), pushover (*colloq.*), walkover (*colloq.*).
adj. *easy*, effortless, undemanding, painless, downhill, cushy (*colloq.*), nothing to it (*colloq.*); *straightforward*, simple, uncomplicated, convenient; *obvious*, clear, readable; *feasible*, manageable; *pleasant*, short, light; *helpful*, easy-going, willing.
vb. *be easy*, etc., present no difficulties, give no trouble, require no effort, make no demands; *go well*, go like clockwork, run smoothly; *have no trouble*, make short work of, sail through, cruise; *ease*, facilitate, smooth, oil the wheels, not stand in the way; *free*, unharness, unfetter; *simplify*, clarify, facilitate, deregulate.
adv. *easily*, readily, standing on one's head (*colloq.*), like falling off a log, with one hand tied behind one's back, blindfold (*colloq.*); *smoothly*, like clockwork (*colloq.*), like a dream (*colloq.*).

630 HINDRANCE

See also **114** (lateness); **628** (difficulty); **668** (restraint).
n. *hindrance*, impedance, impediment, nuisance, handicap, encumbrance; *obstructiveness*, picketing, boycott, blacking, filibustering; *restraint*, check, curb, resistance; *retardation*, drag, friction, headwind, tide; *prohibition*, bar, ban, embargo; *restriction*, limitation, control; *obstacle*, barrier, hurdle, hazard, bunker; *interruption*, intervention, interference; *hitch*, hold-up, setback, spanner in the works (*colloq.*); *obstruction*, blockage, constriction, jam, traffic jam, tailback, snarl-up (*colloq.*); *dam*, barrage, lock, weir; *bandage*, tourniquet, compress; *defence*, moat, wall, portcullis, drawbridge, fence, barricade, stockade; *gate*, tollgate, checkpoint, road block, stile, cattle-grid.
adj. *hindering*, obstructive; *unfavourable*, unhelpful; *restrictive*, limiting, controlling; *prohibitive*, preventive, preventative.
vb. *hinder*, impede, obstruct, hamper, handicap, encumber; restrain, check, resist, retard, brake; *prohibit*, bar, ban; *restrict*, limit, curb, control, clamp down on; *repress*, quell, dam (up), cramp one's style; *constrict*, bandage, bind, cramp, hem in, hedge in; *interrupt*, intervene, interfere, meddle; *thwart*, frustrate, snooker, hamstring, stymie; *block/clog/jam (up)*, filibuster, stonewall, throw a spanner in the works (*colloq.*); *cripple*, paralyse, hobble, fetter; *picket*, boycott, black.

631 HELP

See also **138** (instrumentality); **578** (usefulness); **629** (easiness).
n. *help*, aid, assistance, succour, helping hand, charity; *relief*, easing, alleviation; *advice*, guidance, comfort, feedback; *encouragement*, moral support, backing; *medical assistance*, first aid, treatment, nursing; *financial help/aid/assistance*, foreign aid, loan, sponsorship; *grant*, bursary, scholarship, exhibition, allowance, honorarium; *subsidy*, maintenance, benefit, social security, subsistence, hand-out; *helper*, help, assistant, aide; *right-hand man*, henchman, sidekick (*colloq.*), girl/man Friday, aide-de-camp, lieutenant; *adviser*, counsellor, think-tank, tower of strength; *good Samaritan*, neighbour, fairy godmother; *sponsor*, supporter, champion, promoter.
adj. *helpful*, of assistance, auxiliary; *supportive*, encouraging, obliging.
vb. *help (out)*, aid, assist, succour, render assistance, do one a good turn, lend a hand (*colloq.*), give one a leg-up (*colloq.*), put in a word for; *relieve*, ease, alleviate, comfort; *advise*, guide, show the ropes; *encourage*, support, endorse, back, sustain; *treat*, minister to, nurse; *pay for*, finance, sponsor, subsidize, maintain, promote, patronize.

632 OPPOSITION

See also **14** (oppositeness); **137** (counteraction); **637** (defiance); **638** (resistance); **682** (protest).
n. *opposition*, antagonism, hostility; *noncooperation*, contrariness, recalci-

trance, obstinacy; *denial*, counterargument, contradiction, objection; *disagreement*, dissension, dispute, conflict, clash; *defiance*, resistance, challenge; *competition*, struggle, rivalry; *opposite*, polarity, contrast, antithesis, dichotomy; *opponent*, adversary, antagonist, enemy; *contender*, contestant, rival, competitor, challenger, candidate.

adj. *opposing*, conflicting, antagonistic, adversarial, hostile, unfriendly, defiant; *uncooperative*, contrary, negative, bloody-minded, recalcitrant, obstinate, dissenting; *opposed to*, against, out of sympathy with.

vb. *oppose*, be dead against, disagree, dissent; *dispute*, deny, object, protest, argue against, contradict; *challenge*, resist, defy, fly in the face of, conflict with; *counter*, withstand, confront, hinder, obstruct; *compete against/with*, rival, contend, take up the cudgels.

633 COOPERATION

See also **40** (union); **43** (adhesion); **45** (combination).

n. *cooperation*, mutual assistance, fellowship, support; *working together*, joint/concerted effort, collaboration, teamwork, synergy, combined effort/operation; *merger*, amalgamation, union, coalition; *common aim*, solidarity, fellow feeling, sympathy; *league*, partnership, compact, treaty, alliance, détente; *concurrence*, unanimity, agreement, harmony, concert; *conspiracy*, collusion, connivance, complicity.

adj. *cooperative*, helpful, positive, constructive; *joint*, combined, mutual, bilateral; *sympathetic*, well-disposed, favourable, in sympathy with, concurrent; *in league*, synergic; *unanimous*, solid, united.

vb. *cooperate*, help one another, settle one's differences; *collaborate*, work together, combine/join forces, work in tandem, pull together; *help*, play ball, go along with, join in, muck in; *join together*, club together, team up, merge, amalgamate, unite, coalesce, combine; *agree*, concur, harmonize, see eye to eye; *conspire*, collude, connive, go into a huddle.

634 PARTY

See also 66 (assembly).

n. *party*, group, body, band; *member*, partner, adherent, follower, activist; *organization*, movement, political party, federation, association, society, circle, club; *council*, congress, parliament, legislature; *confederation*, alliance, Axis, coalition, league; *community*, fellowship, brotherhood, sisterhood, order; *confession*, church, religion, denomination, sect; *concern*, establishment, company, firm, corporation, partnership, syndicate, subsidiary, offshoot; *committee*, board of directors/governors, cabinet, junta, executive, administration; *faction*, splinter group, clique, in-group.

adj. *cooperative*, social, communal; *federal*, confederate, affiliated, associated; *corporate*, joint; *factional*, sectional, denominational, sectarian; *committed*, card-carrying, fully paid-up, militant.

vb. *join*, subscribe, enrol, sign on/up; *associate*, ally, federate, affiliate; *take sides*, side with, throw in one's lot with.

635 DISAGREEMENT

See also **18** (dissimilarity); **20** (disparity); **410** (argument); **437** (dissent); **643** (contention).

n. *disagreement*, nonagreement, difference of opinion; *dispute*, strife, contention, controversy, dissidence, dissent, dissension; *fight*, quarrel, squabble, wrangle, clash, row, tiff, feud, vendetta; *defiance*, rebellion, mutiny; *division*, split, breach, rift, schism, infighting; *disunity*, disharmony, discord, dissonance; *litigation*, legal battle, lawsuit, court action; *argument*, words, set-to, bickering, barney (*colloq.*), slanging match (*colloq.*); *bone of contention*, sore point, point at issue, talking point, hot potato (*colloq.*); *polemicist*, young Turk, rebel, firebrand, hothead.

adj. *disagreeing*, in disagreement, dissenting, nonconformist, at odds, at variance, at sixes and sevens, at loggerheads; *quarrelling*, warring, feuding, antagonistic, hostile; *contentious*,

polemical, controversial, provocative, litigious, in dispute; *divided*, split, internecine; *rebellious*, mutinous, quarrelsome; *discordant*, disunited, dissonant; *conflicting*, clashing, divisive.
vb. *disagree*, differ, agree to differ, not go along with (*colloq.*), stick one's neck out; *dispute*, reject, contend, dissent, object, have a bone to pick with (*colloq.*), take issue with, clash; *fight*, quarrel, squabble, wrangle, row, feud; *divide*, split, go one's separate ways; *sue*, lodge a complaint, take to court; *argue*, bicker, fall out, have words.

636 AGREEMENT

See also **17** (similarity); **19** (accord); **436** (assent).
n. *agreement*, concurrence, consent; *contract*, compact, treaty, concordat, entente (cordiale), pact, convention, settlement; *approval*, acceptance, assent; *unanimity*, unity, solidarity, consensus, general agreement; *détente*, reconciliation; *peace*, harmony, accord, mutual understanding, rapport, sweetness and light; *consistency*, symmetry, match, coincidence, correspondence.
adj. *in agreement*, agreed, undisputed, concurring, of one mind, like-minded; *agreeable*, acquiescent, favourable, consenting; *unanimous*, united, allied, solid; *peaceful*, peaceable, harmonious, reconciled; *consistent*, symmetrical, matching, compatible, corresponding.
vb. *agree*, concur, accord, go along with (*colloq.*); *see eye to eye*, get along, hit it off (*colloq.*); *be reconciled*, bury the hatchet, make it up, mend one's fences; *consent*, acquiesce, accept; *assent*, approve, condone, give one's blessing; *correspond*, match, coincide, harmonize.

637 DEFIANCE

See also **632** (opposition); **662** (disobedience).
n. *defiance*, provocation, disobedience; *challenge*, dare, gauntlet, clenched fist; *revolt*, rebellion, mutiny, insubordination.
adj. *defiant*, provocative, challenging; *rebellious*, mutinous, insubordinate, disobedient.
vb. *defy*, disobey, challenge, stand up to; *throw down the gauntlet*, provoke, dare; *scorn*, toss aside, snap one's fingers at; *revolt*, rebel, mutiny.

638 RESISTANCE

See also **137** (counteraction); **301** (friction); **632** (opposition).
n. *resistance*, stand, withstanding, retaliation; *objection*, opposition, protest, civil disobedience; *obstinacy*, reluctance, recalcitrance, unwillingness; *friction*, load, resistor.
adj. *resistant*, unyielding, proof; *obstinate*, reluctant, recalcitrant, unwilling.
vb. *resist*, withstand, stand up to, repel, hold off; *challenge*, not take lying down, put up a fight, not submit, hold out, stand one's ground, dig in one's heels, refuse to budge; *object*, protest, oppose, kick against; *frustrate*, stem, thwart, foil.

639 ATTACK

See also **147** (violence); **828** (disparagement).
n. *attack*, aggression, assault, first strike, offensive, onslaught; *push*, strike, charge, thrust, advance, storming, invasion, blitzkrieg, counterattack; *storming*, siege, blockade, bombardment, investment; *foray*, skirmish, sortie, sally; *raid*, air raid, blitz, barrage, broadside, volley, salvo; *mugging*, robbery with violence, grievous bodily harm, rape; *attacker*, aggressor, assailant; *besieger*, invader, raider, bomber; *terrorist*, gunman, mugger, rapist.
adj. *attacking*, aggressive, offensive.
vb. *attack*, assault, assail; *set upon*, go for, let fly at, fall upon, lay into (*colloq.*); *besiege*, lay siege to, blockade, invest; *bombard*, shell, bomb, strafe; *invade*, advance on, board, storm; *raid*, skirmish, foray, sortie, sally; *mug*, rape, beat up, jump on.

640 DEFENCE

See also **598** (safety); **600** (refuge); **649** (weapon).
n. *defence*, protection, safekeeping,

guard, preservation; *defensive measure*, safety precaution; *rampart*, bulwark, earthworks, wall, moat, bunker, trenches; *barbed wire*, minefield, tripwire, barrage balloon; *fort*, fortification, strongpoint, fortress, castle, keep, donjon, citadel, acropolis, barbican; *armour*, protective clothing, flak jacket, gas mask, helmet; *defender*, protector, champion; *armed forces*, security forces, civil defence, Home Guard; *guard*, sentry, patrol, watch, escort, convoy.
adj. *defensive*, protective, anti-aircract; *defended*, armed, armoured, dug in; *fortified*, barricaded, walled, bombproof.
vb. *defend*, protect, keep, safeguard, guard, preserve, shelter, screen; *garrison*, arm, munition, mobilize; *fortify*, reinforce, wall, fence; *fend off*, ward off, withstand, resist.

641 RETALIATION

n. *retaliation*, self-defence, counterattack, second strike, reprisal, backlash, boomerang; *revenge*, retribution, vengeance, recrimination; *punishment*, comeuppance, just deserts, a dose of one's own medicine; *vindictiveness*, revengefulness, spite; *tit for tat*, an eye for an eye and a tooth for a tooth, feud, vendetta, gangland killing; *rejoinder*, retort, riposte, repartee, counter, counterargument; *avenger*.
adj. *retaliatory*, second-strike; *recriminatory*, retributive, punitive; *vindictive*, revengeful, vengeful, spiteful.
vb. *retaliate*, counterattack, fight back, give as good as one gets; *take one's revenge*, get one's own back, avenge, get even with, pay back; *exact retribution/compensation*, punish, repay; *rejoin*, retort, riposte, counter; *get one's just deserts/comeuppance*, have had it coming to one, get what one deserved.

642 SUBMISSION

See also **72** (conformity); **663** (obedience); **782** (servility).
n. *submission*, compliance, acquiescence, acceptance; *surrender*, capitulation, yielding; *subservience*, slavishness, deference, submissiveness; *fatalism*, resignation, defeatism; *docility*, humility, passivity, meekness.
adj. *submissive*, compliant, acquiescent, obedient; *amenable*, pliant, tractable; *subservient*, deferential, slavish, crawling; *fatalistic*, resigned, defeatist; *docile*, tame, humble, passive, meek.
vb. *submit*, comply, acquiesce, accept; *knuckle under*, bend, kow-tow, take it lying down (*colloq.*); *surrender*, capitulate, yield, give in, cave in, show the white flag, throw in the towel (*colloq.*); *admit defeat*, swallow one's pride, back down, eat humble pie; *defer to*, crawl, lick someone's boots (*colloq.*), lick someone's arse (*vulg.*).

643 CONTENTION

See also **635** (disagreement); **645** (war).
n. *contention*, conflict, clash, strife, dispute; *fighting*, force, combat, war, warfare, battle, hostilities; (*pitched*) *battle*, action, encounter, incident; *fracas*, affray, mêlée, fisticuffs, brawl, scuffle, scrap, punch-up (*colloq.*), dustup (*colloq.*), aggro (*colloq.*); *argument*, war of words, altercation, debate; *duel*, sparring match, joust, fencing; *boxing*, wrestling, judo, ju-jitsu, kung fu, karate, aikido; *contest*, competition, event, tournament, race; *game*, set, match, bout, round, rubber; *contender*, contestant, challenger, rival, competitor, candidate, nominee.
adj. *contending*, warring, competing, rival; *competitive*, sporting; *contentious*, aggressive, combative, pugnacious, bellicose, belligerent.
vb. *contend*, contest, confront, challenge, dispute, struggle, strive, tussle; *fight*, combat, battle, take on, do battle with, engage; *brawl*, spar, scrap, scuffle, come to blows; *compete*, rival, race.

644 PEACE

See also **235** (motionlessness); **354** (silence).
n. *peace*, freedom from war, absence of hostilities, peacetime, peace process;

truce, armistice, amnesty, ceasefire, lull; *cold war*, balance of power, peaceful, coexistence; *neutrality*, nonalignment, armed neutrality; *peace treaty/agreement*, nonaggression pact, nuclear freeze; *agreement*, friendship, cordiality; *pacifism*, nonviolence, nonaggression, appeasement, disarmament, nonintervention; *pacifist*, dove, conscientious objector, peacemaker, disarmer, neutral.

adj. *peaceful*, at peace, peacetime; *nonviolent*, bloodless; *neutral*, nonaligned, noninterventionist, peace-loving, peaceable; *friendly*, cordial.

vb. *keep the peace*, observe neutrality, call a truce, cease hostilities, make peace, disarm.

645 WAR

See also **643** (contention).

n. *war*, warfare, fighting, hostilities, armed conflict, combat, mobilization, call-up, conscription; *battle*, campaign, offensive, attack, strategy, tactics; *operation*, mission, invasion, raid, action; *world war*, global war, nuclear war, civil war, war of independence; *crusade*, holy war, jihad; *war of attrition*, trench/jungle/desert/guerrilla warfare, naval/submarine warfare, germ/chemical warfare; *psychological warfare*, war of nerves, propaganda war, cold war; *theatre of war*, battlefield, battleground, front (line), battle zone, no-man's land, arena; *belligerence*, hostility, aggressiveness, warmongering, sabre-rattling, aggression, militancy, militarism; *warmonger*, hawk, aggressor, belligerent.

adj. *warring*, hostile, at war, belligerent; *martial*, military, strategic, tactical; *armed*, under arms, on active service, mobilized; *bellicose*, militant, aggressive, hawkish, militaristic, warmongering.

vb. *wage war*, war, fight, battle, campaign; *attack*, raid, invade, engage; *declare war*, go to war, use force; *arm*, mobilize, call up, conscript, put on a war footing.

646 PACIFICATION

n. *pacification*, mollification, appeasement, peacemaking, conciliation, mediation; *agreement*, understanding, satisfaction, reparation, reconciliation; *truce*, armistice, ceasefire, amnesty; *treaty*, pact, convention; *disarmament*, demobilization, arms freeze, MBFR (Mutual Balanced Force Reduction), SALT (Strategic Arms Limitation Talks); *white flag*, peace offering, olive branch, overture, pipe of peace.

adj. *pacificatory*, placatory, conciliatory, propitiatory.

vb. *pacify*, mollify, appease, placate; *conciliate*, mediate, propitiate, reconcile; *force to negotiate*, bomb to the conference table; *agree*, settle one's differences; *disarm*, demobilize; *make peace*, bury the hatchet, shake hands, forgive and forget, let bygones be bygones; *sue for peace*, offer the hand of friendship, hold out the olive branch.

647 MEDIATION

See also **148** (moderation).

n. *mediation*, arbitration, good offices, shuttle diplomacy, interposition, intervention, intercession; *broking*, computer dating, matchmaking; *mediator*, intermediary, middleman, peacemaker, negotiator, broker, matchmaker, go-between; *arbiter*, arbitrator, umpire, referee, adjudicator, assessor, third party, neutral; *press officer/secretary*, public relations officer, spokesman, spokeswoman, spokesperson, intercessor, advocate, ombudsman.

adj. *mediatory*, intercessory.

vb. *mediate*, intercede, intervene, interpose; *arbitrate*, umpire, referee, adjudicate.

648 COMBATANT

n. *combatant*, soldier, conscript, volunteer, fighter, warrior, legionnaire, centurion; *gunner*, rifleman, sniper, bombardier, grenadier, artilleryman, infantryman; *seaman*, sailor, marine, submariner; *pilot*, navigator, bomb-aimer; *paratrooper*, commando; *guerrilla*, underground, freedom fighter, resistance fighter; *swordsman*, man-at-arms, knight, archer, lancer, hussar, cavalry; *reservist*, territorial, militiaman, irregular; *mercenary*, soldier of fortune, adventurer, freebooter, pirate; *private*, corporal, lance corporal, sergeant, sergeant major, second lieutenant, lieutenant, captain, major, lieutenant colonel, colonel, brigadier, major general, lieutenant general, general, field marshal; *able seaman*, leading seaman, petty office, sublieutenant, lieutenant, lieutenant commander, commander, captain, rear admiral, vice admiral, admiral; *flight sergeant*, pilot officer, flying officer, flight lieutenant, squadron leader, wing commander, group captain, air commodore, air vice marshal, air marshal; *platoon*, company, battalion, brigade, division, corps, regiment, unit, troop, squadron, flight, group, wing; *armed forces*, services, army, navy, air force, marines.

649 WEAPON

See also **640** (defence).

n. *weapon*, arms, armaments, weaponry, arsenal, armoury; *club*, truncheon, cosh, mace, cudgel, shillelagh; *bow and arrow*, longbow, crossbow, bolt, javelin; *spear*, pike, lance, axe, sword, rapier, cutlass, sabre, scimitar, kukri, dagger, stiletto, bayonet, cold steel (*colloq.*); *explosive*, high explosive, TNT (trinitrotoluene), nitroglycerine, gunpowder, dynamite, cordite, gelignite, jelly (*colloq.*); *bomb*, atomic bomb, A-bomb, hydrogen bomb, H-bomb, nuclear bomb, neutron bomb, incendiary bomb, flying bomb, (hand) grenade, depth charge, torpedo, mine; *gun*, firearm, small arms, handgun, pistol, revolver, rifle, machine gun, sub-machine gun, shotgun, musket, shooter (*colloq.*); *field gun*, cannon, mortar, howitzer; *ammunition*, munitions, round, cartridge; *projectile*, rocket, shell, bullet, shot, slug, pellet, cannonball, grapeshot, shrapnel, flak, tracer; *guided missile*, cruise missile, ICBM (intercontinental ballistic missile), MIRV (multiple independently targeted re-entry vehicle).

650 TROPHY

See also **448** (memory); **774** (repute); **859** (reward).

n. *trophy*, prize, award, reward, kudos; *cup*, plate, shield, badge, blue rosette, palm, laurels; *decoration*, medal, cross, star, ribbon, gong (*colloq.*); *mention* (in dispatches), honourable mention, citation; *honour(s)*, title, order; *spoils*, plunder, loot, booty; *consolation prize*, booby prize, wooden spoon.

651 SUCCESS

See also **31** (superiority); **653** (completion); **655** (prosperity).

n. *success*, happy/favourable outcome, happy ending, good fortune; *feat*, achievement, attainment, accomplishment, pass, graduation, good shot, (smash) hit (*colloq.*); *progress*, advance, lead; *good luck*, run of luck, lucky break, beginner's luck, fluke (*colloq.*); *flash in the pan*, nine days' wonder; *triumph*, victory, win, result, defeat, conquest, checkmate, game, set, and match, walkover, beating, thrashing (*colloq.*); *winner*, victor, conqueror, champion, prizewinner, roaring/runaway success, successful candidate, bestseller, blockbuster.

adj. *successful*, lucky, happy, fortunate; *profitable*, fruitful, beneficial, advantageous; *prosperous*, thriving, flourishing; *winning*, victorious, prizewinning, record-breaking, bestselling, conquering, triumphant, unbeaten, undisputed.

vb. *succeed*, achieve, accomplish, attain, fulfil; *pass*, graduate, make a success of, make a go of, pull off (*colloq.*), bring off (*colloq.*); *bear fruit*, do well, pay off, work out, come off (*colloq.*); *prosper*, profit, progress, advance, thrive, flourish, be/score a hit, make it big (*colloq.*), arrive (*colloq.*); *win*, be victorious, conquer, triumph, prevail, beat, defeat, trounce, crush, get the better of, thrash (*colloq.*), come out on top (*colloq.*).

652 FAILURE

See also **32** (inferiority); **654** (noncompletion).

n. *failure*, lack of success, disaster,

débâcle, fiasco, bankruptcy, collapse, insolvency, flop (*colloq.*), washout (*colloq.*), damp squib (*colloq.*); *inefficacy*, ineffectiveness, breakdown, engine failure, fault; *negligence*, omission, neglect, oversight, faux pas, slip; *futility*, wasted effort, Pyrrhic victory, wild-goose chase; *defeat*, downfall, rout, overthrow, checkmate, beating, thrashing (*colloq.*); *loser*, no-hoper, unsuccessful candidate/competitor, underdog; *failure*, dud, lame duck, also-ran (*colloq.*), has-been (*colloq.*), bankrupt.

adj. *unsuccessful*, disastrous, abortive, miscarried, misfired, failed, would-be, manqué, insolvent, bankrupt; *unfortunate*, unlucky; *ineffectual*, ineffective, dud, defunct, kaput; *unprofitable*, futile, fruitless, bootless, (in) vain; *defeated*, beaten, overthrown, foiled, done for, hoist with one's own petard.

vb. *fail*, be unsuccessful, have no success; *not make the grade*, fall down, fall short, miss, flunk (*colloq.*), come a cropper (*colloq.*); *stop working*, malfunction, seize up, break down, falter, stall, get stuck, pack up (*colloq.*), conk out (*colloq.*); *fall flat*, come to nothing, come unstuck, fizzle out, fall through, flop (*colloq.*); *go down*, go under, go to the wall, go bankrupt, crash, go bust (*colloq.*); *lose*, be defeated, suffer defeat, come last, come second, be pipped at the post.

653 COMPLETION

See also **49** (completeness); **584** (perfection); **651** (success).

n. *completion*, finishing off, rounding off; *perfection*, realization, fulfilment, consummation, culmination; *end*, finish, ending, conclusion, termination; *achievement*, accomplishment; *readiness*, ripeness, maturity, fruition; *final stroke*, coup de grâce, finishing touch; *last straw*, breaking point, bitter end.

adj. *completed*, finished, fulfilled, done, sewn up (*colloq.*); *finishing*, concluding, conclusive, final, culminating, crowning.

vb. *complete*, finish off, round off, finalize; *perfect*, fulfil, consummate, put the finishing touches to, polish off, wrap up (*colloq.*), see through, wind up; *end*, finish, conclude, culminate, terminate, come to a head; *achieve*, accomplish, realize, work out; *mature*, ripen.

654 NONCOMPLETION

See also **50** (incompleteness); **652** (failure).

n. *noncompletion*, nonfulfilment, job half-done, labour of Sisyphus, wild goose chase; *imperfection*, fault, blemish; *deficiency*, deficit, arrears, shortfall; *immaturity*, rawness, unripeness; *circular argument*, vicious circle; *stalemate*, draw; *postponement*, deferment, cold storage.

adj. *uncompleted*, unfinished, half-finished, half-done; *imperfect*, deficient, unrealized, not finalized, in the air, half-baked (*colloq.*); *immature*, unripe, underdone, parboiled; *never-ending*, endless, Sisyphean.

vb. *not complete*, leave undone, skimp, not follow through; *give up*, not stay the course, skip, drop out; *postpone*, defer, hold over, shelve, put on ice, put off.

655 PROSPERITY

See also **651** (success); **712** (wealth).

n. *prosperity*, success, welfare, wellbeing, happiness, good fortune; *milk and honey*, fat of the land, blessings, high life, life of Riley; *wealth*, riches, affluence, Easy Street, luxury, boom; *prime*, halcyon days, salad days, summer, golden age, heyday; *place in the sun*, bed of roses, clover.

adj. *prosperous*, successful, thriving, flourishing, booming, in clover; *wealthy*, affluent, fat, well-to-do, well-off, comfortable; *rising*, up and coming, on the up and up; *golden*, halcyon, sunny, rosy, blissful; *promising*, auspicious, cloudless, fair.

vb. *prosper*, do well, fare well, thrive, flourish, boom, do a roaring trade; *make a fortune*, make one's pile, grow fat, win the jackpot; *be on the up and up*, work one's way up, make it, blossom; *have it made*, never have had it so good, live like a lord, be rolling in money.

656 ADVERSITY

See also **628** (difficulty).

n. *adversity*, trouble, difficulty, struggle; *trial*, ordeal, adverse conditions, burden, pressure, opposition; *hardship*, hard/lean times, tough time, dark age, winter, cold wind, bad patch; *misfortune*, bad luck, hard lines; *misadventure*, disaster, accident, catastrophe; *evil influence*, curse, unlucky star, jinx.

adj. *adverse*, unfavourable, inauspicious; *opposed*, hostile, unfriendly, malign; *unfortunate*, unlucky, wretched; *troubled*, afflicted, burdened, plagued, beleaguered, bedevilled, stricken, fraught, hard pressed, up against it; *disastrous*, catastrophic, ruinous; *bleak*, cold, hard, lean.

vb. *be in trouble*, have a hard/thin time (of it), have been in the wars, go through it, be put through it, hit a bad patch, fall on hard times, feel the pinch, tighten one's belt.

657 AUTHORITY

See also **71** (rule); **622** (management); **661** (command); **672** (commission); **854** (jurisdiction).

n. *authority*, prestige, influence, sway, leadership; *power*, rule, jurisdiction, command, control, patronage, mandate, sovereignty; *right*, seniority, priority, prerogative; *supremacy*, ascendancy, hegemony, upper hand, dominion; *council*, panel, board, committee, cabinet, convocation, congress, convention, county/borough/town/parish council; *legislature*, legislative assembly, parliament, house, senate, administration, government; *democracy*, majority/minority rule, pluralism; *republicanism*, constitutional monarchy; *communism*, socialism; *dictatorship*, autocracy, tyranny, totalitarianism, police state, big brother; *officialdom*, bureaucracy, powers that be, they, them, Establishment, civil service; *councillor*, member of parliament, minister, statesman, parliamentarian, senator, representative, delegate, congressman/-woman; *symbol of authority*, badge of office, insignia, regalia, crown, sceptre, standard, staff, wand, baton, crosier, mitre, bat; *uniform*, epaulette, tab, stripe, star, crown, gold braid, scrambled egg (*colloq.*).

adj. *authoritative*, influential, prestigious, commanding, leading, dominant; *empowered*, ruling, governing, constitutional, in command, in control, reigning, on the throne, sovereign, in power, in office; *democratic*, pluralist, republican, monarchical, communist, socialist; *governmental*, gubernatorial, bureaucratic, administrative, official.

vb. *rule*, have power over, hold sway, reign, have control, govern, control; *tyrannize*, dictate, oppress, lord it over, domineer, have the whip hand, call the tune; *take command*, assume control/command, accede to the throne, gain power, (be asked to) form a government; *seize power*, usurp, overthrow.

658 ANARCHY

See also **56** (disorder); **853** (illegality).

n. *anarchy*, lawlessness, breakdown of law and order, mob rule, rioting, civil disobedience, indiscipline, disruption; *disorder*, chaos, turmoil, pandemonium; *laissez-faire*, noninterference, nonintervention, permissiveness, indulgence, tolerance, licence; *laxity*, easing, relaxation, derestriction, deregulation, legalization, free-for-all.

adj. *anarchic*, lawless, uncontrolled, disruptive, undisciplined; *disordered*, chaotic, riotous; *permissive*, tolerant, indulgent, flexible, free-and-easy; *lax*, relaxed, loose, soft, negligent, easy, ineffectual.

vb. *take the law into one's own hands*, be a law unto oneself, kick over the traces, run amuck; *misgovern*, lose control, abdicate responsibility; *tolerate*, permit, indulge, not enforce, give free rein to, waive the rules, turn a blind eye to.

659 SEVERITY

See also **745** (seriousness).

n. *severity*, strictness, rigour, rigorousness; *discipline*, firmness, rod of iron, heavy hand; *harshness*, oppression, cruelty, draconian measures, tyranny, suppression; *intolerance*, bigotry, pedantry; *intransigence*, pound of flesh, no quarter, no compromise, inflexibility, full weight of the law, letter of the law; *austerity*, asceticism, self-denial, puritanism; *disciplinarian*, martinet, stickler, terror, scourge; *dictator*, despot, persecutor, oppressor; *extremist*, bigot, pedant, ascetic, puritan.

adj. *severe*, strict, rigorous, extreme; *disciplined*, firm, stern, uncompromising, hard-boiled, hard-headed; *harsh*, oppressive, cruel, draconian, drastic; *tyrannical*, autocratic, dictatorial, despotic; *intolerant*, bigoted, hidebound, pedantic, censorious; *inflexible*, unbending, rigid; *austere*, ascetic, puritanical.

vb. *be severe*, etc., tighten up on, clamp down on, crack down on; *discipline*, deal firmly with, get tough with, throw the book at, come down like a ton of bricks on (*colloq.*); *oppress*, tyrannize, suppress, intimidate, domineer, bully, persecute; *not tolerate*, not countenance, stand no nonsense; *insist*, put one's foot down, stand one's ground, hold out for.

660 LENIENCY

See also **813** (forgiveness).

n. *leniency*, mildness, softness, gentleness, kindness; *forgiveness*, pardon; *mercy*, clemency, quarter; *tolerance*, indulgence, sufferance, forbearance; *humanity*, compassion, sympathy, charity.

adj. *lenient*, mild, soft, gentle; *forgiving*, merciful, clement; *tolerant*, indulgent, enlightened, liberal, forbearing, easy-going, long-suffering; *humane*, compassionate, kindly, charitable, soft-hearted, sympathetic.

vb. *be lenient*, etc., pull one's punches, go easy on (*colloq.*), handle with kid gloves; *show forgiveness*, etc., overlook, forgive, pardon; *have mercy*, relent, take pity, spare the rod; *tolerate*, indulge, allow, put up with; *refrain*, forbear.

661 COMMAND

See also **622** (management); **657** (authority); **672** (commission); **681** (request).

n. *command*, order, direction, directive, instruction, (three-line) whip; *charge*, mandate, dictate; *decree*, proclamation, edict, papal bull, ordinance, prescription; *law*, act, injunction, writ, ruling; *summons*, subpoena, habeas corpus, order in council, sequestration; *(tax) demand*, requirement, passport.

adj. *mandatory*, compulsory, obligatory, statutory; *commanding*, imperative, peremptory, compelling.

vb. *command*, give/issue a command, etc., order, direct, instruct; *charge*, mandate, dictate, make compulsory, compel; *decree*, proclaim, ordain, prescribe, lay down; *rule*, enjoin, enforce, issue a writ, lay down the law; *summon*, subpoena, sequestrate; *demand*, require.

662 DISOBEDIENCE

See also **127** (revolution); **637** (defiance); **680** (refusal); **832** (improbity).

n. *disobedience*, refusal to obey, insubordination, noncompliance; *misbehaviour*, naughtiness, mischief; *awkwardness*, contrariness, cussedness, waywardness; *crime*, breach of the peace, disturbance, trespass, contempt of court, lawlessness; *violation*, transgression, infringement, delinquency; *mutiny*, rebellion, revolt, insurrection, defection, desertion, truancy; *defiance*, intractability, recalcitrance; *insurgence*, sedition, subversion, treason; *naughty child*, mischief-maker, trouble-maker, rascal, holy terror (*colloq.*), handful (*colloq.*); *criminal*, delinquent, hooligan, tearaway; *rebel*, mutineer, deserter; *revolutionary*, radical, insurrectionist, anarchist, hothead, firebrand; *insurgent*, subversive, rioter, terrorist.

adj. *disobedient*, insubordinate;

naughty, mischievous, unruly; *mutinous*, rebellious, riotous, dissident; *defiant*, intractable, awkward, difficult; *wayward*, contrary, bolshie, obstreperous, recalcitrant, refractory, bloody-minded; *traitorous*, treacherous, disloyal, duplicitous; *subversive*, disruptive, anarchic.
vb. *disobey*, defy, fail to comply, disregard; *misbehave*, play up, cause trouble; *violate*, break, transgress, infringe, trespass; *mutiny*, rebel, revolt, defect, desert, play truant.

663 OBEDIENCE

See also **642** (submission); **670** (subjection).
n. *obedience*, compliance, good behaviour, acquiescence; *deference*, slavishness, obsequiousness, submission, subservience, docility; *dutifulness*, devotion, loyalty, fidelity.
adj. *obedient*, compliant, acquiescent, law-abiding, well-behaved; *deferential*, slavish, obsequious, subservient; *docile*, submissive, tractable, meek, henpecked, under one's thumb (*colloq.*); *dutiful*, devoted, loyal, faithful.
vb. *obey*, comply, observe, heed, keep, acquiesce, agree; *behave*, do as one is told, submit, do one's duty, follow the party line, toe the line; *defer*, grovel, crawl, tug one's forelock, bow and scrape.
adv. *obediently*, quietly, with good grace, unquestioningly.

664 COMPULSION

See also **143** (strength); **536** (necessity); **558** (requirement).
n. *compulsion*, constraint, obligation, no choice; *pressure*, force, coercion, violence, duress, arm-twisting, strong-arm tactics; *drive*, need, necessity, urgency; *threat*, blackmail, sanction, gunboat diplomacy; *conscription*, call-up, impressment, draft; *forced labour*, slavery, servitude.
adj. *compulsory*, obligatory, mandatory, binding; *compelling*, compulsive, driving, coercive, irresistible; *necessary*, imperative, unavoidable.
vb. *compel*, oblige, constrain, leave no choice; *force*, coerce, lean on, pressurize; *drive*, push, propel, urge; *require*, necessitate, dictate.
adv. *compulsorily*, bodily, under duress, under protest, of necessity.

665 MASTER

See also **31** (superiority); **622** (management).
n. *master*, mistress, lord, lady, lord of the manor, lady of the house; *director*, leader, governor, controller, overlord, superior, principal; *boss*, manager, supervisor, foreman, overseer, gaffer (*colloq.*), guv'nor (*colloq.*); *monarch*, sovereign, king, queen, prince, princess, regent, tsar, emperor, empress, grand duke; *president*, ruler, viceroy, potentate, chief, chieftain, margrave, elector, sheikh, sultan, proconsul, headman, maharajah, mogul, nawab; *despot*, tyrant, autocrat, Führer, Gauleiter, Duce, commissar; *official*, mayor, mayoress, provost, alderman, prefect, commissioner, civil servant, councillor, bureaucrat; *judge*, magistrate, sheriff, justice (of the peace), beak (*colloq.*).

666 SERVANT

See also **32** (inferiority).
n. *servant*, factotum, majordomo, butler, footman, flunky, maid, parlour maid, chambermaid; *nursery nurse*, nursemaid, nanny, ayah, wet nurse, au pair; *valet*, manservant, gentleman's gentleman, scout, lady's maid, lady-in-waiting, page; *steward*, stewardess, waiter, waitress; *housekeeper*, cook, kitchen maid, tweeny, skivvy; *daily* (woman), domestic, help, char(woman/lady), cleaning lady; *concierge*, doorman, porter, janitor, caretaker; *worker*, employee, staff, crew; *menial*, drudge, fag, dogsbody, handyman, odd-job man, chief cook and bottle-washer (*colloq.*); *slave*, serf, bondsman, villein, galley slave; *assistant*, secretary, amanuensis, aide, right-hand man, bodyguard, attendant, equerry, chaplain; *subaltern*, aide-de-camp, lieutenant, batman; *underling*, henchman, lackey, minion, junior.

adj. *serving*, in service, menial, below stairs; *working*, in employment.
vb. *serve*, wait on/upon, look after, minister to, attend, make oneself useful, work for, do for (*colloq.*).

667 FREEDOM

See also **669** (liberation); **677** (permission).
n. *freedom*, liberty, independence, freedom of action/choice, free will; *free speech*, civil rights, democracy, franchise, emancipation, universal suffrage, freedom of the press; *exemption*, immunity, special dispensation; *liberalism*, libertarianism, egalitarianism; *nonintervention*, autonomy, self-government, home rule; *free enterprise*, laissez-faire, market economy, free port, free trade; *room to manoeuvre*, play, Lebensraum, elbowroom, latitude, leeway, margin; *free hand*, blank cheque, carte blanche, free rein, licence; *freeman*, freedman, freedwoman, ex-convict, escapee; *independent*, freethinker, freelancer; *liberal*, libertarian, egalitarian; *gratuity*, free gift, freebie (*colloq.*), freesheet.
adj. *free*, at liberty, on the loose, at large; *independent*, self-governing, autonomous, democratic; *unattached*, self-employed, freelance; *exempt*, immune, unaffected; *emancipated*, enfranchised, liberated; *liberal*, libertarian, egalitarian; *unbiased*, unprejudiced, freethinking, enlightened; *free of charge*, gratis, complimentary; *unchecked*, unrestrained, unfettered, unshackled, unbridled, unhindered, uninhibited.
vb. *be free*, etc., have a free hand, be a free agent, please oneself, have the freedom/run of, make free with, feel free; *loosen up*, cut loose, let oneself go, let one's hair down (*colloq.*), let it all hang out (*colloq.*); *not interfere*, let alone, let be, live and let live, leave someone to their own devices.

668 RESTRAINT

See also **148** (moderation); **601** (trap); **630** (hindrance); **695** (retention); **843** (self-restraint).
n. *restraint*, prohibition, ban, bar, veto; *suppression*, repression, constraint, control, clampdown; *slowing*, deceleration, retardation, drag, curb, brake; *rein*, leash, bit, gag, muzzle, straitjacket; *arrest*, detention, remand, custody, house arrest; *imprisonment*, custodial sentence, incarceration, (solitary) confinement, internment, captivity, quarantine, care, time (*colloq.*), stretch (*colloq.*), porridge (*colloq.*); *restriction*, speed limit, curfew, roadblock; *boundary*, upper limit, ceiling, cut-off point; *economy*, freeze, cutback, credit squeeze, retrenchment, price control, prices and incomes policy; *price-fixing*, cartel, monopoly, closed shop, protectionism, tariff, restrictive practice; *gaoler*, jailer, (prison) warder/wardress, prison officer, (prison) governor, screw (*colloq.*); *keeper*, curator, custodian, attendant; *guard*, escort, bodyguard, garrison; *warden*, ranger, gamekeeper; *concierge*, porter, caretaker, housekeeper, janitor; *watchman*, coastguard, firewatcher, sentry, lookout, scout; *guardian*, foster/adoptive parent, tutor; *nanny*, nursery nurse, nursemaid, governess, childminder, baby-sitter.
adj. *restraining*, suppressive, repressive, restrictive, limiting; *restrained*, limited, controlled, disciplined; *inhibited*, straitlaced, reserved, uptight (*colloq.*); *custodial*, captive, imprisoned, under arrest, in detention, confined to barracks, gated; *in custody*, behind bars, in clink/jug (*colloq.*), inside (*colloq.*); *fettered*, handcuffed, manacled, in the stocks, in irons, bound, gagged; *protectionist*, monopolistic.
vb. *restrain*, limit, control, restrict; *prohibit*, ban, bar, veto; *suppress*, repress, clamp down on, inhibit; *subdue*, muzzle, silence, gag, censor; *slow*, decelerate, retard, curb, be a drag on, hold back, check; *fight back/down*, dam up, bottle up; *block*, hinder, impede, cramp, hamper; *arrest*, apprehend, detain, run in, pick up; *imprison*, remand in custody, put in prison, intern, incarcerate, confine, put behind bars (*colloq.*), put away (*colloq.*); *chain up*, fetter, manacle, handcuff, clap in

irons; *economize*, freeze, cut back, control prices, tighten one's belt (*colloq.*), live within one's income.

669 LIBERATION

See also **606** (deliverance); **667** (freedom); **696** (disposal).

n. *liberation*, freeing, rescue, deliverance, salvation; *release*, discharge, acquittal, parole, bail; *demobilization*, disbanding; *extrication*, loosing, disengagement; *redemption*, forgiveness, absolution; *emancipation*, enfranchisement, liberalization, relaxation, easing.

vb. *liberate*, free, set free, turn loose, rescue, deliver, save; *release*, discharge, acquit, parole, bail; *demobilize*, disband, break up, demob (*colloq.*); *extricate*, disentangle, unravel, loose, disengage, unleash, let out, let off the lead; *redeem*, forgive, pardon, absolve; *emancipate*, enfranchise, give the vote, liberalize, relax, ease, deregulate.

670 SUBJECTION

See also **32** (inferiority); **663** (obedience).

n. *subjection*, subordination, subjugation, conquest, colonization, exploitation, annexation; *inferiority*, dependence; *allegiance*, nationality, subjecthood, service; *oppression*, hegemony, dominance, yoke; *enslavement*, slavery, servitude, bondage, feudalism; *slave labour*, forced labour, conscription, sweatshop.

adj. *subject*, subordinate; *inferior*, junior, subsidiary; *bound*, dependent, tied; *enslaved*, colonized, tributary, colonial; *oppressed*, downtrodden, under the yoke/jackboot, in the clutches of, under the sway of.

vb. *subjugate*, subject, conquer, subdue, reduce, subordinate, colonize, enslave, exploit; *oppress*, dominate, cow, have under one's thumb.

671 PRISON

See also **861** (means of punishment).

n. *prison*, gaol, jail, lockup, penitentiary, maximum-security prison, open prison, clink (*colloq.*), stir (*colloq.*), jug (*colloq.*), nick (*colloq.*); *detention centre*, remand centre/home, internment camp, rehabilitation centre; *Borstal*, approved school, reformatory, reform school; *cell*, dungeon, guardroom, oubliette, cage; *condemned cell*, death row; *prisoner-of-war camp*, P.O.W. camp, concentration camp, death camp, gulag; *prisoner*, convict, inmate, jail/gaolbird (*colloq.*), con (*colloq.*), old lag (*colloq.*), guest of Her Majesty (*colloq.*), lifer (*colloq.*); *detainee*, accused, prisoner in the dock; *captive*, prisoner of war, P.O.W., political prisoner; *hostage*, kidnap victim.

672 COMMISSION

See also **657** (authority); **661** (command); **675** (delegate).

n. *commission*, mandate, charge, task, errand, assignment; *delegation*, deputation, legation, embassy, representation, mission, people's bureau; *appointment*, nomination, installation, induction, enthronement, ordination, consecration, coronation, inauguration, investment, investiture; *election*, return; *sequestration*, trusteeship, power of attorney, charter, licence, proxy; *regency*, protectorate.

adj. *commissioned*, deputed, empowered, entrusted, vicarious.

vb. *commission*, delegate, depute, mandate, charge, assign; *entrust*, commit, consign; *appoint*, nominate, install, induct, enthrone, anoint, ordain, consecrate, crown, inaugurate, invest; *authorize*, empower, charter, sanction, accredit, license; *elect*, return.

673 CANCELLATION

See also **474** (negation).

n. *cancellation*, cancelling, abrogation; *annulment*, nullification, invalidation; *revoking*, revocation, repudiation, retraction, rescission; *abolition*, dissolution, repeal, countermand, reprieve, reversal; *dismissal*, removal from office, unfrocking, suspension, sacking (*colloq.*), the sack (*colloq.*), the heave (*colloq.*), the boot (*colloq.*); *discharge*, court martial, recall, relief; *demotion*, downgrading; *redundancy*, natural

wastage, layoff, job losses; *dethronement*, deposal, deposition, overthrow.
adj. *cancelled*, null and void, invalid, quashed.
vb. *cancel*, abrogate, scrub out; *annul*, nullify, invalidate, render null and void, void; *revoke*, repudiate, retract, rescind; *abolish*, dissolve, repeal, countermand, reprieve, reverse, quash, overrule, set aside; *dismiss*, remove from office, unfrock, strike off, suspend, give someone their cards, sack (*colloq.*), give someone notice, fire (*colloq.*), lay off, make redundant; *discharge*, cashier, court-martial, recall, relieve; *demote*, downgrade, kick upstairs, reduce to the ranks; *dethrone*, depose, unseat, overthrow.

674 RESIGNATION

See also **563** (relinquishment).
n. *resignation*, leaving, withdrawal, retirement, abdication, desertion; *renunciation*, relinquishment, abandonment; *pension*, golden handshake, superannuation, gold watch, redundancy money.
adj. *retiring*, outgoing; *retired*, ex-, former, sometime, one-time, emeritus.
vb. *resign*, leave, withdraw, retire, take early retirement, abdicate, stand down, not stand for re-election, tender one's resignation, apply for the Chiltern Hundreds, hand in one's notice, ask for one's cards; *renounce*, relinquish, abandon, desert, give up, throw up, quit.

675 DELEGATE

See also **672** (commission).
n. *delegate*, representative, consignee, deputy, agent; *delegation*, mission, deputation, committee, working party; *broker*, middleman, stockbroker, negotiator; *nominee*, appointee, proxy, stakeholder; *trustee*, executor, licensee; *legal representative*, advocate, attorney, counsel; *diplomat*, envoy, ambassador, plenipotentiary, consul, attaché, resident, high commissioner, chargé d'affaires; *mission*, embassy, legation, consulate, high commission; *legate*, nuncio.

676 DEPUTY

See also **128** (substitution).
n. *deputy*, second-in-command, right-hand man, lieutenant, assistant, second; *representative*, proxy, substitute, stand-in, agent, understudy, double; *spokesman*, spokeswoman, spokesperson, mouthpiece.
adj. *deputy*, vice-, pro-, acting.
vb. *deputize*, represent, act for, speak for, stand in for, substitute for, replace.

677 PERMISSION

See also **436** (assent); **667** (freedom); **852** (legality).
n. *permission*, authority, leave, freedom, liberty, consent; *authorization*, approval, clearance, sanction, legalization, go-ahead (*colloq.*), green light (*colloq.*); *dispensation*, concession, allowance; *free hand*, blank cheque, carte blanche; *permit*, licence, royal charter, franchise, certificate, grant; *pass*, passport, visa, safe-conduct, passbook, ticket, chit.
adj. *permissive*, tolerant, indulgent, lenient; *permitted*, allowed, free, permissible, printable; *licensed*, chartered, authorized, approved.
vb. *permit*, allow, let, consent, give permission, grant leave, vouchsafe; *authorize*, clear, sanction, pass, rubber-stamp, legalize, decontrol; *license*, charter, certify, franchise; *approve*, give the go-ahead (*colloq.*), encourage; *tolerate*, brook, suffer.

678 VETO

See also **853** (illegality).
n. *veto*, prohibition, forbiddance, interdiction, (blanket) refusal, countermand, proscription, disqualification, taboo; *interference*, intervention; *ban*, bar, embargo, boycott, blacklist; *licensing laws*; *censorship*, suppression, news blackout, D-notice.
adj. *prohibitory*, prohibiting; *prohibitive*, restrictive; *prohibited*, forbidden, not allowed; *illegal*, unlawful, illicit, against the law; *banned*, barred, embargoed, blacked; *censored*, sup-

pressed, blacked out, unprintable; *taboo*, frowned on.
vb. *veto*, prohibit, forbid, refuse, refuse permission, interdict, countermand, disqualify, restrict; *ban*, bar, boycott, embargo, proscribe, outlaw, black, blacklist; *debar*, shut out, blackball, exclude; *suppress*, censor, blue-pencil, cut.

679 OFFER

See also **537** (willingness).
n. *offer*, proffer, proffering; *bid*, tender; *proposal*, proposition, suggestion, submission, application; *approach*, advance, overture, invitation.
adj. *offered*, on offer, advertised; *for sale*, available, for hire, to let, on the market, up for grabs (*colloq.*).
vb. *offer*, proffer, make available; *bid*, tender; *propose*, suggest, put forward, submit, apply; *approach*, make advances/overtures, invite; *advertise*, put on the market, offer for sale, put up for auction, invite tenders; *offer one's services*, come forward, stand, run for, volunteer, run.

680 REFUSAL

See also **538** (unwillingness); **662** (disobedience); **682** (protest).
n. *refusal*, failure to obey/comply, noncompliance, reluctance, recalcitrance; *rejection*, thumb's-down, nonacceptance, denial, withholding, disallowance; *ban*, veto, prohibition; *rebuff*, snub, slap in the face.
adj. *noncompliant*, negative, recalcitrant, reluctant.
vb. *refuse*, fail to obey/comply; *reject*, decline, turn down, not accept, deny, withhold, disallow, not hear of; *ban*, veto, prohibit; *rebuff*, snub, cut, scorn, not listen, turn a deaf ear, ignore; *repel*, repulse, dismiss; *harden one's heart*, have nothing to do with, turn one's back on, wash one's hands of, set one's face against.

681 REQUEST

See also **661** (command).
n. *request*, appeal, plea, entreaty, begging; *demand*, requisition, ultimatum, blackmail; *invitation*, invite, solicitation, canvassing; *petition*, call, application, claim, counterclaim; *prayer*, supplication, intercession, invocation; *suggestion*, proposal, motion, approach; *fund-raising*, begging letter, charity appeal, flag day, benefit game/performance; *advertising*, advertisement, circular, small ad, personal column; *petitioner*, lobby, lobbyist, pressure group; *appellant*, plaintiff, applicant, suppliant, claimant; *advertiser*, salesman, customer, enquirer; *canvasser*, solicitor, hawker, tout, barker, pedlar; *beggar*, scrounger, tramp, bum, sponger, hitch-hiker, mendicant.
adj. *supplicatory*, imprecatory, prayerful, suppliant, on bended knee, grovelling, with cap in hand, imploring, beseeching; *begging*, mendicant, charitable, fund-raising; *urgent*, insistent.
vb. *request*, ask for, call for, invite, express a wish, ask a favour; *demand*, requisition, blackmail; *petition*, appeal, apply, claim; *appeal for funds*, pass the hat round, have a whip-round (*colloq.*); *canvass*, solicit, hawk, tout, peddle; *beg*, entreat, plead, beseech, crave; *cadge*, sponge, scrounge, hitch-hike, bum (*colloq.*), touch (*colloq.*); *pray*, supplicate, intercede, invoke, call on; *suggest*, propose, move, approach.

682 PROTEST

See also **538** (unwillingness); **632** (opposition); **680** (refusal).
n. *protest*, remonstration, deprecation, expostulation, dissent; *exception*, objection, demur, demurral; *murmur*, complaint, howl, squeal, raised voices, outcry, storm of protest, heckling; *demonstration*, protest meeting, sit-in, walkout, work-in, picket, secondary picketing, march, strike, civil disobedience, demo (*colloq.*); *disapproval*, dissatisfaction, raised eyebrows, jeers, slow handclap; *protester*, demonstrator, objecter, dissenter, heckler.
adj. *protesting*, dissatisfied, dissenting, protestant, deprecatory.
vb. *protest*, lodge/register a protest, remonstrate, deprecate, ask not to;

expostulate, take exception, raise objections, raise one's voice against; *object*, demur, kick, jib; *murmur*, complain, howl, squeal, grumble, moan, kick up a fuss, beef, heckle; *demonstrate*, march, go on strike, walk out, hold a sit-in, picket; *disapprove*, raise one's eyebrows, jeer, slow-handclap.

683 PROMISE

See also **473** (affirmation); **562** (undertaking); **684** (contract); **821** (duty).

n. *promise*, word (of honour), vow, pledge, credit, oath, troth, parole, assurance, signature; *profession*, declaration; *guarantee*, warranty, promissory note, banknote, bill, treasury note, IOU; *covenant*, bond, pact, contract, undertaking, agreement, commitment; *engagement*, betrothal.

adj. *promised*, pledged, covenanted, guaranteed, promissory; *committed*, on/under oath; *engaged*, betrothed, affianced.

vb. *promise*, give one's word, agree, engage, undertake, commit oneself, make a vow, pledge, swear; *profess*, declare, vow; *contract*, covenant, sign on the dotted line, set down in black and white; *guarantee*, assure, give an assurance; *get engaged*, exchange vows, plight one's troth.

684 CONTRACT

See also **562** (undertaking); **683** (promise).

n. *contract*, (binding) agreement, compact, conspiracy; *undertaking*, ratification, pact, covenant, arrangement, understanding; *settlement*, deal, bargain, compromise; *peace treaty*, convention, nonagression pact, concordat, entente, charter, alliance, league.

adj. *contractual*, binding; *contracted*, agreed (to), arranged, settled, negotiated, covenanted; *consenting*, agreeable.

vb. *contract*, agree (terms), enter into/make/sign a contract, strike a bargain, do/clinch/make a deal, shake hands, come to an arrangement, reach a compromise, covenant, ratify.

685 NEGOTIATION

See also **422** (qualification); **571** (provision); **707** (trade).

n. *negotiation*, bargaining, making terms, barter, collective bargaining, horse-trading, haggling, wheeler-dealing; *condition*, terms, small print, stipulation, frame of reference, contingency, provision, clause, proviso; *limitation*, strings, exclusion, exception, escape clause, loophole, catch, restriction, reservation, penalty.

adj. *conditional*, contingent, provisional, dependent, subject; *limiting*, qualifying, with strings attached.

vb. *negotiate*, bargain, haggle, barter, discuss, parley, treat; *propose conditions*, attach strings, stipulate, impose, hold out for, insist on, make demands, require.

686 COMPROMISE

See also **250** (middle way).

n. *compromise*, give and take, concessions on both sides, mutual concessions, compromise solution, working arrangement, modus vivendi, middle ground, middle course.

vb. *compromise*, give and take, make concessions, lower one's sights, meet halfway, back down, climb down; *split the difference*, split down the middle, go Dutch, go half and half; *steer a middle course*, make the best of a bad job, cut one's losses.

adv. *knock for knock*, fifty-fifty.

687 SECURITY

See also **598** (safety).

n. *security*, guarantee, warranty, surety; *bond*, pledge, covenant; *collateral*, mortgage, pawn, token, indemnity, cover, hostage, forfeit; *caution money*, deposit, down payment, bail, recognizance, stake; *guarantor*, mortgagor, backer, referee.

adj. *secured*, insured, covered; *pledged*, pawned, mortgaged, deposited, in hock (*colloq.*).

vb. *secure*, insure, cover; *guarantee*, warrant, indemnify, assure, underwrite, endorse; *pledge*, pawn, mortgage, deposit, pop (*colloq.*); *give security*, go bail, bail out, stand surety.

688 OBSERVANCE

See also **72** (conformity); **549** (habit).

n. *observance*, keeping, practice, habit, carrying out, performance, execution; *adherence*, conformity, orthodoxy, heeding, regard, respect, the done thing; *conscientiousness*, diligence, pedantry, scrupulousness, punctiliousness; *fidelity*, faithfulness, devotion, loyalty, dependability, compliance, obedience.

adj. *observant*, professing, practising, religious, orthodox, conformist; *conscientious*, diligent, pedantic, scrupulous, punctilious; *faithful*, loyal, devoted, dependable, responsible, compliant, obedient.

vb. *observe*, keep, practise, carry out, perform, execute; *heed*, respect, regard, pay due attention to; *conform*, abide by, follow, adopt, adhere; *be faithful to*, do one's duty, honour one's obligations, comply, obey, fulfil, keep faith, be as good as one's word.

689 NONOBSERVANCE

See also **73** (nonconformity); **407** (negligence).

n. *nonobservance*, nonperformance, nonfulfilment; *disregard*, disrespect, inattention, indifference; *nonconformity*, nonconformism; *unreliability*, negligence, neglect, laxity, omission, carelessness; *disobedience*, noncompliance, contravention, violation, transgression, infringement, sin, breach; *disloyalty*, unfaithfulness, infidelity, breach of faith.

adj. *nonobservant*, nonpractising; *inattentive*, indifferent; *nonconformist*, unorthodox; *unreliable*, negligent, lax, careless, irresponsible; *disobedient*, noncompliant, out of line, sinning; *disloyal*, unfaithful.

vb. *not observe*, disregard, omit, neglect; *disobey*, break, contravene, violate, transgress, infringe, sin, breach; *renege*, break faith, go back on one's word.

690 GAIN

See also **33** (increase); **35** (addition); **703** (taking); **719** (receipt).

n. *gain*, acquisition, obtaining, procurement, purchase, theft; *benefit*, yield, advantage, reward; *earnings*, income, earned income, pay, salary, wage(s), emolument, remuneration, stipend; *grant*, bursary, scholarship, exhibition, allowance, expenses, perks; *takings*, receipts, turnover, revenue, proceeds; *windfall*, jackpot, bonus, winnings, inheritance, legacy, bequest; *profit*, interest, dividend, yield, unearned income, return; *growth*, capital gain, savings, accumulation; *realization*, encashment, redemption, recouping.

adj. *gainful*, profitable, paid, salaried, paying, money-spinning, remunerative, lucrative, worthwhile, advantageous; *acquisitive*, on the make, covetous, greedy.

vb. *gain*, acquire, get, come by; *obtain*, procure, get hold of, lay one's hands on, appropriate, take possession of, buy, steal; *store up*, hoard, save, put by; *inherit*, come into, win; *pocket*, catch, net, land, secure; *earn*, make, benefit, glean, reap, accumulate, make money; *take*, turn over, gross, bring in; *profit*, capitalize on, cash in on (*colloq.*); *realize*, encash, redeem, recoup; *show a gain/profit*, pay a dividend, yield.

691 LOSS

See also **34** (decrease); **36** (subtraction).

n. *loss*, deprivation, lack, privation, bereavement; *forfeit*, forfeiture, eviction; *wastage*, leakage, shortfall, deficit, debit.

adj. *lost*, mislaid, missing, untraced; *deprived*, bereaved, bereft, shorn, denuded, stripped; *lacking*, wanting; *forfeit*, forfeited; *wasted*, down the drain (*colloq.*), irretrievable, irrecoverable.

vb. *lose*, miss, mislay; *let slip through one's fingers*, throw away, fritter away, say goodbye to, forfeit, squander; *go* *to waste*, leak, go down the drain (*colloq.*).

692 POSSESSION

See also **694** (property).

n. *possession*, ownership, proprietorship, custody, enjoyment; *mastery*, monopoly, domination, control, hold, grasp, clutches; *occupancy*, residence, tenancy, tenure, squatting, nine tenths of the law; *possessor*, owner, owner-occupier, proprietor, man of property, landowner, landlord, landlady, freeholder, leaseholder, lessee, householder; *occupier*, occupant, resident, tenant, squatter, lodger; *holder*, hirer.

adj. *proprietorial*, possessive, monopolistic; *propertied*, landed, to one's name.

vb. *possess*, be possessed of, own, have; *control*, monopolize, command, get one's hands on, grab, corner, hog (*colloq.*); *occupy*, fill, hold, enjoy.

693 JOINT POSSESSION

n. *joint possession*, joint ownership, co-ownership, partnership, participation; *public ownership*, nationalization, collectivism; *joint account*, (joint-stock) company, profit-sharing; *condominium*, time-sharing, housing association; *commune*, kibbutz, collective, kolkhoz, cooperative, coop; *common* (land), public property; *partner*, shareholder, stockholder, member, participant; *flatmate*, roommate; *communard*, kibbutznik, collectivist.

adj. *jointly owned*, joint, common, communal, participating, cooperative, collective; *public*, state-owned, nationalized.

vb. *share*, have a share in, have shares in, be in partnership with, go in with, participate, hold in common; *nationalize*, collectivize.

694 PROPERTY

See also **692** (possession).

n. *property*, possessions, belongings, impedimenta, trappings, accoutrements, goods and chattels, movables, effects, valuables, consumer durables, things, bits and pieces (*colloq.*), paraphernalia, clobber (*colloq.*), stuff (*colloq.*); *land*, real estate, realty, hereditament, immovables; *estate*, assets, means, capital, reserves, equity; *investment*, securities, stocks and shares, unit trusts; *rights*, interest, stake.

adj. *propertied*, landed; *proprietary*; *movable*, immovable, real, material.

695 RETENTION

See also **40** (union); **668** (restraint).

n. *retention*, holding, tenacity, adhesion; *hold*, grip, grasp, clasp, embrace, hug, bearhug, clinch; *clutches*, stranglehold, half-nelson, armlock.

adj. *retentive*, tenacious, tight, vicelike, fast; *sticky*, tacky, clinging, adhesive, fusible.

vb. *retain*, hold, keep a firm hold of, grip, grasp, clench, pin, clasp, embrace, hug, clinch; *secure*, fix, lock, clamp, fasten; *cling*, stick, adhere, fuse, hang on; *detain*, confine, withhold, contain.

696 DISPOSAL

See also **41** (separation); **563** (relinquishment); **669** (liberation).

n. *disposal*, abandonment, relinquishment, renunciation, alienation, cession; *release*, discharge, dumping, recycling, on the scrapheap; *refuse*, flotsam and jetsam, castoffs, waste.

adj. *abandoned*, derelict, cast-off; *disposable*, throwaway, soluble, biodegradable; *dispensable*, expendable, transferable, saleable.

vb. *dispose of*, throw away, discard, chuck out (*colloq.*); *pass on*, bequeath, part with; *sell off*, alienate, transfer; *jettison*, ditch, dump, drop, shed; *let go*, release, free, unhand, loose; *release*, discharge, lay off, pension off; *abandon*, relinquish, renounce, yield, cede; *do without*, forgo, dispense with, spare, waive; *disown*, disinherit, cut off without a penny.

697 TRANSFER OF PROPERTY

See also **239** (transfer); **707** (trade); **716** (payment).

n. *transfer of property*, assignment,

conveyancing, alienation, change of ownership, handover, consignment; *bequest*, inheritance, legacy, capital transfer, settlement, endowment; *purchase*, sale, lease, hire, letting, rental, exchange, barter, trade.
adj. *transferable*, alienable, exchangeable, negotiable.
vb. *transfer*, assign, convey, alienate, hand over, consign, sign over, make over, pass on; *bequeath*, will, leave, settle, endow, grant, hand down; *inherit*, succeed to, come into; *buy*, purchase, sell, lease, hire (out), let, rent, exchange, convert, barter, trade; *dispossess*, expropriate, nationalize; *change hands*, pass, revert.

698 GIVING
See also **725** (generosity).
n. *giving*, donation, conferral, bestowal; *charity*, alms, handout, food parcel, poor box; *gift*, present, presentation, golden handshake; *prize*, award, reward; *contribution*, subscription; *aid*, grant, subsidy, support, sponsorship; *tip*, gratuity, Christmas box; *bequest*, legacy, covenant; *largesse*, bounty, generosity; *offering*, sacrifice, church collection, offertory; *giver*, donor, contributor, subscriber, benefactor, tipper.
adj. *charitable*, votive, sacrificial; *bountiful*, generous, liberal, open-handed; *free*, gratis, complimentary.
vb. *give*, donate, confer, bestow, vouchsafe, render, afford, accord, allot, remit; *hand out*, distribute, dole out, share out; *present*, honour, award; *aid*, subsidize, support, sponsor, grant, endow; *contribute*, subscribe, help, shell out (*colloq.*), fork out (*colloq.*), put one's hand in one's pocket; *tip*; *bequeath*, leave; *offer*, sacrifice.

699 RECEIVING
See also **265** (admittance); **719** (receipt).
n. *receiving*, reception, admittance, admission, acceptance; *acquisition*, getting, gain, collection, assumption; *receipts*, winnings, proceeds, takings, income, gate; *toll*, tribute, tax, levy; *recipient*, receiver, acceptor, accepting house; *trustee*, assignee, licensee, lessee, payee; *devisee*, legatee, heir(ess), inheritor, beneficiary; *winner*, grantee; *treasurer*, bursar, tax collector, exciseman, customs officer.
adj. *receptive*, welcoming, acquisitive.
vb. *receive*, acknowledge receipt of, admit, accept, be given, attract, land; *acquire*, obtain, derive, get, gain, win, collect, assume; *take in*, pocket, gross, net, make; *inherit*, succeed to, come into; *levy*, tax, charge; *be received*, come one's way, accrue, fall into one's lap.

700 ALLOCATION
See also **48** (part).
n. *allotment*, apportionment, distribution, administration, sharing, share-out, rationing; *division*, partition, demarcation, carve-up (*colloq.*); *share*, portion, allocation, quota, allowance; *ration*, dose, dosage, measure; *serving*, helping, slice, cut, whack (*colloq.*), dollop (*colloq.*); *lot*, parcel, batch.
vb. *allocate*, appoint, assign, detail; *allot*, apportion, distribute, administer, dispense, dole out, share (out), deal, farm out, dish out (*colloq.*); *ration*, dose, measure (out), mete out; *divide up*, divvy up, lot, parcel out, zone, partition, carve up (*colloq.*); *demarcate*, delimit.
adv. *proportionately*, pro rata, per head, per capita.

701 LENDING
See also **714** (credit).
n. *lending*, hiring, letting, subletting, leasing; *loan*, advance, mortgage, overdraft, bridging loan, pawnbroking, credit; *investment*, backing, finance, (start-up) capital; *let*, sublet, lease; *lender*, moneylender, creditor, usurer, Shylock (*colloq.*), loan shark (*colloq.*); *finance house*, credit institution, bank, building society; *investor*, financier, banker, mortgagee, pawnbroker.
vb. *lend*, hire out, let, sublet, lease; *loan*, advance, extend credit, put out at interest; *invest*, finance, back, subsidize, put money up, speculate.

702 BORROWING

See also **715** (debt).

n. *borrowing*, hire, rental, leasing, chartering; *mortgage*, loan, credit card, overdraft; *hire purchase*, HP, instalment plan, easy terms (*colloq.*), the never-never (*colloq.*); *pawn*, pledge; *copying*, plagiarism, imitation; *borrower*, mortgage, debtor, sponge, leech.

vb. *borrow*, hire, rent, lease, charter; *mortgage*, have an overdraft, be creditworthy, be in the red; *sponge*, cadge, bum (*colloq.*), touch (*colloq.*); *pawn*, pledge, pop (*colloq.*); *copy*, plagiarize, lift, crib (*colloq.*).

703 TAKING

See also **690** (gain); **705** (stealing).

n. *taking*, assumption, appropriation, exploitation, extortion, blackmail; *seizure*, grab, snatch, confiscation, impounding; *requisition*, requisitioning, commandeering, compulsory purchase, nationalization; *occupation*, settlement, colonization, annexation; *expropriation*, dispossession, exaction, disinheritance, distraint, foreclosure; *capture*, apprehension, arrest; *kidnap*, kidnapping, abduction, rape, slave trade; *receipt*, acceptance; *booty*, spoils, capture, haul, prize; *kidnapper*, abductor, rapist, captor, slaver; *predator*, parasite, bloodsucker, leech.

adj. *grasping*, grabbing, acquisitive, rapacious, predatory; *extortionate*, exploitative, parasitical.

vb. *take*, assume, take over, appropriate, grasp, grab, snatch, wrest, extort; *seize*, confiscate, impound; *bag*, pocket, net; *requisition*, commandeer, nationalize; *occupy*, settle, colonize, annex; *expropriate*, dispossess, deprive, exact, disinherit, divest; *capture*, take by storm, lead captive, apprehend, arrest, nab (*colloq.*); *kidnap*, abduct, rape, impress, press-gang; *receive*, accept.

704 GIVING BACK

See also **28** (compensation).

n. *giving back*, restitution, restoration, return; *repayment*, reimbursement, indemnification, refund, rebate; *amends*, reparation, compensation, recompense, damages; *reinstatement*, rehabilitation, privatization, denationalization; *recovery*, retrieval, repossession, clawback.

adj. *restitutory*, indemnificatory, compensatory.

vb. *give back*, restitute, make restitution, restore, return; *repay*, reimburse, indemnify, refund, rebate; *make amends*, make reparations, compensate, recompense; *reinstate*, rehabilitate, privatize, denationalize; *get back*, recover, retrieve, repossess, recoup, regain, claw back.

705 STEALING

See also **703** (taking).

n. *stealing*, theft, robbery, grand/petty larceny, kleptomania, pilfering; *burglary*, housebreaking, breaking and entering, safe-blowing/-breaking/-cracking, raid, smash-and-grab raid (*colloq.*), heist (*colloq.*); *shoplifting*, pickpocketing, bag-snatching, hold-up (*colloq.*), stick-up (*colloq.*), mugging, robbery with violence; *looting*, pillage, plunder, rustling, poaching; *hijack*, hijacking, skyjacking, kidnapping, abduction, piracy, body-snatching; *embezzlement*, misappropriation, tax evasion, smuggling, moonlighting, black economy, fiddle (*colloq.*); *fraud*, swindle, con (*colloq.*), diddle (*colloq.*), rip-off (*colloq.*); *thief*, robber, burglar, cat burglar, safe-blower/-breaker/-cracker, cracksman, raider; *shoplifter*, pickpocket, Artful Dodger, bag-snatcher, mugger; *highwayman*, bandit, brigand, footpad; *looter*, pillager, rustler, poacher; *hijacker*, skyjacker, kidnapper, abductor, pirate, body-snatcher; *embezzler*, tax evader, smuggler; *fraud*, swindler, con, crook, rogue, shark, fiddler (*colloq.*), rip-off merchant (*colloq.*).

adj. *thieving*, thievish, light-fingered, kleptomaniac, on the fiddle (*colloq.*); *marauding*, piratical, buccaneering.

vb. *steal*, thieve, rob, burgle, pilfer, filch, purloin, help oneself to, walk off with, nick (*colloq.*), pinch (*colloq.*), nobble (*colloq.*), swipe (*colloq.*), heist (*colloq.*), snaffle (*colloq.*), knock off (*colloq.*), rip off (*colloq.*); *shoplift*, pick pockets, hold up, mug; *loot*, pillage, plunder, sack, raid, rustle, poach; *hijack*, skyjack, kidnap, abduct, shanghai; *embezzle*, misappropriate, smuggle, moonlight, fiddle (*colloq.*), cook the books (*colloq.*); *defraud*, cheat, swindle, con, diddle (*colloq.*), rook (*colloq.*), fleece (*colloq.*), rip off (*colloq.*); *fall off the back of a lorry* (*colloq.*).

706 BOOTY
See also **650** (trophy).

n. *booty*, loot, spoils, plunder, stolen goods, contraband, swag (*colloq.*), perks (*colloq.*); *haul*, catch, find, prize, winnings, ransom, treasure trove; *kidnap victim*, hostage.

707 TRADE
See also **685** (negotiation); **697** (transfer of property); **708** (purchase); **709** (sale); **710** (market).

n. *trade*, commerce, business; *trading*, barter, buying and selling, traffic, trafficking, dealing; *speculation*, brokerage, jobbing, transaction; *exchange*, swap, trade-in, payment in kind; *bargaining*, haggling, negotiations; *export*, import; *trader*, merchant, businessman, entrepreneur, trafficker, dealer, speculator, pedlar; *wholesaler*, middleman, retailer, shopkeeper, tradesman, chandler; *exporter*, importer; *broker*, jobber, stockbroker, estate agent; *business*, dealership, brokerage; *racketeer*, black marketeer, wheeler-dealer, slave trader, drug trafficker, fence (*colloq.*), tout (*colloq.*), cowboy (*colloq.*); *merchandise*, wares, goods, stock, supplies, stuff (*colloq.*); *article*, range, line, commodity; *durables*, consumer goods, consumer durables, perishables.

adj. *trading*, commercial, entrepreneurial, mercantile; *wholesale*, retail, marketable.

vb. *trade*, barter, merchandise, buy and sell, traffic, deal, transact; *exchange*, swap, trade in; *export*, import; *bargain*, negotiate, haggle, wheel and deal, beat down; *racketeer*, profiteer, fence (*colloq.*), tout (*colloq.*).

708 PURCHASE
See also **707** (trade).

n. *purchase*, buying, shopping, mail order; *hire purchase*, easy terms, tick (*colloq.*), the never-never (*colloq.*); *shopping spree*, buy, bargain, impulse buy; *takeover*, merger, dawn raid; *purchaser*, buyer, highest bidder, consignee; *customer*, client, shopper, clientele, patron, market, consumer; *custom*, trade, patronage, goodwill.

vb. *purchase*, make a purchase, buy, shop, go shopping, window-shop, patronize; *invest in*, put one's money into, bid for, buy up; *take over*, buy out, corner, stockpile.

709 SALE
See also **697** (transfer of property).

n. *sale*, auction, selling; *clearance sale*, auction, stocktaking sale, closing-down sale, end-of-season sale, January sales, special purchase; *bazaar*, jumble/rummage sale, sale of work, fête, bring-and-buy sale; *dumping*; *boom*, sell-out, high turnover; *marketing*, merchandising, sales talk/pitch, high-pressure salesmanship, hard/soft sell, spiel (*colloq.*); *seller*, vendor, tout (*colloq.*); *shopkeeper*, retailer, trader, purveyor; *sales representative*, rep, commercial traveller; *salesman*, saleswoman, shop assistant, shop walker, shop girl; *booking clerk*, travel/ticket agent.

adj. *saleable*, marketable; for/on sale, available; *in demand*, called for, sought after; *sold out*, fresh out of (*colloq.*), off (*colloq.*).

vb. *sell*, make a sale, vend, auction, knock down, flog (*colloq.*); *market*, advertise, put up for sale, put on the market; *wholesale*, retail; *peddle*, hawk, tout (*colloq.*); *dump*, unload, sell off, clear out, remainder; *be sold off*, come under the hammer; *be in demand*, sell well, sell like hot cakes, do a roaring trade.

710 MARKET
See also **707** (trade).

n. *market*, bazaar, arcade, covered market, flea market; *mart*, exchange, entrepôt, depot, warehouse; *fair*, fayre, trade fair, show; *stall*, stand, kiosk, booth, barrow; *shop*, store, department store, chain store, boutique, emporium, supermarket, hypermarket, cash-and-carry, shopping centre/precinct, shopping mall; *free trade area*, market economy.

711 MONEY

See also **712** (wealth).

n. *money*, currency, Lsd, sterling, bullion, filthy lucre (*colloq.*), dough (*colloq.*), bread (*colloq.*), lolly (*colloq.*), brass (*colloq.*), shekels (*colloq.*); *cash*, small change, coin, banknote, treasury note, bill, hard cash, greenback, ready money, the ready (*colloq.*); *cheque*, credit card, postal order, money order, banker's order/draft, traveller's cheque, letter of credit, promissory note, IOU; *funds*, finances, capital, reserves, liquidity, bank account, bank balance, wherewithal (*colloq.*), the needful (*colloq.*); *pay*, salary, wages, remuneration, emolument, expenses, petty cash, pocket money, savings, nest egg; *cash flow*, turnover, profit; *forgery*, dud cheque (*colloq.*), rubber cheque (*colloq.*); *banker*, treasurer, keeper of the purse; *bursar*, purser, controller, comptroller, purse strings, paymaster; *cashier*, teller, croupier; *accountant*, bookkeeper; *bank*, savings bank, building society, cash dispenser; *treasury*, strongroom, vault, coffer, safe; *till*, cash register, checkout, gate; *money box*, piggybank, kitty, purse, wallet.

adj. *monetary*, financial, fiscal, pecuniary.

vb. *mint*, issue, coin, monetize, circulate; *cash*, encash, draw out, change; *forge*, counterfeit; *withdraw*, demonetize, call in; *finance*, capitalize, fund, bankroll (*colloq.*); *save*, amass, put by.

712 WEALTH

See also **655** (prosperity); **694** (property); **711** (money).

n. *wealth*, affluence, prosperity, comfort, ease, creditworthiness, high income bracket; *luxury*, opulence, fleshpots; *riches*, fortune, king's ransom, substance, assets, money, means, pile (*colloq.*), mint (*colloq.*), tidy sum (*colloq.*), packet (*colloq.*), pots of money (*colloq*); *rich person*, multimillionaire(ess), man/woman of means, Croesus, Midas, moneybags (*colloq.*), fat cat (*colloq.*), plutocrat, nouveau riche, new rich, idle rich, haves (*colloq.*).

adj. *rich*, wealthy, affluent, prosperous, well-off, comfortably off, comfortable, well-to-do, propertied, moneyed, well-heeled, born with a silver spoon in one's mouth, in the money, flush (*colloq.*), made of money, rolling in it (*colloq.*), filthy/stinking rich (*colloq.*), loaded (*colloq.*); *luxurious*, opulent, plush, palatial, up-market.

vb. *be rich*, have money to burn (*colloq.*), have a bob or two (*colloq.*); *afford*, make ends meet, keep the wolf from the door, do all right (*colloq.*), get by (*colloq.*); *get rich*, prosper, make money, come into money, rake it in (*colloq.*), laugh all the way to the bank (*colloq.*), make a bomb/fortune/packet/pile (*colloq.*), strike it rich (*colloq.*), line one's pocket (*colloq.*).

713 POVERTY

See also **558** (requirement).

n. *poverty*, impoverishment, impecuniousness; *beggary*, mendicancy, penury, destitution, pennilessness, indigence, privation, subsistence level, breadline (*colloq.*); *insolvency*, bankruptcy, ruin, collapse, queer street; *financial difficulty*, reduced/straitened circumstances, poverty trap; *pauper*, the poor, down-and-out, slum dweller, have-nots (*colloq.*); *beggar*, mendicant; *insolvent*, bankrupt.

adj. *poor*, impoverished, impecunious, poverty-stricken, penurious, straitened, on one's beam ends, on one's uppers, hard up (*colloq.*), short (*colloq.*); *destitute*, penniless, indigent, needy, on the breadline (*colloq.*), clean/flat/stony broke (*colloq.*), skint (*colloq.*); *deprived*, underprivileged, disadvantaged, under-

developed, low-paid, underpaid, exploited; *insolvent*, bankrupt, ruined; *down at heel*, in rags, barefoot, starving, down and out.
vb. *be poor*, live from hand to mouth, have to watch the pennies, feel the pinch, fall on hard times, go broke/bust (*colloq.*); *impoverish*, beggar, ruin.

714 CREDIT

See also **701** (lending).
n. *credit*, loan, mortgage, credit facilities, credit account, charge account, credit card, credit note, hire purchase, deferred payment, easy terms, tick (*colloq.*); *creditworthiness*, reputation, trust, confidence, reliability; *creditor*, mortgagee, lender, investor, depositor.
vb. *credit*, allow/give credit, charge to one's account, credit one's account, lend, defer payment, grant a loan, put on the slate (*colloq.*), be in the black (*colloq.*); *take credit*, pay by credit card, keep an account with, borrow, mortgage.

715 DEBT

See also **702** (borrowing); **819** (entitlement).
n. *debt*, indebtedness, commitment, obligation, duty; *liability*, debit, mortgage, amount due/outstanding/owing, bill, arrears, back pay, bad debt; *debtor*, borrower, mortgagor, bad debtor.
adj. *indebted*, committed, obliged, bound, under an obligation; *in debt*, mortgaged, overdrawn, in the red (*colloq.*); *owed*, owing, outstanding, due, overdue, in arrears, unsettled, unpaid, payable, on credit.
vb. *owe*, be in debt, be overdrawn; *mortgage*, overdraw one's account, run up a debt/bill, get credit; *pay by credit card*, buy on hire purchase, buy on the never-never (*colloq.*), get on tick (*colloq.*).

716 PAYMENT

See also **697** (transfer of property).
n. *payment*, settlement, liquidation, reckoning, discharge; *remittance*, defrayment, disbursement, subsidy, subvention; *repayment*, reimbursement, recompense, restitution, refund, damages; *contribution*, subscription, donation, tribute; *deposit*, down payment, outlay, instalment; *pay*, wages, salary, emolument, honorarium, fee, remuneration, stipend, earnings, commission, pension; *payer*, paymaster, cashier, wages clerk.
vb. *pay*, settle, liquidate, reckon, discharge, honour, clear, square accounts with; *pay out*, foot the bill, pick up the tab (*colloq.*), bear the cost of, meet, stand, spend, expend, pay up, fork out (*colloq.*), shell out (*colloq.*), *cough up* (*colloq.*), stump up (*colloq.*); *remit*, defray, remunerate, disburse, subsidize; *repay*, reimburse, recompense, refund, pay damages; *contribute*, subscribe, donate, chip in (*colloq.*).

717 NONPAYMENT

n. *nonpayment*, default, failure to pay, withholding payment; *stoppage*, deduction; *tax evasion*, dishonoured/dud cheque; *insolvency*, run on a bank, crash, failure, collapse, bankruptcy, liquidation; *defaulter*, bankrupt, tax dodger.
adj. *defaulting*, in arrears, behind; *insolvent*, bankrupt, unable to pay, bust (*colloq.*), on the rocks (*colloq.*), washed up.
vb. *default*, fail to pay, fall into arrears; *stop*, deduct, dock, refuse/withhold payment; *welsh*, fiddle one's income tax, do a moonlight flit (*colloq.*); *stop a cheque*, refer to drawer, bounce, freeze, dishonour, repudiate; *fail*, crash, go under, go to the wall, fold, go bankrupt, go bust (*colloq.*); *bankrupt*, ruin; *go into liquidation*, be wound up; *wind up*, liquidate, put in the hands of a receiver.

718 EXPENDITURE

See also **716** (payment).
n. *expenditure*, spending, payment, outlay, disbursement, outgoings, investment; *extravagance*, overspend, spending spree, blowout (*colloq.*); *costs*, overheads, (out-of-pocket) expenses.

vb. *expend*, spend, pay, lay out, invest, disburse, bear the cost, meet, foot the bill; *incur*, run up; *stand*, treat; *draw on one's savings*, splash out, overspend, blow, get through, use up, consume.

719 RECEIPT
See also **690** (gain); **699** (receiving).
n. *receipt*, acknowledgment, ticket, voucher, chit, coupon, counterfoil, stub; *receipts*, income, revenue, takings, monies, proceeds, box office receipts, gate money, returns, royalty, rent; *income*, earnings, pay, salary, wages, remuneration, emolument; *dividend*, pension, annuity, capital gain; *grant*, scholarship, exhibition, bursary, maintenance, allowance, pocket money; *winnings*, prize, legacy, inheritance, windfall, bonus.

720 ACCOUNTS
See also **486** (record).
n. *accounts*, accounting, accountancy, auditing, audit; *creative accounting*, fiddling; *account*, profit-and-loss account, balance sheet, budget, budget forecast; *bookkeeping*, single entry, double entry, books, journal, day book, cash book, ledger, trial balance; *statement*, bill, manifest, invoice, receipt; *accountant*, actuary, chartered accountant, certified accountant, bookkeeper, auditor.
adj. *accounting*, budgetary, actuarial; *accountable*.
vb. *account*, keep accounts, keep the books, enter, debit, credit, post, book, balance; *present*, charge, invoice, bill; *budget*, cost; *falsify the accounts*, cook the books (*colloq.*), massage the figures; *audit*, examine, inspect.

721 PRICE
See also **582** (worth).
n. *price*, cost/selling price, quotation, estimate, price label/tag/ticket; *list price*, recommended retail price (RRP), retail price index (RPI), price control, price freeze; *toll*, entrance/admission charge, rent, hire charge, rental, ground rent, cover charge, postage, corkage; *interest rate*, commission, introduction fee, retainer; *surcharge*, supplement, currency surcharge; *tax*, taxation, duty, levy, impost, tribute, tithe, direct/indirect taxation, inland revenue; *customs duty*, excise duty, tariff, purchase tax, sales tax, value-added tax (VAT); *capital gains tax* (CGT), capital transfer tax (CTT), stamp duty, estate duty, death duties, wealth tax; *income tax*, pay-as-you-earn (PAYE), National Insurance (NI), surtax, supertax, investment surcharge, tax credit, local income tax, corporation tax; *rates*, general rate, water rate, rating assessment, rateable value; *poll tax*, salt tax, window tax, danegeld.
adj. *taxable*, dutiable, gross.
vb. *price*, assess, cost, value, put a price on, estimate, quote, rate; *cost*, fetch, realize, go/sell for, change hands for, be priced at; *tax*, levy, impose, raise, put a tax on.

722 DISCOUNT
See also **36** (subtraction).
n. *discount*, reduction, rebate, deduction; *commission*, percentage, brokerage, cut, margin, mark-up, rake-off (*colloq.*); *concession*, special price/rate, bargain/cut price, special offer, bargain.
adj. *concessionary*, tax-free, duty-free, tax-deductible, net.
vb. *discount*, reduce, deduct, rebate, allow, knock off; *reduce*, cut, slash (*colloq.*).

723 DEARNESS
n. *dearness*, expensiveness, costliness, expense, sellers' market; *extravagance*, exorbitance, extortion, rip-off (*colloq.*), overcharging; *inflation*, inflationary spiral, rising/spiralling prices, sellers' market.
adj. *dear*, expensive, pricey, priceless, precious, up-market, extravagant, costly; *extortionate*, exorbitant, prohibitive, unreasonable, excessive, overpriced, stiff, steep; *inflationary*, rising, spiralling, soaring, climbing.
vb. *be dear*, cost a lot, cost a packet/pretty penny/fortune/the earth (*col-*

loq.); *extort*, profiteer, overcharge, short-change, exploit, sting, fleece, bleed, rip off (*colloq.*); *pay through the nose* (*colloq.*), be done (*colloq.*), be had (*colloq.*); *go up*, rise, soar, climb, rocket, go through the roof, appreciate; *put up*, increase, revalue, mark up.

724 CHEAPNESS

n. *cheapness*, inexpensiveness, reasonableness, competitiveness; *bargain*, good buy, snip (*colloq.*), good value, value for money, sale goods, rejects, seconds; *price reduction*, sale price, cheap rate, reduced rate, concessionary fare, cheap day return, package (holiday), excursion fare; *deflation*, slump, glut, buyers' market; *no charge*, free gift, labour of love, free delivery, Freepost, Freefone, reversed charges, complimentary tickets, comps (*colloq.*).
adj. *cheap*, inexpensive, reasonable, competitive, affordable, down-market; *reduced*, cut-price, cut, half-price, rock-bottom, knock-down, concessionary, marked down, to clear; *economical*, economy, budget, family-size, own-brand; *cheap and nasty*, shoddy, cheapo (*colloq.*); *free of charge*, gratis, complimentary, for nothing, on the house, tax-free, reply-paid, toll-free, collect (*US*).
vb. *be cheap*, go cheap, go for a song; *cheapen*, reduce, cut, mark down, slash; *fall in price*, depreciate, decline, slump, drop; *flood the market*, dump, undersell, undercut; *cost nothing*, be had for the asking; *economize*, budget, shop around, bulk-buy.

725 GENEROSITY

See also **698** (giving).
n. *generosity*, munificence, liberality, lavishness, free hand; *largesse*, bounty, gifts; *hospitality*, charity, open house, kind offer.
adj. *generous*, munificent, liberal, bounteous, bountiful, free-handed, open-handed; *lavish*, right royal, handsome, fit for a king/queen, slap-up (*colloq.*); *hospitable*, charitable, kind, philanthropic, big-hearted, unselfish, unstinting.
vb. *be generous*, give generously, spare no expense, not count the cost; *lavish*, not stint, heap/shower upon, do proud, push the boat out (*colloq.*), kill the fatted calf, do things in style.

726 THRIFT

n. *thrift*, economy, frugality; *care*, prudence, husbandry, careful management, good housekeeping, conservation; *savings*, cuts, cheeseparing, economies, retrenchment.
adj. *thrifty*, economical, frugal, meagre, sparing; *careful*, prudent, canny; *money-saving*, energy-saving, labour-saving.
vb. *be thrifty*, economize, keep costs down, live within one's means/income, make ends meet; *manage*, husband, save, conserve, recycle, waste nothing; *make savings*, cut costs, cut corners, cut back, retrench, tighten one's belt (*colloq.*)

727 EXTRAVAGANCE

See also **572** (waste), **575** (excess).
n. *extravagance*, wastefulness, profligacy, dissipation, improvidence, no thought for tomorrow; *lavishness*, prodigality, profusion, conspicuous consumption, money to burn; *overspending*, permanent overdraft, deficit finance, splurge, spree; *squanderer*, wastrel, prodigal son, spendthrift, big spender.
adj. *extravagant*, wasteful, profligate, improvident, reckless, immoderate, spendthrift; *lavish*, prodigal, profuse, over-generous.
vb. *overspend*, overdraw, fritter away, dissipate, live beyond one's means; *blow/blue one's money*, splurge, lash out, not count the cost, hang the expense, spend money like water (*colloq.*), think money grows on trees (*colloq.*), spend money as if it were going out of fashion (*colloq.*); *squander*, waste, throw away, pour money down the drain, throw good money after bad.

728 MEANNESS

See also **834** (selfishness).

n. *meanness*, minginess, miserliness, stinginess, niggardliness, illiberality, cheeseparing, false economy; *skinflint*, miser, niggard, cheapskate, scrooge; *greed*, avarice, acquisitiveness, venality, voracity, avidity, covetousness, gluttony.

adj. *mean*, mingy, miserly, stingy, niggardly, illiberal, cheeseparing, penny-pinching, parsimonious, close, tight, tight-/close-fisted, grudging, sparing; *greedy*, avaricious, acquisitive, grasping, money-grubbing, mercenary, venal, voracious, avid, covetous, gluttonous, usurious, rapacious.

vb. *be mean*, begrudge; *scrimp*, scrape, skimp, do on the cheap (*colloq.*), pinch, stint, count the pennies; *be greedy*, hoard.

729 FEELING

See also **334** (sensation); **732** (strong emotion).

n. *feeling*, emotion, affection, sentiment, passion; *sensation*, experience, perception, sense of, consciousness, impression; *sympathy*, empathy, fellow feeling, vibes (*colloq.*), friendliness, understanding, appreciation, sensitivity, tenderness, warmth; *agitation*, commotion, trembling, tremor, tingling, quiver, flutter; *sentimentality*, emotion, lump in one's throat; *excitement*, thrill, kick (*colloq.*), buzz (*colloq.*); *enthusiasm*, vigour, ardour, zeal, fervour, fire, keenness, impatience, fanaticism, obsessiveness, mania.

adj. *feeling*, sentient, sensitive, sensible, sensuous, sensual; *sentimental*, romantic, passionate, emotional, affectionate, tender; *sympathetic*, understanding, appreciative, tender, warm; *agitated*, tense, nervous, edgy; *impressed*, influenced, affected, moved, stirred, touched, heart-felt; *enthusiastic*, vigorous, ardent, zealous, burning, keen, earnest, avid, impatient, fanatical, obsessive, manic; *excited*, worked up, keyed up, breathless, panting, exuberant, hysterical, overwrought, feverish, impassioned, dramatic.

vb. *feel*, sense, entertain, experience, endure, go through, undergo, bear, taste, enjoy; *sympathize*, empathize, suffer with, feel for, commiserate, appreciate, know the feeling; *move*, affect, impress, touch, stir, influence, fire, quicken, excite; *respond*, react, warm to, catch, thrill.

730 SENSITIVITY

See also **334** (sensation).

n. *sensitivity*, sensibility, sensitiveness, awareness, responsiveness, alertness, consciousness; *susceptibility*, vulnerability, hypersensitivity; *touchiness*, prickliness, irritability, soft spot, sore point; *soft touch*, easy mark, softie (*colloq.*).

adj. *sensitive*, aware, conscious, sensible, responsive, alive, awake, alert, on one's toes; *susceptible*, vulnerable, impressionable, malleable; *compassionate*, tender-hearted, soft, romantic, emotional, soppy (*colloq.*); *tender*, bruised, painful, hypersensitive, delicate; *oversensitive*, touchy, prickly, thin-skinned; *nervous*, highly strung, irritable, impatient.

731 INSENSITIVITY

See also **335** (insensibility).

n. *insensitivity*, insensibility, unresponsiveness, unawareness, obliviousness, insentience, thick skin; *lethargy*, torpor, stupor, numbness, paralysis, coma, hypnosis; *calmness*, stolidness, imperturbability, impassiveness, coldness, sangfroid, detachment; *stupidity*, obtuseness, dullness; *callousness*, dourness, ruthlessness, brutality, no heart, heartlessness; *stoic*, ascetic, iceberg, robot, automaton.

adj. *insensitive*, unfeeling, insensible, unresponsive, unaware, oblivious, insentient, thick-skinned; *lethargic*, torpid, numb, paralysed, comatose, hypnotized, punchdrunk; *calm*, stolid, imperturbable, impassive, cold, unemotional, unruffled, expressionless, detached, stoical; *stupid*, obtuse, dull, bovine, unimaginative; *dead to*, blind to, deaf to, impervious; *hard-bitten*, hard-nosed, tough, inured, invulnerable; *callous*, dour, ruthless, brutal, hard-hearted, heartless, inhuman.

vb. *be unaffected*, feel no emotion,

leave cold, not turn a hair, not bat an eyelid; *harden oneself*, steel oneself, harden one's heart against, disregard, ignore, switch off (*colloq.*); *not see*, miss the point of; *benumb*, numb, deaden, toughen, harden, sear, stupefy, dull.

732 STRONG EMOTION

See also **729** (feeling).

n. *strong emotion*, excitement, animation, fever, frenzy, delirium; *hullabaloo*, to-do, flurry, fuss, scene, song and dance (*colloq.*); *exhilaration*, elation, euphoria, intoxication, abandon, thrill, ecstasy, ebullience, fever pitch, orgasm, high (*colloq.*); *anger*, rage, fury, temper, outburst, fit, hysterics, tantrum; *passion*, emotion, romanticism, lyricism, sensationalism, melodrama; *excitation*, agitation, stimulation, galvanization, activation, arousal; *inspiration*, invitation, incitement, appeal, provocation, encouragement; *fascination*, bewitching, interest, enchantment, captivation; *excitability*, impetuousness, impetuosity, restlessness, irritability, instability, explosiveness, hot blood, intolerance; *vehemence*, turbulence, boisterousness, recklessness, high spirits.

adj. *excited*, animated, thrilled, inspired, impassioned, stimulated, moved; *feverish*, delirious, effervescent, wound up, crazy, keyed up, a-quiver; *exhilarated*, elated, euphoric, intoxicated, ebullient, ecstatic, turned on (*colloq.*), high (*colloq.*); *angry*, furious, raging, in a temper, hysterical, on the rampage, on the warpath; *passionate*, emotional, romantic, lyrical; *exciting*, exhilarating, thrilling, stimulating, rousing; *stirring*, inspiring, moving, affecting, evocative; *gripping*, enthralling, heart-stopping, nerve-wracking, nail-biting; *interesting*, absorbing, fascinating, captivating, enchanting, bewitching, compelling; *dramatic*, momentous, sensational, melodramatic, mind-boggling; *provocative*, titillating, saucy, spicy, racy, tantalizing; *excitable*, volatile, mercurial, quicksilver, temperamental, turbulent; *highly strung*, nervous, edgy, on edge, tense, jumpy, jittery, restless; *impetuous*, impulsive, hot-headed, headstrong; *impatient*, intolerant, irritable, quick-tempered; *enthusiastic*, keen, boisterous, high-spirited.

vb. *excite*, arouse, inflame, work up, wind up, incite, provoke, incense, impassion, fire, fuel, goad; *stimulate*, activate, awaken, animate, electrify, energize, galvanize, summon up, quicken, turn on (*colloq.*), switch on (*colloq.*); *enthuse*, inspire, stir, move, encourage, hearten, urge; *interest*, absorb, fascinate, intrigue, engage, captivate; *enthral*, enchant, bewitch, compel, delight, thrill; *anger*, enrage, make one's blood boil; *startle*, amaze, take one's breath away, arrest, impress; *get excited*, fret, fume, work oneself up, get on one's high horse, rage, explode, fly off the handle, create (*colloq.*), freak out (*colloq.*).

733 IMPASSIVITY

See also **148** (moderation); **335** (insensibility); **731** (insensitivity; **756** (indifference); **760** (lack of wonder).

n. *impassivity*, inexcitability, imperturbability, steadiness, level-headedness, sangfroid, phlegm; *calmness*, coolness, composure, self-control, self-restraint; *equanimity*, serenity, tranquillity, placidity; *mildness*, meekness, submissiveness, resignation, acquiescence; *detachment*, aloofness, nonchalance, dispassionateness; *apathy*, indifference, unconcern; *sobriety*, gravity, staidness, sedateness; *patience*, forbearance, stoicism, tolerance.

adj. *impassive*, inexcitable, imperturbable, phlegmatic, level-headed, unflappable (*colloq.*); *calm*, cool, collected, composed, self-possessed; *even-tempered*, serene, tranquil, placid, cool as a cucumber (*colloq.*); *mild*, meek, submissive, uncomplaining, resigned, acquiescent; *detached*, aloof, nonchalant, dispassionate, blasé; *apathetic*, indifferent, unconcerned, uninterested; *sober*, grave, staid, sedate, reserved;

patient, forbearing, long-suffering, stoical, tolerant, easy-going.
vb. *keep calm/cool*, keep one's temper, control oneself, master one's feelings, not excite oneself, keep a cool head, keep one's hair/shirt on (*colloq.*), keep one's cool (*colloq.*), not flap (*colloq.*), not bat an eyelid (*colloq.*); *resign oneself*, submit, swallow, take, stomach; *be patient*, tolerate, put up with, brook, abide, endure, support, suffer.

734 JOY

See also **336** (physical pleasure); **742** (cheerfulness); **746** (rejoicing).
n. *joy*, pleasure, delight, enjoyment, thrill, enchantment, kick (*colloq.*); *fun*, jollity, merriment, good time; *ecstasy*, rapture, elation, exhilaration, bliss, euphoria, exaltation; *glee*, relish, gusto, zest; *happiness*, gladness, felicity, satisfaction, fulfilment; *comfort*, ease, well-being, convenience, bed of roses, luxury, paradise; *indulgence*, self-indulgence, hedonism, self-gratification; *malice*, gloating, schadenfreude.
adj. *joyful*, happy, glad, delighted, pleased, satisfied, gratified, pleased as Punch; *joyous*, thrilled, excited, on top of the world; *ecstatic*, rapturous, elated, euphoric, overjoyed, enraptured, delirious, carried away, over the moon (*colloq.*), in seventh heaven; *jolly*, merry, cheery, gladsome; *pleasant*, enjoyable, comfortable, pleasurable, convenient, satisfying, cosy, welcome; *delightful*, adorable, blissful, divine (*colloq.*), heavenly (*colloq.*); *self-indulgent*, hedonistic, luxurious, palatial; *malicious*.
vb. *rejoice*, jump for joy, celebrate, congratulate oneself; *enjoy*, get pleasure from, take pleasure in, delight in, relish, have fun; *revel in*, bask in, adore, rave about, get a kick out of (*colloq.*), get off on (*colloq.*).

735 SORROW

See also **337** (physical pain); **743** (dejection); **747** (lamentation).
n. *sorrow*, sadness, melancholy, unhappiness, wretchedness, misery, gloom, woe; *despair*, distress, dejection, despondency, depression, dolour, desolation; *torment*, heartache, agony, anguish, suffering; *mourning*, bereavement, grieving, grief, regret, remorse; *homesickness*, nostalgia, longing, yearning; *worry*, anxiety, care, disquiet, something on one's mind, concern, burden; *problem*, headache, bother, trouble; *phobia*, neurosis, hang-up (*colloq.*).
adj. *sorrowful*, sad, melancholy, unhappy, depressed, disconsolate; *gloomy*, woeful, down in the dumps (*colloq.*); *wretched*, miserable, pitiable, pathetic; *desperate*, despairing, dejected, despondent; *distressed*, upset, distraught, anguished; *troubled*, afflicted, vexed, burdened; *worried*, anxious, fretful; *sorrowing*, mournful, grief-stricken, heart-broken, cut up (*colloq.*); *homesick*, nostalgic; *distressing*, harrowing, agonizing, painful; *neurotic*, hung-up (*colloq.*), driven.
vb. *sorrow*, be unhappy, grieve, mourn, pine, yearn, eat one's heart out; *depress*, distress, upset, agonize; *worry*, trouble, torment, harrow.

736 PLEASANTNESS

See also **336** (physical pleasure).
n. *pleasantness*, pleasurableness, niceness, delightfulness, attractiveness, enjoyableness; *charm*, fascination, winsomeness, allure, loveliness, beauty; *amiability*, friendliness, affability; *treat*, joy, delight, fun, lark (*colloq.*); *melody*, harmony.
adj. *pleasant*, pleasurable, pleasing, genial, agreeable, nice, delightful, acceptable, welcome, enjoyable; *charming*, fascinating, winsome, ravishing, exquisite, lovely, beautiful, fetching; *good*, wonderful, marvellous, excellent; *amiable*, friendly, affable, likeable; *enchanting*, alluring, seductive, enticing, bewitching; *melodious*, harmonious, mellow, soothing; *delicious*, tasty, luscious, delectable, choice, refreshing.
vb. *please*, delight, give/afford pleasure, amuse, entertain, make happy, gladden; *comfort*, soothe, put at ease, stroke, pet; *attract*, interest, allure;

charm, bewitch, captivate, entrance; *gratify*, satisfy, indulge, pander to, pamper, coddle; *excite*, stimulate, thrill.

737 UNPLEASANTNESS

See also **337** (physical pain); **604** (harm).

n. *unpleasantness*, disagreeableness; *hatefulness*, loathsomeness, nastiness, ugliness; *disappointment*, difficulty, trouble, worry, thorn in the flesh; *persecution*, harassment, molestation; *soreness*, tenderness, inflammation; *bitterness*, unpalatability, sharpness, tastelessness, disgust; *annoyance*, nuisance, vexation, embarrassment; *curse*, pest, plague; *burden*, cross, load, affliction.

adj. *unpleasant*, disagreeable, undesirable, displeasing; *hateful*, repellent, loathsome, beastly, foul, nasty, obnoxious, disgusting, nauseating, revolting, offensive; *hideous*, ugly, dismal, dreary, grim, unattractive, uninviting, depressing, unappealing; *unpalatable*, tasteless; *painful*, inflamed, sore, tender; *annoying*, troublesome, bothersome, irritating, trying, tiresome, irksome, wearisome; *onerous*, burdensome, oppressive; *upsetting*, off-putting, disturbing.

vb. *displease*, dissatisfy, go against the grain, rub up the wrong way; *repel*, put one off, nauseate, disgust, sicken; *shock*, horrify, scandalize, offend; *trouble*, worry, afflict, upset, disturb, distress; *bother*, incommode, inconvenience, put out, put to trouble; *torment*, harass, bait, bully, persecute, victimize; *tease*, pester, annoy, irritate, vex, obsess, haunt, molest, peeve, needle.

738 SATISFACTION

See also **573** (sufficiency); **825** (approval).

n. *satisfaction*, contentment, ease of mind, peace of mind, happiness; *comfort*, snugness, rest, ease, tranquillity, serenity; *complacency*, self-satisfaction, smugness.

adj. *satisfied*, content, contented, happy, carefree; *comfortable*, snug, relaxed, at ease, tranquil, serene, peaceful; *uncomplaining*, unenvious, easily pleased, undemanding; *complacent*, self-satisfied, smug, pleased with oneself; *satisfactory*, satisfying, acceptable, passable, unobjectionable.

vb. *be satisfied*, etc., have all that one could wish for, achieve one's heart's desire, have no complaints; *satisfy*, content, gratify, please, meet with approval, go down well, meet one's needs; *appease*, mollify, pacify, propitiate, reconcile.

739 DISSATISFACTION

See also **574** (insufficiency); **747** (lamentation); **826** (disapproval).

n. *dissatisfaction*, discontent, displeasure; *irritation*, resentment, regret, pique; *depression*, sadness, unhappiness, grief, vexation; *tension*, strain, unrest, uneasiness, restlessness, restiveness; *grudge*, ill will, grievance; *criticism*, fault-finding, nit-picking; *complaint*, murmur; *critic*, fault-finder, nit-picker; *dissident*, malcontent, angry young man, protester.

adj. *dissatisfied*, discontented, displeased, disgruntled, browned/cheesed off (*colloq.*); *uneasy*, restless, tense; *cross*, piqued, sulky, tetchy, peevish, testy; *critical*, querulous, hard to please, exacting, captious, censorious; *disconsolate*, disappointed; *grudging*, jealous, envious, resentful.

vb. *be dissatisfied*, etc., complain, harp, nag, grouse, grumble, moan (*colloq.*), beef (*colloq.*), bellyache (*colloq.*), mutter under one's breath; *criticize*, carp, split hairs, quibble.

740 RELIEF

See also **620** (refreshment).

n. *relief*, easing, alleviation, mitigation, abatement, assuagement; *help*, comfort, load off one's mind, consolation; *break in the clouds*, lull, respite, ray of sunshine; *painkiller*, sedative, analgesic, balm, anaesthetic; *remedy*, cure.

adj. *relieving*, easing, mitigating; *comforting*, consoling; *soothing*, analgesic,

anodyne, anaesthetic; *remedial*, curative, restorative.
vb. *relieve*, ease, alleviate, mitigate, abate, assuage; *soften*, cushion, take the strain; *help*, comfort, console; *encourage*, buck, hearten; *lighten*, lift, unburden; *soothe*, deaden, still, lull, anaesthetize; *remedy*, cure; *be relieved*, feel relief, relieve oneself, feel better, take comfort, take heart; *breathe again*, heave a sigh of relief, thank one's lucky stars.

741 AGGRAVATION

See also **593** (deterioration).
n. *aggravation*, exacerbation, deterioration, worsening, degeneration; *augmentation*, intensification, strengthening, deepening, sharpening, heightening; *exasperation*, irritation, annoyance, embittering.
adj. *aggravated*, etc., unmitigated, unrelieved.
vb. *aggravate*, exacerbate, deteriorate, worsen, degenerate; *augment*, intensify, strengthen, deepen, sharpen, heighten, magnify, multiply; *exasperate*, irritate, annoy, embitter, sour, inflame, fuel, make matters worse.

742 CHEERFULNESS

See also **734** (joy); **748** (hope).
n. *cheerfulness*, cheeriness, high spirits, blitheness, light-heartedness, levity; *happiness*, satisfaction, contentment; *optimism*, hopefulness, positive thinking; *vitality*, animation, liveliness, joie de vivre, vivacity; *mirth*, merriment, glee, laughter, mischief, gaiety, jollity, good humour, jocularity, joviality; *good nature*, geniality, amiability, affability, life and soul of the party, conviviality.
adj. *cheerful*, cheery, high-spirited, blithe, sunny, light-hearted, chirpy, breezy, carefree, easy-going; *happy*, satisfied, content, on top of the world; *optimistic*, hopeful, sanguine, in good heart; *vital*, animated, lively, vivacious, radiant, sparkling, bouncy, ebullient, bright-eyed and bushy-tailed (*colloq.*), full of beans (*colloq.*); *merry*, mirthful, gleeful, mischievous, laughing, gay, jolly, good-humoured, jocular, jovial; *good-natured*, genial, amiable, affable, convivial; *cheering*, warming, encouraging, heartening.
vb. *be cheerful*, etc., keep smiling, keep a stiff upper lip, put on a brave face, grin and bear it, keep one's chin/end/pecker up (*colloq.*); *cheer up*, perk up, take heart, pull oneself together, look on the bright side, snap out of it (*colloq.*); *cheer* (up), humour, jolly along, hearten, encourage; *console*, comfort.

743 DEJECTION

See also **735** (sorrow); **749** (hopelessness).
n. *dejection*, despondency, gloom, cheerlessness, low spirits, weltschmerz, the doldrums, the blues (*colloq.*); *despair*, defeatism, pessimism; *depression*, unhappiness, joylessness, misery, melancholy; *disappointment*, chagrin, disillusionment.
adj. *dejected*, despondent, sad, gloomy, cheerless, low, down, down in the mouth, morose, glum, blue (*colloq.*), down in the dumps (*colloq.*); *despairing*, defeatist, negative, pessimistic, downhearted; *depressed*, unhappy, suicidal, miserable, melancholy, dismal, world-weary, browned/cheesed off (*colloq.*); *disappointed*, dispirited, disheartened, disillusioned, crestfallen, hangdog, downcast, crushed; *upset*, put out, cut up (*colloq.*), pissed off (*colloq.*).
vb. *be dejected*, etc., mope, brood, languish, pine, moan, sulk, droop, pull a long face; *despair*, give up, lose heart, eat one's heart out; *depress*, dishearten, discourage, demoralize, dismay, sadden, get down; *dampen*, disappoint, put a damper on, pour cold water on.

744 HUMOUR

n. *humour*, sense of humour, wit, wittiness, jocularity; *satire*, burlesque, farce, spoof, take-off (*colloq.*); *sarcasm*, flippancy, facetiousness, irony, whimsy; *repartee*, banter, badinage, joking, buffoonery; *joke*, witticism, pun, play on words, jest, quip, wisecrack, gag, one-liner, shaggy-dog story; *dirty joke*, double entendre, innuendo, sick joke, black comedy; *practical joke*, hoax; *cartoon*, comic strip, caricature; *comedy*, slapstick, situation comedy, sit com; *limerick*, clerihew, epigram, aphorism; *laughter*, mirth, gales/roar/shriek of laughter, giggle, the giggles, snigger, titter, chuckle, chortle, guffaw, cackle; *smile*, grin, smirk, simper; *humorist*, wit, wag, card (*colloq.*), satirist, comic writer, cartoonist; *joker*, practical joker, clown, buffoon, jester, comic, (stand-up) comedian, comedienne.

adj. *humorous*, funny, droll, amusing, comic, comical, farcical, funny ha-ha (*colloq.*); *witty*, satirical, sarcastic, ironic, sardonic; *ridiculous*, laughable, side-splitting, hilarious, uproarious, killing, killingly funny; *jocular*, jokey, joking, flippant, whimsical, facetious, tongue-in-cheek; *risqué*, near the bone, off-colour, blue.

vb. *joke*, jest, crack a joke, quip, pun, bring the house down (*colloq.*); *tease*, chaff, pull someone's leg, kid (*colloq.*); *ridicule*, make fun of, poke fun at, mock, caricature, satirize, lampoon, take off, ham up (*colloq.*), camp up (*colloq.*); *have a sense of humour*, see the funny side of, enjoy a joke; *laugh*, hoot, giggle, snigger, titter, chuckle, chortle, guffaw, cackle; *split one's sides*, roar with laughter, crease (*colloq.*), be in stiches, fall about, laugh like a drain, roll in the aisles (*colloq.*), nearly die (laughing) (*colloq.*); *smile*, grin, smirk, simper.

745 SERIOUSNESS

See also **659** (severity); **743** (dejection); **747** (lamentation); **762** (boredom).

n. *seriousness*, solemnity, earnestness, gravity, grimness; *sedateness*, sobriety, staidness, demureness, primness, sternness, puritanism; *dullness*, dryness, stuffiness, colourlessness; *killjoy*, sobersides, wet blanket (*colloq.*), spoilsport, party pooper (*colloq.*).

adj. *serious*, solemn, earnest, grave, unfunny; *grim*, forbidding, frowning, stern, po-faced; *sedate*, sober, stolid, staid, demure, prim, straitlaced, stern, puritanical; *straight-faced*, deadpan, poker-faced; *dull*, dry, stuffy, colourless, dreary.

vb. *take things (too) seriously*, not get the joke, not have a sense of humour, keep a straight face.

746 REJOICING

See also **734** (joy).

n. *rejoicing*, exultation, celebration, jubilation, triumph; *revelling*, revels, revelry, festivity, merrymaking, street party, carnival, thanksgiving; *clapping*, cheering, hallelujah, three cheers, hurrah, hooray.

adj. *rejoicing*, cock-a-hoop, over the moon (*colloq.*), exultant, jubilant; *celebratory*, triumphal, triumphant.

vb. *rejoice*, exult, celebrate, triumph; *revel*, make merry, carouse, dance/leap for joy, skip, dance in the streets, let one's hair down (*colloq.*), paint the town red (*colloq.*); *clap*, cheer, shout, whoop, yell; *gloat*, crow, rub one's hands.

747 LAMENTATION

See also **735** (sorrow); **739** (dissatisfaction); **745** (seriousness).

n. *lamentation*, mourning, wailing, weeping, sobbing, tears, gnashing of teeth; *cry*, sob, weep, whimper, bawl; *widow's weeds*, sackcloth and ashes, black; *grief*, regret, sorrow; *lament*, threnody, elegy, dirge, requiem, funeral march, wake.

adj. *lamenting*, mourning, grief-stricken, tearful, inconsolable; *mournful*, lugubrious, plaintive; *lamentable*, pathetic, woeful, pitiable.

vb. *lament*, mourn, keen, beat one's breast; *grieve*, sorrow, go into mourning, elegize; *bemoan*, regret, deplore; *condole*, commiserate, comfort; *weep*, wail, sob, cry, burst into tears, break down; *sob*, sigh, moan, whimper, groan.

748 HOPE

See also **742** (cheerfulness); **755** (desire).

n. *hope*, aspiration, ambition, high hopes; *dream*, pipe-dream, wishful thinking, heart's desire, promised land, utopia; *trust*, confidence, faith, reliance, optimism; *expectation*, assumption, presumption, anticipation; *promise*, good omen; *hopeful*, young hopeful, candidate, aspirant, competitor; *dreamer*, visionary, optimist.
adj. *hopeful*, aspiring, ambitious, would-be; *trusting*, confident, expectant, buoyant, optimistic, sanguine; *promising*, encouraging, favourable, auspicious, rosy.
vb. *hope*, aspire, set one's heart on, aim, long for; *trust*, rely, have faith, believe, feel confident, be in hopes of, rest assured; *expect*, assume, presume, anticipate; *look on the bright side*, live in hope, hope against hope, keep one's fingers crossed; *raise someone's hopes*, give to believe, encourage; *show promise*, have the makings of, augur well, bid fair, bode well.

749 HOPELESSNESS

See also **743** (dejection).
n. *hopelessness*, despondency, defeatism, despair, desperation, pessimism, cynicism, resignation, dashed hopes; *impossibility*, no chance, irrevocability; *hopeless case*, poor lookout, dead duck (*colloq.*), goner (*colloq.*); *pessimist*, Job's comforter, defeatist.
adj. *hopeless*, desperate, despondent, defeatist, pessimistic, cynical, resigned, past hoping; *vain*, futile, to no avail, impossible, irrevocable, irredeemable; *inauspicious*, unpropitious, unfavourable, ominous, bleak.
vb. *lose hope*, despair, give up, resign oneself, abandon hope, write off; *dash someone's hopes*, hold out no hope, discourage.

750 FEAR

See also **752** (cowardice).
n. *fear*, dread, awe, horror, fright, trepidation, terror, phobia, blue funk (*colloq.*); *panic*, alarm, scare, stampede; *intimidation*, threats, deterrence, sabre-rattling, reign of terror; *timidity*, timorousness, fearfulness, nervousness; *diffidence*, shyness, hesitation; *cold feet*, misgivings, qualms, apprehension, uneasiness, disquiet; *worry*, concern, anxiety; *tremor*, flutter, fear and trembling, adrenalin, cold sweat, butterflies (*colloq.*), heebie-jeebies (*colloq.*), collywobbles (*colloq.*), the creeps (*colloq.*), the willies (*colloq.*).

adj. *afraid*, frightened, terrified, petrified, horrified, scared (stiff), alarmed, panicky, panic-stricken, white as a sheet; *timid*, timorous, fearful, nervous, jittery, jumpy, uptight (*colloq.*); *diffident*, shy, hesitant, wary; *apprehensive*, uneasy; *worried*, concerned, anxious; *frightening*, frightful, alarming, awesome, horrifying, terrible, hair-raising, bloodcurdling, ghastly, grisly, gruesome, macabre; *creepy*, weird, scary, eerie.

vb. *fear*, be afraid, dread, stand in fear of; *get/have the wind up*, take fright, panic, lose one's nerve, break out in a cold sweat; *quake*, tremble, shake, quiver, shudder; *quail*, shrink, cower, funk, not be able to face, chicken out (*colloq.*); *freeze*, feel one's blood run cold/one's knees knock/one's hair stand on end; *frighten*, affright, scare, terrify, petrify, alarm; *intimidate*, menace, terrorize, put the fear of God into, browbeat, cow; *make nervous*, unnerve, put the wind up, shake, rattle, disquiet.

751 COURAGE

See also **539** (resolution).

n. *courage*, bravery, valour, heroism, fearlessness, intrepidity; *boldness*, audacity, daring, nerve, bottle (*colloq.*); *manliness*, prowess, chivalry, gallantry; *spirit*, dash, derring-do, pluck, mettle, backbone, guts (*colloq.*), spunk (*colloq.*); *fortitude*, resolution, morale, determination, courage of one's convictions; *hero*, heroine, brave, Amazon, daredevil, VC, lionheart.

adj. *courageous*, brave, valiant, heroic, ready for anything; *bold*, audacious, daring, spirited, dashing, plucky, spunky; *unafraid*, intrepid, fearless, dauntless, doughty, stout-hearted,

unflinching; *manly*, chivalrous, gallant, macho.
vb. *be courageous*, have the courage/nerve to, venture, brave, beard, confront, face (the music), defy, dare to, show one's mettle, have what it takes, take it like a man, keep one's chin up (*colloq.*); *take courage*, pluck up courage, take heart, screw up one's courage, nerve oneself, brace oneself, put a brave face on; *hearten*, nerve, embolden, inspire, rally, boost, bolster, strengthen, give confidence, buck up.

752 COWARDICE

See also **541** (vacillation); **750** (fear).
n. *cowardice*, cowardliness, pusillanimity, faint-heartedness, timidity, weakness, spinelessness, white feather, yellow streak, funk (*colloq.*); quitting, defeatism; *boasting*, braggadocio, Dutch courage; *coward*, poltroon, dastard, cowardy custard (*colloq.*), rabbit (*colloq.*), chicken (*colloq.*), scaredy (*colloq.*), sissy (*colloq.*), *deserter*, quitter, defeatist, shirker, braggart.
adj. *cowardly*, craven, pusillanimous, faint-hearted, timid, lily-livered, gutless, spineless, yellow-bellied (*colloq.*), sissy (*colloq.*), yellow (*colloq.*), chicken (*colloq.*); *dastardly*, mean, cowering, defeatist.
vb. *lack courage*, not dare, have no stomach for, funk (*colloq.*); *cringe*, quail, shrink, cower, skulk; *panic*, desert, turn tail, slink away, cut and run; *get cold feet*, quit, lose one's nerve, bottle/chicken out (*colloq.*).

753 RASHNESS

See also **445** (folly); **615** (haste).
n. *rashness*, recklessness, carelessness, thoughtlessness, heedlessness, imprudence; *indiscipline*, irresponsibility, wildness, temerity, audacity; *folly*, indiscretion, foolhardiness, brinksmanship, gamble, a leap in the dark; *impulsiveness*, impetuosity, haste, hotheadedness; *daredevil*, hothead, tearaway, fire-eater, gambler, madcap, harum-scarum.
adj. *rash*, incautious, reckless, thoughtless, heedless, ill-considered, inconsiderate, unthinking; *undisciplined*, irresponsible, wild, buccaneering, trigger-happy; *careless*, slap-happy, hit-and-miss, devil-may-care; *foolish*, foolhardy, imprudent, indiscreet; *impulsive*, impetuous, overenthusiastic, hotheaded, headstrong, overhasty; *precipitous*, headlong, breakneck, do-or-die, suicidal.
vb. *be rash*, etc., not care, take the plunge, throw caution to the winds, damn the consequences, stick one's neck out; *rush into*, tempt providence, ask for trouble; *gamble*, take unnecessary risks, play with fire, risk one's neck, go out on a limb, dice with danger, court disaster.

754 CAUTION

See also **406** (carefulness); **453** (foresight).
n. *caution*, cautiousness, heed, heedfulness, wariness, care, safety first, prudence; *circumspection*, reverence, respect, discretion; *deliberation*, planning, forethought, foresight, precaution, prophylaxis, prophylactic; *vigilance*, watchfulness, alertness, suspicion.
adj. *cautious*, wary, careful, heedful, prudent; *circumspect*, gingerly, respectful, suspicious, nervous; *precautionary*, prophylactic; *vigilant*, watchful, alert, canny.
vb. *take care*, play safe, think twice, look before one leaps; *take preventive measures*, keep well out of, give a wide berth, keep one's head down; *look out*, watch one's step, tread warily, be on one's guard; *cover oneself*, see how the wind blows, feel one's way, leave nothing to chance.

755 DESIRE

See also **553** (intention); **681** (request); **748** (hope)
n. *desire*, wish, want, fancy; *requirement*, need; *longing*, yearning, hankering, yen, ambition, aspiration; *curiosity*, inquisitiveness, thirst for knowledge; *urge*, inclination, motivation, eagerness, keenness, itch, bug

(*colloq.*); *craving*, covetousness, lust, mania, addiction, craze; *greed*, voracity, gluttony, rapacity; *hunger*, thirst, appetite, famine, starvation, drought; *object of one's desire*, desideratum, ambition, dream, fantasy.

adj. *desirous*, wishful; *aspiring*, would-be, hopeful, ambitious; *eager*, keen, avid, itching, bent on; *curious*, inquisitive; *covetous*, lusting, lecherous, crazy for; *greedy*, voracious, insatiable, rapacious; *hungry*, starving, ravenous, famished, empty, peckish (*colloq.*); *thirsty*, dry, parched; *desirable*, acceptable, welcome, enviable, appetizing, attractive.

vb. *desire*, wish, want, pray for; *welcome*, be glad of, fancy, could do with; *require*, need, must have; *long*, yearn, hanker, thirst, itch, set one's heart on, aspire, be dying for (*colloq.*); *covet*, lust after, crave, have designs on; *hunger*, thirst, starve, drool, could eat a horse (*colloq.*).

756 INDIFFERENCE

See also **403** (lack of curiosity); **733** (impassivity).

n. *indifference*, lack of interest, unconcern, apathy; *insensitivity*, coldness, impassivity; *half-heartedness*; *neutrality*, impartiality, disinterest; *promiscuousness*.

adj. *indifferent*, unconcerned, uninterested, apathetic, blasé, cool (*colloq.*); *insensitive*, cold, unimpressed, unmoved, uninvolved, impassive, unresponsive; *half-hearted*, lukewarm, not bothered, easy (*colloq.*); *neutral*, impartial, disinterested, impersonal, dispassionate; *unambitious*, easy-going, laid back (*colloq.*); *promiscuous*; *unwanted*, de trop, unwelcome, unasked, unbidden, uninvited; *undesirable*, unattractive.

vb. *not care* (less), not mind, be all the same to, can take it or leave it, not give a damn/hoot (*colloq.*); *leave one cold*, take no interest in, not care for, hold no brief for.

757 LIKING

See also **336** (physical pleasure); **795** (love).

n. *liking*, fondness, fancy, relish, weakness, partiality, sympathy, affinity, soft spot; *leaning*, inclination, penchant, propensity, proclivity; *preference*, predilection; *attraction*, fascination, appeal.

adj. *fond of*, partial to, keen on, sympathetic to; *likable*, popular, in favour, attractive, appealing, fetching, catchy.

vb. *like*, be fond of, care for, go for, fancy, relish, be partial to, have a weakness for, take pleasure in, be into (*colloq.*); *prefer*, favour, choose, incline.

758 DISLIKE

See also **796** (hate).

n. *dislike*, disinclination, distaste; *dissatisfaction*, displeasure; *repulsion*, repugnance, disgust, abhorrence, loathing; *aversion*, allergy, antipathy, prejudice; *bête noire*, bugbear, pet hate.

adj. *displeased*, dissatisfied, disenchanted, disgusted, fed up; *averse*, allergic, antipathetic, loath, anti; *undesirable*, disagreeable, objectionable, obnoxious; *repulsive*, repugnant, abhorrent, loathsome, rebarbative; *unpopular*, out of favour, unloved.

vb. *dislike*, not care for, not find to one's taste, have no time for, have no stomach for, not go for; *take a dislike to*, turn one's nose up at, not take kindly to; *shrink from*, shudder at, detest, abhor, loathe, can't abide/bear/stand; *displease*, antagonize, go against the grain, rub up the wrong way, put off, repel, disgust, make one's gorge rise.

759 WONDER

See also **451** (surprise).

n. *wonder*, wonderment, amazement, shock, astonishment, awe, fascination, stupefaction, bewilderment, bafflement, incredulity; *sensation*, drama, miracle, marvel, prodigy, phenomenon, seven wonders of the world; *oddity*, curiosity, rarity, freak, monster, monstrosity; *wizard*, miracle-worker, genius, child prodigy.

adj. *wondrous*, amazing, astonishing, astounding, remarkable, mind-boggling, breathtaking, stupefying, bewildering, baffling, unbelievable, out of this world; *sensational*, dramatic, miraculous, prodigious, phenomenal, extraordinary, unparalleled, monstrous, stupendous, fantastic, wonderful, fabulous, tremendous; *odd*, curious, strange, rare, freaky, freakish, weird, mysterious; *amazed*, astonished, astounded, rapt, spellbound, dumbfounded, struck dumb, speechless, open-mouthed, bewildered, stupefied, flabbergasted, bowled over, thunderstruck, transfixed.
vb. *wonder*, marvel, gasp, whistle, not get over; *stare*, gape, gaze, goggle, gawk, gawp, not believe one's eyes, rub one's eyes; *amaze*, astonish, astound; *bowl over*, stagger, take one's breath away, flabbergast, overwhelm, dumbfound; *confound*, baffle, bewilder.

760 LACK OF WONDER

See also **733** (impassivity); **756** (indifference).
n. *lack of wonder/astonishment*, etc., composure, blankness, impassivity; *expectation*, what one expected, just as one thought, nothing to write home about, nothing new under the sun, old hat (*colloq.*).
adj. *unsurprised*, unimpressed, unmoved, unperturbed; *expected*, foreseen, accustomed, common, usual.
vb. *not wonder*, not be surprised, see nothing remarkable, take in one's stride, not bat an eyelid, have seen it all before; *expect*, assume, take for granted, take as read.

761 RECREATION

See also **165** (habitat); **236** (land travel); **237** (water travel); **555** (pursuit); **612** (leisure).
n. *recreation*, amusement, pleasure, fun, leisure, spare time, diversion, relaxation, rest, (activity) holiday; *activity*, interest, pastime, hobby, pursuit, sport, game, play; *entertainment*, theatre, television, video, radio, music, opera, musical; *festival*, fiesta, carnival, gala; *fair*, funfair, circus; *party*, housewarming party, bottle party, picnic, barbecue, street party, dinner, banquet, feast; *outing*, trip, day trip, excursion, jaunt; *camping*, pony-trekking, hiking, orienteering, mountaineering, rock-climbing; *athletics*, running, jogging, keep-fit, aerobics, cycling; *swimming*, diving, boating, rowing, sculling, canoeing, sailing, yachting, windsurfing, waterskiing, surfing; *skiing*, ski-jumping, tobogganning, skating, ice hockey; *flying*, gliding, parachuting, skydiving, parascending, hang-gliding; *equestrianism*, horseracing, showjumping, steeplechasing, dressage; *football*, soccer, rugby (football), volleyball, cricket, baseball, tennis, squash (rackets), badminton, golf, hockey, lacrosse, polo, croquet, snooker, billiards; *party game*, musical chairs, sardines, charades; *hopscotch*, leapfrog, hide-and-seek; *crossword*, jigsaw (puzzle), noughts and crosses, Rubik's cube, solitaire, video game; *chess*, draughts, checkers, backgammon, mah jong, ludo, snakes and ladders, Monopoly, Scrabble; *card game*, bridge, rummy, canasta, patience, whist, snap, pontoon, brag, poker; *roulette*, dice, bingo, tombola; *dancing*, ballet, folk/tap/morris/ballroom/old-time dancing; *waltz*, polka, mazurka, cancan, quickstep, foxtrot, flamenco, Charleston, cha-cha, conga, rumba, samba, jive, rock 'n' roll, twist, disco, breakdancing; *toy*, plaything, ball, balloon, rattle, bricks, marbles, water pistol, popgun, airgun, toy soldier; *doll*, teddy bear, golliwog, action man; *bicycle*, tricycle, fairy cycle, roller skates, skateboard, pedal car; *model railway*, train set, model, Meccano, Lego; *blood sport*, hunt, meet, fox-hunting, coursing, beagling, falconry, angling, fishing; *park*, gardens, playing field, recreation ground; *pitch*, ground, court, field, green, course; *theatre*, opera house, concert hall, dance hall, discotheque, night club, casino, bingo hall; *player*, sportsman, sportswoman, champion, grandmaster.
adj. *recreational*, sporting, sporty; *festive*, out to enjoy oneself, jovial, jolly;

amusing, entertaining, diverting, pleasant, enjoyable.

vb. *amuse*, entertain, divert, delight, cheer, make one laugh, tickle; *relax*, have fun, pursue, enjoy oneself, go on holiday; *have fun*, give/throw a party, have a good time, go out, celebrate, picnic, go dancing, let off steam (*colloq.*), paint the town red (*colloq.*), have a ball (*colloq.*); *camp*, climb, hike, ramble; *play games*, do sport, gamble, run, jump, jog, cycle, swim, dive, sail, ski, toboggan, skate; *hunt*, shoot, ride to hounds, course, fish, go fishing.

762 BOREDOM

See also **745** (seriousness).

n. *boredom*, tedium, monotony, sameness; *dreariness*, drabness, deadliness, dullness, banality; *stodginess*, flatness, colourlessness, heaviness, slowness; *weariness*, world-weariness, languor, ennui, time to kill; *bore*, bind, chore, grind, treadmill, daily round, drag (*colloq.*); *pub bore*, buttonholer, pain in the neck (*colloq.*).

adj. *boring*, tedious, monotonous, uneventful, repetitive, repetitious, same; *dreary*, drab, deadly, dull, unexciting, uninteresting, unfunny, unimaginative; *stodgy*, flat, colourless, heavy, ponderous, slow, turgid; *plain*, prosaic, mundane, humdrum, banal, commonplace, trite, pedestrian; *long-winded*, wordy, verbose, prolix; *wearisome*, tiresome, irksome; *bored*, at a loose end, twiddling one's thumbs; *sick of*, fed up to the back teeth; *weary*, world-weary, stale, cloyed, jaded.

vb. *bore stiff/rigid*, bore to tears/to death, go on and on, never vary; *weary*, try, irk; *pall*, cloy, jade, lose its novelty.

763 BEAUTY

See also **218** (symmetry); **511** (elegance); **765** (beautification).

n. *beauty*, pulchritude, loveliness, comeliness, prettiness, good looks, handsomeness, fairness, attractiveness, shapeliness; *glamour*, sex appeal, vital statistics, attractions; *grace*, charm, elegance, chic; *grandeur*, magnificence, splendour, resplendence, radiance, brilliance, glory; *thing of beauty*, masterpiece, work of art, showpiece; *beauty spot*, view, landscape, seascape; *idol*, vision, dream, knockout, picture, fine figure of a man/woman, cheesecake (*colloq.*), beefcake (*colloq.*); *belle*, beauty queen, Venus, pin-up, stunner (*colloq.*), cracker (*colloq.*), dolly bird (*colloq.*), peach (*colloq.*), dish (*colloq.*), sight for sore eyes, dreamboat (*colloq.*), heartthrob (*colloq.*).

adj. *beautiful*, lovely, attractive, comely, fair; *pretty*, bonny, sweet, pretty as a picture; *good-looking*, handsome, husky, tall, dark, and handsome; *glamorous*, alluring, stunning, dishy (*colloq.*); *shapely*, well-formed, curvaceous, rounded, slim, slinky; *neat*, trim, well-kept, spruce, smart, natty, dapper; *graceful*, charming, exquisite, stylish, elegant, chic; *grand*, magnificent, splendid, resplendent, gracious, radiant, ravishing, gorgeous, brilliant, dazzling, glorious; *picturesque*, scenic, eye-catching.

764 UGLINESS

See also **219** (distortion); **512** (inelegance); **767** (blemish).

n. *ugliness*, hideousness, unsightliness, repulsiveness; *inelegance*, gracelessness, clumsiness; *deformity*, distortion, mutilation, defacement, disfigurement; *eyesore*, sight, fright (*colloq.*), blot on the landscape, horror, mess; *ugly duckling*, witch, scarecrow, no oil painting, plain Jane.

adj. *ugly*, hideous, unsightly, nasty, grotty (*colloq.*); *plain*, ill-favoured, frumpy, mousy; *repulsive*, horrible, ghastly, frightful, monstrous, loathsome, offensive; *deformed*, distorted, malformed, mutilated, defaced, disfigured, grotesque, misshapen; *unbecoming*, inelegant, graceless, unprepossessing, garish, gaudy; *coarse*, ungainly, cumbersome, clumsy, ill-fitting.

vb. *look a fright*, pull a face; *disfigure*, deface, mar, mutilate, distort.

765 BEAUTIFICATION

See also **510** (ornament); **763** (beauty); **766** (decoration).

n. *beautification*, face-lift, plastic surgery, skin graft, nose job (*colloq.*); *beauty treatment*, face mask, facial, manicure, pedicure; *tanning*, sun tan, sun bed, solarium; *grooming*, wash and brush-up; *hairdressing*, hair cut, trim, shave, styling, coiffure, hairdo; *short back and sides*, crewcut, pageboy, bouffant, Afro, Mohican, fringe, curls, ringlets, plait, pigtail, ponytail, bun; *shampoo and set*, perm, blow-dry, highlights, streaks; *beard*, goatee, imperial, moustache, toothbrush moustache, soup-strainer, handlebar moustache, muttonchops, sideboards, sideburns; *wig*, toupee, hairpiece, false eyelashes; *hairbrush*, comb, curlers, rollers, curling tongs, hairpin, hairgrip, kirby grip, slide, hairnet, hair dryer; *razor*, shaver, depilatory; *shampoo*, rinse, dye, henna, conditioner, hair spray, hair lacquer, hair cream; *make-up*, cosmetic, lipstick, lip gloss, eye shadow, eyeliner, mascara, rouge, blusher, foundation, moisturizer, face powder; *nail scissors*, nail clippers, nail file, nail polish; *beautician*, plastic surgeon, make-up artist, visagist, manicurist; *hairdresser*, barber, coiffeur, coiffeuse, stylist.

vb. *beautify*, prettify, improve the appearance of, dress up, primp, smarten, preen, groom, make up, titivate, doll up (*colloq.*), tart up (*colloq.*).

766 DECORATION

See also **510** (ornament); **765** (beautification).

n. *decoration*, adornment, ornamentation, embellishment, enrichment, finery; *interior decoration*, paint, wallpaper, furnishings; *flower arranging*, floral display, bouquet, posy, buttonhole, garland, wreath; *pattern*, design, detail, motif, tracery, scrollwork, check, pinstripe, herringbone, hound's tooth, polka dot, paisley; *needlework*, embroidery, tapestry, appliqué, smocking, broderie anglaise; *crochet*, lace, tatting, macramé, knitting; *trimming*, frill, fringe, tassel, braid, bead, bow, bobble, ribbon, sequin, diamante; *jewellery*, bracelet, bangle, ring, engagement/wedding ring, signet ring, necklace, pendant, locket, charm, crucifix, earring, tiara, clasp, brooch, cameo, medallion; *jewel*, gem, precious stone, diamond, ruby, pearl, opal, sapphire, turquoise, emerald, beryl, garnet, amethyst, topaz, agate, onyx, coral, jet, mother of pearl, moonstone, lapis lazuli.

adj. *decorative*, ornamental, just for show, cosmetic; *ornate*, fancy, elaborate, intricate; *gaudy*, garish, florid; *decorated*, adorned, ornamented, embellished, patterned, inlaid, enamelled, engraved, tooled, embossed, studded; *worked*, embroidered, trimmed; *festooned*, garlanded, wreathed, hung; *bejewelled*, decked out, dressed to kill, sporting.

vb. *decorate*, ornament, adorn, embellish, enrich, enhance, set off, pick out, smarten up; *bedeck*, deck out, hang, trim, festoon; *paint*, wallpaper, varnish, whitewash, grain, lacquer; *embroider*, work, crochet; *inlay*, enamel, engrave, tool, emboss, gild.

767 BLEMISH

See also **219** (distortion); **585** (imperfection); **764** (ugliness).

n. *blemish*, flaw, defect, imperfection; *smudge*, smear, blur, tarnish, rust; *mark*, spot, daub, stain, speck, blot, blotch; *crack*, chip, dent; *mole*, birthmark, strawberry mark, freckle; *wart*, carbuncle, pimple, acne.

adj. *blemished*, flawed, defective, impaired, imperfect, shop-soiled; *smudged*, blurred, tarnished, rusty; *marked*, stained, foxed, spotted; *cracked*, dented, pitted.

vb. *blemish*, flaw, spoil, impair, mar, sully, deface; *smudge*, smear, blur, tarnish, rust; *mark*, daub, stain, speck, blot; *crack*, dent, pit, chip.

768 REFINEMENT

See also **418** (discrimination); **791** (courtesy).

n. *refinement*, tastefulness, good taste,

discrimination, discernment, good judgment; *connoisseurship*, epicureanism, palate, nose, flair; *tact*, tactfulness, euphemism, civility, courtesy, delicacy; *grace*, polish, sophistication, breeding, urbanity, manners, etiquette, culture, savoir faire; *decency*, propriety, decorum, respectability; *connoisseur*, epicurean, gourmet, sophisticate, cognoscente, dilettante, amateur, aesthete, critic.
adj. *refined*, discriminating, discerning, fastidious, epicurean; *tasteful*, in good taste, appreciative, aesthetic, critical; *tactful*, delicate, civil, decorous, seemly, respectable; *graceful*, dignified, polished, sophisticated, well-bred, urbane.
vb. *have good taste*, discriminate, criticize; *appreciate*, value.

769 VULGARITY

See also **419** (lack of discrimination); **785** (showiness); **792** (discourtesy).
n. *vulgarity*, tastelessness, bad/poor taste; *gaudiness*, garishness, brashness, loudness, ostentation; *tactlessness*, uncivility, discourtesy, rudeness, crassness, boorishness, shamelessness; *artificiality*, pretension, shoddiness, kitsch; *indecency*, impropriety, indecorum, indelicacy, obscenity; *bad form*, no breeding, commonness, incorrectness; *snob*, nouveau riche, parvenu, social climber, rough diamond, cad, lout, yob (*colloq.*).
adj. *vulgar*, tasteless, in bad/poor taste, non-U, naff (*colloq.*); *gaudy*, garish, brash, loud, meretricious, ostentatious, flash (*colloq.*); *tactless*, uncivil, discourteous, rude, crass, boorish, caddish, loutish, yobbish (*colloq.*); *artificial*, pretentious, shoddy, cheap and nasty, kitschy; *indecent*, indecorous, indelicate, obscene, improper; *unpolished*, gauche, unpresentable, uncultured, unsophisticated, common.

770 FASHION

See also **72** (conformity); **502** (style).
n. *fashion*, style, mode, trend, vogue; *craze*, fad, rage, cult; *latest fashion*, latest, last word, dernier cri; *fashionableness*, stylishness, chic, elegance; *society*, fashionable society, high society, smart set, jet set, bright young things, beautiful people; *upper crust*, cream, crème de la crème; *man/woman about town*, jetsetter, leader of fashion, trendsetter, swinger, playboy, swell, dandy, toff, peacock, blood, blade, beau, debutante, deb, deb's delight (*colloq.*).
adj. *fashionable*, modish, trendy, in vogue, all the rage, à la mode, up to the minute, with it (*colloq.*), groovy (*colloq.*), swinging (*colloq.*), in (*colloq.*); *stylish*, elegant, chic, exquisite, well-dressed; *posh*, smart, classy, swish (*colloq.*); *flashy*, dashing, foppish, rakish, snazzy (*colloq.*).
vb. *become popular*, find favour, catch on; *follow the fashion*, jump on the bandwagon, move with the times, follow the crowd, keep up with the Joneses, move in the right circles, get with it (*colloq.*); *lead the fashion*, set trends.

771 AFFECTATION

See also **480** (deception); **783** (vanity).
n. *affectation*, pretentiousness, pretension; *pose*, airs, act, image, façade, front, show, bluff; *artificiality*, mannerism, sham, humbug, insincerity, put-on (*colloq.*); *boast*, boastfulness, ostentation, bragging, swanking, self-glorification; *bravado*, bluster, bombast, hot air, grandiloquence; *charlatan*, humbug, impostor, bluffer, poser, poseur; *boaster*, braggart, big-mouth (*colloq.*), show-off.
adj. *affected*, pretentious, studied, mannered, contrived, stilted; *posing*, posturing, attitudinizing, for effect, ostentatious, poncy (*colloq.*); *superficial*, insincere, hypocritical, hollow, empty; *artificial*, sham, phoney, tongue-in-cheek; *self-righteous*, sanctimonious, mealy-mouthed, prim, stuck up, snobbish; *boastful*, big-mouthed (*colloq.*), loud-mouthed; *bombastic*, blustering, grandiloquent.

vb. *affect*, pretend, put on; *pose*, posture, attitudinize, put on airs, ponce around (*colloq.*); *fake*, sham, feign, make a show of, bluff; *overact*, ham it up, camp it up; *boast*, brag, vaunt, show off, swank, strut; *bluster*, rant.

772 RIDICULOUSNESS

See also **443** (nonsense); **744** (humour).

n. *ridiculousness*, ludicrousness, laughableness, risibility, absurdity; *extravagance*, exaggeration, caricature; *mimicry*, parody, travesty; *paradox*, catch-22 situation; *buffoonery*, fooling about/around, tomfoolery, horseplay, clowning; *escapade*, monkey tricks, nonsense, scrape.

adj. *ridiculous*, ludicrous, laughable, risible, farcical, mad, daft, silly; *absurd*, grotesque, bizarre, outlandish; *monstrous*, preposterous, outrageous; *contemptible*, derisory; *extravagant*, exaggerated, over the top (*colloq.*); *paradoxical*; *tomfool*, asinine, idiotic.

vb. *go from the sublime to the ridiculous*; *play the fool*, fool/lark about/around, clown, be a laughing stock, make an exhibition of oneself, go way over the top (*colloq.*); *caricature*, mimic, parody, make a fool of.

773 DERISION

See also **772** (ridiculousness); **824** (disrespect).

n. *derision*, ridicule, mockery, scoffing, scorn; *teasing*, ribbing, leg-pulling, ragging, banter; *snigger*, titter, smirk; *irony*, sarcasm, caricature, parody, lampoon, burlesque, spoof, send-up, take-off; *butt*, figure of fun, laughing stock, fair game; *stooge*, straight man, foil.

adj. *derisive*, mocking, scoffing, scornful; *ironic*, sarcastic, satirical.

vb. *deride*, ridicule, mock, scoff, scorn, jeer; *make fun of*, poke fun at, tease, rib, chaff, rag, twit; *snigger*, titter, smirk; *fool*, kid, pull someone's leg, take the mickey out of, have on (*colloq.*); *caricature*, satirize, lampoon, pillory, send up; *deflate*, debunk, puncture.

774 REPUTE

See also **650** (trophy); **778** (title); **823** (respect); **831** (probity).

n. *repute*, reputation, good standing, good name; *regard*, esteem, admiration, estimation; *favour*, good odour, popularity; *prestige*, glory, acclaim, honour, kudos, cachet, dignity, illustriousness; *eminence*, prominence, distinction, position, status; *renown*, fame, celebrity; *reliability*, respectability, trustworthiness, dependability; *worthy*, somebody, dignitary, pillar of society, doyen, leading light, celebrity, star, luminary, grand old man.

adj. *reputable*, of good repute, estimable, worthy, meritorious, admirable; *esteemed*, highly regarded, well thought of, highly acclaimed, celebrated, of note; *reliable*, trustworthy, dependable; *famous*, renowned, celebrated; *in favour*, popular; *illustrious*, eminent, prominent, distinguished, of distinction, leading, ranking, prestigious, august; *grand*, imposing, dignified, majestic, royal, regal, princely, lordly, superior, noble, aristocratic.

vb. *have a reputation*, have one's position to consider, command respect, be looked up to, go down in history; *gain a reputation*, do oneself credit, win one's spurs, gain recognition, make one's mark; *rank*, excel, shine, star; *outshine*, overshadow, eclipse; *respect*, pay respect to, regard, esteem, honour, look up to, admire; *praise*, acclaim, glorify, lionize, revere, put on a pedestal; *prize*, value, treasure; *reward*, crown, enthrone, ennoble, elevate to the peerage; *beatify*, canonize, deify, worship.

775 DISREPUTE

See also **824** (disrespect); **832** (improbity).

n. *disrepute*, ill repute, bad name, discredit; *notoriety*, infamy; *disfavour*, unpopularity, bad odour; *unreliability*, untrustworthiness; *disparagement*, slur, slight; *opprobrium*, disgrace, humiliation, shame, dishonour, ignominy, obloquy; *smear*, stain, tarnish, blot, slur; *scandal*, calumny, gossip, slander, defamation, libel.

adj. *disreputable*, shady, shifty; *notorious*, infamous; *unreliable*, untrustworthy; *questionable*, dubious, doubtful; *humiliating*, degrading, infra dig; *despised*, held in contempt; *despicable*, mean, base; *inglorious*, shameful, dishonourable, ignominious, disgraceful; *disgraced*, humiliated; *shabby*, squalid, scruffy; *obscure*, unknown, unheard-of.

vb. *bring into disrepute*, take away one's good name, disparage, tarnish, smear, cast aspersions on, blot, sully, mar, taint, blemish, dishonour, bring shame upon, disgrace, discredit, put to shame, expose, cut down to size (*colloq.*), take down a peg (*colloq.*); *fall into disrepute*, disgrace oneself, get a bad name, blot one's copybook, lose one's reputation, come down in the world, lose face; *stoop*, lower oneself, demean oneself, degrade oneself.

776 ARISTOCRAT

n. *aristocrat*, nobleman, noblewoman, noble, titled person, noble lord/lady, peer, peeress, peer of the realm, hereditary peer, life peer; *lords temporal*, duke, archduke, duchess, marquis, marquess, marchioness, earl, count, countess, viscount, viscountess, baron, baroness, baronet, dowager; *lords spiritual*, archbishop, bishop; *knight*, dame, don, squire, laird, Junker, boyar, grandee, patrician, grande dame; *king*, queen, prince, princess, monarch, sovereign, emperor, tsar, sultan, rajah, nawab, nabob, sheikh, emir, bey, khan; *aristocracy*, nobility, gentry, landed gentry, peerage, elite, privileged class, ruling class, establishment, high society, upper classes, upper crust (*colloq.*), toff (*colloq.*), nob (*colloq.*), Sloane Ranger, hooray Henry; *royalty*, court; *nobility*, high birth, blue blood, descent, ancestry, family, house, dynasty, caste, pedigree; *rank*, distinction, position, station, majesty, prerogative, privilege.

adj. *aristocratic*, noble, titled, in Burke's Peerage, ducal, baronial; *of high birth*, well-born, blue-blooded, of good family, patrician; *royal*, regal, monarchical, majestic, kingly, queenly, princely, of royal blood; *upper-class*, respectable, top-drawer (*colloq.*), double-barrelled, posh, county, U.

777 COMMONER

n. *commoner*, pleb, plebeian, citizen; *ordinary person*, Joe Bloggs, John Doe, man in the street, man on the Clapham omnibus, common man; *worker*, housewife, blue-collar worker, white-collar worker; *nobody*, nonentity; *peasant*, yeoman, villein, serf, yokel, country bumpkin, country cousin; *tramp*, down-and-out, vagabond, bum, hobo, vagrant, outcast, untouchable; *commonality*, commons, bourgeoisie, citizenry, the people, populace, community, general public, the masses, the rank and file, hoi polloi, proletariat, Tom, Dick, and Harry; *rabble*, herd, mob, riffraff, scum, dregs of society, the great unwashed (*colloq.*); *middle class*, bourgeoisie, salaried classes, professional classes, yuppies (*colloq.*), intelligentsia; *lower classes*, working class, lower orders, have-nots, underdogs, poor whites, the underprivileged; *underworld*, demi-monde.

adj. *common*, average, ordinary; *working-class*, plebeian, proletarian; *middle-class*, (petit) bourgeois, upwardly mobile, suburban, provincial, gentrified; *lowly*, obscure, humble, mean, low, base.

778 TITLE

See also 774 (repute).

n. *title*, honorific, courtesy title, designation, handle (*colloq.*); *Majesty*, Royal Highness, Excellency, Grace, Lordship, Ladyship, my lord, my lady, Honourable, Right Honourable, Sir, Lady, Honour, Worship, Worshipful, Reverence; *Reverend*, Very Reverend, Right Reverend, Most Reverend, Monsignor, Holiness, padre; *Brother*, Sister, Reverend Father, Reverend Mother; *sir*, madam, ma'am, mister, Mr, mistress, Mrs, Miss, Ms; *monsieur*, madame, mademoiselle; *Herr*,

Frau, Fräulein; *señor*, señora, señorita; *signore*, signora, signorina; *sahib*, memsahib, bwana, effendi; *comrade*, brother, sister, tovarisch; *academic title*, bachelor, master, doctor, professor.

779 PRIDE

See also **783** (vanity).

n. *pride*, self-esteem, self-respect, self-regard, dignity, reputation; *haughtiness*, condescension, disdain, arrogance, insolence; *snobbery*, conceit, vainglory, self-glorification, big-headedness; *proud person*, snob, swank, prima donna, his nibs, Lord/Lady Muck.

adj. *proud*, self-respecting, house-proud; *lofty*, dignified, commanding, stately; *haughty*, condescending, patronizing, high-and-mighty; *disdainful*, arrogant, overbearing; *conceited*, vainglorious, big-headed, swollen-headed, strutting; *snobbish*, toffee-nosed (*colloq.*), stuck-up (*colloq.*), uppity (*colloq.*).

vb. *be proud*, etc., have one's pride, hold one's head high, stand erect, take pride in, pride oneself on; *be too proud*, give oneself airs, strut, be up on one's high horse; *disdain*, despise, condescend, patronize.

780 HUMILITY

See also **577** (unimportance); **782** (servility); **784** (modesty).

n. *humility*, humbleness, meekness, resignation; *self-abasement*, self-effacement, modesty, unpretentiousness; *lowliness*, inoffensiveness; *servility*, submissiveness, subservience, obedience.

adj. *humble*, meek, resigned; *self-abasing*, self-effacing, modest, unpretentious, unassuming; *lowly*, inoffensive, harmless; *servile*, submissive, subservient, obedient.

vb. *humble oneself*, resign oneself, turn the other cheek; *condescend*, deign, stoop, lower oneself, demean oneself; *submit*, crawl, eat humble pie, knuckle under.

781 INSOLENCE

See also **824** (disrespect).

n. *insolence*, effrontery, impudence, impertinence, rudeness, incivility; *nerve*, cheek (*colloq.*), gall, neck (*colloq.*), sauce (*colloq.*), lip (*colloq.*); *audacity*, temerity, boldness; *shamelessness*, blatancy, brazenness; *arrogance*, presumption; *disdain*, contempt; *upstart*, young pup (*colloq.*), whippersnapper, smart aleck, cheeky devil (*colloq.*).

adj. *insolent*, impudent, impertinent, rude, uncivil, impolite, offensive; *cheeky*, fresh, offhand, flippant, pert, familiar, cocky (*colloq.*), cocksure; *audacious*, bold, defiant; *shameless*, blatant, brazen; *arrogant*, presumptuous; *disdainful*, contemptuous, high-handed, imperious, snotty (*colloq.*).

vb. *get fresh*, have the cheek/nerve to, make bold to, make free with; *answer back*, cheek (*colloq.*); *get above oneself*, step out of line, presume, lord it, come the high and mighty with (*colloq.*); *express contempt*, snort, cock a snook, snap one's fingers at, give a V-sign.

782 SERVILITY

See also **642** (submission); **780** (humility).

n. *servility*, deference, compliance, subservience; *timeserving*, ingratiation, sycophancy, obsequiousness, fawning, crawling, bowing and scraping, bootlicking, arse-licking (*vulg.*), brown-nosing (*vulg.*); *sycophant*, toady, timeserver, Uriah Heep, crawler, bootlicker, arse-licker (*vulg.*), yes-man, smoothie (*colloq.*), lapdog.

adj. *servile*, deferential, compliant, subservient; under the thumb (*colloq.*); *timeserving*, ingratiating, sycophantic, obsequious, smarmy (*colloq.*); *fawning*, crawling, whining, grovelling.

vb. *toady*, ingratiate oneself, fawn, crawl, grovel, curry favour, lick the boots of, suck up to (*colloq.*), lick the arse of (*vulg.*), brown-nose (*vulg.*); *comply*, kowtow, defer, tug one's forelock; *fetch and carry for*, stooge, pander to.

783 VANITY

See also **431** (overestimation); **771** (affectation); **779** (pride).

n. *vanity*, immodesty, conceit, self-importance, egotism, megalomania; *self-congratulation*, self-glorification, smugness, superciliousness, arrogance; *narcissism*, self-worship, self-love; *boastfulness*, boasting, showing off, exhibitionism; *egotist*, show-off, exhibitionist, peacock, Narcissus, God's gift to women (*colloq.*).

adj. *vain*, immodest, conceited, self-important, egotistical, megalomaniac; *self-satisfied*, complacent, smug, supercilious, arrogant, stuck-up (*colloq.*); *narcissistic*, full of oneself; *dogmatic*, opinionated; *cocky*, bumptious, pretentious, pompous, swollen-headed, big-headed, too big for one's boots (*colloq.*).

vb. *have a high opinion of oneself*, think a lot of oneself, be puffed up, think one knows it all, fish for compliments; *get above oneself*, get too big for one's boots (*colloq.*); *show off*, strut, put on airs, talk big, blow one's own trumpet; *go to one's head*, turn one's head.

784 MODESTY

See also **432** (underestimation); **780** (humility).

n. *modesty*, unpretentiousness, unassuming nature, unobtrusiveness, meekness, reserve, restraint; *shyness*, diffidence, timidity, bashfulness, reticence, reluctance; *prudishness*, demureness, coyness, inhibition; *chastity*, virtue; *mouse*, shrinking violet, doormat (*colloq.*).

adj. *modest*, unpretentious, unassuming, unobtrusive; *unassertive*, low-key, unimposing, unimpressive; *meek*, reserved, restrained, self-effacing; *shy*, diffident, timid, retiring, bashful, reticent, sheepish, reluctant, backward in coming forward (*colloq.*), wet (*colloq.*); *prudish*, blushing, demure, coy, inhibited; *chaste*, virtuous.

vb. *be modest*, efface oneself, hide one's light under a bushel, take a back seat, keep a low profile, keep in the background, play second fiddle, shun the limelight; *hang back*, hesitate, shrink, crawl into one's shell; *blush*, colour, flush, go red.

785 SHOWINESS

See also **464** (display); **769** (vulgarity).

n. *showiness*, ostentation, ostentatiousness, blatancy, flagrancy, exhibitionism, showmanship; *flashiness*, gaudiness, glitter, tinsel, garishness, flamboyance; *effect*, window-dressing, show; *splendour*, grandeur, magnificence, brilliance; *pomp*, majesty, pageantry, parade, spectacle; *pomposity*, extravagance, bombast, rhetoric; *dramatics*, histrionics, theatre, theatricality, sensationalism; *heroics*, bravado, stunt; *showman*, exhibitionist.

adj. *showy*, ostentatious, blatant, flagrant, shameless; *painted*, glorified, tarted up (*colloq.*); *flashy*, gaudy, glittering, garish, loud, flamboyant, lurid, conspicuous; *pompous*, extravagant, bombastic, pretentious; *splendid*, grandiose, magnificent, brilliant, splendiferous (*colloq.*); *sumptuous*, de luxe; *dramatic*, histrionic, spectacular, theatrical, stagy, for show, done for effect, cosmetic.

vb. *do for show*, do for effect, put on a show, flaunt, flourish, parade; *splurge*, make a splash, pull out all the stops; *play to the gallery*, show off, take the centre of the stage, upstage, grab the limelight, make an exhibition of oneself; *give oneself airs*, swank.

786 CELEBRATION

See also **746** (rejoicing).

n. *celebration*, festivity, festivities, festive occasion, fête, ceremony, function, occasion, party, beanfeast (*colloq.*), do (*colloq.*); *honouring*, keeping, commemoration, remembrance, observance, ceremonial, solemnization, performance, ritual; *coronation*, enthronement, installation, induction, inauguration; *anniversary*, jubilee, birthday, red-letter day, centenary; *salute*, drum roll, fanfare, fireworks; *cheering*, clapping, ovation, flag-waving, tribute, appreciation;

hero's welcome, red carpet, reception committee, ticker-tape parade; *congratulation(s)*, felicitation(s), toast, compliments, many happy returns, best wishes.

adj. *celebratory*, festive, commemorative, ceremonial; *anniversary*, centennial; *congratulatory*, welcoming, complimentary.

vb. *celebrate*, honour, keep, commemorate, remember, observe, mark; *solemnize*, perform; *crown*, enthrone, install, induct, inaugurate; *come out*, pass out, graduate; *welcome*, salute, fête, chair, lionize, garland; *cheer*, clap; *praise*, pay tribute to, sing the praises of; *throw a party*, kill the fatted calf, roll out the red carpet, hang out the flags; *congratulate*, toast, felicitate, raise one's glass to, drink to the health of.

787 FORMALITY

See also **791** (courtesy); **881** (ritual).

n. *formality*, ceremoniousness, stiffness, dignity, solemnity, etiquette, correct behaviour, the thing to do, protocol, form, ceremony; *ceremonial*, procedure, ritual, drill, practice, routine; *dress*, formal dress, black tie, regalia, formal attire, morning dress, evening dress, dinner jacket, lounge suit, long dress, best bib and tucker, Sunday best.

adj. *formal*, ceremonial, ceremonious, stiff, dignified, solemn, stately; *correct*, precise, punctilious, ritual, procedural.

vb. *observe the formalities*, stand on ceremony, do things by the book.

788 INFORMALITY

n. *informality*, lack of formality, lack of ceremony; *freedom*, licence, indulgence, toleration; *nonobservance*, nonadherence, breach of etiquette, bad form, gaffe; *casual dress*, shirtsleeves, mufti, civvies.

adj. *informal*, unconstrained, relaxed, unstuffy, unceremonious, casual; *unconventional*, lax, loose, tolerant, easy, free and easy.

vb. *not insist*, waive the rules, relax, show no respect for.

789 SOCIABILITY

See also **85** (accompaniment); **793** (friendship).

n. *sociability*, sociableness, gregariousness, friendliness, affability, cordiality, conviviality, geniality, heartiness, bonhomie; *compatibility*, togetherness, companionship, comradeship; *party*, social gathering, get-together, meeting, social, soirée, at home, reception, reunion, visit, date; *dinner party*, banquet, feast, bunfight, beano (*colloq.*), barbecue, picnic; *drinks party*, cocktail party, bottle party, wine-and-cheese party, coffee morning, tea party; *dance*, ball, disco, hop, knees-up (*colloq.*); *visitor*, caller, habitué, guest; *good companion*, good neighbour, good mixer, life and soul of the party; *host*, hostess, master of ceremonies; *gatecrasher*, unwelcome guest, freeloader.

adj. *sociable*, social, gregarious, clubbable, friendly, pally (*colloq.*), affable; *cordial*, convivial, genial, smiling, welcoming; *hospitable*, neighbourly; *compatible*, companionable, comradely; *extrovert*, outgoing, hearty.

vb. *like company*, make friends easily, mix well, get along/on well with; *invite*, entertain, host, throw a party, keep open house; *visit*, call on, drop in on; *go out*, get together, party, go nightclubbing; *gatecrash*, arrive uninvited.

790 UNSOCIABILITY

See also **41** (separation); **52** (exclusion).

n. *unsociability*, standoffishness, aloofness, unapproachability; *unfriendliness*, coolness; *introversion*, shyness; *uncommunicativeness*, reticence, taciturnity; *distance*, withdrawal, isolation, separation, retreat; *loneliness*, solitude, seclusion, retirement; *confinement*, quarantine, purdah; *exile*, banishment, deportation, expulsion, excommunication; *apartheid*, segregation; *ghetto*, enclave, reserve, reservation, homeland, bantustan, concentration camp, prison; *cloister*, ivory tower, desert island, den; *hermit*, loner, isolationist, recluse, stay-at-home, monk; *leper*,

pariah, outsider, untouchable; *castaway*, outcast, deportee, outlaw, displaced person, refugee, evacuee.
adj. *unsociable*, standoffish, distant, aloof, unapproachable, antisocial; *unfriendly*, cool, unneighbourly, unwelcoming; *uncommunicative*, reticent, taciturn, unforthcoming; *introverted*, shy, withdrawn, retiring, stay-at-home; *lonely*, friendless, desolate, solitary, unpopular; *secluded*, off the beaten track, isolated, out of the way, remote, deserted, cloistered.
vb. *keep oneself to oneself*, shun company, stay at home, shut oneself up, retire, take the veil; *cut dead*, cold-shoulder, ignore, snub, rebuff; *confine*, isolate, imprison, quarantine, segregate; *exclude*, blackball, expel, exile, outlaw, excommunicate, ostracize, send to Coventry.

791 COURTESY

See also **787** (formality); **823** (respect).
n. *courtesy*, politeness, good manners, civility, graciousness; *thoughtfulness*, consideration, generosity, decency, tact, discretion; *friendliness*, kindness, kindliness, amiability; *respect*, deference, obeisance; *chivalry*, gallantry, courtliness; *etiquette*, protocol, custom, convention; *culture*, breeding, gentility, correctness, refinement, urbanity, diplomacy; *condescension*, sycophancy, flattery, ingratiation; *act of courtesy*, salutation, salute, greeting, handshake, kiss, hug, embrace, smile, wave; *bow*, nod, curtsy; *presentation*, introduction, welcome, invitation, reception, compliment, acknowledgment, toast; *favour*, good turn.
adj. *courteous*, polite, civil, gracious, good-mannered, well-behaved, on one's best behaviour; *thoughtful*, considerate, generous, decent, tactful, discreet; *friendly*, kind, kindly, obliging, amiable; *respectful*, deferential; *chivalrous*, gallant, courtly; *cultured*, cultivated, well-bred, genteel, correct, refined, urbane, diplomatic, gentlemanly, ladylike; *condescending*, sycophantic, flattering, ingratiating.
vb. *behave oneself / well / properly*, oblige, mind one's P's and Q's, mind one's manners, not give offence; *salute*, greet, hail, raise one's hat, touch one's cap, present arms; *shake hands*, kiss, hug, embrace, smile, wave; *show respect*, bow, nod, curtsy, kiss hands; *present*, introduce, welcome, invite, receive, compliment, acknowledge, drink to, toast.

792 DISCOURTESY

See also **769** (vulgarity); **824** (disrespect).
n. *discourtesy*, impoliteness, bad manners, incivility; *rudeness*, disrespect, insolence, impudence, cheek; *act of discourtesy*, rebuff, insult, snub, abuse, rude word, rude gesture; *vulgarity*, boorishness, lack of refinement, ill breeding, coarseness; *rude person*, boor, lout, brute, yob (*colloq.*), yahoo; *unfriendliness*, brusqueness, unpleasantness, nastiness; *thoughtlessness*, lack of consideration, inattention; *misconduct*, bad behaviour.
adj. *discourteous*, impolite, bad-mannered, uncivil, unmannerly, ungracious; *rude*, disrespectful, insolent, impudent, saucy, cheeky, impertinent, obstreperous; *insulting*, abusive, offensive, crude; *vulgar*, coarse, boorish, unrefined, ill-bred, uncouth, uncultured, ungentlemanly; *brusque*, abrupt, gruff, curt, surly, churlish; *unfriendly*, unpleasant, nasty, unkind, disagreeable; *thoughtless*, tactless, inconsiderate, insensitive, cavalier, offhand.
vb. *be rude*, etc., insult, abuse, affront, outrage; *curse*, swear, damn; *snub*, ignore, cut dead, look right through, give the cold shoulder; *interrupt*, shout down; *frown*, scowl, pout.

793 FRIENDSHIP

See also **789** (sociability); **795** (love).
n. *friendship*, amity, comradeship, fraternity, fellowship, solidarity; *companionship*, togetherness, camaraderie, compatibility, intimacy, familiarity; *friendliness*, amicability, good terms, sociability, neighbourliness; *kindness*,

hospitality, warmth, cordiality, sympathy, understanding; *act of friendship*, handshake, embrace, hug, kiss; *friend*, acquaintance, companion, comrade, crony, pal, mate, chum, buddy, girlfriend, boyfriend, best friend, bosom pal, intimate, confidant, classmate, roommate, playmate.

adj. *friendly*, amicable, sociable, affectionate, warm-hearted, well-meaning, kind, benevolent; *neighbourly*, brotherly, sisterly, fraternal; *intimate*, familiar, inseparable, close, pally (*colloq.*), matey (*colloq.*); *loyal*, faithful, staunch, trustworthy, true, devoted; *cordial*, congenial, hearty.

vb. *befriend*, make friends with, strike up an acquaintance, get to know; *be friendly*, keep company with, be in with (*colloq.*), go around with, be inseparable, be as thick as thieves; *court*, date, take out, go out with, make advances, woo; *be hospitable*, entertain, welcome, greet, embrace, introduce, present.

794 ENMITY

See also **796** (hate).

n. *enmity*, hostility, aggression, antagonism; *antipathy*, dislike, hatred, animosity; *ill feeling*, ill will, acrimony, bitterness, rancour, dissension; *alienation*, estrangement, separation, incompatibility; *hostile act*, conflict, hostilities, state of war, vendetta, feud; *enemy*, foe, traitor, antagonist, opponent, adversary, public enemy, arch enemy, aggressor, invader.

adj. *inimical*, hostile, antagonistic, aggressive; *unfriendly*, aloof, cool, chilly, cold, ill-disposed; *estranged*, irreconcilable, alienated, incompatible; *opposed*, at daggers drawn, at loggerheads, on bad terms; *rancorous*, bitter, acrimonious, grudging, resentful; *disloyal*, unfaithful, traitorous.

vb. *be hostile*, have one's hackles up, snap, snarl, growl; *oppose*, be opposed to, conflict, differ, be at odds with, clash, collide, be incompatible, be worlds apart; *antagonize*, provoke, estrange, alienate, make enemies; *fight*, battle, feud; *oppress*, persecute, hound.

795 LOVE

See also **757** (liking); **800** (endearment).

n. *love*, affection, fondness, attachment, devotion, true love; *adoration*, worship, admiration, fascination; *passion*, lust, desire, amorousness, rapture, ecstasy; *infatuation*, crush (*colloq.*), first love, calf love, puppy love; *Platonic love*, friendship, fellow feeling, sympathy; *predilection*, preference, fancy; *sentiment*, emotion, feeling; *romance*, love affair, relationship, amour, liaison, intrigue, flirtation; *lovableness*, charm, endearment, appeal, attractiveness, sex-appeal, coquetry; *love-making*, courtship, proposal, suit, gallantry; *lover*, flirt, philanderer, paramour, mistress, suitor, beau, escort; *boyfriend*, girlfriend, fiancé, fiancée, date, blind date, steady (*colloq.*), fella (*colloq.*), bird (*colloq.*); *admirer*, fan, aficionado, idol, hero, flame, heart-throb; *loved one*, soul mate, darling, intimate, sweetheart, valentine.

adj. *loving*, fond, affectionate, tender; *romantic*, sentimental, emotional; *devoted*, adoring, admiring; *passionate*, lustful, amorous, ardent; *infatuated*, besotted, crazy about, lovesick; *enamoured*, attracted, keen on, in love; *lovable*, endearing, adorable, lovely, appealing, attractive, seductive, desirable, captivating, enchanting; *beloved*, loved, cherished, adored, darling, pet; *erotic*, sexy, erogenous, amatory.

vb. *love*, like, be fond of, fancy, care for, be partial to, delight in; *cherish*, hold dear, treasure, prize, value, esteem; *adore*, worship, admire, revere; *be in love*, dote on, be crazy about, lose one's heart, be swept off one's feet, be infatuated, have a crush on; *desire*, long, yearn; *make love*, have intercourse, have sex, have it off (*colloq.*), sleep with, sleep together; *attract*, appeal, allure, bewitch, charm, enchant, captivate, fascinate, enrapture; *seduce*, woo, set one's cap at, flirt, philander; *rouse*, stir, excite, turn on (*colloq.*).

796 HATE

See also **758** (dislike); **794** (enmity).

n. *hate*, hatred, loathing, detestation, abhorrence; *repugnance*, revulsion, repulsion, disgust; *aversion*, antipathy, dislike, disfavour, odium; *animosity*, antagonism, hostility, ill feeling; *malevolence*, malice, spite, scorn, grudge; *phobia*, prejudice, bête noire, pet hate; *anathema*, abomination, menace, pest, bugbear.

adj. *hateful*, odious, detestable, obnoxious, loathsome, abhorrent, execrable, accursed, abominable; *repugnant*, revolting, repellent, disgusting, vile, nasty, horrid, beastly; *hostile*, antagonistic, averse, set against; *malicious*, malignant, malevolent, spiteful, vicious, vindictive, rancorous.

vb. *hate*, loathe, detest, abhor, abominate, recoil at; *reject*, spurn, refuse, object to, spit upon; *condemn*, denounce, execrate; *resent*, dislike, bear a grudge, have a down on, have it in for (*colloq.*); *antagonize*, alienate, estrange, set by the ears; *embitter*, poison, exacerbate, sour.

797 MARRIAGE

n. *marriage*, matrimony, conjugality, wedlock, union, alliance, match; *monogamy*, bigamy, polygamy, second marriage, open marriage, marriage of convenience, shotgun wedding, arranged marriage; *wedding*, nuptials, marriage ceremony, wedding service, civil marriage, church wedding, elopement; *reception*, wedding breakfast, marriage feast, honeymoon, anniversary; *bridal party*, best man, bridesmaid, matron of honour, page, attendant, usher; *married couple*, the happy couple, newlyweds, honeymooners, bridegroom, bride, spouse, partner, mate, husband, wife, better half (*colloq.*), trouble and strife (*colloq.*); old man, old lady, old dutch, common-law husband/wife; *matchmaker*, marriage bureau, lonely hearts column, computer dating.

adj. *matrimonial*, marital, conjugal, nuptial, connubial, premarital; *married*, wed, united, newlywed, engaged; *marriageable*, nubile, eligible, suitable.

vb. *marry*, wed, espouse, remarry, intermarry; *get married*, get spliced (*colloq.*), get hitched (*colloq.*), make an honest woman of (*colloq.*), become one, plight one's troth, say 'I do'; *join*, unite, pronounce man and wife; *give in marriage*, give away, marry off, matchmake; *honeymoon*, go away, elope, consummate; *marry well*, find a good match, marry into.

798 DIVORCE; WIDOWHOOD

n. *divorce*, annulment, dissolution of marriage, decree nisi, decree absolute, breakdown of marriage, broken marriage; *separation*, living apart, desertion; *divorce court*, maintenance, alimony, divorcee, corespondent, single parent, broken home; *widowhood*, widow, widower, survivor, relict, dowager, war widow, grass widow, golf widow.

adj. *divorced*, separated, on the rocks, living apart, widowed.

vb. *divorce*, get divorced, separate, split up; *leave*, walk out on, desert.

799 CELIBACY

n. *celibacy*, single state, bachelorhood, spinsterhood; *virginity*, maidenhood, chastity, purity; *celibate*, virgin, single person, bachelor, confirmed bachelor, misogynist, spinster, bachelor girl, old maid, maiden aunt; *monk*, nun, hermit, solitary.

adj. *celibate*, single, bachelor, unmarried, unwed, independent, free, unattached, eligible; *virginal*, chaste, pure, monastic, unconsummated.

vb. *be unmarried*, live alone, be on the shelf, take holy orders.

800 ENDEARMENT

See also **795** (love).

n. *endearment*, affection, fondness, attachment, love; *loving words*, blandishments, sweet nothings, flattery, compliments; *embrace*, hug, kiss, cuddle, stroke, caress, fondling, petting, necking (*colloq.*); *courtship*, suit, lovemaking, wooing, courting, dating; *flir-*

tation, familiarity, pass, advances, proposition; *love-letter*, valentine, proposal, offer of marriage, engagement; *darling*, dear, love, sweetheart, beloved, dearest, angel, pet, poppet, honey (*colloq.*), precious, treasure, jewel, duck (*colloq.*), chicken (*colloq.*), lamb (*colloq.*); *favourite*, teacher's pet, blue-eyed boy, apple of one's eye.

adj. *affectionate*, loving, sentimental, soppy (*colloq.*), lovey-dovey (*colloq.*).

vb. *cherish*, be fond of, love, coddle, cosset, pamper, pet, mother, spoil, spoonfeed, kill with kindness; *court*, woo, go out with, date, go steady, pursue, chase, make overtures; *make advances*, make passes, get fresh (*colloq.*), flirt, ogle, make eyes, leer, proposition; *hug*, embrace, cuddle, clasp, snuggle, nuzzle, kiss, neck (*colloq.*), snog (*colloq.*), smooch (*colloq.*), stroke, fondle, caress, pet; *trifle*, dally, toy, play fast and loose, philander; *propose*, pop the question (*colloq.*), get engaged.

801 CURSE

See also **806** (malevolence).

n. *curse*, malediction, evil eye, spell; *execration*, vilification, abuse, calumny, threat, vituperation, denunciation; *profanity*, oath, obscenity, swearword, four-letter word, expletive, imprecation, invective, bad language, billingsgate; *scurrility*, vulgarity, blasphemy, sacrilege, profanation.

adj. *maledictory*, vituperative, abusive; *scurrilous*, foul-mouthed, ribald, blue, indecent, obscene, vulgar, profane, blasphemous, sacrilegious; *cursed*, accursed, damned, execrable.

vb. *curse*, damn, condemn, wish ill, confound; *execrate*, fulminate, thunder against, inveigh against; *denounce*, abuse, call names, defame, vilify, vituperate, revile; *swear*, cuss, damn, blast, eff and blind (*colloq.*), swear like a trooper, blaspheme.

802 RESENTMENT; ANGER

n. *resentment*, bitterness, acrimony, rancour, spleen, gall; *displeasure*, ill humour, grudge, bone to pick, malice, animosity; *offence*, umbrage, hurt, indignity, wrong, injustice, insult, affront; *anger*, rage, fury, passion, wrath, ire, vexation, indignation, exasperation, annoyance, irritation; *tantrum*, temper, tizzy (*colloq.*), paddy (*colloq.*), outburst, huff; *quarrel*, argument, tiff, fight; *frown*, scowl, glare, black look, snarl, growl.

adj. *resentful*, bitter, embittered, rancorous, acrimonious, smarting, hurt, sore; *grudging*, jealous, envious; *angry*, cross, irate, indignant, livid, furious, enraged, incensed, fuming, hopping mad (*colloq.*), beside oneself, up in arms; *irritated*, annoyed, peeved, vexed, exasperated, infuriated; *riled*, worked up, het up (*colloq.*), shirty (*colloq.*), ratty, hot under the collar (*colloq.*), impatient.

vb. *resent*, bear malice, bear a grudge, have a bone to pick; *take umbrage*, take offence, be insulted, take exception, take amiss; *get angry*, get cross, lose one's temper, lose one's rag (*colloq.*), go mad (*colloq.*), go spare (*colloq.*), see red, throw a tantrum, blow one's top (*colloq.*), hit the roof (*colloq.*), fly off the handle (*colloq.*), explode, go up the wall (*colloq.*), go off the deep end (*colloq.*); *be angry*, rage, fume, rant, roar, thunder, fulminate, seethe, boil, make a scene; *frown*, scowl, glare, glower, growl, snarl, snap, bite someone's head off (*colloq.*); *anger*, enrage, exasperate, madden, incense, infuriate, drive mad, make one's blood boil; *annoy*, irritate, upset, aggravate, needle, nettle, goad, rankle, rile, get on one's nerves, get one's dander up (*colloq.*), rub up the wrong way (*colloq.*); *vex*, bother, harass, pester, provoke, stir, ruffle; *antagonize*, offend, affront, insult.

803 IRASCIBILITY

n. *irascibility*, irritability, short temper, limited patience, temperament, sensitivity, touchiness; *shrew*, scold, virago, termagant, battleaxe, dragon, harridan, Tartar.

adj. *irascible*, choleric, querulous, irritable, prickly, touchy, edgy, short-tempered, tetchy, ratty (*colloq.*), shirty

(*colloq.*); *peevish*, crotchety, testy, crusty, bilious, dyspeptic, cantankerous, gruff, grumpy; *sensitive*, thin-skinned, nervous, jumpy, uptight (*colloq.*); *temperamental*, moody, changeable, fractious, fretful; *snappy*, sharp, waspish, tart; *irritated*, annoyed, riled, nettled.
vb. *be irascible*, be short-tempered, be on a short fuse, snap, bark, fly at, turn on, jump down someone's throat (*colloq.*).

804 SULLENNESS

n. *sullenness*, ill humour, spleen, sourness, gruffness, sulkiness; *glumness*, discontent, melancholy, moroseness; *moodiness*, temperament, unsociability; *grimace*, pout, scowl, frown, glare, black look; *growl*, snarl, snap, snort.
adj. *sullen*, sulky, surly, churlish, curmudgeonly, cantankerous, unsociable; *disagreeable*, ill-humoured, sour, jaundiced, cross, crusty, crabby, grouchy, grumpy, stroppy (*colloq.*); *glum*, morose, mournful, melancholy, lugubrious, hangdog; *gloomy*, dismal, dark, sombre, cheerless; *moody*, temperamental, saturnine, dour; *gruff*, brusque, abrupt, irascible.
vb. *scowl*, glower, glare, lour, frown, grimace, pout, sulk; *snap*, snarl, growl, grunt; *grumble*, mutter, grouch, grouse, carp, complain; *mope*, be dejected, be unsociable.
adv. *sullenly*, with bad grace.

805 BENEVOLENCE

See also **807** (philanthropy); **809** (pity).
n. *benevolence*, kindness, kindheartedness, good will, benignity; *charity*, humanity, fellow feeling, philanthropy; *generosity*, magnanimity, altruism, selflessness; *consideration*, thoughtfulness; *pity*, sympathy, understanding, mercy, forgiveness; *good deed*, good turn, good works, service, favour, benefit; *kind person*, good Samaritan, Christian, good neighbour, philanthropist, altruist, humanitarian, reformer, well-wisher, do-gooder.
adj. *benevolent*, kind, charitable, beneficent, good, kindly, benign; *thoughtful*, considerate, well-meant, well-meaning, well-intentioned; *kindhearted*, warm-hearted, compassionate, sympathetic; *helpful*, obliging, accommodating, neighbourly; *generous*, altruistic, unselfish, philanthropic, humanitarian; *loving*, tender, affectionate, motherly, fatherly; *merciful*, tolerant, forgiving; *gallant*, chivalrous, gracious, courteous.
vb. *be kind*, have a heart of gold, be kindness itself, mean well; *do good*, philanthropize, reform; *help*, oblige, do a good turn, do a favour, render a service; *give one's blessing*, wish well, support, encourage; *comfort*, show concern, relieve, mother, nurse.

806 MALEVOLENCE

See also **808** (misanthropy); **810** (pitilessness); **836** (evil); **838** (wickedness).
n. *malevolence*, ill will, wickedness, unkindness, malignity; *malice*, spite, gall, bitterness, acrimony, rancour; *hate*, animosity, enmity, bad blood; *inhumanity*, callousness, cruelty, barbarity, ferocity, sadism, brutality, savagery, monstrousness; *severity*, harshness, ruthlessness, relentlessness, hardheartedness; *harm*, misfortune, mischief, ill turn, catastrophe, disaster; *atrocity*, foul play, outrage, act of inhumanity, violence, torture, murder; *threat*, menace, intimidation, blackmail.
adj. *malevolent*, ill-natured, wicked, bad, evil, malign, malignant, baleful, hostile; *malicious*, spiteful, catty, caustic, bitter, acrimonious, vindictive; *unkind*, nasty, mean, beastly, ungracious, unfriendly, uncharitable; *cruel*, inhuman, merciless, savage, brutal, barbarous, truculent, fierce; *harsh*, severe, ruthless, cold, callous, hard-hearted, cold-blooded, tough, intolerant; *maleficent*, venomous, treacherous; *fiendish*, devilish, diabolical, satanic, hellish, infernal; *threatening*, menacing, ominous, foreboding, impending, imminent.
vb. *be malevolent*, harm, abuse, maltreat, ill-treat, molest; *hurt*, injure, tor-

ture, torment; *victimize*, persecute, have it in for (*colloq.*), hound, harry, bully, oppress, tyrannize; *bear malice*, bear a grudge, spite; *rankle*, fester, poison; *threaten*, menace, intimidate, blackmail, hold to ransom, frighten, scare; *bode ill*, spell danger.
adv. *malevolently*, with evil intent; *spitefully*, out of spite; *threateningly*, on pain of death.

807 PHILANTHROPY

See also **805** (benevolence).
n. *philanthropy*, humanitarianism, utilitarianism; *benevolence*, humanity, altruism, dedication; public spiritedness, social conscience; *welfare state*, social work, social services, community service, voluntary work, charity, aid, benefit; *campaign*, crusade, worthy cause, good works; *philanthropist*, benefactor, humanitarian, do-gooder, missionary, voluntary worker; *altruist*, idealist, visionary, utopian; *patron*, founder, protector, guardian angel, supporter, fairy godmother, champion, backer; *kind person*, good neighbour, helper, good Samaritan, saint, angel.
adj. *philanthropic*, humanitarian, humane, altruistic, charitable; *enlightened*, liberal, reforming, public-spirited.
vb. *be charitable*, be public-spirited, do good, have a social conscience.

808 MISANTHROPY

n. *misanthropy*, hatred of mankind, misogyny, unsociability, cynicism; *selfishness*, egotism; *misanthrope*, misogynist, man-hater, woman-hater; *loner*, solitary, cynic, egotist.
adj. *misanthropic*, antisocial, unsociable, cynical.
vb. *misanthropize*, lose faith in human nature.

809 PITY

See also **805** (benevolence).
n. *pity*, compassion, charity, humanity, benevolence, soft-heartedness, warmheartedness, understanding, tenderness; *sympathy*, empathy, condolence, fellow feeling, commiseration, comfort, solace, consolation, relief; *mercy*, forbearance, forgiveness, clemency, grace, favour, quarter, second chance; *remorse*, compunction, regret.
adj. *pitying*, sympathetic, comforting, sorry, consoling; *compassionate*, kind, charitable, tender, understanding, softhearted; *merciful*, forbearing, forgiving, lenient, clement, gracious, generous, lax; *pitiful*, piteous, pitiable, pathetic, heart-rending.
vb. *pity*, sympathize, feel for, commiserate, grieve with, weep for, console, comfort, support; *show mercy*, pardon, forgive, spare, reprieve, give a second chance, take pity on, relent, unbend, relax; *ask for mercy*, plead with, move to pity, disarm, melt, thaw.

810 PITILESSNESS

See also **806** (malevolence).
n. *pitilessness*, hardness of heart, callousness, mercilessness, pound of flesh, heartlessness, inhumanity, cruelty, ruthlessness, implacability, relentlessness, remorselessness.
adj. *pitiless*, unfeeling, heartless, impassive, unmoved, cold, unsympathetic, cold-blooded; *relentless*, unrelenting, unbending, inflexible, inexorable, remorseless; *severe*, harsh, hardhearted, stony-hearted, callous, brutal; *merciless*, unforgiving, unmerciful, barbarous, vindictive, vengeful, ruthless, implacable.
vb. *be pitiless*, harden one's heart, give no quarter, turn a deaf ear to, stop at nothing, persecute, avenge.

811 GRATITUDE

n. *gratitude*, gratefulness, thankfulness, appreciation, indebtedness, sense of obligation; *thanks*, thank-you, thank-you letter, leaving present, reward, tip; *acknowledgment*, tribute, credit, recognition, praise, vote of thanks; *thanksgiving*, blessing, benediction, grace, prayer.
adj. *grateful*, thankful, appreciative; *indebted*, obliged, beholden; *gratified*, pleased.
vb. *be grateful*, be in someone's debt, appreciate, receive with open arms,

never forget; *thank*, say thank-you, reward, tip; *requite*, repay, return a favour; *acknowledge*, pay tribute, recognize, praise, applaud; *give thanks*, say grace.

adv. *gratefully*, with thanks.

812 INGRATITUDE

n. *ingratitude*, ungratefulness, lack of appreciation, thanklessness; *thoughtlessness*, selfishness, rudeness, grudging thanks, thankless task, ungrateful wretch.

adj. *ungrateful*, begrudging, unappreciative; *unmindful*, forgetful, selfish, rude, discourteous; *thankless*, unrewarding, unprofitable; *unthanked*, unrewarded, unacknowledged, without credit, unrequited.

vb. *be ungrateful*, show ingratitude, not thank, take for granted, presume upon.

813 FORGIVENESS

See also **660** (leniency); **809** (pity).

n. *forgiveness*, pardon, reprieve, amnesty, indemnity; *mercy*, grace, indulgence, forbearance, patience; *absolution*, remission, acquittal, release, discharge; *exoneration*, exculpation; *reconciliation*, redemption, rehabilitation, atonement.

adj. *forgiving*, merciful, lenient, forbearing, long-suffering, patient; *forgiven*, pardoned, absolved, acquitted, released, excused, let off; *reconciled*, restored, taken back, redeemed, rehabilitated, reinstated; *pardonable*, forgivable, excusable, venial.

vb. *forgive*, pardon, reprieve, grant amnesty to; *show mercy*, forbear, tolerate, bear with, relent, unbend, soften; *absolve*, remit, acquit, clear, discharge, excuse, justify; *exonerate*, exculpate; *ignore*, disregard, shut one's eyes to, wink at, overlook, condone, let pass; *be reconciled*, make it up, forgive and forget, bury the hatchet, let bygones be bygones, redeem; *ask forgiveness*, beg pardon, atone.

814 ATONEMENT

See also **641** (retaliation); **841** (penitence).

n. *atonement*, amends, reparation, indemnity, compensation, redress, satisfaction, repayment, restitution, requital, retribution; *propitiation*, reconciliation, appeasement, redemption, offering, sacrifice, scapegoat, substitute, representative; *expiation*, purgatory, penance, confession, shrift; *repentance*, apology, penitence.

adj. *atoning*, indemnificatory, compensatory, making amends; *propitiatory*, reconciliatory, appeasing, sacrificial, redemptive, representative, vicarious; *penitential*, penitentiary; *apologetic*, sorry, penitent, repentant.

vb. *atone*, make amends, make reparation, indemnify, compensate, redress, repay, requite, give satisfaction; *propitiate*, conciliate, reconcile, appease, apologize, beg pardon, satisfy, offer sacrifice; *expiate*, redeem, do penance, suffer purgatory.

815 JEALOUSY

n. *jealousy*, distrust, mistrust, suspicion, doubt, watchfulness, possessiveness; *envy*, resentment, hostility, unfaithfulness; *rivalry*, competition, competitiveness; *rival*, competitor, eternal triangle.

adj. *jealous*, suspicious, distrustful, possessive, watchful; *envious*, resentful, jaundiced, sour.

vb. *be jealous*, mistrust, distrust, suspect, doubt; *envy*, resent.

816 ENVY

n. *envy*, covetousness, desire, resentment, ill will, spite.

adj. *envious*, covetous, jealous, green with envy, grudging.

vb. *envy*, covet, desire, crave, lust after, hanker, grudge, begrudge.

817 RIGHT

n. *right*, rightfulness, what is right, obligation, duty; *lawfulness*, legality, legitimacy; *justice*, fairness, equity, impartiality, fair play, square deal, equality; *reward*, redress, retribution, just deserts, nemesis, poetic justice; *suitability*, fitness, propriety, etiquette, conformity; *morality*, virtue, decency, rectitude, integrity, probity.

adj. *right*, correct, accurate, precise, true, valid; *appropriate*, suitable, fitting, fit, apt, proper; *lawful*, legitimate, legal, rightful; *just*, fair, equitable, objective, unprejudiced, impartial, unbiased, disinterested, dispassionate, neutral, detached; *honest*, upright, straight, righteous, unimpeachable, straightforward, fair-minded, decent, sporting; *justifiable*, excusable, forgivable.

vb. *be just*, be fair, play the game, do the right thing, see fair play; *be in the right*, have grounds for, have cause to; *put right*, rectify, redress, remedy, mend, reform.

adv. *right*, rightly, equally, fairly, without distinction, without fear or favour.

818 WRONG

n. *wrong*, wrongness, wrongfulness, irregularity; *injustice*, inequity, unfairness; *partiality*, partisanship, prejudice, discrimination, bias, favouritism, preferential treatment, nepotism, old school tie; *grievance*, injury, mischief, foul play, raw deal; *disgrace*, shame, dishonour, slur; *sin*, vice, crime, misdeed, offence, trespass.

adj. *wrong*, wrongful, unreasonable, abnormal, irregular; *unfair*, unjust, inequitable, unsportsmanlike, not cricket (*colloq.*), below the belt; *partial*, partisan, biased, prejudiced, uneven, unbalanced, weighted, one-sided; *incorrect*, inaccurate, erroneous, imprecise, at fault; *injurious*, harmful; *unsuitable*, inappropriate, improper, unseemly; *illegal*, illegitimate, illicit, unlawful, criminal; *wicked*, sinful, bad, vicious, immoral; *unforgivable*, unjustifiable, inexcusable, reprehensible.

vb. *wrong*, harm, hurt, injure, maltreat; *err*, be in the wrong, be at fault; *do wrong*, break the law, transgress, infringe, trespass, cheat, not play fair, hit below the belt; *discriminate*, favour, show partiality, lean towards.

819 ENTITLEMENT

See also **715** (debt).

n. *entitlement*, dueness, due, right, privilege, prerogative; *merits*, deserts, just deserts, come-uppance, punishment, reward, compensation; *payment*, dues, fees, levy, contribution; *duty*, responsibility, obligation; *legal right*, claim, title, birthright, human rights; *bond*, security, title deed, patent, copyright; *warrant*, licence, charter, permit; *heir*, beneficiary, plaintiff.

adj. *entitled*, warranted, just, rightful, legitimate, lawful, legal, inviolable, inalienable; *due*, owing, payable, chargeable, unpaid, unsettled, in arrears, outstanding; *deserving*, worthy, meritorious, needy; *deserved*, merited, well-deserved; *fit*, fitting, right, proper, as it should be.

vb. *be entitled*, warrant, expect, have the right to; *claim*, lay claim to, insist on one's rights, exercise one's prerogative; *justify*, vindicate, exonerate, substantiate; *merit*, be worthy, deserve, earn, have it coming to one (*colloq.*), serve one right; *be due*, fall due, mature; *honour*, pay, discharge, meet an obligation; *assign*, attribute, give every man his due, acknowledge, credit, hand it to; *allot*, apportion, prescribe.

adv. *duly*, by right, by law.

820 LACK OF ENTITLEMENT

See also **272** (overstepping); **575** (excess).

n. *lack of entitlement*, absence of right, presumption, assumption, arrogation, violation; *undueness*, unfittingness, gratuitousness; *disentitlement*, dispossession, forfeiture, disqualification, disestablishment; *usurper*, pretender, impostor, squatter.

adj. *unentitled*, unqualified, unauthorized, presumptuous, without rights; *undue*, unwarranted, uncalled-for, unnecessary, gratuitous; *immoderate*, excessive; *undeserved*, unmerited, unjust, unfair; *undeserving*, unworthy; *improper*, unseemly, inappropriate; *spurious*, false, would-be, fictitious,

bogus; *invalid*, forfeit, illicit, illegal, illegitimate.
vb. *not be entitled to*, have no right to, presume, arrogate, overstep the mark, take liberties, go too far; *usurp*, violate, trespass, encroach, infringe; *disentitle*, disqualify, invalidate, disfranchise, disestablish, expropriate, dispossess, depose.

821 DUTY

See also **683** (promise).
n. *duty*, obligation, responsibility, onus, liability, burden; *commitment*, pledge, promise, contract, engagement, debt, bond, tie, call of duty; *conscience*, sense of duty, moral obligation, moral imperative; *loyalty*, faithfulness, fealty, allegiance; *discharge of duty*, performance, acquittal, observance; *task*, commission, office, charge, station, profession; *precept*, code of duty, morality, ethics.
adj. *liable*, responsible, accountable, answerable, subject to; *obliged*, duty-bound, under obligation; *obligatory*, incumbent, mandatory, compulsory, binding, inescapable, unconditional, categorical; *dutiful*, conscientious, obedient, compliant, submissive, tractable; *ethical*, moral, honourable, decent.
vb. *be the duty of*, fall to, rest with, devolve on, be responsible for, should, ought, had better, behove; *commit oneself*, pledge oneself, engage, shoulder responsibility; *do one's duty*, discharge, fulfil, perform, acquit oneself, honour, pay; *oblige*, bind, saddle with, put under an obligation; *impose a duty*, require, detail, order, call upon, enjoin, look to, expect.

822 EXEMPTION

See also **605** (escape); **857** (acquittal).
n. *exemption*, immunity, nonliability, impunity; *exception*, privilege, special treatment; *freedom*, release, liberation, dispensation, absolution, acquittal, pardon; *permission*, leave, liberty, licence, charter, franchise.
adj. *exempt*, nonliable, immune, not subject to, free, clear; *privileged*, unaccountable, unaffected, independent; *unrestricted*, unbound, unrestrained, uncontrolled.
vb. *exempt*, free, clear, set apart, exclude; *excuse*, exonerate, exculpate, acquit, let off; *absolve*, pardon, forgive; *release*, lift restrictions, grant impunity, liberate; *be exempt*, get off scot-free, get away with it, get away with murder (*colloq.*); *shrug off*, shift the blame, pass the buck (*colloq.*), wash one's hands of.

823 RESPECT

See also **774** (repute); **791** (courtesy).
n. *respect*, regard, esteem, consideration, honour, high opinion, appreciation, favour; *repute*, high standing, authority; *admiration*, worship, veneration, adoration, hero-worship, awe; *praise*, reverence, homage, deference, humility, devotion; *respects*, regards, greeting, salutation, salute; *bow*, curtsy, red carpet, guard of honour.
adj. *respectful*, courteous, polite, ceremonious; *admiring*, awestruck; *reverential*, deferential, standing, kneeling, prostrate; *humble*, submissive, obsequious, servile; *respected*, well thought of, highly regarded, reputable, valued, appreciated, esteemed, venerable, time-honoured; *important*, impressive, imposing, authoritative.
vb. *respect*, think well of, regard highly, have a high opinion of, hold dear, value, appreciate, honour; *admire*, think the world of, take off one's hat to (*colloq.*), revere, look up to, hero-worship, put on a pedestal, pay homage, defer to; *praise*, extol, exalt, pay tribute, lionize; *pay one's respects*, greet, welcome, salute, drink to, toast; *show respect*, bow, curtsy, kneel, scrape, grovel, kowtow, be humble, submit; *command respect*, impress, impose, awe, overawe, overwhelm, humble.

824 DISRESPECT

See also **773** (derision); **781** (insolence); **792** (discourtesy).
n. *disrespect*, irreverence, discourtesy,

impoliteness; *dishonour*, disrepute; *contempt*, scorn, disdain, disparagement, low opinion, low esteem, disapprobation; *insult*, affront, slight, sneer, snub, rebuff, indignity, humiliation, degradation; *ridicule*, mockery, derision, taunt, jeer, hiss, catcall, boo.

adj. *disrespectful*, irreverent, discourteous, impolite, rude; *neglectful*, negligent; *dishonourable*, humiliating, degrading; *contemptible*, disreputable, despicable, worthless, shameful, base; *contemptuous*, scornful, supercilious, haughty, disdainful; *insulting*, offensive, pejorative, slighting, cutting; *impertinent*, cheeky, saucy, insolent, insubordinate; *offhand*, airy, breezy, cavalier.

vb. *have no respect for*, hold in contempt, have no time for; *underrate*, underestimate; *scorn*, despise, look down on, disdain, look down one's nose at (*colloq.*), disparage, denigrate, belittle; *taunt*, mock, scoff, deride, jeer at, sneer at, laugh at, ridicule; *insult*, offend, affront, slight, snub, rebuff, humiliate; *dishonour*, disgrace, put to shame; *show disrespect*, lack courtesy, jostle, tread on someone's toes, brush aside, ride roughshod over; *desecrate*, profane, cheapen, lower, degrade.

825 APPROVAL

See also **738** (satisfaction).

n. *approval*, approbation, satisfaction; *recognition*, acknowledgment, appreciation, gratitude; *permission*, agreement, sanction, acceptance, adoption, blessing, consent, assent, seal of approval, imprimateur; *admiration*, esteem, credit, prestige, honour, favour; *commendation*, compliment, bouquet, citation, favourable review, accolade, tribute; *praise*, adulation, eulogy, panegyric; *applause*, ovation, clapping, curtain call, encore, three cheers, acclaim; *supporter*, advocate, patron, admirer, fan.

adj. *approving*, satisfied, content, appreciative; *complimentary*, commendatory, laudatory, fulsome; *approved*, favourable, satisfactory; *commendable*, praiseworthy, laudable, meritorious, estimable, creditable, admirable, unimpeachable; *approvable*, permissible, admissible, acceptable; *popular*, well thought of, in demand.

vb. *approve*, recognize, acknowledge, favour; *agree*, allow, permit, sanction, adopt; *accept*, pass, rubber-stamp, tick, endorse; *commend*, compliment, admire, take off one's hat to (*colloq.*), pay tribute, sing the praises of, speak well of, rave about, exalt, extol, boost, puff; *overrate*, exaggerate, overestimate, inflate; *applaud*, clap, cheer, stamp, whistle, hail, acclaim, welcome, drink to; *advocate*, recommend, support, back; *win praise*, gain credit, find favour, meet with approval, pass muster.

826 DISAPPROVAL

See also **739** (dissatisfaction).

n. *disapproval*, disapprobation, nonacceptance, rejection, refusal; *dissatisfaction*, discontent, displeasure, disfavour; *disagreement*, objection, opposition, contradiction; *criticism*, hostility, fault-finding, complaint, censure, critical review, attack, diatribe; *reprimand*, reproach, blame, rebuke, reproof, black mark, brickbat, rocket, admonition, telling-off, home truths, lecture, talking to, roasting (*colloq.*); *protest*, outcry, clamour, hiss, boo, catcall, raspberry; *taunt*, sneer, irony, sarcasm, dig; *blacklist*, boycott, bar, ban; *opponent*, critic, knocker (*colloq.*), anti.

adj. *disapproving*, hostile, critical, hypercritical, censorious; *reproving*, reproachful, stern, fault-finding, captious; *disparaging*, uncomplimentary, defamatory, deprecatory, unfavourable, opposed, against; *shocked*, not amused; *caustic*, trenchant, mordant, biting, venomous; *disapproved*, disreputable, insufficient, found wanting, not good enough; *reprehensible*, blameworthy, culpable, objectionable.

vb. *disapprove*, reject, not accept, object to, protest, demur; *disagree*, frown on, oppose, not hold with, take a dim view of; *regret*, deplore, lament; *disparage*, belittle, run down, denigrate, depreciate; *criticize*, complain,

carp, find fault, pick holes, not think much of, censure, knock (*colloq.*), slam (*colloq.*), condemn, damn with faint praise; *reprove*, rebuke, reprimand, reprehend, upbraid, scold, chide, tell off, tick off, lecture, dress down (*colloq.*), tear off a strip (*colloq.*), haul over the coals (*colloq.*), carpet (*colloq.*), give a piece of one's mind; *punish*, castigate, chastise, rap over the knuckles; *reproach*, blame, incriminate, impeach; *boo*, hiss, whistle, heckle, lynch; *blacklist*, boycott, ban, bar; *be open to criticism*, get a bad name, get a bad press, incur blame, have a rough ride.
adv. *disapprovingly*, under protest, against one's better judgment.

827 FLATTERY
See also **782** (servility).
n. flattery, compliment, adulation, blandishments, blarney, soft soap (*colloq.*), flannel (*colloq.*); *insincerity*, false praise, hypocrisy, sham, eyewash (*colloq.*); *fawning*, cajolery, wheedling, obsequiousness; *flatterer*, hypocrite, toady, sycophant, yes-man, creep (*colloq.*), crawler (*colloq.*), hanger-on.
adj. *flattering*, complimentary, fulsome, adulatory; *insincere*, plausible, bland, mealy-mouthed, honeyed, sugary, saccharine; *smooth*, unctuous, smarmy (*colloq.*), slimy; *obsequious*, servile, ingratiating, sycophantic.
vb. *flatter*, compliment, praise, puff, boost, soft-soap (*colloq.*), lay it on thick (*colloq.*), overdo it; *cajole*, wheedle, coax, inveigle, suck up to (*colloq.*), sweet-talk, butter up (*colloq.*), massage someone's ego; *fawn*, court, curry favour, be servile, ingratiate oneself.

828 DISPARAGEMENT
See also **595** (damage); **639** (attack).
n. *disparagement*, depreciation, detraction, denigration, belittling; *degradation*, debasement, vilification; *defamation*, calumny, slander, libel, mud-slinging, smear campaign, character assassination; *criticism*, bad press, attack, hatchet job (*colloq.*), brickbat, knocking copy; *aspersion*, slur, stigma, brand, smear, innuendo, insinuation; *scandal*, muck-raking, backbiting, gossip; *ridicule*, caricature, skit, satire, lampoon; *detractor*, critic, knocker (*colloq.*), mud-slinger; *slanderer*, libeller, defamer; *scandalmonger*, muckraker, backbiter, gossip columnist, gutter press; *mocker*, scoffer, cynic, satirist.
adj. *disparaging*, deprecatory, derogatory, denigratory, pejorative; *defamatory*, slanderous, libellous; *contemptuous*, slighting, mocking, sarcastic, cynical, catty, snide; *caustic*, bitter, venomous, destructive.
vb. *disparage*, deprecate, detract, depreciate, belittle, play down, sell short, run down (*colloq.*); *discredit*, dishonour, defame, denigrate, blacken, vilify, malign, sully, defile, tarnish, smear, besmirch; *criticize*, slur, cast aspersions on, slight, knock (*colloq.*), pan, slate; *denounce*, decry, revile, expose, pillory; *slander*, libel, calumniate; *deride*, mock, ridicule, lampoon, satirize, guy, sneer at.

829 VINDICATION
n. *vindication*, justification, mitigation, extenuation, defence, apologia, excuse; *grounds*, right, basis, plea, alibi; *pretext*, whitewash, gloss; *exoneration*, exculpation, acquittal; *apologist*, witness, defendant, advocate, champion.
adj. *vindicating*, justifying, extenuating, mitigating, excusing; *justifiable*, arguable, defensible, plausible, allowable; *excusable*, pardonable.
vb. *vindicate*, justify, warrant, give grounds for, make excuses for; *whitewash*, varnish, gloss; *confirm*, bear out, support, show, demonstrate, prove; *uphold*, maintain, defend, plead; *exonerate*, exculpate, excuse, acquit, absolve, clear; *palliate*, mitigate, soften.

830 ACCUSATION
n. *accusation*, indictment, arraignment, prosecution, impeachment, denunciation; *charge*, allegation, complaint, imputation, incrimination, blame, censure; *insinuation*, slur, smear; *false*

charge, frame-up (*colloq.*), put-up job (*colloq.*), libel, slander, calumny, perjury; *action*, suit, case, count, plaint, citation, summons; *accuser*, plaintiff, prosecutor, accused, defendant, suspect, informer, witness.

adj. *accusing*, accusatory, condemnatory; *denunciatory*, incriminating; *defamatory*, calumnious; *accused*, charged, suspect; *accusable*, chargeable, liable to prosecution, inexcusable, indefensible.

vb. *accuse*, charge, bring charges, challenge, arraign, indict, impeach; *arrest*, book, prosecute, sue; *impute*, incriminate, blame, censure, point the finger at, lay at one's door; *denounce*, expose, inform, tell, blab (*colloq.*); *implicate*, involve; *complain*, find fault with, reprove; *slander*, libel, slur, calumniate, defame; *fabricate*, trump up, concoct, invent, frame (*colloq.*), perjure oneself, bear false witness.

831 PROBITY

See also **774** (repute); **837** (virtue).

n. *probity*, rectitude, uprightness, good character; *honesty*, integrity, truthfulness, genuineness, conscientiousness, good faith; *fidelity*, faithfulness, loyalty, reliability, constancy; *morality*, moral fibre, scruples, standards; *virtue*, goodness, purity; *honour*, nobility, chivalry; *principle*, point of honour; *honourable person*, man of honour, trusty soul, good sort, brick (*colloq.*); *good sport*, sportsman, fair play, good loser.

adj. *honourable*, upright, straight, erect, right, square; *honest*, truthful, law-abiding, incorruptible; *sincere*, frank, candid, straightforward; *loyal*, faithful, dependable, reliable, trusty, sterling, trustworthy, genuine, dutiful, conscientious; *moral*, principled, ethical, scrupulous, reputable, respectable; *fair*, just, equitable, impartial; *noble*, high-minded, idealistic, chivalrous; *virtuous*, good; *immaculate*, spotless, stainless, clean, pure; *innocent*, ingenuous, artless, guileless.

vb. *be honourable*, play fair, be in good faith, keep faith, do the decent thing; *go straight* (*colloq.*), reform.

832 IMPROBITY

See also **662** (disobedience).

n. *improbity*, dishonesty, immorality, corruption, evil, wickedness; *guile*, cunning, artfulness, disingenuousness; *dishonour*, shame, disgrace, disrepute; *disloyalty*, infidelity, faithlessness, bad faith, double standard, duplicity, double-dealing, betrayal, sell-out; *perfidy*, treachery, treason, sedition, defection; *villainy*, roguery, foul play, skulduggery; *dishonest act*, racket, fiddle, wangle, dirty tricks.

adj. *immoral*, corrupt, evil, wicked, bad; *dishonest*, deceitful, fraudulent, criminal, bent (*colloq.*), crooked; *insincere*, two-faced, disingenuous, double-dealing; *unprincipled*, unscrupulous, unethical; *disreputable*, ignominious, ignoble; *unreliable*, faithless, unfaithful, inconstant; *perfidious*, treacherous, insidious; *sly*, underhand, crafty, devious, artful, foxy, cunning; *dubious*, shady, suspicious, questionable, fishy (*colloq.*), shifty; *base*, vile, mean, shabby, abject.

vb. *be dishonest*, deceive, lie, fib, cheat, swindle, defraud, double-cross, two-time (*colloq.*), do the dirty on (*colloq.*); *betray*, sell out, sell down the river.

833 DISINTERESTEDNESS

n. *disinterestedness*, selflessness, unselfishness, self-sacrifice, dedication, self-denial, altruism, martyrdom; *magnanimity*, generosity, liberality, nobility, philanthropy; *impartiality*, indifference; *neutrality*, objectivity, non-involvement, detachment, unconcern.

adj. *disinterested*, impartial, unbiased, unprejudiced, objective, fair, just; *indifferent*, unconcerned, dispassionate; *unselfish*, selfless, dedicated, self-sacrificing, self-effacing, humble; *magnanimous*, generous, liberal, unsparing; *noble*, high-minded, quixotic, chivalrous.

vb. *be disinterested*, put oneself last, take a back seat.

834 SELFISHNESS

See also **728** (meanness).

n. *selfishness*, self-interest, egoism, egotism, self-absorption, opportunism, individualism; *vanity*, narcissism, self-indulgence, self-worship; *greed*, meanness, avarice; *egoist*, egotist, narcissist, individualist, opportunist, gold-digger; *miser*, niggard.

adj. *selfish*, egocentric, self-centred, self-absorbed, self-seeking, egoistic, egotistic; *greedy*, miserly, mean, avaricious; *vain*, narcissistic, self-indulgent, conceited; *covetous*, envious, jealous, possessive, dog-in-the-manger.

vb. *be selfish*, put oneself first, look after number one; *monopolize*, hog, keep to oneself; *look out for oneself*, be on the make, have an eye for the main chance.

835 GOOD

See also **805** (benevolence); **837** (virtue).

n. *good*, benefit, advantage, interest; *good fortune*, providence, luck, boon, windfall, godsend, pennies from heaven, treasure trove; *gain*, profit, harvest, success, prosperity, wealth; *welfare*, wellbeing, fortune, weal; *improvement*, betterment, edification; *good turn*, help, service, favour, convenience; *common good*, public weal.

adj. *good*, beneficial, advantageous, gainful; *helpful*, useful, heaven-sent; *worthwhile*, valuable, profitable; *thriving*, successful, prosperous.

vb. *do good*, benefit, favour, bless; *be useful*, avail, serve, help; *make better*, edify, improve, do one a power of good; *do well*, flourish, thrive, prosper, succeed.

836 EVIL

See also **806** (malevolence); **838** (wickedness).

n. *evil*, ill; *accident*, tragedy, disaster, catastrophe, calamity, ruin; *nuisance*, trial, affliction; *misfortune*, ill luck, crying shame, raw deal; *harm*, mischief, damage, hurt, injury, pain, anguish, distress, trouble; *wrong*, disservice, dirty trick, foul play, outrage; *wickedness*, corruption; *scourge*, pest, plague, bane; *disadvantage*, setback, hitch.

adj. *evil*, bad, ill, adverse, nefarious; *unfortunate*, catastrophic, disastrous, ruinous, calamitous; *distressing*, tragic, painful, hurtful; *wicked*, vicious, sinister, maleficent; *fatal*, fell, mortal, deadly.

vb. *do evil*, harm, damage, do mischief, do a disservice; *afflict*, ruin, trouble.

adv. *amiss*, awry, wrong.

837 VIRTUE

See also **582** (worth); **805** (benevolence); **831** (probity).

n. *virtue*, goodness, morality, uprightness, rectitude, righteousness, good behaviour; *kindness*, compassion, magnanimity; *honesty*, integrity, character, honour, probity; *temperance*, sanctity, saintliness, holiness; *purity*, chastity, innocence; *morals*, principles, ethics; *worth*, merit, saving grace; *good person*, good neighbour, salt of the earth, one in a million, good sort, brick (*colloq.*), pillar of society, saint, angel; *good example*, model, paragon.

adj. *virtuous*, good, upright, righteous, proper, moral, principled; *saintly*, angelic, holy; *kind*, kindly, generous, dutiful, conscientious, well-intentioned; *honest*, worthy, sterling, exemplary, unimpeachable; *perfect*, irreproachable, immaculate, impeccable, unblemished, excellent; *pure*, chaste, innocent.

vb. *be good*, behave oneself, have a clear conscience, set a good example, keep to the straight and narrow; *be virtuous*, resist temptation, go straight.

838 WICKEDNESS

See also **806** (malevolence); **810** (pitilessness); **836** (evil).

n. *wickedness*, vice, evil, unrighteousness, wrongdoing; *immorality*, corruption, depravity, wantonness, baseness; *iniquity*, sin, wrong, perversity, sin, transgression, trespass, offence; *outrage*, atrocity, enormity; *crime*, felony, underworld, den of vice; *malignity*, malevolence, villainy, roguery; *fault*, weakness, foible, bad habit, failing, demerit, shortcoming, peccadillo; *bad person*, wrongdoer, malefactor, evildoer, sinner, miscreant, reprobate; *scoundrel*, wretch, villain, vagabond, rogue, rascal, knave, blackguard, bounder, blighter; *bad child*, terror, imp, scamp, monkey, scallywag; *bully*, ugly customer, nasty piece of work, ruffian, thug, lout, hoodlum, tough, yobbo (*colloq.*), brute, monster, beast, savage, barbarian; *idler*, loafer, wastrel, prodigal, good-for-nothing, ne'er-do-well, layabout, bad lot, riffraff, black sheep, troublemaker, mischief-maker; *crook*, liar, cheat, conman, twister, racketeer, impostor, traitor; *criminal*, felon, lawbreaker, offender, public enemy, thief, pickpocket, housebreaker, delinquent, vandal, pirate, gangster, desperado, murderer, assassin; *rake*, profligate, pimp, wanton, hussy; *cad*, rotter, heel (*colloq.*), bastard, worm, rat, louse, swine.

adj. *wicked*, evil, bad, wrong; *immoral*, corrupt, dissolute, degenerate, perverted, depraved, indecent, wanton; *naughty*, disobedient; *wayward*, perverse; *unscrupulous*, unprincipled; *mean*, despicable, base, vile, malevolent, callous, vicious, brutal, cruel; *outrageous*, shocking, scandalous, abominable, atrocious, heinous, monstrous, unforgivable, inexcusable; *offensive*, repugnant, distasteful; *hellish*, infernal, diabolic, fiendish; *criminal*, lawless, nefarious.

vb. *be wicked*, err, transgress, do wrong; *lapse*, stray, fall, backslide, degenerate, go off the rails (*colloq.*); *misbehave*, be naughty; *make wicked*, corrupt, pervert, lead astray, defile, tempt, seduce.

839 INNOCENCE

n. *innocence*, guiltlessness, blamelessness, irreproachability, faultlessness; *clear conscience*, clean hands, clean slate; *purity*, impeccability, stainlessness, virtue; *artlessness*, inexperience, unworldliness, naivety; *probity*, integrity, uprightness, incorruptibility; *innocent*, child, babe, lamb, dove; *innocent party*, injured party.

adj. *innocent*, not guilty, not responsible, guiltless, blameless, in the clear, acquitted; *pure*, clean, stainless, spotless, unsoiled, untainted, immaculate, undefiled; *perfect*, impeccable, faultless, above suspicion, sinless, unimpeachable, incorruptible; *ignorant*, simple, unsophisticated, inexperienced, naive, unworldly, green; *guileless*, artless; *harmless*, inoffensive, innocuous; *pardonable*, forgivable, excusable.

vb. *be innocent*, have a clear conscience, have nothing to confess; *mean no harm*, know no better.

840 GUILT

n. *guilt*, blame, culpability, charge, reproach; *responsibility*, liability, accountability *criminality*, delinquency, illegality, sinfulness; *guilty conscience*, bad conscience, remorse; *involvement*, complicity; *guilty act*, crime, offence, sin, transgression, trespass, misdemeanour; *misconduct*, misbehaviour, malpractice; *indiscretion*, peccadillo, impropriety; *error*, fault, lapse, slip, blunder.

adj. *guilty*, found guilty, condemned, judged, convicted, incriminated; *wrong*, at fault, to blame, culpable, reproachable; *suspected*, blamed, censured; *responsible*, liable, answerable, accountable; *red-handed*, caught in the act, caught in flagrante delicto; *sheepish*, shamefaced, embarrassed.

vb. *be guilty*, be caught in the act, plead guilty; *find guilty*, incriminate, charge, condemn.

841 PENITENCE

n. *penitence*, repentance, change of heart, contrition, compunction, confession; *remorse*, shame, self-reproach, regret; *self-accusation*, self-condemnation; *penance*, sackcloth and ashes, hair shirt; *apology*, atonement; *penitent*, prodigal son, reformed character, convert.

adj. *penitent*, repentant, contrite, remorseful, ashamed; *regretful*, full of regrets, sorry, apologetic; *conscience-stricken*, chastened, self-reproachful, self-accusing; *reformed*, converted.

vb. *repent*, feel shame, confess, acknowledge, own up, admit, plead guilty; *be penitent*, be contrite, regret, apologize, excuse oneself; *recant*, see the light, be converted, turn over a new leaf.

842 IMPENITENCE

n. *impenitence*, noncontrition, refusal to recant, obduracy, stubbornness; *hardness*, hardness of heart, heart of stone, pitilessness; *no regrets*, no apologies; *incorrigibility*, hardened sinner.

adj. *impenitent*, unrepentant, uncontrite, unashamed, unabashed, recusant; *hard*, obdurate, insensitive, callous, stubborn; *incorrigible*, irredeemable, hopeless, despaired of, lost.

vb. *be impenitent*, have no regrets, show no remorse, harden one's heart, refuse to recant, feel no compunction.

843 SELF-RESTRAINT

See also **668** (restraint).

n. *self-restraint*, self-control, self-discipline, restraint, asceticism, temperance, moderation, abstemiousness; *self-denial*, abstinence, continence, teetotalism, prohibitionism, vegetarianism, veganism; *abstainer*, total abstainer, teetotaller. prohibitionist, vegetarian, vegan, ascetic.

adj. *self-restrained*, self-controlled, ascetic, self-disciplined; *temperate*, moderate, restrained, measured, disciplined, careful, continent; *sparing*, plain, frugal, spartan; *abstemious*, sober.

vb. *be self-restrained*, restrain oneself, exercise self-control, control oneself, contain oneself, deny oneself, ration oneself, be moderate, abstain, refrain; *watch oneself*, know when to stop, know when one has had enough, keep within bounds; *give up*, swear off, go on a diet; *be sober*, keep sober, go on the wagon (*colloq.*).

844 SELF-INDULGENCE

See also **575** (excess).

n. *self-indulgence*, intemperance, immoderation, want of moderation, lack of restraint; *excess*, excessiveness, extravagance, overindulgence; *incontinence*, lack of self control, want of self control, indiscipline, addiction; *wastefulness*, waste; *sensuality*, voluptuousness, carnality, the fleshpots; *gluttony*, debauchery, dissoluteness, dissipation; *high living*, luxury, epicureanism, hedonism.

adj. *self-indulgent*, intemperate, immoderate, unrestrained; *excessive*, unlimited, overindulgent, extravagant; *incontinent*, uncontrolled, undisciplined; *wasteful*, spendthrift, uneconomical; *sensual*, sensuous, voluptuous, carnal, bodily, fleshly; *gluttonous*, debauched, dissolute, dissipated, hungover; *high-living*, pleasure-seeking, fun-loving, epicurean, hedonistic.

vb. *be self-indulgent*, indulge (oneself), be intemperate, be immoderate, luxuriate, wallow, deny oneself nothing; *have one's fling*, paint the town red (*colloq.*), sow one's wild oats; *overeat*, eat to excess, gorge, overindulge (oneself), binge; *drink too much*, drink to excess, go on a bender (*colloq.*); *not know when to stop*, burn the candle at both ends; *lack self-control*, lack discipline.

845 FASTING

n. *fasting*, abstinence from food, fast, bread and water, hunger strike; *starvation*, hunger, malnutrition, anorexia, famishment; *dieting*, slimming, diet, war rations; *fast day*, Lent, Ramadan, Yom Kippur.

adj. *fasting*, abstinent, abstaining, not eating; *starving*, hungry, famished; *underfed*, undernourished, poorly fed, half starved.

vb. *fast*, eat nothing, go without food; *starve*, go hungry, famish; *diet*, slim, reduce weight, lose weight, go on a diet; *go on hunger strike*, refuse food.

846 GLUTTONY

n. *gluttony*, greed, greediness, insatiability, voracity, intemperance, excess, overindulgence, overeating, insatiable appetite; *glutton*, gourmand, pig, hog, locust, gannet (*colloq.*), greedy pig,

greedy guts (*colloq.*); *gourmet*, gastronome, epicure; *feast*, blowout (*colloq.*).
adj. *gluttonous*, greedy, insatiable, overfed; *ravenous*, voracious, omnivorous; *gastronomic*, epicurean.
vb. *overeat*, stuff oneself, make a pig of oneself, eat like a horse, eat out of house and home; *guzzle*, gulp down, bolt down, wolf, scoff, demolish, polish off, gobble up, devour, gorge, cram, stuff.

847 SOBRIETY

n. *sobriety*, soberness, temperance, teetotalism, prohibition, abstinence; *sober person*, moderate drinker, teetotaller, abstainer, total abstainer, prohibitionist; *Band of Hope*, temperance society.
adj. *sober*, temperate, abstinent, abstemious; *teetotal*, on the wagon (*colloq.*); *clear-headed*, in one's right mind, in possession of one's senses, stone-cold sober, sober as a judge; *sobered*, sobered up, dried out.
vb. *be sober*, be temperate, drink moderately, not drink, not imbibe; *become teetotal*, give up alcohol, sign the pledge, go on the wagon (*colloq.*), dry out; *hold one's drink*, have a good head for drink; *sober up*, sleep it off (*colloq.*), get rid of a hangover, clear one's head.

848 DRUNKENNESS

n. *drunkenness*, intoxication, inebriation, insobriety, intemperance; *alcoholism*, drink problem, dipsomania, dt's, pink elephants; *tipsiness*, a drop too much, one over the limit, one too many; *drunkard*, drunk, heavy drinker, hard drinker, alcoholic, boozer (*colloq.*), inebriate, old soak, tippler, wino (*colloq.*), dypso (*colloq.*), lush (*colloq.*); *drinking bout*, pub-crawl, booze-up (*colloq.*), bender (*colloq.*), blind (*colloq.*); *Dutch courage*, a hair of the dog that bit you; *hangover*, head, headache, morning after the night before feeling.
adj. *drunk*, intoxicated, inebriated, under the influence, the worse for drink, boozed up (*colloq.*), dead drunk, blind drunk, drunk and disorderly; *tipsy*, squiffy (*colloq.*), merry, high, befuddled, feeling no pain, sozzled (*colloq.*), sloshed (*colloq.*), tight (*colloq.*), pickled (*colloq.*), plastered (*colloq.*), woozy, stoned (*colloq.*), blotto (*colloq.*), canned (*colloq.*), legless (*colloq.*), pissed (*colloq.*), Brahms and Liszt; *seeing double*, glassy-eyed.
vb. *drink*, booze (*colloq.*), tipple, swig, guzzle, drink like a fish, hit the bottle, go pub-crawling, knock back a few, bend the elbow, drown one's sorrows, wet one's whistle (*colloq.*); *be drunk*, be merry, be tipsy, be under the influence of drink, have had one too many; *see double*, lurch, stagger, get stoned out of one's mind, pass out, crash out; *intoxicate*, inebriate, go to one's head.

849 DRUG-TAKING

n. *drug-taking*, smoking; *drug dependence*, drug addiction, drug abuse, habit, narcotism, solvent abuse, glue-sniffing; *drug*, narcotic, dope, hard drug; *joint*, reefer, shot, fix; *tobacco*, nicotine; *cannabis*, hemp, marijuana, hash, hashish, pot, grass, ganja; *cocaine*, coke, snow; *morphine*, opium, opium den; *heroin*, horse (*colloq.*), smack (*colloq.*), brown sugar (*colloq.*); *LSD*, acid, mescalin; *amphetamine*, speed (*colloq.*), bennies (*colloq.*); high (*colloq.*), buzz (*colloq.*), rush (*colloq.*).
adj. *drugged*, high (*colloq.*), stoned (*colloq.*); *stimulant*, opiate, narcotic, mind-blowing (*colloq.*).
vb. *drug* (oneself), smoke, turn on (*colloq.*), inject (oneself), mainline (*colloq.*), snort, sniff, pop (*colloq.*), take a trip.

850 MORALITY

See also **586** (cleanness); **831** probity); **837** (virtue).
n. *morality*, morals, virtue, decency, decorum, propriety, delicacy, chastity, virginity, continence, celibacy; *purity*, cleanness, cleanliness, spotlessness, untaintedness, immaculateness; *sinlessness*, perfection; *prudery*, primness, false shame, false modesty, prudishness; *prude*, prig, old maid; *Victorian*,

Puritan; *guardian of morality*, Mrs Grundy, censor; *celibate*, monk, nun.
adj. *moral*, good, virtuous, decent, honourable, decorous, demure, abstemious, platonic, continent; *pure*, clean, spotless, untainted, immaculate, innocent, sinless, perfect; *chaste*, celibate, virgin, virginal, white; *prudish*, prim, priggish, squeamish, shockable, narrow-minded, Victorian, straitlaced, puritanical, old-maidish.
vb. *moralize*, censor.

851 IMMORALITY

See also **587** (dirtiness).
n. *immorality*, indecency, shamelessness, immodesty, unchastity, looseness of morals, easy virtue, permissive society; *impurity*, imperfection, uncleanness, filthiness, taintedness, contamination, pollution, sinfulness; *lewdness*, lasciviousness, prurience, salaciousness, dissoluteness, dissipation, debauchery, licentiousness; *ribaldry*, bawdiness; *lust*, sensuality, eroticism, libido; *obscenity*, pornography, filth, smut, soft porn, blue film; *rape*, violation, indecent assault, sexual assault, incest; *promiscuity*, sleeping around (*colloq.*), dirty weekend (*colloq.*), free love, affair, extramarital relations, adultery, fornication, carnal knowledge, infidelity, unfaithfulness, eternal triangle; *prostitution*, street-walking, whoredom; *brothel*, house of ill repute, red-light district; *libertine*, lecher, womanizer, rake, playboy, stud; *whore*, harlot, tramp, trollop, slut, slag (*colloq.*), bint (*colloq.*); *voyeur*, pervert, flasher (*colloq.*), dirty old man (*colloq.*).
adj. *immoral*, amoral, indecent, wanton, shameless, immodest, unchaste, loose; *impure*, unclean, dirty, contaminated, polluted, sullied; *lewd*, lascivious, prurient, salacious, dissolute, lecherous, licentious, debauched, randy (*colloq.*); *sensual*, erotic, libidinous; *obscene*, filthy, smutty, dirty, lurid, pornographic, porno, blue; *vulgar*, coarse, risqué; *adulterous*, extramarital, illicit, unfaithful, incestuous.
vb. *be immoral*, sleep around (*colloq.*), commit adultery, fornicate, womanize; *seduce*, debauch, take advantage of; *rape*, assault, violate.

852 LEGALITY

See also **677** (permission).
n. *legality*, lawfulness, permissibility, legitimacy; *legislation*, law-making, regulation, authorization, codification, sanction, enactment; *justice*, authority, right; *law*, body of law, statute book, constitution, charter, statute, legal code, code; *ordinance*, act, edict, regulation, rule, bylaw; *jurisprudence*, science of law, legal learning; *legislator*, law-maker, jurist.
adj. *legal*, lawful, legitimate, right, just; *permissible*, permitted, allowable, sanctioned, authorized, codified, statutory, within the law, constitutional; *jurisprudential*, nomothetic.
vb. *make legal*, enact, pass, put into effect.
adv. *legally*, by law, by order, legitimately, in the eyes of the law.

853 ILLEGALITY

See also **658** (anarchy); **678** (veto).
n. *illegality*, unlawfulness, unconstitutionality, miscarriage of justice, injustice, wrong verdict, loophole; *lawbreaking*, breach of law, trespass, offence, wrong, violation, transgression, contravention, encroachment, infringement, foul play, malpractice; *criminal offence*, crime, misdemeanour, felony; *lawlessness*, street violence, crime wave, anarchy, terrorism, mob rule, gang rule; *riot*, rebellion, revolt, breakdown of law and order, chaos, disorder; *illegitimacy*, bastardy; *illegitimate child*, bastard, love child.
adj. *illegal*, unlawful, illicit, prohibited, banned, forbidden, not allowed, unauthorized, outside the law, contrary to the law, wrong; *contraband*, smuggled, hot (*colloq.*), stolen, black-market; *lawless*, anarchic, irresponsible, without law, riotous; *illegitimate*, bastard, born out of wedlock, born on the wrong side of the blanket.
vb. *be illegal*, break the law, do wrong, disobey, violate, transgress, contravene, infringe; *take the law into one's*

own hands, be a law unto oneself, stand above the law; *suspend*, annul, cancel, nullify, abrogate, void.
adv. *illegally*, illicitly, unlawfully, criminally, illegitimately.

854 JURISDICTION

See also **657** (authority).
n. *jurisdiction*, authority, control, law and order, arm of the law, direction, supervision; *responsibility*, competence, capacity, power; *executive*, corporation, administration; *domain*, range, territory; *law officer*, judge, mayor, sheriff, legal administrator; *police*, police force, constabulary; *police officer*, policeman, policewoman, constable, cop (*colloq.*), copper (*colloq.*), bobby (*colloq.*), rozzer (*colloq.*), fuzz (*colloq.*), filth (*colloq.*); *traffic warden*, meter maid.
adj. *jurisdictional*, competent, executive, administrative, directive, judiciary, judicial.
vb. *administer*, direct, supervise; *judge*, administer/dispense justice, sit in judgment; *police*, keep order, control.

855 TRIBUNAL

n. *tribunal*, court, bench, board, judicial assembly, assizes, session, council; *throne*, woolsack, seat of justice; *dock*, witness box, bar, courthouse, lawcourt.

856 LITIGATION

n. *litigation*, going to law, judicature; *lawsuit*, case, suit, action, legal proceedings; *summons*, citation, subpoena, writ, search warrant, charge, indictment; *inquest*, inquiry, hearing, prosecution, defence, affidavit, examination, cross-examination, testimony, pleadings, arguments, reasoning, summing up; *ruling*, verdict, judgment, finding, decision; *acquittal*, favourable verdict; *condemnation*, unfavourable verdict; *appeal*, retrial, reversal of judgment; *litigant*, party, suitor, claimant, plaintiff, defendant, objector, accused, prisoner at the bar, accuser, prosecutor.
adj. *litigating*, suing, accusing, litigant; *going to law*, contesting, objecting, disputing, arguing, litigious.
vb. *litigate*, go to law, appeal to law, prosecute, sue, charge, indict, bring to trial, bring to justice, bring a suit, file a suit, file a claim, petition, bring an action against; *prepare a case*, prepare a brief; *try*, hear, give a hearing to, judge, rule, arbitrate, adjudicate; *sum up*, close the pleadings, charge the jury; *pass sentence*, sentence, return a verdict, rule, find, declare, pronounce, convict.

857 ACQUITTAL

n. *acquittal*, favourable verdict, verdict of not guilty, innocence; *discharge*, reprieve, release, remission, suspended sentence, pardon, clearance, case dismissed, exoneration, exculpation, let-off (*colloq.*).
adj. *acquitted*, not guilty, guiltless, innocent, in the clear, cleared, exonerated, exculpated, vindicated; *discharged*, set free, released, liberated; *reprieved*, forgiven.
vb. *acquit*, find not guilty, declare not guilty, prove innocent, vindicate, clear someone's name; *reprieve*, pardon, absolve, forgive, clear, dismiss, grant remission, discharge, let off (*colloq.*); *release*, set free.

858 CONVICTION

n. *conviction*, unfavourable verdict, condemnation, denunciation; *death sentence*, death warrant, condemned cell.
adj. *convicted*, found guilty, condemned, sentenced; *condemnatory*, damnatory.
vb. *convict*, find guilty, prove guilty, condemn, bring home the charge, judge, sentence, pass sentence on; *punish*, denounce, damn, curse; *sentence to death*, sign someone's death warrant, put on the black cap.

859 REWARD

See also **650** (trophy).
n. *reward*, award, prize, trophy, honour, decoration, accolade, bonus, premium, tribute; *recognition*, acknowledgment, thanks; *recompense*, compensation, remuneration, fee, pay,

payment, guerdon, reparation, reimbursement; *profit*, return, gain; *tip*, gratuity, golden handshake, honorarium; *deserts*, just deserts; *reward for service*, pension; *bribe*, bait, kickback (*colloq.*).

adj. *rewarding*, profitable, worthwhile, advantageous, remunerative; *generous*, open-handed, charitable, unsparing, liberal.

vb. *reward*, award, honour, decorate, present, bestow a title, confer, grant; *recognize*, acknowledge, pay tribute, be grateful, thank, show one's gratitude; *recompense*, compensate, remunerate, pay, reimburse, redress, indemnify, make reparation; *bribe*, offer a bribe.

adv. *rewardingly*, profitably; *as a reward*, in compensation.

860 PUNISHMENT

See also **826** (disapproval).

n. *punishment*, chastisement, castigation, discipline, disciplinary action, reprimand, condemnation, reproof, correction, retribution; *penalty*, fine, damages, costs, liability; *banishment*, exile, expulsion, transportation; *prison sentence*, hard labour, solitary confinement, Borstal; *corporal punishment*, blow, clout, cane, rap, cuff, slap, smack, whip; *torture*, third degree; *capital punishment*, execution, death sentence, gallows, hanging, electrocution, decapitation, beheading, guillotining, garrotting, strangling, strangulation, impalement, crucifixion, drowning, burning; *mass execution*, mass murder, massacre, genocide, slaughter, annihilation; *martyrization*, martyrdom; *punisher*, chastiser, castigator, persecutor, torturer, inquisitor; *executioner*, hangman, firing squad.

adj. *punitive*, penal, castigatory, disciplinary, corrective; *punishable*, liable.

vb. *punish*, correct, chastise, castigate, discipline, reprimand, rebuke, sentence; *penalize*, fine, deprive, confiscate, take away, endorse one's licence; *demote*, suspend, downgrade, unfrock, cashier, reduce to the ranks; *slap*, smack, spank, wallop, cuff, clout, box on the ears, rap over the knuckles; *belt*, beat, strap, tan, cane, birch, flog, whip, whack, thrash, thrash the living daylights out of, give a good hiding; *exile*, banish, deport, transport, expel; *isolate*, ostracize, send to Coventry, outlaw; *imprison*, jail, confine; *torture*, rack, break on the wheel, tar and feather, kneecap, martyr; *execute*, put to death, kill, crucify, stone to death, hang, hang draw and quarter, behead, decapitate, guillotine, garrotte, electrocute, gas, shoot, strangle, burn alive, impale, drown, poison; *massacre*, slaughter, annihilate; *be punished*, suffer punishment, face the music (*colloq.*), take one's medicine, pay the penalty, get one's just deserts.

861 MEANS OF PUNISHMENT

See also **671** (prison).

n. *scourge*, whip, horsewhip, belt, strap, cat o' nine tails, birch, cane, stick, rod, ruler; *pillory*, stocks, ducking stool, whipping post; *prison*, jail; *instrument of torture*, rack, wheel, thumbscrew, maiden, water torture, torture chamber; *scaffold*, gallows, gibbet, noose, rope, halter, garrotte, cross, stake, bullet, poison, guillotine, axe, electric chair, gas chamber, death chamber.

862 DIVINITY

n. *divinity*, divineness, deity; *God*, godhead, Spirit, Supreme Being, Creator, Providence, Preserver, prime mover, Alpha and Omega, the Eternal, Almighty, Allah, Brahma, Buddha; *Trinity*, three in one; *Father*, Lord, Yahweh, Jehovah, King of Kings, Lord of Lords, Lord of Hosts; *Jesus Christ*, Son of God, Son of Man, Emmanuel, Messiah, Saviour, Redeemer, Lamb of God, Good Shepherd, Friend, Prince of Peace; *Holy Spirit*, Holy Ghost, Comforter, Paraclete, Dove; *supreme deity*, the gods, Zeus, Jupiter, Apollo, Mars, Hermes, Mercury, Poseidon, Neptune, Bacchus, Hades, Pluto, Eros, Cupid, Venus, Pan; *object of worship*, god, goddess, idol, false god, golden calf, mumbo jumbo, cargo cult; *divine manifestation*,

theophany, incarnation, transfiguration, glory; *divine task*, creation, preservation, judgment, mercy, grace, salvation, propitiation, atonement, redemption, mediation, intercession.
adj. *divine*, godlike; *heavenly*, celestial, sublime, ineffable; *infinite*, supreme, absolute, omnipresent, sovereign; *transcendent*, immanent, self-existent, changeless; *eternal*, everlasting, immortal, timeless; *almighty*, omnipotent, all-powerful; *omniscient*, all-knowing, all-wise; *just*, merciful; *gracious*, loving, forgiving, providential; *holy*, godly, hallowed, sanctified, sacred; *religious*, mystical, spiritual, superhuman, supernatural, not of this world.

863 SAINT

See also **872** (holiness).
n. *saint*, believer, convert, man of prayer, man of God, holy man, patron saint; *the saints*, children of God, the righteous, the just, chosen people, the elect; *follower*, disciple, apostle; *saintliness*, sanctity, beatitude; *mystic*, holy person, fakir, dervish, ascetic; *good spirit*, angel, archangel, ministering spirit, guardian angel, seraph, cherub, (heavenly) host, principalities, authorities, powers, dominions.
adj. *saintly*, sanctified, beatified, blessed, holy, pious, righteous, just; *angelic*, ministering, guardian, heavenly, celestial.

864 DEVIL

see also **876** (sorcery); **877** (occultism).
n. *devil*, Satan, the Evil One, fallen angel, Mephistopheles, Beelzebub, Prince of Darkness, Lord of Misrule, Lucifer, serpent, Tempter, Accuser, Adversary, Antichrist, Old Harry (*colloq.*), Old Nick (*colloq.*); *evil spirit*, devil, demon, unclean spirit, succubus, incubus, fiend, powers of darkness; *devil worship*, demonism, Satanism, witchcraft, black magic, voodoo; *devil-worshipper*, Satanist.
adj. *satanic*, devilish, Mephistopholean; *wicked*, diabolical, fiendish; *infernal*, hellish.

865 FAIRY

n. *fairy*, spirit, little people, fairy godmother, fairy queen; *elf*, brownie, goblin, gnome, dwarf, pixie, sprite, hobgoblin, imp, puck, leprechaun, troll, gremlin; *genie*, centaur, satyr, faun, mermaid, Lorelei, nymph, yeti, Abominable Snowman, Green Man; *fairy tale*, fair story, folklore; *ghost*, spectre, phantom, spirit, poltergeist, spook (*colloq.*), dybbuk, wraith, visitant, departed spirit, presence, zombie; *apparition*, vision, appearance; *vampire*, ghoul, werewolf, ghoul, ogre, bogey (man).
adj. *fairylike*, elfish, impish; *mythical*, imaginary; *ghostly*, spooky (*colloq.*), eerie, haunted, weird, uncanny, supernatural, phantom, ghoulish, nightmarish.
vb. *haunt*, visit, walk, return from the dead.

866 HEAVEN

n. *heaven*, paradise, bliss, glory, Abraham's bosom, heavenly city, holy city, kingdom of heaven, kingdom of God, next world, the hereafter, world to come, eternal rest, celestial bliss, presence of God, new Jerusalem, kingdom come (*colloq.*), happy hunting grounds (*colloq.*), seventh heaven, cloud nine (*colloq.*), Elysium, Garden of Eden, nirvana; *resurrection*, afterlife, rapture, glorification, translation, ascension, assumption, millennium.
adj. *heavenly*, celestial, eternal, blessed, blissful, glorious, glorified.

867 HELL

n. *hell*, underworld, lower world, nether regions, abyss, bottomless pit, inferno, everlasting fire, hellfire, lake of fire and brimstone, place of departed spirits, Sheol, Gehenna, Hades, perdition, purgatory, limbo; *judgment*, punishment, darkness, separation, destruction, wrath, weeping and gnashing of teeth.
adj. *hellish*, infernal, damned.

868 RELIGION

See also **434** (belief).

n. *religion*, natural religion, revealed religion; *deism*, theism, monotheism, polytheism, pantheism, animism, gnosticism; *religious teaching*, Christianity, Judaism, Islam, Hinduism, Buddhism, Brahminism, Baha'ism, Zoroastrianism, Zen, Confucianism, Shintoism, Taoism; *revelation*, declaration, inspiration, illumination, prophecy; *sacred writings*, truth, word of God, Holy Writ, (Holy) Scriptures, (Holy) Bible, the Good Book (*colloq.*), canon, Old Testament, Talmud, Torah, Pentateuch, ten commandments, the Law and the Prophets, Psalms, Apocrypha, New Testament, Gospel, Good News, Acts (of the Apostles), Epistles, Revelation, Apocalypse, Koran, Vedas; *vision*, sign, miracle, theophany, incarnation, Word made flesh; *belief*, faith, teaching, doctrine, faith, creed, dogma, tenet, articles of faith, 39 Articles, confession; *study of religion*, theology, divinity, religious education, R.E., religious knowledge, R.K.; *religious teacher*, apostle, prophet, rabbi, preacher, lay-preacher, interpreter, commentator, expositor, evangelist, missionary, guru; *theologian*, scholar, divine.

adj. *religious*, holy, spiritual, divine, devout, godly; *revealed*, scriptural, holy, sacred, inspired, prophetic, biblical, canonical, apostolic, authoritative, infallible, trustworthy, evangelical, evangelistic, devotional; *theological*, doctrinal, dogmatic.

869 UNBELIEF

See also **435** (disbelief)

n. *unbelief*, atheism; *irreligion*, godlessness, unholiness, nothing sacred, profaneness, ungodliness; *wickedness*, sinfulness; *false religion*, idolatry, heresy; *heathenism*, paganism; *disbelief*, scepticism, doubt, agnosticism; *lack of faith*, lapse from faith; *freethinking*, rationalism, humanism, secularism, materialism, worldliness; *unbeliever*, dissenter, rationalist, freethinker, atheist; *agnostic*, sceptic, doubter, doubting Thomas; *idolater*, heretic; *materialist*, worldling; *heathen*, pagan; *infidel*, apostate.

adj. *unbelieving*, atheistic; *irreligious*, godless, unholy, profane, ungodly, unspiritual; *wicked*, sinful; *disbelieving*, doubting, agnostic; *heathen*, pagan, idolatrous; *heretical*, unorthodox; *freethinking*, rationalistic, humanistic, secular, materialistic, worldly; *apostate*, unfaithful, lapsed, dissenting; *non-practising*, unconverted, lost.

870 ORTHODOXY

n. *orthodoxy*, strictness, soundness, fundamentalism; *heresy-hunting*, persecution, witch hunt; *conformist*, traditionalist, fundamentalist; *believer*, true believer; *the faithful*, congregation, flock, pillar of the church, communicant.

adj. *orthodox*, sound, pure, true, right-minded, non-heretical; *loyal*, devout, obedient; *practising*, committed, conforming, card-carrying (*colloq.*); *conventional*, traditional, conservative; *scriptural*, canonical, strict; *fundamentalist*, evangelical.

871 HETERODOXY

n. *heterodoxy*, unorthodoxy, wrong belief, modernism, liberalism; *sectarianism*, separatism, partisanship, schismatism, party spirit; *bigotry*, prejudice; *denominationalism*, nonconformism; *division*, dissociation, secession, separation, withdrawal, excommunication; *heresy*, divergence, distortion, perversion; *sect*, schism, division, split, faction, branch, offshoot; *denomination*, tradition; *separatist*, rebel, dissident, dissenter, nonconformist, heretic.

adj. *heterodox*, unorthodox, unsound, unconventional, nonconformist, unauthorized; *heretical*, divergent, perverted; *sectarian*, partisan, schismatic, breakaway, exclusive, denominational.

vb. *declare heretical*, condemn, excommunicate; *secede*, separate, withdraw, break away.

872 HOLINESS

See also **863** (saint).

n. *holiness*, sanctity, consecration, godliness, saintliness, sacredness, goodness, spirituality, unworldliness, piety, devotion; *loyalty*, dutifulness, faithfulness, zeal, commitment, dedication, perseverance, allegiance, earnestness; *reverence*, worship, awe, fear of God, humility, prayerfulness, meditation, contemplation, communion, mysticism; *sanctimoniousness*, pietism, show of piety, religiosity, formalism; *fanaticism*, fundamentalism, bibliolatry; *the saints*, the righteous, the just, man of prayer, believer; *fanatic*, zealot, bigot, Pharisee, scribe, fundamentalist, Bible puncher (*colloq.*), hot-gospeller (*colloq.*), missionary, evangelical, revivalist, pilgrim.

adj. *holy*, pious, devout, consecrated, godly, saintly, sacred, solemn, spiritual, unworldly, otherworldly; *loyal*, faithful, zealous, committed, practising, dedicated, earnest; *reverent*, worshipful, prayerful, humble, meek, pure in heart, God-fearing; *meditative*, contemplative; *sanctimonious*, self-righteous, holier-than-thou, goody-goody (*colloq.*); *fanatical*, fundamentalist, Pharisaic, evangelical, born-again, crusading, fervent, enthusiastic.

vb. *be holy*, fear God, worship, praise, pray, say one's prayers, go to church, persevere, keep the faith, fight the good fight (*colloq.*); *become holy*, repent and believe, be converted, see the error of one's ways, see the light; *make holy*, sanctify, consecrate, dedicate, hallow; *bring to God*, convert, proselytize; *canonize*, beatify.

873 PROFANITY

n. *profanity*, impiety, godlessness, irreverence; *blasphemy*, sacrilege, desecration, violation, defilement; *scoffing*, derision; *worldliness*, materialism; *hypocrisy*, false piety, self-righteousness, cant, lip service; *profane person*, blasphemer, sinner, reprobate; *scoffer*, mocker; *worldling*, materialist; *hypocrite*; *unbeliever*, backslider, apostate.

adj. *profane*, unholy; *impious*, godless, ungodly, unrighteous, sinful, irreverent, irreligious, worldly, earthbound; *hardened*, brazen; *blasphemous*, sacrilegious, swearing; *hypocritical*, self-righteous, insincere, deceitful; *apostate*, unregenerate.

vb. *profane*, desecrate, violate, defile, commit sacrilege; *blaspheme*, swear, take the name of the Lord in vain; *backslide*, apostasize, harden one's heart.

874 WORSHIP

n. *worship*, honour, reverence, homage, respect, adoration, veneration, exaltation, devotion, praise; *act of worship*, service, rite, liturgy; *prayer*, prayer for the day, intercession, vigils, rogation, supplication, litany, benediction, collect, blessing, grace, petition, request, invocation, thanksgiving; *private devotion*, meditation, quiet time, prayer; *hymn*, song, song of praise, psalm, chant, anthem, canticle, chorus; *worshipper*, adorer, venerator; *churchgoer*, Christian, communicant; *congregation*, church, flock, assembly; *supplicant*, intercessor, petitioner, man of prayer.

adj. *worshipping*, devoted, reverent, supplicant, devout, prayerful, religious; *worshipful*, reverential, solemn, sacred, holy, devotional, liturgical; *meditating*, praying, interceding, communicating, kneeling; *worshipped*, revered, adored.

vb. *worship*, revere, honour, adore, venerate, exalt, praise, glorify, respect, do worship to, pay homage to, homage, laud, humble oneself, prostrate oneself, kneel, genuflect; *pray*, say a prayer, say one's prayers, meditate; *give thanks*, thank, bless; *petition*, supplicate, intercede, entreat, ask, invoke, beseech; *idolize*, deify; *sing hymns*, sing psalms, chant.

875 IDOLATRY

n. *idolatry*, false worship, idolism, idol-worship, image-worship, iconolatry; *heathenism*, paganism, irreligion, fetishism, anthropomorphism, demonism, demonolatry, devil-worship, sun-worship, hero-worship, animal-worship, mumbo jumbo, hocus-pocus, sorcery; *idolization*, apotheosis, deification; *idol*, graven image, false god, image, icon, statue, fetish, totem; *idolater*, idol-worshipper, pagan, heathen, idolizer, fetishist, demonist, devil-worshipper; *idol-maker*, image-maker.

adj. *idolatrous*, heathen, pagan, fetishistic, idol-worshipping, devil-worshipping.

vb. *idolatrize*, worship idols, worship the golden calf; *enshrine*, deify, apotheosize; *idolize*, worship, put on a pedestal, sing the praises of, dote on, treasure.

876 SORCERY

See also **864** (devil).

n. *sorcery*, witchcraft, wizardry, magic, superstition, occultism, diabolism, black magic, black art; *miracle-working*, thaumaturgy; *witch-doctoring*, voodooism; *exorcism*, ghost-laying; *magic rite*, invocation, incantation, spell; *enchantment*, bewitchment, curse, hoodoo, evil eye, jinx, influence, possession, trance; *magic word*, hocus-pocus, abracadabra, open sesame, mumbo jumbo; *charm*, fetish, amulet, talisman, mascot, lucky charm; *sorcerer*, witch, wizard, enchanter, spellbinder; *magician*, conjuror, juggler, illusionist; *witch-doctor*, medicine-man, shaman, voodoo; *seer*, soothsayer, wise man, diviner, clairvoyant; *astrologer*, alchemist; *miracle worker*, thaumaturgist; *spiritualist*, medium, spirit raiser, occultist, necromancer, exorcist; *spiritism*, spiritualism, spirit communication; *séance*, ouija board, planchette, automatic writing, table-turning.

adj. *sorcerous*, devilish, diabolic, occult, necromantic; *magical*, spellbinding, enchanting, supernatural, uncanny, weird, eerie; *bewitched*, enchanted, spellbound, charmed; *cursed*, under the evil eye.

vb. *practise sorcery*, do magic, divine, conjure; *exorcise*, lay ghosts; *raise spirits*, call up spirits; *recite a spell*, recite an incantation, wave a wand; *bewitch*, enchant, charm, fascinate, spellbind; *possess*, curse, put under a curse; *hold a séance*.

877 OCCULTISM

See also **455** (prediction); **864** (devil).

n. *occultism*, mysticism, religion, occult lore; *astrology*, alchemy, divination, prediction; *hypnotism*, hypnosis; *spiritualism*, spirit communication, sitting, séance; *spirit manifestation*, ghost, automatic writing, spirit message; *psychics*, parapsychology, psychic science, ESP, clairvoyance, intuition, second sight, telepathy, psychokinesis, spoon-bending; *mystic*, yogi, esoteric; *fortune-teller*, crystal-gazer, palmist; *spiritualist*, medium; *psychic*, clairvoyant, telepathist, mind-reader; *seer*, prophet, oracle.

adj. *occult*, cabbalistic, religious, mystic, mysterious, dark, transcendental, supernatural, paranormal; *psychic*, psychical, telepathic, clairvoyant, fey.

vb. *practise occultism*, alchemize, astrologize, transform, divine; *practise spiritualism*, study spiritualism; *hold a séance*, attend a séance; *materialize*, dematerialize; *hypnotize*, mesmerize.

878 ECCLESIASTICISM

n. *ecclesiasticism*, churchdom, the church, ministry; *call*, vocation, mission; *holy orders*, ordination, induction, appointment, installation; *Holy Office*, priesthood, pastorship, papacy, primacy, incumbency; *parish*, diocese, bishopric, see; *preaching*, spiritual guidance, pastoral care, confession, absolution, ministration; *prayer*, fellowship, communion; *synod*, convocation, council, chapter, tribunal.

adj. *ecclesiastical*, orthodox, authoritative, apostolic, spiritual; *priestly*, sacerdotal, ministerial, pastoral, pontifical, papal, episcopal, clerical.

vb. *ordain*, order, enthrone, frock; *consecrate*, sanctify; *take holy orders*, be ordained.

879 CLERGY

n. *clergy*, hierarchy, clerical order; *clergyman*, servant of God, preacher, minister, pastor, vicar, parson, rector, parish priest; *curate*, chaplain, cleric, padre; *priest*, prelate, bishop, arch-

bishop, deacon, archdeacon, dean, canon, prior, primate, patriarch, cardinal; *pope*, pontiff, Holy Father; *monk*, friar, prior, abbot, superior, Trappist, Benedictine; *nun*, sister, bride of Christ, abbess, Mother Superior; *missionary*, evangelist; *rabbi*, imam, lama.
adj. *clerical*, ordained, pastoral, episcopal, papal, monastic.
vb. *be ordained*, enter the ministry, take holy orders, take the veil.

880 LAITY

n. *laity*, layman, lay people, lay brethren; *parish*, flock, sheep, fold, community, church, congregation, assembly; *parishioner*, church member, elder, deacon, lay-preacher, lay-reader, novice, altar boy, chorister, beadle, verger, sexton.
adj. *lay*, laical, secular, non-clerical, unordained; *temporal*, of the world, civil; *irreligious*, unholy, profane, unsacred, unconsecrated.
vb. *laicize*, secularize, deconsecrate.

881 RITUAL

See also **787** (formality).
n. *ritual*, custom, institution, observance, practice; *order*, form, litany, liturgy, ordinance; *rite*, ceremony, celebration; *service*, divine worship, matins, evensong, vespers, mass, prayer meeting, Bible study, Sunday School; *sacrament*, Holy Communion, Lord's Supper, Eucharist, baptism, christening, marriage service, nuptial mass, requiem mass; *ritual object*, cross, crucifix, altar, candle, chalice, incense, holy water, sacred relics, prayer wheel, prayer book, hymn book, psalter; *clerical dress*, canonicals, surplice, vestment, cassock, chasuble, cope, mitre, staff, crook, crosier; *holy day*, feast day, festival, Sabbath, Lord's Day, Advent, Christmas, Epiphany, Lent, Shrove Tuesday, Ash Wednesday, Easter, Good Friday, Whitsun, Pentecost, Passover.
adj. *ritual*, formal, solemn, ceremonial, customary, liturgical.
vb. *perform ritual*, celebrate, observe, keep; *officiate*, minister, baptize, confirm, ordain, excommunicate; *worship*, pray, take communion; *bless*, dedicate, consecrate; *kneel*, genuflect, bow, cross oneself.

882 TEMPLE

n. *temple*, shrine, sanctuary, pantheon, place of worship, house of prayer, holy place; *church*, house of God, kirk, chapel, tabernacle, meeting-house, mission; *cathedral*, minster, abbey; *synagogue*, mosque; *monastery*, friary, priory, nunnery, convent; *parsonage*, presbytery, rectory, manse, vicarage, deanery, Vatican; *cemetery*, graveyard, churchyard; *altar*, font, pulpit, lectern, pew; *nave*, aisle, transept, chancel, choir, vestry, crypt; *tower*, steeple, belfry, buttress, cloister, lychgate.

A

B

C

D

E

F

G

H

I

J

K

L

M

O

P

Q

R

S

U

V

W

X

Y

Z

MORE ABOUT PENGUINS, PELICANS AND PUFFINS

THE PENGUIN ENGLISH DICTIONARY

The Penguin English Dictionary has been created specially for today's needs. It features:

* More entries than any other popularly priced dictionary
* Exceptionally clear and precise definitions
* For the first time in an equivalent dictionary, the internationally recognised IPA pronunciation system
* Emphasis on contemporary usage
* Extended coverage of both the spoken and the written word
* Scientific tables
* Technical words
* Informal and colloquial expressions
* Vocabulary most widely used *wherever* English is spoken
* Most commonly used abbreviations

It is twenty years since the publication of the last English dictionary by Penguin and the compilation of this entirely new *Penguin English Dictionary* is the result of a special collaboration between Longman, one of the world's leading dictionary publishers, and Penguin Books. The material is based entirely on the database of the acclaimed *Longman Dictionary of the English Language.*

PENGUIN REFERENCE BOOKS

☐ ***The Penguin Map of the World*** £2.50

Clear, colourful, crammed with information and fully up-to-date, this is a useful map to stick on your wall at home, at school or in the office.

☐ ***The Penguin Map of Europe*** £2.95

Covers all land eastwards to the Urals, southwards to North Africa and up to Syria, Iraq and Iran * Scale = 1:5,500,000 * 4-colour artwork * Features main roads, railways, oil and gas pipelines, plus extra information including national flags, currencies and populations.

☐ ***The Penguin Map of the British Isles*** £1.95

Including the Orkneys, the Shetlands, the Channel Islands and much of Normandy, this excellent map is ideal for planning routes and touring holidays, or as a study aid.

☐ ***The Penguin Dictionary of Quotations*** £3.95

A treasure-trove of over 12,000 new gems and old favourites, from Aesop and Matthew Arnold to Xenophon and Zola.

☐ ***The Penguin Dictionary of Art and Artists*** £3.95

Fifth Edition. 'A vast amount of information intelligently presented, carefully detailed, abreast of current thought and scholarship and easy to read' – *The Times Literary Supplement*

☐ ***The Penguin Pocket Thesaurus*** £1.95

A pocket-sized version of Roget's classic, and an essential companion for all commuters, crossword addicts, students, journalists and the stuck-for-words.